# Macintosh and You
## System 7 Basics

# Macintosh and You
## System 7 Basics

Patricia L. Sullivan

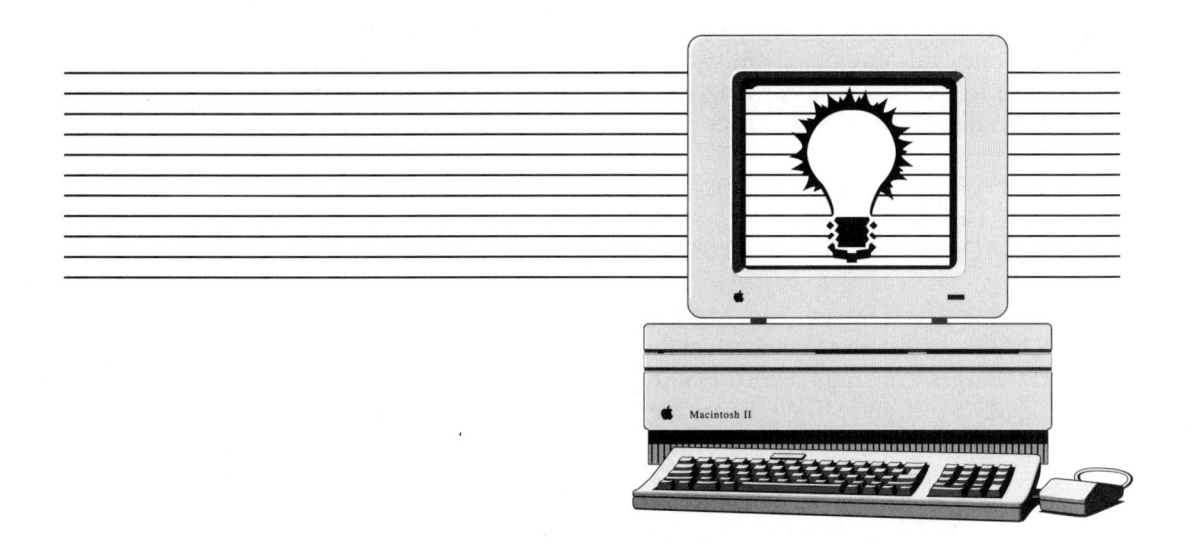

FRANKLIN, BEEDLE & ASSOCIATES INCORPORATED
8536 SW St. Helens Drive, Suite D
Wilsonville, Oregon 97070

*To my best friend and husband, Michael Sullivan.*

| | |
|---|---|
| Publisher | James F. Leisy, Jr. |
| Developmental Editor | Samantha Soma |
| Interior Design & Production | Lisa Cannon |
| Proofreading | Bill DeRouchey |
| Cover Design | Neo Nova |
| Cover Photograph | Kathryn Kreider, *Rapid Ribbon Repeat* Quilt |

© 1993 Franklin, Beedle & Associates, Incorporated. No part of this book may be reproduced, stored in a retrieval system, transmitted, or transcribed in any form or by any means, electronic, mechanical, telepathic, photocopying, recording or otherwise, without prior written permission of the publisher. Permission requests should be addressed as follows:

Rights and Permissions, FRANKLIN, BEEDLE & ASSOCIATES INCORPORATED
8536 SW St. Helens Drive, Suite D
Wilsonville, Oregon 97070   (503) 682-7668   (503) 682-7638 (FAX)

Apple, Macintosh and System 7 are registered trademarks of the Apple Corporation.
ClarisWorks is a registered trademark of the Claris Corporation.
ClickArt® Images Copyright© 1987, 1988 T/Maker company. All Rights Reserved.
MS Excel, MS Word, and MS Works are registered trademarks of the Microsoft Corporation.
PageMaker is a registered trademark of the Aldus Corporation.

### Library of Congress Cataloging-in-Publication Data

Sullivan, Patricia L.
    Macintosh and you : System 7 basics / Patricia L. Sullivan.
        p.    cm.
    Includes index.
    ISBN 0-938661-48-5
    1. Operating systems (Computers)    2. System 7.    3. Macintosh (Computer)--Programming.    I. Title.
QA76.76.O63S86   1993
005.469--dc20                                                     93-283
                                                                  CIP

# Preface

## *Macintosh & You: System 7 Basics* is for Beginning to Advanced Computer Users

This book is intended for computer novices through experienced Macintosh application users. It assumes no prior computer experience. Students who begin with no knowledge of computers will be led through the learning process using step-by-step instructions. By the time they complete the book they will have a strong understanding of how to use the Macintosh computer as well as core system operations and commands. Frequently, experienced Macintosh users have learned several application programs but know little about the operating system. The step-by-step approach offered in this book will help students to organize their previous operating system knowledge and will challenge them with new information. This book has been extensively class-tested—no prior experience is assumed.

## Intended for use in Operating System 7.1, but also compatible with other versions

This textbook was written on and about System 7.1. The Macintosh hardware operations and core system commands covered in this book are common to all versions of the operating system and can be used in any Macintosh environment. However, Operating System 7.1 handles fonts and control panels differently, and provides additional capabilities. If you are using System 6.x, see *Macintosh and You: The Basics*, also published by Franklin, Beedle & Associates, Inc.

## Introduction to Application Programs

The Macintosh operating system is easy and fun to use but students are anxious to see how the Macintosh is going to add to their productivity at work, school and/or home. Therefore, the last four chapters of this book introduce application programs: word processing, database management, spreadsheet, and desktop publishing. Simple step-by-step instructions are provided on a variety of software packages. The word processing chapter provides instruction in ClarisWorks, Microsoft Works, and Microsoft Word. The database management chapter provides instruction in ClarisWorks, Microsoft Works. The spreadsheet program provides instruction in ClarisWorks, Microsoft Works, and Excel. The desktop publishing chapter provides instruction in PageMaker. Application Chapters 14 through 17 can be introduced anytime after Chapter 8.

## A Step-by-step Approach is Used in this Book

I suggest students read each chapter or attend a classroom lecture on the chapter before sitting down at the computer. Students should then complete each Activity within the chapter and all assignments at the end of the chapter on the computer. Each Activity in the chapter is presented in a careful student-oriented, step-by-step approach. Explanations for the operation/command and the results are interspersed within the steps when necessary.

A handy reference feature of this book is the Quick Reference Appendix, which shows all the menus and the commands and shortcuts used most often. Key Terms and questions appear at the end of every chapter to help reinforce the material presented in the chapter. Key terms can be found in the Glossary and all questions are answered in the Instructor's Manual.

## Data Disk Included

I have found that by using a prepared data disk containing sample files, students quickly learn how to copy a disk or document, duplicate icons, rename icons, delete icons, create file folders, request and print directories, and so on. A data disk is provided with the textbook for two reasons; students can practice on the data disk without disturbing the hard disk, and it is helpful for students' data disk to exactly match the screen captures in the textbook.

## Necessary Hardware and Software

Students need access to the following hardware:
    A Macintosh with at least 2MB of Ram, a hard drive and a floppy drive.
    A keyboard
    A mouse
    A printer
    Four floppy disks

Students need access to the following software:
    Operating System 7.0 through 7.1
    TeachText (comes with the Macintosh)

Word Processing (any of the following):
Microsoft Works 3.0, ClarisWorks 1.0v2, Microsoft Word 5.0.
Database Management (any of the following):
Microsoft Works 3.0, ClarisWorks 1.0v2.
Spreadsheet (any of the following):
Microsoft Works 3.0, ClarisWorks 1.0v2, Microsoft Excel 4.0.
Desktop Publishing: PageMaker 4.1.

## Supplementary Material

An Instructor's Manual is available to the teacher upon adoption of this book for the classroom. It includes:
- A syllabus for an eight/nine-week course.
- An outline for each chapter.
- Answers to all end-of-chapter questions and assignments.
- Midterm and Final exams.

## Acknowledgements

A book is never the product of one person working alone—it is a collaborative effort. Thank you to all who have contributed. A special Thanks to:

Michael Sullivan, my husband, for his love, encouragement, and patience. Thanks for working through every activity and exercise in this book at least twice, for your suggestions and for adding a lot of "spice" to my life.

Chris Sullivan, my son, for maintaining his sense of humor even during the ordeal of living with an author.

Larry Boyd, a life-long family friend, thanks for keyboard testing and critiquing this book.

To the students at Saddleback College, who have taken my numerous Macintosh courses and are always requesting/demanding more. Their enthusiasm and thirst for knowledge "lights my fire" even when I'm exhausted.

To my colleagues in the Computer Information Management Department at Saddleback College for their support.

Jim Leisy, my publisher, for his encouragement, wisdom, patience and knowledge. A special thanks to Lisa Cannon, and everyone at Franklin, Beedle & Associates for their cheerfulness and optimism.

Many thanks also to the following reviewers of the manuscript for their insights: Scott Hill, *San Ramon Valley Center for Higher Education*; Karen Jolly, *Portland Community College*; Christina Olds, *Jackson Community College*; Sally Peterson, *University of Wisconsin, Madison*; Cyndi Reese, *Santa Rosa Junior College*; Jim Schroeder, *Dodge City Community College*; and Constance Schueneman, *Delta College*.

# Introduction to Application Software

The primary focus of this book in Chapters 1 through 13 is the Macintosh Operating System 7. The Macintosh and System 7 are fun to use, but without application software few of us would have a need for the computer. Therefore, Chapters 14 through 17 briefly introduce four major types of application software. The emphasis is on *briefly*. These chapters will provide you with a brief glimpse at application programs and their power. Complete books and courses are available on each of these programs, and I encourage you to continue studying the Macintosh and related application programs.

A variety of programs are used in each chapter. This gives you the opportunity to see how similar the programs are. Hopefully you have computer access to at least one program for each chapter. The following list specifies the programs and version number used in each chapter. These programs were selected because of their availability in most schools.

CHAPTER 14   **Word Processing Applications**
　　　　　　　ClarisWorks 1.0v2
　　　　　　　Microsoft Works 3.0
　　　　　　　Microsoft Word 5.0

CHAPTER 15   **Database Management Applications**
　　　　　　　ClarisWorks 1.0v2
　　　　　　　Microsoft Works 3.0

CHAPTER 16   **Spreadsheet Applications**
　　　　　　　ClarisWorks 1.0v2
　　　　　　　Microsoft Works 3.0
　　　　　　　Microsoft Excel 4.0

CHAPTER 17   **Desktop Publishing Applications**
　　　　　　　Aldus PageMaker 4.01

# Overview

| | | |
|---|---|---|
| CHAPTER 1 | Introducing Computer Hardware and Software | 1 |
| CHAPTER 2 | Getting Started: Basic Macintosh Operations | 19 |
| CHAPTER 3 | Handling Floppy Disks | 49 |
| CHAPTER 4 | Windows | 69 |
| CHAPTER 5 | The Apple Menu and Desk Accessories | 94 |
| CHAPTER 6 | The Finder Menu Bar | 114 |
| CHAPTER 7 | Printing | 151 |
| CHAPTER 8 | Working with TeachText and the Finder | 177 |
| CHAPTER 9 | File Manipulation: Duplicating, Copying, Renaming, Locking, Erasing, and Customizing Files | 199 |
| CHAPTER 10 | File and Disk Management | 221 |
| CHAPTER 11 | The Control Panels | 253 |
| CHAPTER 12 | The System Folder | 290 |
| CHAPTER 13 | Security Issues | 306 |
| CHAPTER 14 | Word Processing Applications | 317 |
| CHAPTER 15 | Database Management Applications | 334 |
| CHAPTER 16 | Spreadsheet Applications | 349 |
| CHAPTER 17 | Desktop Publishing Applications | 363 |
| APPENDIX | Quick Lookup | 377 |
| | Glossary | 391 |
| | Index | 410 |

**Related Books from Franklin, Beedle & Associates**

**Macintosh and You : The Basics**
*Patricia L. Sullivan*

**Excel for the Macintosh**
*Karen Jolly*

# Contents

**CHAPTER 1  Introducing Computer Hardware and Software .. 1**
Learning Objectives ............................................................. 1
Introduction ......................................................................... 1
Computer Hardware ........................................................... 3
Macintosh System Configuration ..................................... 11
Computer Software ........................................................... 11
Key Terms ............................................................................ 15
Discussion Questions ......................................................... 16
True/False Questions ......................................................... 16
Completion Questions ...................................................... 17
Matching Questions .......................................................... 17
Assignments ....................................................................... 18

**CHAPTER 2  Getting Started: Basic Macintosh Operations .... 19**
Learning Objectives ........................................................... 19
Introduction ....................................................................... 19
Starting a Computer Session ............................................ 20
The Desktop ....................................................................... 21
Mouse Operations ............................................................. 23
Selecting and Moving Single Icons ................................. 24
Selecting and Moving Multiple Icons ............................. 29
Using Menus ....................................................................... 31
Select All ............................................................................. 36
Getting Help ...................................................................... 37
Ending a Computer Session ............................................. 40
Key Terms ............................................................................ 42
Discussion Questions ......................................................... 43
True/False Questions ......................................................... 44
Completion Questions ...................................................... 44
Matching Questions .......................................................... 45
Assignments ....................................................................... 46

**CHAPTER 3** **Handling Floppy Disks** .................................................. **49**
Learning Objectives ................................................................. 49
Introduction ............................................................................ 49
Inserting Floppy Disks .............................................................. 50
Ejecting Floppy Disks ............................................................... 50
Locking Floppy Disks ................................................................ 52
Formatting Floppy Disks ........................................................... 53
Copying Floppy Disks ............................................................... 57
Erasing Floppy Disks ................................................................. 62
Renaming Floppy Disks ............................................................ 65
Key Terms ................................................................................ 66
Discussion Questions ............................................................... 66
True/False Questions ............................................................... 66
Completion Questions ............................................................. 67
Assignments ............................................................................ 68

**CHAPTER 4** **Windows** .................................................................. **69**
Learning Objectives ................................................................. 69
Introduction ............................................................................ 69
Opening an Icon ..................................................................... 70
Closing An Icon ....................................................................... 72
Switching Between Icon and List Views .................................... 73
Common Windows Features and Operations ......................... 75
Executing Window Operations ................................................ 77
Selecting Icons in the Active Window ...................................... 87
Key Terms ................................................................................ 89
Discussion Questions ............................................................... 89
True/False Questions ............................................................... 89
Completion Questions ............................................................. 90
Matching Questions ................................................................ 90
Assignments ............................................................................ 91

**CHAPTER 5** **The Apple Menu and Desk Accessories** ............. **94**
Learning Objectives ................................................................. 94
Introduction ............................................................................ 94
Activating and Closing Desk Accessories ................................. 95

About This Macintosh ............................................................... 96
The Alarm Clock ....................................................................... 97
The Calculator ........................................................................ 101
The Chooser ........................................................................... 103
Key Caps ................................................................................ 103
Note Pad ................................................................................ 107
Puzzle ..................................................................................... 107
Scrapbook .............................................................................. 108
Key Terms ............................................................................... 109
Discussion Questions ............................................................. 109
True/False Questions .............................................................. 110
Completion Questions ........................................................... 110
Assignments ........................................................................... 111

## CHAPTER 6  The Finder Menu Bar ............................................... 114
Learning Objectives ............................................................... 114
Introduction ............................................................................ 114
The File Menu ......................................................................... 115
The Edit Menu ........................................................................ 125
The View Menu ...................................................................... 130
The Label Menu ..................................................................... 135
The Special Menu .................................................................. 135
The Help Menu ....................................................................... 139
The Application Menu ........................................................... 140
Key Terms ............................................................................... 143
Discussion Questions ............................................................. 144
True/False Questions .............................................................. 145
Completion Questions ........................................................... 145
Matching Questions .............................................................. 146
Assignments ........................................................................... 146

## CHAPTER 7  Printing ........................................................................ 151
Learning Objectives ............................................................... 151
Introduction ............................................................................ 151
Printers .................................................................................... 152
ImageWriter ........................................................................... 153
The Chooser Desk Accessory ................................................ 154

Printing a Directory on the Macintosh ............................ 159
Printing from within an Application Program ................. 169
Key Terms .................................................................... 173
Discussion Questions .................................................... 174
True/False Questions .................................................... 174
Completion Questions .................................................. 175
Assignments ................................................................. 175

## CHAPTER 8  Working with TeachText and the Finder ............ 177
Learning Objectives ..................................................... 177
Introduction ................................................................. 177
Creating a New Document in TeachText ..................... 178
Opening an Existing Document, Modifying it,
    and Saving it as a New Document ......................... 186
Pasting In The Scrapbook ............................................ 189
Copying from the Scrapbook ...................................... 190
Printing the Letters ....................................................... 193
Removing The Entry From Your Scrapbook .................. 194
Key Terms .................................................................... 194
Discussion Questions .................................................... 195
True/False Questions .................................................... 195
Completion Questions .................................................. 195
Assignments ................................................................. 196

## CHAPTER 9  File Manipulation: Duplicating, Copying, Renaming, Locking, Erasing, and Customizing Files ................................................ 199
Learning Objectives ..................................................... 199
Introduction ................................................................. 199
Locking and Unlocking Files ........................................ 200
Duplicate Command .................................................... 201
Copying Files From One Disk to Another ..................... 203
Renaming Files ............................................................. 206
Customizing Icons ........................................................ 208
Erasing Files ................................................................. 213
Summary ...................................................................... 215

xiv

Key Terms .................................................................. 218
Discussion Questions ................................................ 218
True/False Questions ................................................ 218
Completion Questions .............................................. 219
Assignments ............................................................. 219

CHAPTER 10 **File and Disk Management** ............................. 221
Learning Objectives ................................................. 221
Introduction ............................................................. 221
Hierarchical File System ........................................... 222
Moving through the HFS .......................................... 223
Copying the HFS to Another Floppy Disk ............... 229
Dismantling the HFS ................................................ 232
Creating A Hierarchical Filing System .................... 234
Duplicating a File Folder ......................................... 239
The Find Command ................................................. 242
Key Terms .................................................................. 247
Discussion Questions ................................................ 248
True/False Questions ................................................ 248
Completion Questions .............................................. 248
Assignments ............................................................. 249

CHAPTER 11 **The Control Panels** ........................................... 253
Learning Objectives ................................................. 253
Introduction ............................................................. 253
Monitors ................................................................... 255
General Controls ...................................................... 256
Startup Disk .............................................................. 262
Keyboard .................................................................. 263
Mouse ....................................................................... 263
Sound ....................................................................... 265
Color ......................................................................... 268
Memory .................................................................... 271
Views ........................................................................ 273
Labels ....................................................................... 278
Numbers ................................................................... 279
Date & Time ............................................................. 281

Computer Network Control Panels ..............................285
Key Terms ........................................................287
Discussion Questions ..........................................287
True/False Questions ..........................................288
Completion Questions .........................................288
Assignments ....................................................289

CHAPTER 12 **The System Folder** ..................................**290**
Learning Objectives ...........................................290
Introduction ....................................................290
The Startup Disk ...............................................291
The System Folder .............................................292
The Finder File .................................................294
The System File .................................................294
Preferences ....................................................295
Extensions .....................................................295
PrintMonitor Documents ......................................296
Fonts Folder ....................................................299
The Apple Menu Items Folder .................................301
The Startup Items Folder .....................................301
Alias Files ......................................................302
Key Terms ........................................................304
Discussion Questions ..........................................304
True/False Questions ..........................................304
Completion Questions .........................................305

CHAPTER 13 **Security Issues** ......................................**306**
Learning Objectives ...........................................306
Introduction ....................................................306
Computer Viruses ..............................................307
Original Program Issues .......................................310
Data File Issues ................................................311
Backing Up .....................................................313
Key Terms ........................................................314
Discussion Questions ..........................................315
True/False Questions ..........................................315

Completion Questions .......................................................316
Assignment .....................................................................316

### CHAPTER 14 — Word Processing Applications ..........................317
Learning Objectives ........................................................317
Introduction ...................................................................317
Word Processing .............................................................318
Key Terms .......................................................................332
Discussion Questions .......................................................333
Assignments ...................................................................333

### CHAPTER 15 — Database Management Applications ..............334
Learning Objectives ........................................................334
Introduction ...................................................................334
Database Uses ................................................................335
ClarisWorks .....................................................................336
Microsoft Works ..............................................................342
Key Terms .......................................................................347
Discussion Questions .......................................................347
Assignments ...................................................................347

### CHAPTER 16 — Spreadsheet Applications ...................................349
Learning Objectives ........................................................349
Introduction ...................................................................349
Using ClarisWorks, Microsoft Works, or Microsoft Excel ..350
Key Terms .......................................................................361
Discussion Questions .......................................................361
Assignments ...................................................................361

### CHAPTER 17 — Desktop Publishing Applications .......................363
Learning Objectives ........................................................363
Introduction ...................................................................363
Using PageMaker 4.01 ....................................................363
Key Terms .......................................................................376
Discussion Questions .......................................................376
Assignment .....................................................................376

**APPENDIX**

**Quick Lookup ..................................................................... 377**
The Finder Menu Bar ......................................................... 377
Finder Menu Bar Commands ........................................... 378
Basic Menu Operations ..................................................... 379
Working with Icons ............................................................ 380
Manipulating Files and Folders ......................................... 381
Trash Hints ......................................................................... 382
Customizing Icons ............................................................. 383
Locating Files and Folders Using the Find and
    Find Again Commands ................................................ 383
Handling Floppy Disks ....................................................... 384
Windows ............................................................................ 387
Parts of the Window ......................................................... 388
Hierarchical Filing System Pop-up Menus ....................... 389
Hierarchical Filing System Keyboard Shortcuts .............. 389
Opening, Closing, and Activating Windows ................... 390
Powering Down ................................................................. 390

**Glossary ............................................................................. 391**

**Index .................................................................................. 410**

xviii

# Introducing Computer Hardware and Software

## Learning Objectives

**After completing this Chapter you will be able to:**

1. Explain the difference between hardware and software.
2. Compare and contrast system software and application software.
3. Name and explain the purposes of the four components of a computer system.
4. Compare and contrast RAM and ROM.
5. Explain how information is stored in RAM and on disk.
6. Explain how RAM and disk storage are measured.
7. Explain and give examples of input devices.
8. Explain and give examples of output devices.
9. Explain the difference between impact and non-impact printers.
10. Explain the purposes of a floppy disk.
11. Compare and contrast floppy disks and hard disks.
12. Explain version numbers.
13. Describe the minimum configuration for a Macintosh system.

## Introduction

Congratulations on your choice of computers, and welcome to the Macintosh computing environment. You are beginning a great adventure—you will be astounded at how quickly you become a productive computer user.

There are many reasons for learning how, why, and when to use computers. In today's society it is becoming a required skill. Computers abound in our schools, banks, government offices, doctors' offices, stores and restaurants. A computer is a tool we can use to calculate complex mathematical formulas, to maintain financial records, to teach children how to read, to write books, to draw pictures, to write and produce music, to entertain, to store vast amounts of information for quick access later... the possibilities are only limited by our imaginations.

New computer users frequently say that their main goal in learning to use the computer is to save time and effort—to make their life easier. Using a computer may save you time and will provide accurate results, but it will not necessarily save time on all projects. Sometimes the total amount of time you budgeted for the project is used redoing and cleaning up the product. For example, if you type a letter on the typewriter and later find a small mistake in punctuation, would you retype the letter? Perhaps you would if it was a formal business letter. Otherwise you could be tempted to ignore the mistake and mail the letter. If you had used a computer to write the letter, it would only take seconds to correct the mistake. The ability to modify computer documents quickly and easily encourages users to polish their documents before printing. The computer-produced document is cleaner, but do you save time? On the other hand, if you need to proof the letter for spelling, grammar or punctuation errors, the computer can perform these tasks quickly, inserting the corrections at your command.

Computers are simple devices that follow instructions without question—you are in command. You provide and input data, you instruct the computer to store and to manipulate the data, and you direct the computer to produce the desired output. All computers require hardware and software to operate.

**Hardware** refers to the physical components of the system, including the main system, monitor, keyboard, mouse, printer, and cables. You can see them and touch them.

**Software**, or programs, contain a set of detailed instructions that tell the computer hardware what to do. There are two primary categories of software. **System software** coordinates and supervises the operation of the physical components of the computer and allows the hardware to run application programs. **Application software** refers to programs that are developed to perform and solve specific problems. For instance, word-processing software allows you to create, edit, and print the letter we discussed earlier.

Obviously, both hardware and software are necessary to a working computer system—they are dependent on each other. To become a productive Macintosh user, you must learn the system software as well as application software. This book is designed to teach you the concepts of operating systems in general, and specifically the **Macintosh System 7.1.** Chapters 14 through 17 will guide you through several brief hands-on activities using application software packages.

# Computer Hardware

## Overview

Computer systems consist of four components: input devices, the processor, storage devices and output devices. These components allow you to convert raw data into useful information. The process is simple: you provide the necessary raw data using an input device, the Central Processing Unit (CPU) processes the data and transforms it into useful information using software stored on storage devices, and then the CPU sends the results to an output device. Input, output, and storage devices are **peripherals**—devices used to access the CPU. (See Figure 1.1)

1. **Processor.** The **Central Processing Unit (CPU)** is the engine and brain of the computer hardware. By itself it is powerless, but when software is added, it controls all computer operations and carries out each instruction one at a time.

2. **Input devices.** These peripherals are used to provide data to the CPU. They convert the data to electronic pulses and transmit the pulses to the CPU. The keyboard, mouse, and trackball are examples of input devices.

3. **Storage devices.** These peripherals are used to store data and programs for later access. Storage devices are input/output devices; you can read information stored on them into the CPU and you can write information to them from the CPU. Disk drives are examples of storage devices.

4. **Output devices.** These peripherals are used to produce or display the useful information. Printers and monitors are examples of output devices.

Figure 1.1—Components of a Computer System Showing the Flow of Data

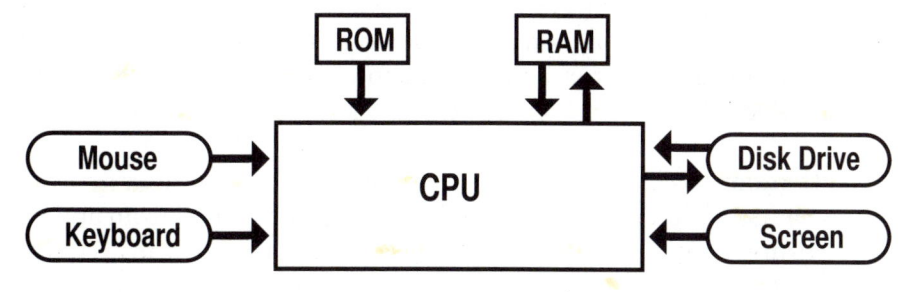

Figure labels: Monitor, Floppy Drive, System Unit, Keyboard, Mouse

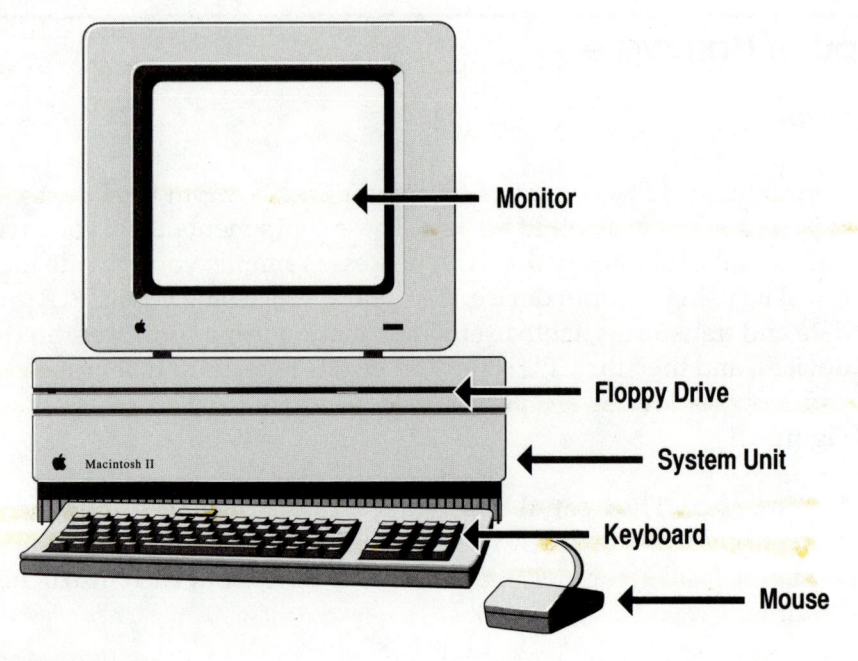

## The System Unit

The box that houses the electronic and mechanical parts of the computer system is known as the system unit. The system unit contains the power supply, the fan, the CPU, primary and secondary storage, expansion cards, expansion slots, and, on some Macintoshes, the monitor as well.

1. **Power supply and fan**. Computers need a source of power, either from an electrical power cable or from a battery. The fan cools your computer system while in use.

2. **Central Processing Unit (CPU)**. The CPU includes a microprocessor chip and primary memory. The microprocessor chip is less than an inch square and is etched with electronic circuitry. Different chips are available for different Macintosh models. Apple Computer, Inc. is currently installing the Motorola 68000 series chips in Macintoshes. Generally, the higher the chip number, the more advanced the chip's capabilities.

3. **Random-Access Memory (RAM)**. RAM is the computer system's primary storage. It can be modified by the user. You can read from and write to this portion of memory. **Random-access** means the CPU can access any storage location in RAM. It can jump ahead or go back and read information in another storage location without reading the information stored in between. A variety of information is stored in RAM when the computer is on: parts of

the operating system, application programs, the Finder, desk accessories, disk directories, utility programs, and data you key in. RAM is **volatile** memory. It is erased on command or when the power to the computer system is disrupted or turned off.

A single storage position in memory or on a disk is known as a **byte**. A byte is a single character such as a letter, number, special character (. , : ; ? / * > < ), or a space. It is important to know the amount of RAM in your computer. The amount of RAM available on your computer system will determine which application programs you can run and how much data the system can process at one time. If your system only has 1 MB of RAM memory, you cannot run application programs that require 2 MB. Macintoshes come with a minimum of 2 MB, with varying expansion capabilities. Figure 1.2 shows some common abbreviations used to describe memory and disk storage capacity.

*Figure 1.2—Memory and Disk Memory Storage*

| | |
|---|---|
| **Byte (B)** | One storage position |
| **Kilobyte (KB)** | Approximately one thousand storage positions (1024) |
| **Megabyte (MB)** | Approximately one million storage positions |
| **Gigabyte (GB)** | Approximately one billion storage positions |
| **Terabyte (TB)** | Approximately one trillion storage positions |

4. **Read Only Memory (ROM)**. ROM has programs permanently fixed (burned in) by the manufacturer. They cannot be altered by the user. ROM stores the initial instructions on how to start the computer, how to control disk drives, how to interpret input from the keyboard and the mouse, and how to draw graphics and text on the screen. You can read this portion of memory but you cannot alter or write to it. It can only be changed by removing the chip and inserting a new one. This portion of memory is **nonvolatile** and therefore is not affected by turning the power off.

5. **Expansion cards**. Expansion cards allow you to expand the capabilities of your Macintosh. Several different types of cards are available: coprocessor cards, memory cards, graphic and video cards, communication cards. Your computer may come with some expansion cards already installed in **expansion slots** inside the system unit. The number of expansion slots vary from one Macintosh model to the next.

## Input Devices

### Keyboard

Apple Computer, Inc. markets two different keyboards for the Macintosh—the **Apple Keyboard** and the **Apple Extended Keyboard.** (Figure 1.3) Both keyboards have the standard **QWERTY** layout (named for the first row of letters) consisting of 94 **alphanumeric** characters (letters, numbers, and symbols) and a separate **numeric keypad** that is arranged like a calculator for rapid number input. Some special keys that can be found on the keyboard are: Power-on, Control, Option, Command⌘ ⌘ , Clear, and Esc. The Shift, Control, Option, and Command keys are used in conjunction with other keys to perform special functions. The Clear and Esc keys have a variety of functions that vary from one application program to the next.

The Apple Extended Keyboard has two additional sets of keys. The **function** keys, located across the top of the keyboard, are numbered F1 through F15. They can be assigned specific tasks by different application programs. The **cursor control** keys are located between the main keyboard and the numeric keypad: Help, Home, Page up, Del, End, Page down, and the four directional arrow keys. The extended keyboard has three **status lights**: Num lock, Caps lock, and Scroll lock. When the status light is on, it infers a true condition. A green Caps lock light would mean that you have pressed the **Caps Lock** key. If you are typing, all letters will be capitalized.

*Figure 1.3—Apple Standard and Extended Keyboards*

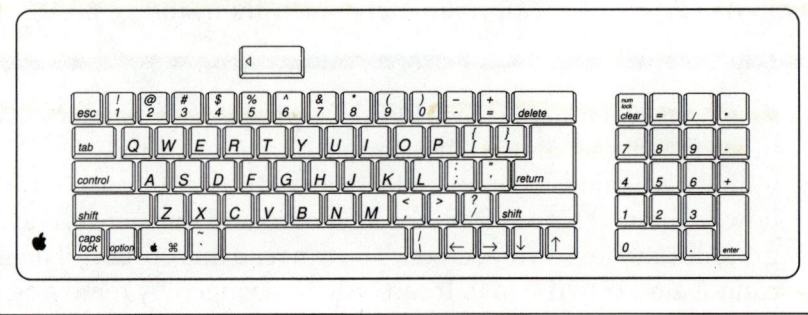

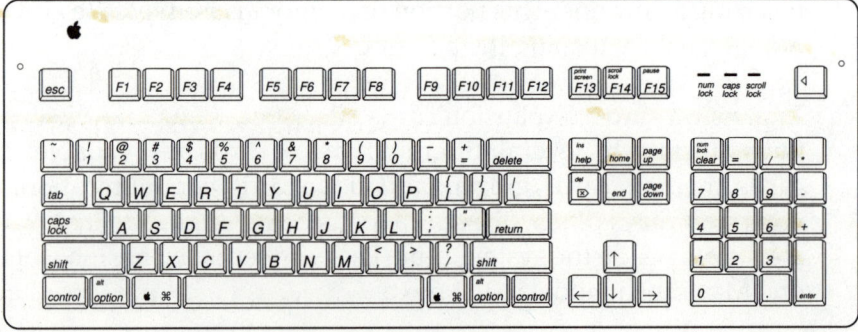

## Mouse and the Trackball

A **mouse** is a hand-held device with a ball-type roller on the bottom and one or more buttons on the top. A **trackball** is another popular pointing device with a ball-type roller on top and one or more buttons. (Figure 1.4) You can use a mouse or trackball to point to items on the screen, to choose a menu option, to mark text for editing, to select items for further action, or to draw.

To operate the mouse, you move the entire mouse unit across the table top in order to move a pointer on the screen. The trackball on the other hand is a stationary unit. To operate the trackball, you roll the ball on the top of the unit to move the pointer on the screen. Trackballs use little desk space, are good for fine detailed work, and can be found on many laptop (portable) computers.

*Figure 1.4—Pointing Devices*

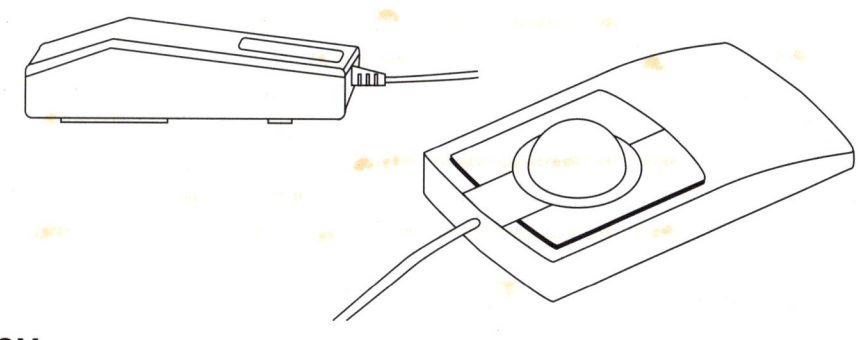

## CD-ROM

**CD-ROM** (pronounced "see-dee-rom") is an acronym for Compact Disk-Read Only Memory. CD-ROM disks use the same technology as CD audio disks. The advantage of CD-ROM disks is their storage capacity. A 5-inch diameter CD-ROM disk can store 800 MB of information. The disadvantage is that the disks are currently read-only and they are slow. CD-ROM disks are useful for storing large amounts of information that doesn't change. Reference materials are good examples of this—encyclopedias, medical journals, magazines, and so on.

## Output Devices

### Monitors

A monitor is a **Cathode-Ray Tube (CRT)** similar to your television but with higher resolution and sharper images. **Monochrome, gray-scale** or **color** monitors are available for the Macintosh. Monochrome monitors display only black and white. Gray-scale monitors display from one to 256 shades of gray. Color monitors can display from 16 to 16.7 million colors. Monitors come in a variety of shapes and sizes. A 12-inch **landscape** (wide) monitor will display the full width of a 8.5 by 11-inch page and more than half the length. A 15-inch **portrait** (tall) monitor will display a full 8.5 by 11-inch page. A two-page, 21-inch monitor will display two full 8.5 by 11-inch pages.

### Printers

Printers can be divided into two classifications—impact or non-impact. **Impact printers** use a strike-on method to press a fabric or carbon ribbon against the paper, leaving a mark. The most common type of impact printer is a **dot matrix printer**. It creates characters from a rectangular grid of pins. If you look at a document created by a dot matrix printer, you can see that each character consists of many tiny individual dots. A **near-letter-quality (NLQ)** dot-matrix printer will print a character and then overprint the same character in a slightly offset pattern, filling in some of the blank spots between the dots, producing a sharper character.

Three common non-impact printers are: **thermal printers, ink-jet printers,** and **laser printers**. Thermal printers use heat produced by the printer to create whole characters. Thermal printers are not extremely popular because they require expensive heat-sensitive paper that fades over time. Ink-jet printers form characters by shooting tiny dots of ink onto the paper. Laser printers use a process similar to xerographic copiers. They beam complete pages onto a drum, and when the paper is passed over the drum, it picks up the image with toner.

## Secondary Storage Devices

### Floppy Disks

**Floppy disks**, also known as **microfloppy disks**, have two primary purposes—permanent storage and portability. For example, as you write a business report, the characters you key in are stored in RAM. If you turn the computer off, RAM will be wiped out. Therefore, you need a medium (floppy disk) on which to store the report in order to be able to recover it later. Since the disk is portable, you can easily transport the disk between work and home.

A 3.5 inch, one-sided floppy disk stores approximately 400 KB, a two-sided floppy stores 800 KB, while a high density two-sided floppy stores 1.4 MB. To put this in to more familiar terms, let's estimate that each 8 1/2 by 11 inch page of a manuscript can store 3600 characters. How many pages of the manuscript could each type of floppy store? A one-sided disk could store 113 pages (409,600/3600). Figure 1.5 illustrates this storage capacity.

If you look at a disk, can you tell what is stored there? No, and neither can the computer system without a disk drive. **Disk drives** are the physical devices that can read and write to disks. Not all disk drives can read a high density disk (1.4 MB). A special Floppy Drive High Density **(FDHD)** drive is required. A high-density disk drive reads and writes to one-sided, two-sided and high-density disks. Why are there different types of floppy disks and drives? The answer is an excellent example of how rapidly technology changes. When the original Macintosh arrived on the market in 1984, only one-sided floppy disks were available. Two-sided disks were later released and now high-density disks are popular. High-density drives (FDHD) are included in all new Macintoshes. Eventually high density drives will replace all previous formats. Who knows what will replace them.

*Figure 1.5—Disk Storage Capacity*

| Disk type | Storage | | Capacity | Max. Pages |
|---|---|---|---|---|
| One-sided | 400 KB | = | 409,600 | 113 pages |
| Two-sided | 800 KB | = | 819,200 | 227 pages |
| High density | 1.4 MB | = | 1,433,600 | 398 pages |

Floppy disks are enclosed in rigid plastic coverings that have movable **write-protect tabs**. (Figure 1.6) The write-protect tab prevents anyone from writing to or erasing information from the disk. High density disks have an additional hole on the opposite side of the disk. A directional arrow appears on the shutter end of the disk directing you to insert that end of the disk in the drive first. When you insert the floppy into a disk drive, the spring-loaded shutter is opened, exposing a thin, flexible, magnetic recording surface called a floppy disk. A separate read/write head is required for each side of the disk. One disk drive motor moves the heads radially across the disk, while another motor spins the disk, in a way similar to a record player. How to care for your floppy disks is discussed in Figure 1.7.

*Figure 1.6—A Floppy Disk*

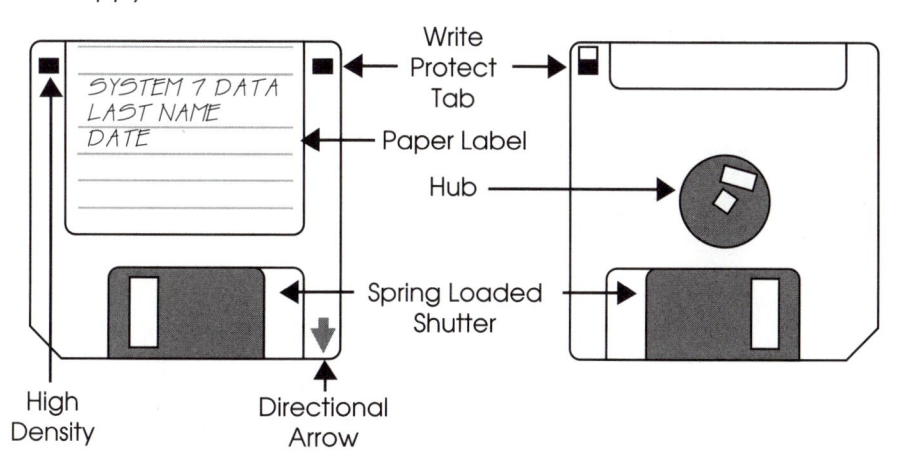

*Figure 1.7—Caring for your Floppy Disks*

---

**These precautions will make your disks last longer**

1. Do not expose the disks to extreme heat, sunlight, cold or humidity.
2. Do not expose your disks to magnetic fields. Keep them away from magnets, telephones, television sets, and copiers.
3. Do not play with the shutter!
4. Keep food and drink away from your disks and your computer.

---

**Hard Disk**

**Hard disks,** or **fixed drives,** are also used to record and store information. There are, however, some major differences between floppy and hard disks. Instead of a single flexible plastic disk, hard disk drives use several magnetic coated, rigid metal or glass recording surfaces, called **platters,** enclosed in a sterile chamber. The read/write heads float above the platters, while on floppies, the heads come in contact with the surfaces. When a head touches a hard drive platter, it is called a **head crash.** The disk is then no longer usable. Head crashes can be caused by a tiny piece of dust, hair, or an ash coming between the platter and the read/write head. Hard drives spin continuously, while floppies only spin when being written to or read from.

Compared to floppy disks, hard drives are capable of storing larger amounts of information, and have faster **access time** (the time necessary to move the read/write head and the disk to the desired location to retrieve or write information), and **transfer rates** (the time necessary to transfer information from the disk to main memory). Most Macintosh users store application programs on their hard disks, in order to use the storage capacity and access speed of the disk. Hard drives may be installed internally (within your system unit) or externally (sitting next to it). Obviously, it is not practical to use internal hard drives to transport information. (Figure 1.8) You do not want to take your Macintosh apart and remove the internal hard drive just to transport information.

*Figure 1.8—Hard Disk Drive*

## Macintosh System Configuration

In summary, let's examine the minimum Macintosh configuration.

A minimum Macintosh system consists of:
- A system unit with 2 to 3 MB RAM
- A floppy drive
- A hard drive
- A keyboard
- A mouse or trackball
- A monitor
- A box of unused or new floppy disks
- System software
- Application software, purchased separately

The following items are almost a necessity:
- More RAM (4 or more)
- A printer and cables to connect the printer to the system unit
- A surge-protector unit (provides a consistent power level for the system)

## Computer Software

### Overview

**Software**, or **programs**, contain a set of detailed instructions that tell the computer hardware what to do. System and application software are the two types of software necessary to turn your Macintosh hardware into a useful tool. Software, just like hardware, is constantly being improved. **Version numbers are assigned to different releases of the same program to distinguish the latest release from earlier ones.** (It would be impractical to change the name of a program just because a minor improvement was included in the latest release.) The highest-numbered release is the one that is the most current. Jumps in whole numbers indicate a major improvement or change from the last release, while fractional increases in the version number indicates a small improvement or a "fix" to an existing problem.

The Macintosh Operating System (OS) for example, has been using the version numbers 6.02, 6.05, 6.07, and so on, for the last few years. These releases have provided minor changes in the operating system. However, in the spring of 1991, Apple Computer, Inc. released version 7.0. This version of the operating system has some major advantages over the old system as well as a few disadvantages. The advantages include the ability to use two or more application programs at the same time, to be able to quickly move between them (**multitasking,** which is similar to MultiFinder in System 6), easier and quicker access to folders and documents, a virtual memory capability that allows you to use hard-disk space as temporary RAM, on-line Balloon Help, and the ability to link documents so that changes made in one document will be automatically reflected in the other document (Publish and Subscribe). The major drawbacks of System 7 are that it requires 1 to 2 MB of RAM for the operating system, it requires a hard drive, it is not totally compatible with all existing application programs, and some Macintosh users complain that it runs slower than System 6.07.

Version 7.1 of the operating system was released in the fall of 1992. System 7.1 allows you to customize the way dates, times, numbers and currency are displayed on the screen. Other new features include: improved memory management, increased file sharing security, and a new folder to store fonts. These features will be examined in future chapters.

It is necessary for you to know the version number of the operating system you are using. All application programs interact with the operating system and may require features that are missing from certain versions of the operating system.

### System Software

**System software** is a set of programs that allow you to interact with the hardware. System software coordinates and supervises all the input/output operations of the physical components of the computer and allows the hardware to run application software. Apple Computer, Inc. provides the operating system for the Macintosh family of computers.

### Application Software

**Application software** is a set of programs that have been developed to perform and solve a specific problem. **Packaged application programs** are relatively inexpensive programs that are designed for a large variety of users. They provide good how-to-use instructions (**documentation**), and can be purchased at many computer stores. **Customized application programs** are written by computer programmers to satisfy the needs of a specific user. They can be time-consuming to develop and are therefore far more expensive than packaged software.

We will discuss a few of the many types of application programs available.

1. **Word Processing** software allows you to create, manipulate (edit/change), store, and output a finished document. Do you remember typing a long report, proofing the finished document and finding that you left out a

paragraph? With a typewritten paper you would be forced to type it over or leave out the missing paragraph. On a computer, you need only enter the document once, proof the document, make as many changes as necessary on the screen, and print all or part of the document at any time.

2. **Database Management** software, also known as record management, enables you to take a file cabinet full of information and to computerize the information for quick access. Let's examine a simple and familiar database example—a personal phone book. Imagine that you used 3 by 5 cards to store information about each of your friends. Each card lists a name, address, telephone number, birth date, and so on. Each individual data item would be called a **field**. The whole card would be considered a **record** of information on that friend. A group of cards describing different friends is called a **file**. Figure 1.9 shows an example of a friend's record. There are twenty fields listed, and more could be added.

*Figure 1.9—Example of a friend's record.*

| Salutation | Mrs. | First Name | Anne | Last Name | Smith |
|---|---|---|---|---|---|
| Street Address | 10 Palm Avenue | | | | |
| City | Pleasant Ville | State | CA | Zip | 90000 |
| Home Phone | (333) 444-5555 | Work Phone | (333) 444-5544 | | |
| Birthday | 9/23/60 | Favorite Color | Blue | Hobbies | Hiking, Camping, Gourmet Cook |
| Spouse Salutation | Mr. | Spouse Name | Michael | Anniversary Date | 6/24/82 |
| Child 1 | Chris | Child 2 | Brooke | Child 3 | | Child 4 | |
| Relationship | Friend | | | | |

If you forgot your friend's address you could easily look it up whether it was on a card or in a computerized database file. However, if you were going to the store to buy birthday cards, and you wanted a list of all friends who were celebrating their birthdays this month, would you want to shuffle through your cards to find them? How long would that take? Instead, you could tell the database program to look for all friends with a birthday in September (**search criteria**), and allow the computer to do your searching and generate a paper report listing the names and addresses of those friends.

3. **Spreadsheet** software is used to manipulate numbers. A spreadsheet document, called a worksheet, can replace large paper ledger sheets filled with financial transaction figures or any other type of numerical information. A worksheet is divided into rows (identified by numbers) and columns (identified by letters). The intersection of a row and column is called a **cell**. Each position on the worksheet has its own address consisting of a column letter and a row number. For example, the intersection point of column B (second column) and row 10 would be called B10. Figure 1.10 shows an example of a home spreadsheet. Each column shows how much was spent during that month. For example, cell B10 shows $400.00 was spent for food in January.

*Figure 1.10—A Sample Home Expense Spreadsheet*

|    | A         | B         | C         | D         | E         | F           |
|----|-----------|-----------|-----------|-----------|-----------|-------------|
| 1  |           | Jan       | Feb       | Mar       | Average   | Qtr. Totals |
| 2  | Mortgage  | 1000.00   | 1000.00   | 1000.00   | 1000.00   | 3000.00     |
| 3  | Electric  | 50.00     | 60.00     | 57.00     | 55.67     | 172.67      |
| 4  | Gas       | 60.00     | 63.00     | 55.00     | 59.33     | 177.33      |
| 5  | Water     | 32.00     | 37.00     | 35.00     | 34.67     | 106.67      |
| 6  | Rubbish   | 23.00     | 23.00     | 23.00     | 23.00     | 69.00       |
| 7  | Phone     | 25.70     | 10.90     | 8.50      | 15.03     | 34.43       |
| 8  | Insurance | 125.00    | 125.00    | 125.00    | 125.00    | 375.00      |
| 9  | Newspaper | 9.75      | 9.75      | 9.75      | 9.75      | 29.25       |
| 10 | Food      | 400.00    | 356.00    | 425.00    | 393.67    | 1174.67     |
| 11 | Savings   | 250.00    | 250.00    | 250.00    | 250.00    | 750.00      |
| 12 |           | $1975.45  | $1934.65  | $1988.25  | $1966.12  | $5889.02    |
| 13 |           |           |           |           |           |             |

Spreadsheets have built in functions that allow you to create your own formulas. In Figure 1.10 the spreadsheet program calculated the total dollar amount spent each month (row 12), the average amount spent each month by category (column E), and the total for the quarter spent in each category (column F). Since spreadsheets can quickly recalculate, they lend themselves to the what-if game. For example, what if I could reduce my utility bills by 4%? How much money would I save? To find out, I would simply enter the new figures and allow the spreadsheet program to recalculate the totals and averages.

4. **Desktop Publishing** is page layout software. This specialized software permits the users to easily combine text and graphic images on the screen and to print the finished document. It is used in the publishing industry to create and design the layout of books, magazines, brochures, fliers and so on.

# Key Terms

Access time
Alphanumeric
Apple Extended Keyboard
Apple Standard Keyboard
Application software
Byte
Caps lock key
Cathode Ray Tube
Cell
Central Processing Unit
CD-ROM
Clear key
Color monitor
Computers
Control key
Cursor control keys
Customized application programs
CPU
Data
Database Management
Desktop Publishing
Disk drive
Disk storage
Documentation
Dot-matrix printer
Esc key
Expansion cards
Expansion slots
FDHD
Field
File
Finder
Fixed drives
Floppy disk
Function keys
Gigabyte
Gray-scale monitor
Hard disk
Hardware
Head crash

Impact printer
Ink-jet printer
Input device
Keyboard
Kilobyte
Landscape monitor
Laser printers
Macintosh
Main Memory
Megabyte
Micro floppy disks
Monitors
Monochrome monitor
Mouse
Multitasking
NLQ printer
Nonvolatile
Numeric keypad
Operating system
Output devices
Packaged application programs
Platters
Peripherals
Permanent storage
Portrait monitor
Power-on
Programs
QWERTY
RAM
Random Access Memory
Read-Only Memory
Record
ROM
Search criteria
Secondary storage devices
Software
Spreadsheet
Status light
Storage devices
System software

System Unit
Terabyte
Thermal printer
Trackball
Transfer pates
Version numbers
Volatile
Word Processing
Write-protect tab

## Discussion Questions

1. Define Hardware.
2. What is the purpose of System Software?
3. Describe a typical computer configuration.
4. What is inside the system unit?
5. What is RAM, and how is it different from ROM?
6. What is a mouse used for?
7. What is ROM-BIOS?
8. What is the primary purpose of a floppy disk?
9. Do you need a floppy disk drive if you have a hard drive?
10. When do you need a hard drive?
11. What are the advantages and disadvantages of storing information on the hard drive?
12. Describe the four major types of application software.
13. Explain version numbers and how they are assigned.

## True/False Questions

For each question, circle the letter T if the statement is true and the letter F if the statement is false.

T  F  1. RAM is volatile memory.
T  F  2. Version numbers are always whole numbers.
T  F  3. The CPU, monitor, and keyboard are examples of peripherals.
T  F  4. A Byte is a single storage position in memory.
T  F  5. Application software is required to coordinate and supervise the operations of all physical components of the Macintosh.
T  F  6. Memory and disk storage are measured in kilobytes, megabytes, gigabytes, terabytes.

MATCHING QUESTIONS  17

T F 7. CPU is an acronym for Computer Processing Unit.
T F 8. Access time is the amount of time you have to work on the Macintosh.
T F 9. FDHD disks may be used in all 3.5 inch floppy drives.
T F 10. If the read/write heads come in contact with the platters on a hard disk, a head crash will occur.

## Completion Questions

Write the correct answer in each blank space.

1. The two primary purposes of a floppy disk are _____ and _____.
2. The _____ controls all computer operations and carries out each instruction one at a time.
3. The keyboard and mouse are examples of _____ devices.
4. Devices used to access the CPU are known as _____.
5. The non-volatile portion of memory is called _____.
6. Two examples of storage devices are _____ and _____.
7. A _____ is a hand held device used to point to objects on the screen.
8. _____ is the physical components of the Macintosh.
9. _____, or programs, contain detailed instructions that tell the Macintosh what to do.
10. _____ is an input device that is read-only and stores a vast amount of information.

## Matching Questions

For each question, place the letter of the correct answer on the line provided.

A. Laser Printer         B. Operating System        C. Database Management
D. Word Processing       E. Mouse                   F. Dot-matrix Printer
G. Spreadsheet           H. Desktop Publishing      I. Trackball

___ 1. Application software used to create, modify, save, and print text.
___ 2. An impact printer.
___ 3. A non-impact printer.
___ 4. Software used by the publishing industry to combine text and graphic images on the same page.
___ 5. Application software also known as record management.

___ 6. Application software used to create a numerical worksheet.
___ 7. A hand-held input device with a ball-type roller on the bottom and one or more buttons on top.
___ 8. System software that supervises all input/output operations on the Macintosh.
___ 9. An input device with a ball-type roller on top and one or more buttons.

## Assignments

1. Write a short paragraph describing what tasks you will be performing on your computer system, if you own one, or what you would use one for, if you did.

2. Cut out a minimum of two computer ads from your local newspaper and/or magazine advertising Macintosh computer systems for sale. Bring these ads to class.

# 2 Getting Started: Basic Macintosh Operations

## Learning Objectives

**After completing this Chapter you will be able to:**

1. Explain what visually oriented computing means.
2. List and explain the steps necessary to boot up the Macintosh.
3. List and describe the items on the Macintosh desktop after booting.
4. Explain the three basic mouse techniques used on the Macintosh.
5. Explain how and why you would select or deselect an icon.
6. Describe how to move one or more icons on the desktop.
7. List and explain the three ways to select multiple icons.
8. Explain how to access a menu and execute a command.
9. Explain how to access a menu without executing a command.
10. Explain the following characteristics of menus: dimmed menu commands, three dots after a menu command, a check mark next to a menu option, and the ⌘ followed by a letter.
11. List and briefly explain the purpose of the eight Finder menus.
12. List and explain the steps necessary to power down the system.

## Introduction

The first Macintosh computer was introduced in 1984. It was not the first computer with a graphical interface, but the Macintosh computer is responsible for increasing the popularity of the graphical environment and for inspiring many people who would never have touched a computer to become avid computer users. Computing became easier and more fun with the introduction of the Macintosh. (When I first saw the Macintosh in 1984, I was not overly impressed. I thought of the computer as little more than a toy, with cute pictures, or icons, on the screen. The Macintosh was so simple to use compared to other available systems, I thought, how could it be as powerful? I was certainly wrong!)

The Macintosh uses a **visually oriented computing** technique. The interaction between human and computer takes place in visual ways. This is known as a **graphical user interface** (abbreviated GUI, pronounced "gooey"), in which humans and machines interact (communicate) through graphics. As you perform an operation, you see the effects of your actions on the screen. Computers using this form of communication have a **windowing environment**. Other computer manufacturers have introduced this windowing technique on their computers because it is easy to use. There is one major difference between the windowing environment on the Macintosh and on other computers: the Macintosh Operating System centers on the graphics and the windowing environment—it is an integral part of the operating system. Other computers load their operating system into computer memory and then provide the option to run the windowing environment program. Their windowing environment program was not written in conjunction with the operating system—it runs on top of it.

This chapter will introduce you to visually oriented computing. You will learn how to power the computer on, how to start a computer session, and how to insert a floppy disk in the disk drive. You will be exposed to the Macintosh desktop, and you will learn how to operate the mouse. Menus will be introduced, as well as how to access and select menu commands. Finally, you will learn the proper technique to end your computer session.

To do the exercises and assignments in this chapter, you will need the System 7-Data disk that came with the book.

## Starting a Computer Session

The process of starting a computer is often called **starting up** or **booting up** (the process of pulling oneself up by the bootstraps). This includes supplying the computer with power, loading the necessary operating software into RAM, and starting the Finder program. The operating system program **Finder** creates and maintains the desktop, which is your work area on the computer. The **operating system** is stored in two locations: in ROM and on the disk. A group of programs called **ROM-BIOS**, short for Read Only Memory-Basic Input Output System, is stored in ROM by the manufacturer. ROM-BIOS stores the initial instructions on how to start the computer, how to control disk drives, how to interpret input from the keyboard and the mouse, and how to draw graphics and text on the screen. Is ROM-BIOS hardware or software? The answer is both, since the ROM chip(s) is hardware but the set of instructions is software. The term **firmware** has been given to this chip. Most of the operating system programs are stored in a **System Folder** on your **Startup disk**.

## Activity 2.1—Booting your Macintosh

Note 1   Whenever you see Activities with numbered steps, you should be sitting at the Macintosh computer performing the steps as you read.

Note 2   The Boot process varies slightly from one Macintosh configuration to the next. For example, if you are in a computer-equipped classroom or lab, the Macintosh may already be on. Therefore, verify the proper booting process with your instructor before doing this activity.

Step 1   If your Macintosh has an external hard disk drive, turn it on.

Step 2   Power on your Macintosh. Press the power on key (◁) on the keyboard. If this does not work, locate the Macintosh power switch to turn it on. If your monitor did not power on, press the monitor's power on switch.

### What's Happening

Electricity is supplied to the Macintosh. The computer reads and executes the ROM-BIOS chip.

If you do not have a Startup floppy disk in the disk drive, a floppy disk icon flashes on the screen as the Macintosh searches for the operating system files. The Macintosh will search the hard disk next. A smiling Macintosh flashes on the screen as the programs are located in the System Folder of the Startup disk and read into RAM. (Figure 2.1) A quick *Welcome to Macintosh* message appears, and the computer desktop appears on your screen.

*Figure 2.1—Loading the Operating System*

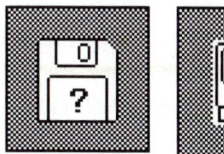

## The Desktop

The Macintosh desktop will appear after a successful boot. The desktop is where you will start and end all work sessions. It is designed to resemble a table top work area. It includes a menu bar, a surface to work on, an arrow pointer, a trash can, and one or more disks. (Figure 2.2) The disk that was used for booting (Startup disk) will appear in the top right corner. Disks are used to store documents (files) and folders (similar to a file cabinet). The trash can will appear wherever it was left when the Macintosh was last powered down. The trash can is used to remove unwanted items.

*Figure 2.2—The Macintosh Desktop*

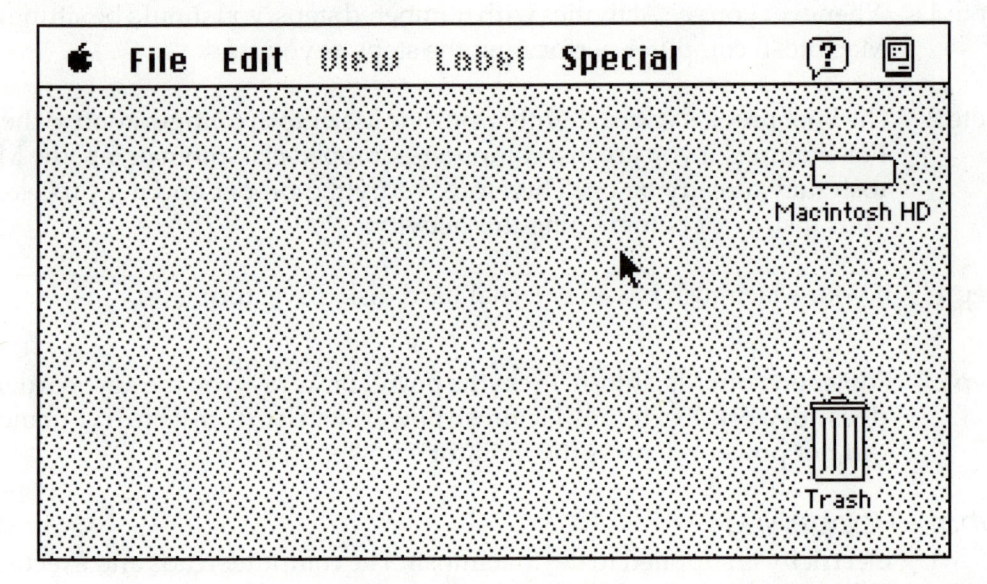

The Finder menu bar is displayed across the top of the screen. The **menu bar** consists of menu titles. Inside each menu you will find a list of **commands** (operations) that you can direct the Macintosh to perform. Menu bars vary from one program to the next.

The drawings on the desktop are called icons. **Icons** are symbols representing objects on your desktop. The shape and name of an icon provides clues about the type of object it represents. For instance, the Trash icon looks like a real trash can, the hard disk icon appears in the shape of a rectangle, and a floppy disk icon resembles the shape of a real floppy disk. When you create a letter, picture, or database document in an application program, the document will be assigned the appropriate icon by the application program. (Figure 2.3) In Chapter 9, you will learn how to customize icons by creating and assigning your own icons to documents.

*Figure 2.3—Sample icons*

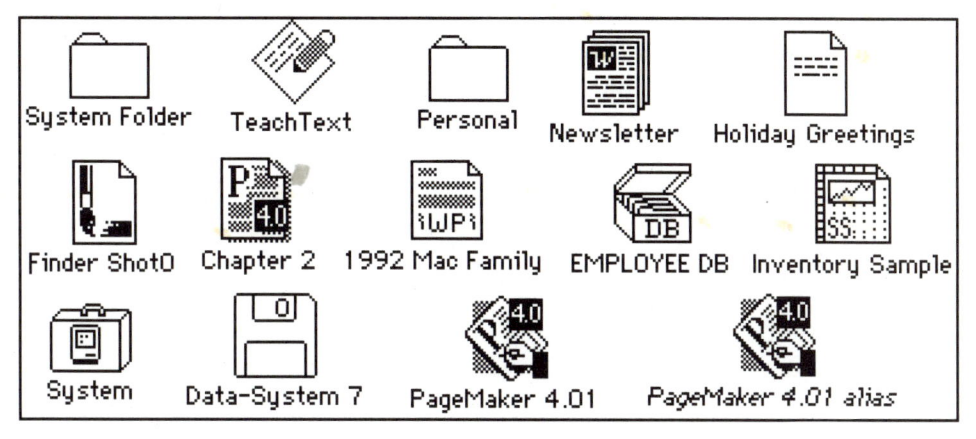

*Figure 2.4—Sample Pointers*

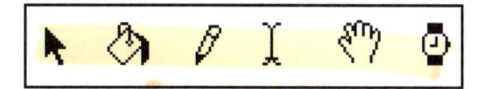

The desktop **arrow** is your **pointer.** As you move the mouse, the arrow on the screen moves in the same direction. The **pointer** will change shapes depending on what you are doing. It may assume the shape of an arrow, a stop watch, a revolving ball, an I-beam, and so on. (Figure 2.4)

## Mouse Operations

The hand-held mouse allows you to point to objects or locations on the computer desktop. There are three basic mouse techniques you need to know to be a productive Macintosh user.

1. **Pointing** is the process of moving the mouse across your table top to position the arrow on the screen at the desired location. If you are using a trackball instead of a mouse, use your fingertips to roll the ball on the top of the trackball. When pointing at an icon, make sure the tip of the arrow pointer is touching the icon. You may pick the mouse up and put it back down on the table top without disturbing the position of the pointer on the computer desktop.

2. **Clicking** is the process of pressing and releasing the mouse button. This will select an icon for further action or initiate an action. The object the pointer is on and the number of times you click the button will determine the action.

For example, clicking once on an application program icon will select the icon for further action. Clicking twice on an application program icon will execute the program. It is also important to mention that where you click on the icon is significant. Clicking once on an icon selects the icon for further action, but clicking once on the icon name allows you to rename the icon.

3. **Dragging** is the process of moving the mouse while holding down the mouse button. This allows you to move icons on the desktop, use pull-down menus, and highlight text.

To use the mouse, hold it with the cable exiting away from your fingertips. Your fingertips should be resting on the mouse button.

## Selecting and Moving Single Icons

In the following exercises you will use the three basic mouse techniques to select, deselect, and move icons on your desktop. Keyboard shortcuts to select an icon will also be discussed. A **selected icon** and its associated text will appear highlighted (dark) on your desktop. (Figure 2.5)

*Figure 2.5—Selected and Deselected Trash Icon*

Selected Icon     Deselected Icon

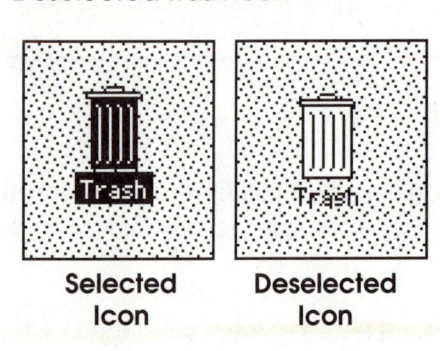

*Figure 2.6—Correct Pointer Placement*

### Activity 2.2—Arrow Pointer Hot Spot

Step 1  Move the mouse across a flat surface until the tip of the arrow on the screen is touching the Trash icon. (Figure 2.6) Click the mouse button once.

*What's Happening*
   The Trash icon will be highlighted. It will turn dark.

Step 2  Move the arrow to an empty spot on the desktop and click once.

*What's Happening*
   The Trash icon is deselected (no longer active or highlighted).

Step 3  Place the arrow pointer so that the arrow is on the Trash icon but the tip of the arrow is not. (Figure 2.7) Click once.

## What's Happening

The arrow pointer's **hot spot** is the tip of the arrow. Since the tip of the arrow was not on the icon, the icon was not selected. All pointers have a hot spot that must be on the icon to work correctly.

*Figure 2.7—Incorrect Pointer Placement*

### Activity 2.3—Making different icons active

Step 1   Move the mouse across a flat surface (the table top) until the arrow on the screen is touching the disk icon in the upper right corner of the screen. Click the mouse button once.

## What's Happening

If the disk icon is not already dark, it will turn dark. You have selected that object for further action. The disk icon is now your **selected** or **active object**.

Step 2   Move the mouse across a flat surface until the arrow on the screen is touching the Trash icon. Click the mouse button once.

## What's Happening

The Trash icon will be highlighted. It will turn dark. The disk icon will be **deselected** (no longer active or highlighted). The Trash icon is now your selected or active object.

Step 3   Press the Tab key on the keyboard.

## What's Happening

The icon above the Trash icon will be activated. The Trash icon will be deselected.

Step 4   Press the letter T key.

## What's Happening

The Trash icon will be highlighted and the disk icon will be deselected. Pressing a letter key activates the first icon with a name beginning with that letter.

Step 5   Press the Down Arrow key on the keyboard.

*What's Happening*

Pressing the Down Arrow key will cause the icon immediately below the Trash icon to become active. If there is no icon below the Trash icon, nothing will happen because there is no icon on the desktop in the direction the arrow is pointing (down). The Trash icon remains the active icon.

Step 6    Press the Up Arrow key on the keyboard.

*What's Happening*

If there is an icon immediately above the current active icon (Trash) it will be selected. Your disk icon may become the active icon.

Step 7    Move the mouse until the arrow is on an empty area of the desktop. Click the mouse button once.

*What's Happening*

By clicking on an empty area of the open desktop you have deselected, or unactivated, all objects. Figures 2.8 and 2.9 summarize how to select and deselect an icon.

*Figure 2.8—Selecting an Icon*

| Method | Action |
| --- | --- |
| Click on the icon | That icon becomes active. |
| Press an arrow key | The next desktop icon in that direction becomes active. |
| Press the Tab key | The next desktop icon in alphabetic order becomes active. |
| Press a letter key | The first desktop icon with a name beginning with that letter becomes active. |

*Figure 2.9—Deselecting an Icon*

| Method | Action |
| --- | --- |
| Click on another icon | That icon becomes active and the original icon is deselected. |
| Click on any empty desktop area | Everything becomes inactive. All icons become deselected. |

## Inserting Floppy Disks

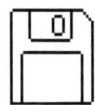

Locate the System 7-Data disk that came with the book. Let's examine this disk. (Figure 2.10)

*Figure 2.10—Parts of a Floppy Disk*

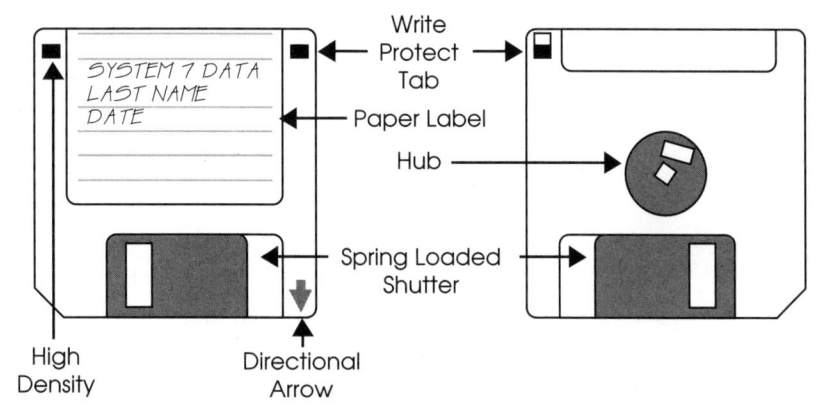

The front side of this disk contains:
1. A disk label containing the name of the disk (used to identify the disk).
2. The write-protect hole in the top right corner.
3. A hole in the top left corner, if the disk is high density.
4. The spring-loaded shutter along the bottom of the disk. Do not open this shutter. Opening the shutter will expose the floppy disk inside to unnecessary contamination.
5. A directional arrow next to the shutter. This directional arrow indicates which end of the disk should be inserted in the floppy disk drive first.

The back side of this disk contains:
1. The write-protect tab in the top left corner.

2. A hub or center spindle which is used by the disk drive to spin the floppy disk.
3. The spring-loaded shutter along the bottom of the disk.

To insert a floppy disk in the disk drive, hold the floppy disk with the disk label facing up. With your thumb on the label (opposite the shuttered end), insert the shutter end into the disk drive and push gently. If your disk does not have a label attached, the side with the write-protect tab and hub should face down. The directional arrow next to the shutter also indicates the side and end of the disk that should be inserted into the disk drive first.

### Activity 2.4—Insert the System 7-Data Floppy Disk

Step 1  Place your thumb on the disk label opposite the shuttered end of the System 7-Data disk. Insert the shuttered end of the disk into the drive and push gently.

*Figure 2.11-Disk Icon*

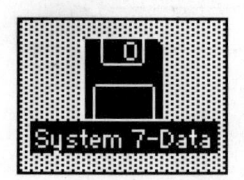

*What's Happening*

Your Macintosh grabs the disk and pulls it into the disk drive. The System 7-Data disk icon appears on your desktop. (Figure 2.11)

### Activity 2.5—Moving Icons on the Desktop

Step 1  Position the arrow pointer on the System 7-Data disk icon, hold the mouse button down and drag the disk icon to the opposite side of the screen. Release the button.

*What's Happening*

You have selected this icon for action and have moved it to another location on your desktop. The icon will stay at this location until you move it to another location or until you power down the Macintosh.

Step 2  Position the arrow pointer on the Trash icon, hold the mouse button down and drag the Trash icon next to the System 7-Data disk icon. Release the mouse button.

*What's Happening*

You selected this icon for action and have moved it to a new location on your desktop. Obviously you can arrange the icons on your desktop according to your needs. However, you may not be able to move the Startup hard disk icon. There are several programs available that provide security for this disk that will prevent anyone from moving the icon.

Step 3   Drag the icons back to their original positions.

Step 4   Click on an open area of the desktop to deselect all icons.

## Selecting and Moving Multiple Icons

Frequently, Macintosh users want to select a group of icons for further action. Any action taken on one will occur to the group. For example, you can copy a group of icons from one disk to another, you can throw away a group of icons, you can move a group of icons, and so on. There are three ways to accomplish this task: the Shift-click technique, the box technique and the menu technique.

1. **Shift-Click.** Hold down the Shift key while clicking once on each icon to be included in the group.

2. **Box.** Position the arrow pointer at one corner of the group of icons you want to select, hold the mouse button down, and drag the arrow diagonally across the screen to the other corner of the group. A box (also called a marquee) will form around the icons and any icon inside the box or touched by it will be included in the group of selected icons.

3. **Menu.** This technique does not allow you to select certain icons to be included in the group, rather, all icons on the desktop or active window will be selected. A **window** is a region on the desktop associated with a specific icon, hardware device, application program, document and so on. (If you were in an application program, everything in the open document would be selected. If you were viewing a list of available documents on a disk, all documents on the disk would be selected.) Windows will be discussed further in Chapter 4. To execute the Select All command, point to the Edit menu and choose **Select All** or use the keyboard equivalent—**Command A.** The Command key is located next to the Space Bar. This key is easily identifiable because one or both of these symbols will be located on it. ( ⌘ )

### Activity 2.6—Selecting Multiple Icons

Step 1   While holding down the Shift key, point and click on the Trash icon and the System 7-Data disk icon. Release the Shift key.

*What's Happening*

Both icons have been selected for further action. Both icons are highlighted.

Step 2   Click anywhere on the open desktop.

## What's Happening

You have deselected all objects. The disk and Trash icons are no longer highlighted.

Step 3   Move the System 7-Data disk icon to the middle of the desktop. If the Trash icon is not in the lower right corner, move it there.

Step 4   Position your arrow above and to the left of the System 7-Data disk icon. Hold the mouse button down, drag the mouse down and to the right until the disk and Trash icons are within the box. Release the button.

## What's Happening

Both icons are selected for further action and are highlighted.

Step 5   Click anywhere on the open desktop to deselect both icons.

Step 6   Position your arrow just below and to the right of the Trash icon. Hold the mouse button down, drag the mouse up and to the left until the Trash and System 7-Data disk icons are inside the box. Release the button.

## What's Happening

Both icons are selected. You can draw the box up, down, left or right. Simply start at one corner and drag.

Step 7   Click anywhere on the open desktop to deselect both icons.

The third technique to select multiple icons requires you to execute the Select All command in the Edit menu. The Select All command will be discussed in Activity 2.14 and 2.15. Figure 2.12 summarizes how to select multiple icons.

*Figure 2.12—Selecting Multiple Icons*

| Method | Group includes |
| --- | --- |
| Shift-Click | Each icon clicked on. |
| Box | Any icon in or touched by the box. |
| Edit menu command Select All | All icons on the desktop or active window. |

## Activity 2.7—Moving Multiple Icons

Step 1   Your System 7-Data disk icon should be in the middle of the screen. Drag your Trash icon next to this disk icon. Click on the open desktop to deselect all icons.

Step 2   Use the Shift-click technique to select and move both icons. Hold your Shift key down and click on the System 7-Data disk icon. Point to the Trash icon, hold your Shift key down and press and hold the mouse button down. Drag the two icons to the bottom left corner of your screen.

Step 3   Click anywhere on the open desktop to deselect both icons.

Step 4   Use the Box technique to select and move both icons. Draw a Box around both icons. Point to one of the icons and drag the group to the top left corner of your screen.

Step 5   Click anywhere on the open desktop to deselect both icons.

Step 6   Drag the Trash icon to the bottom right corner of the desktop.

Step 7   Drag the System 7-Data disk icon below the Startup disk icon in the top right corner of the desktop.

## Using Menus

The **Finder Menu Bar** is displayed across the top of your desktop. The **Finder** is a special **Utility** program. Why is it special? Unlike other Utility programs, it is loaded during the booting process and remains working as long as your system is on. Most Utility programs are only loaded into memory at your request and are cancelled (stopped) at your command. Each utility and application program has its own menu bar with commands, although some commands are available in all application programs. The Finder Menu Bar consists of at least eight separate pull-down menus: Apple, File, Edit, View, Label, Special, Help and Application. (Figure 2.13) A pull-down menu drops down from the menu bar, and only remains open as long as you hold it open. If you have customized your Macintosh, it is possible that you may have additional menus.

*Figure 2.13—Finder Menu Bar*

 File   Edit   View   Label   Special

The following information will help you work with menus.

- **Displaying a menu.** Point to the menu title and hold down the mouse button. The commands available in that menu will be displayed in a **pull-down menu**.

- **Dimmed menu commands**. The menu commands that are not as dark as others are dimmed. Dimmed menu commands are not executable at the moment. The reason for this will vary.

- **Three dots after a menu command.** Three dots after a menu command indicates that the Macintosh operating system will require additional information to execute this command.

- **Check Mark.** A check mark next to a menu command indicates the command is the active, selected command.

- **Keyboard Shortcuts**. You can use the keyboard instead of using your mouse to execute a command. Hold down the **Command** ( ⌘) key while typing the specified characters to do this. For example, holding down the ⌘ key while pressing the A key will select all icons on the active desktop.

- **Executing a menu command.** To execute a command, position the pointer on the menu title, press and hold the mouse button, drag the pointer down the menu until the command you want is highlighted, and release the mouse button.

- **Not selecting any command on the menu.** If you change your mind after displaying the pull-down menu and you decide you do not want to execute a command, simply move the arrow pointer back to the menu title and release the mouse button.

- **A triangle at the bottom of the menu.** On some application program menus, you will find a downward pointing triangle at the bottom of the menu. The arrow indicates there are additional commands available that would not fit in the menu. Placing the pointer on the downward triangle will cause the commands to appear or to **scroll** by (roll past you).

Display each of the Finder Bar menus. These menus will be discussed in more detail in Chapter 6. Some of the commands on your menus may be dimmed. Don't worry about this now.

USING MENUS 33

### Activity 2.8—Examining the Apple Menu

Step 1  Display the **Apple menu.** Move the arrow on the desktop until it is touching the Apple icon in the top left corner. Hold down the mouse button to display the Apple pull-down menu. Your Apple menu may have different entries on it. (Figure 2.14)

*What's Happening*

The Apple menu will be displayed. Notice the three dots after the About This Macintosh command, indicating that additional information will be provided or required. The Apple menu contains Desk Accessories, which are useful programs available from within almost any Macintosh application.

*Figure 2.14—The Apple Menu*

- About This Macintosh...
- Alarm Clock
- Calculator
- Chooser
- Control Panels
- Key Caps
- Note Pad
- Puzzle
- Scrapbook

Step 2  Release the mouse button.

*What's Happening*

When you release the mouse button the menu disappears.

### Activity 2.9—Examining the File Menu

Step 1  Display the **File menu.** Move the arrow on the desktop until it is touching the word File on the menu bar. Hold down the mouse button to display the File pull-down menu. (Figure 2.15)

*What's Happening*

The File menu is displayed. Notice that some commands have keyboard equivalents. For instance, Open has the **keyboard equivalent** ⌘ O. The File menu allows you to find, open, close, print, duplicate or obtain information on files.

*Figure 2.15—The File Menu*

| File | |
|---|---|
| New Folder | ⌘N |
| Open | ⌘O |
| Print | ⌘P |
| Close Window | ⌘W |
| Get Info | ⌘I |
| Sharing... | |
| Duplicate | ⌘D |
| Make Alias | |
| Put Away | ⌘Y |
| Find... | ⌘F |
| Find Again | ⌘G |
| Page Setup... | |
| Print Desktop... | |

Step 2  Release the mouse button.

Step 3   Click on the Trash icon.

*What's Happening*

The Trash icon is highlighted.

Step 4   Move the arrow on the desktop until it is touching the word File in the menu bar. Hold down the mouse button to display the File pull-down menu. While holding the mouse button down, drag the arrow pointer down the list of menu commands until the **Open** command is highlighted. Release the mouse button.

*What's Happening*

Since the Trash icon was highlighted, a Trash window opens on your desktop. In Figure 2.16, the Trash window contains 0 items—it's empty. An in-depth discussion of windows is presented in Chapter 4.

*Figure 2.16—The Trash Window*

*Figure 2.17—The Edit Menu*

Step 5   Move the arrow on the desktop until it is touching File in the menu bar. Hold down the mouse button to display the File pull-down menu. While holding the mouse button down, drag the arrow down the list of menu commands until the **Close Window** command is highlighted. Release the mouse button.

*What's Happening*

The Trash window closes and disappears from the desktop.

### Activity 2.10—Examining the Edit Menu

Step 1   Display the **Edit menu.** (Figure 2.17)

*What's Happening*

The Edit menu lets you cut or copy information from one location in a document and place it in a new location in the same document or in a different document.

### Activity 2.11—Examining the View Menu

Step 1   Display the **View menu**. (Figure 2.18)

*What's Happening*

The View menu permits you to decide how to display the contents of a Macintosh window. The check mark identifies the selected view.

### Activity 2.12—Examining the Label Menu

Step 1   Display the **Label menu**. (Figure 2.19)

*What's Happening*

You may assign labels to icons. This can help you quickly identify and separate icons. If your monitor is capable of showing at least sixteen colors or shades of gray, each label can be assigned a different color/gray shade. The check mark identifies the current selection.

### Activity 2.13—Examining the Special Menu

Step 1   Display the **Special menu**. (Figure 2.20)

*What's Happening*

The Special menu provides unique commands that simply do not belong in any of the other menus.

### Activity 2.14—Examining the Help Menu

Step 1   Move the arrow on the desktop until it is touching the question mark (?) icon on the menu bar. Hold down the mouse button to display the Help pull-down menu. (Figure 2.21)

*Figure 2.18—The View Menu*

```
View
   by Small Icon
 ✓ by Icon
   by Name
   by Size
   by Kind
   by Label
   by Date
```

*Figure 2.19—The Label Menu*

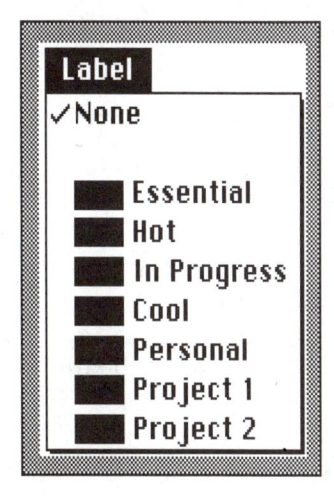

```
Label
 ✓ None

 ■ Essential
 ■ Hot
 ■ In Progress
 ■ Cool
 ■ Personal
 ■ Project 1
 ■ Project 2
```

*Figure 2.20—The Special Menu*

```
Special
 Clean Up Window
 Empty Trash...

 Eject Disk      ⌘E
 Erase Disk...

 Restart
 Shut Down
```

*Figure 2.21—The Help Menu*

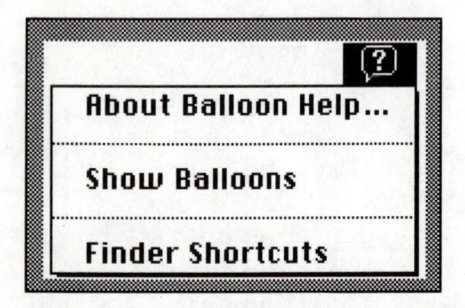

[Menu showing: About Balloon Help..., Show Balloons, Finder Shortcuts]

*Figure 2.22—Application Menu*

[Menu showing: Hide Finder, Hide Others, Show All, ✓ Finder]

*What's Happening*

The **Help menu** may be used to obtain information on most items on the computer screen.

### Activity 2.15—Examining the Application Menu

Step 1   Move the arrow on the desktop until it is touching the current application icon (a tiny Macintosh) on the far right end of the menu bar. Hold down the mouse button to display the Application pull-down menu. (Figure 2.22)

*What's Happening*

The **Application menu** lists all open programs. The check mark identifies the active program.

## Select All

Remember, the third way to select multiple icons is to use the menu command Select All.

### Activity 2.16—Executing the Select All Command in the Edit Menu

Step 1   Move the arrow on the desktop until it is touching the word Edit in the menu bar. Hold down the mouse button to display the Edit pull-down menu. While holding the mouse button down, drag the arrow down the list of menu commands until the Select All command is highlighted. Release the mouse button.

*What's Happening*

All icons on the screen are highlighted. They have been selected for further action.

Step 2   Click anywhere on the open desktop to deselect all icons.

### Activity 2.17—Executing the Select All Command using the Keyboard

Step 1    Use the keyboard equivalent for this command: ⌘ A. (While holding down the Command key, press the A letter key.)

*What's Happening*

All icons on the screen are highlighted. They have been selected for further action. Keyboard equivalent commands are not **case-sensitive**—upper or lower case letters may be used.

Step 2    Click anywhere on the open desktop to deselect all icons.

## Getting Help [?]

One of the many new features of the Macintosh System 7 Operating Software is a built-in help program. Explanations are available for most items that appear on the desktop: icons, menus, menu commands, and so on. The Help menu is always available. Many application programs use this feature to explain objects within the program.

### Activity 2.18—Executing the About Balloon Help Command

Step 1    Move the arrow on the desktop until it is touching the Help [?] icon in the menu bar. Hold down the mouse button to display the Help menu. While holding the mouse button down, drag the arrow down the list of menu commands until the **About Balloon Help** command is highlighted. Release the mouse button.

*What's Happening*

A description on how **Balloon Help** works is displayed. (Figure 2.23)

*Figure 2.23—About Balloon Help Command*

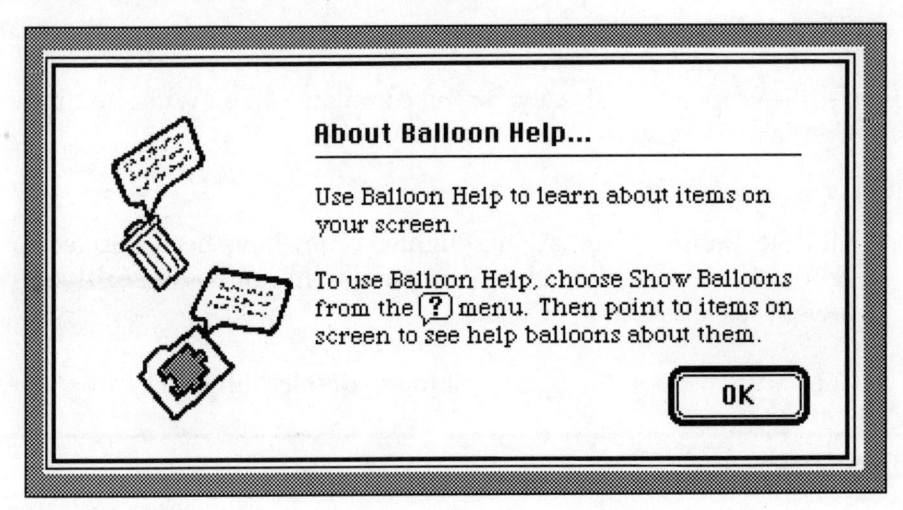

**About Balloon Help...**

Use Balloon Help to learn about items on your screen.

To use Balloon Help, choose Show Balloons from the [?] menu. Then point to items on screen to see help balloons about them.

OK

Step 2   Press the Return key on the keyboard.

*What's Happening*

Pressing the Return key directs the Macintosh to accept the answer in the bold button (OK). The description disappears from the desktop. Positioning the tip of the arrow pointer in the OK button and clicking the mouse button once also enters this answer.

### Activity 2.19—Turning Balloon Help On

Step 1   Move the arrow on the desktop until it is touching the Help icon in the menu bar. Hold down the mouse button to display the Help menu. While holding the mouse button down, drag the arrow down the list of menu commands until the **Show Balloons** command is highlighted. Release the mouse button.

*Figure 2.24—Hard Disk Balloon*

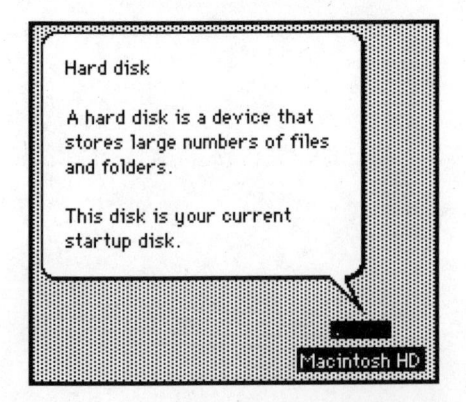

Hard disk

A hard disk is a device that stores large numbers of files and folders.

This disk is your current startup disk.

Macintosh HD

*What's Happening*

Balloon help has been turned on.

### Activity 2.20—Using Balloon Help

Step 1   Move the arrow pointer on the desktop until it is touching the hard disk icon.

*What's Happening*

A help balloon appears for the hard disk icon. (Figure 2.24)

Step 2    Move the arrow pointer on top of the Trash icon.

*What's Happening*

Balloon help appears for the Trash icon. (Figure 2.25)

Step 3    Position the arrow pointer on the Help menu icon, but do not click on it.

*What's Happening*

A balloon appears displaying information about the Help menu. (Figure 2.26) This works for any menu title.

Step 4    Position the arrow pointer on the Special menu, but do not click on it.

*What's Happening*

A balloon containing a brief description on the Special menu appears. (Figure 2.27)

Step 5    Click anywhere on the open desktop to deselect all icons.

Step 6    Position the arrow pointer on the Special menu, hold the mouse button to display the menu, and slowly drag the pointer down the list of commands. *Do Not* release the mouse button while a command is highlighted. You do not want to execute one of these commands. Move the arrow pointer back to the menu title before releasing the mouse button.

*Figure 2.25—Trash Balloon*

Trash

To discard an item, eject a disk, or remove a hard disk or shared disk icon from your desktop, drag it to the Trash. To permanently remove items in the Trash, choose Empty Trash from the Special menu.

*Figure 2.26—Help Menu Balloon*

Help menu

Use this menu to get information that helps you use your computer.

*Figure 2.27—Special Menu Balloon*

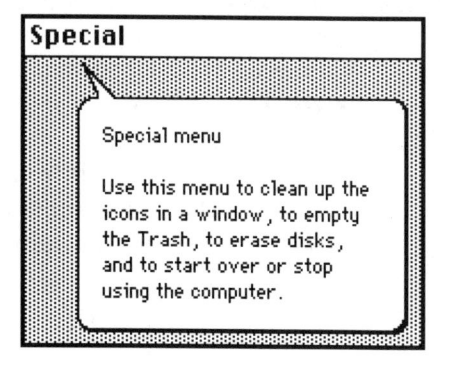

Special

Special menu

Use this menu to clean up the icons in a window, to empty the Trash, to erase disks, and to start over or stop using the computer.

*What's Happening*

A new balloon appears as you drag over each command. For example, Figure 2.28 shows the help balloon for the Shut Down command.

*Figure 2.28—Shut Down Command Balloon*

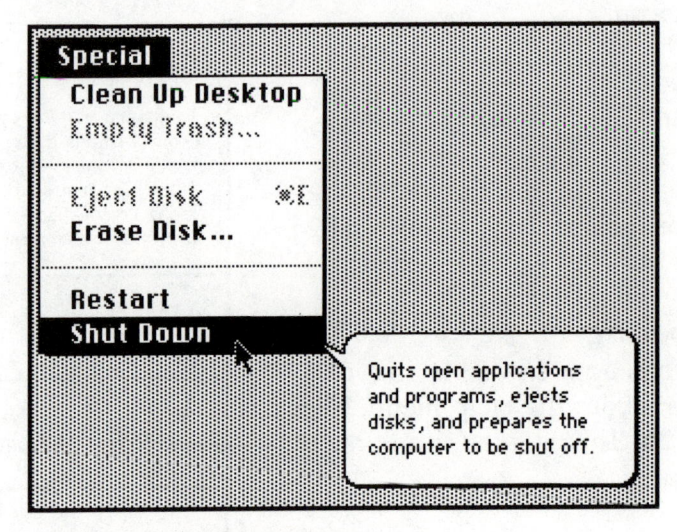

```
Special
  Clean Up Desktop
  Empty Trash...

  Eject Disk    ⌘E
  Erase Disk...

  Restart
  Shut Down
```

Quits open applications and programs, ejects disks, and prepares the computer to be shut off.

### Activity 2.21—Turning Balloon Help Off

Step 1   Display the Help menu. Drag the mouse down the menu until the **Hide Balloons** command is highlighted. Release the mouse button.

*What's Happening*

Balloon Help has been turned off. Balloon Help is great for beginners or when you are trying to learn a new program and can be turned off as needed.

## Ending a Computer Session

When you are finished working with your computer system it is time to **power-down**. This is different from turning the computer off. You do not want to abruptly cut power. This can damage your open files and disks. Of course, if a power failure occurs while you are using your computer system, the power will be cut abruptly—you don't have any control over it. You can only hope nothing is damaged. Figure 2.29 summarizes the steps necessary to perform an orderly power-down.

*Figure 2.29—Steps to Powering-down the Macintosh*

1. Close any open document files you have been working on.
2. Quit all open application programs.
3. Close all open windows.
4. Select the Shut Down command in the Special menu.

Figure 2.30 summarizes the actions automatically performed by the Shut Down command.

*Figure 2.30—Steps Performed by the Shut Down Command*

1. Closes all open application program documents and programs (if you accidentally left any open).
2. Closes all operating system files in an orderly fashion.
3. Adjusts the hard drive's read/write heads so that the drive can safely be powered down.
4. Ejects all floppy disks from the drives.
5. Turns off the power on some Macintosh models or directs you to do it manually.

## Activity 2.22—Shutting Down the Computer

*Very Important: Read Carefully.*

Note 1   If you are not working on your own Macintosh, check with the person in charge of the computer before powering-down. Some Macintosh users, and computer-equipped classrooms and labs prefer to leave the computer powered-on all day. It is easier on the hardware to leave the Macintosh on if someone will be using it within the next two to three hours.

Note 2   The way you leave your Macintosh desktop will vary depending on whether you are using a Macintosh that is shared with others or not.

For example, let's say you share a normal wooden desk with others at work. You use the desk as a work area during the day but someone else uses the desk in the evening. You would probably make sure to remove your work from the desktop before going home in the evening. There are several reasons for this: you do not want the evening person to disturb your documents, the documents may be confidential, and it is courteous to leave a clean work area for the next employee. On the other hand, if you have your own desk, you are more likely to leave non-confidential items on the desktop when you go home.

The same scenario exists with the Macintosh computer. If you are working on a Macintosh that is used by others, you should be courteous. Leave the desktop clean, (close all open windows) empty the Trash, and return the Trash icon to the bottom right corner of the desktop.

If you are working on your own personal Macintosh, you may choose to leave open windows on the desktop. For example, if the Startup disk window is left open when you shutdown the Macintosh, it will appear on your desktop the next time you boot.

Step 1   Click anywhere on the open desktop to deselect any active icons.

Step 2   If this is a shared Macintosh, clear the desktop. Close all open windows, and return the Trash icon to its original location (lower right corner). Empty the Trash. (Discussed in a later chapter.)

Step 3   Move the arrow on the desktop until it is touching the Special menu. Hold down the mouse button to display the Special pull-down menu. While holding the button down, drag the arrow down the menu commands until the **Shut Down** command is highlighted. Release the mouse button.

### What's Happening
Your system has gone through the shut-down sequence.

Step 4   If the power is still on, use the power switch to turn off the power.

Step 5   Remove the System 7-Data disk from the floppy drive.

Whenever you end a work session, follow this shut-down procedure or the procedure outlined for you by the person responsible for the Macintosh system you are using.

---

# Key Terms

| | |
|---|---|
| ⌘ ⌘ | Commands |
| About Balloon Help | Deselected icon |
| Active icon | Desktop |
| Apple menu | Dimmed command |
| Application menu | Dragging |
| Arrow pointer | Edit menu |
| Balloon Help | Eject |
| Booting-up | External hard drive |
| Box/Marquee | File menu |
| Case-sensitive | Finder |
| Clicking | Finder menu bar |
| Close Window command | Firmware |

GUI
Graphical User Interface
Help Menu
Hide Balloons
Hot spot
Icons
Keyboard equivalents
Label menu
Menu bar
Menu command
Open command ⌘ O
Operating System (OS)
Pointer
Pointing
Power-down
Pull-down menu
ROM-BIOS

Scroll
Select All ⌘ A
Selected icon
Shift-click
Show Balloons
Shut Down
Special menu
Startup disk
System boot disk
System Folder
Trash
Utility programs
View menu
Visually oriented computing
Window
Windowing environment

## Discussion Questions

1. What is meant by visually oriented computing?
2. Describe what happens during the booting process.
3. Discuss how to access a menu, how to execute a command and how to not execute a command once the menu has been displayed.
4. Describe the three basic mouse techniques.
5. Describe the steps necessary to move an icon on the desktop.
6. Explain how to select multiple icons.
7. Why is it important to shut down the Macintosh properly?
8. Describe these common menu characteristics: dimmed commands, 3 dots following a command, a check mark next to a command, keyboard equivalents.
9. Why aren't keyboard equivalents available for all commands?
10. If you have multiple disk icons on the desktop, can you tell which one was accessed during the booting process? If so, how?
11. Describe System 7's help feature.
12. Explain what is meant by the arrow pointer's hot spot and why it is important.

## True/False Questions

For each question, circle the letter T if the statement is true and the letter F if the statement is false.

T F 1. Operating System 7 is stored in the System Folder of the Startup disk.
T F 2. The phrase "Macintosh desktop" refers to the area on your tabletop where your Macintosh computer sits.
T F 3. The Finder menu bar and all application menu bars contain the same menu commands.
T F 4. You should use the keyboard arrow keys to move the arrow pointer on your desktop.
T F 5. Dragging is the process of holding the mouse button down and dragging an object across the desktop.
T F 6. You design and assign icons to files as they are created.
T F 7. You should hold the mouse so that the mouse button is under your fingertips and the cable is exiting away from your fingers.
T F 8. You should allow plenty of room on your tabletop for mouse movements, because you can't pick up the mouse without disturbing the arrow pointer on the screen.
T F 9. ⌘ S is the keyboard equivalent for the Shut Down command.
T F 10. A group of selected icons act as one.

## Completion Questions

Write the correct answer in each blank space.

1. The three basic mouse techniques are _____, _____, and _____.
2. The process of starting your Macintosh is known as _____.
3. The operating system is stored in two locations:_____ and _____.
4. _____ and_____ on an icon selects it for future action.
5. Two methods to deselect an icon are _____ and _____.
6. To execute a command using a keyboard equivalent, hold down the _____ key while typing another character.
7. The drawings that appear on your desktop are called_____.
8. A selected icon will appear_____on your desktop.
9. List four methods to select multiple icons.
   a.
   b.
   c.
   d.

10. ⌘ _____ will select all icons on the desktop.
11. To use System 7's help feature, execute the _____ _____ command of the _____ menu.

## Matching Questions

For each question, place the letter of the correct answer on the line provided. Some answers will be used more than once.

    A. Apple Menu    B. Application Menu    C. File Menu
    D. Edit Menu    E. Help Menu    F. Label Menu
    G. View Menu    H. Special Menu

___ 1. Use a command in this menu to shut down the Macintosh.
___ 2. The Select All command is included in this menu.
___ 3. Use this menu to switch between showing objects by icon, name, date, size, and kind.
___ 4. This menu consists of unique commands that simply do not belong on any other menu.
___ 5. Desk accessories are available in this menu.
___ 6. This menu includes commands to Open, Close, or duplicate files.
___ 7. Use the commands in this menu to cut, copy, and paste text.
___ 8. The Show Balloons and Hide Balloons commands are on this menu.
___ 9. Use this menu to display a list of all open application programs.
___ 10. Use the commands on this menu to assign a color to icons for easy identification.

For each question, place the letter of the correct answer (relating to pull-down menus) on the line provided.

    A. Check-mark    B. Three Dots    C. ⌘
    D. Dimmed commands

___ 1. Indicates that you can't execute this command at this time.
___ 2. Indicates that the Macintosh will need additional information before executing this command.
___ 3. Identifies the active menu option.
___ 4. Indicates that a keyboard equivalent exists for this command.

## Assignments

Take a seat in front of the Macintosh computer system. If the computer is not already on, do not power the system on yet. Examine the Macintosh hardware you are using and answer the following questions.

1. \_\_\_\_ The Macintosh Computer System you will use to complete this assignment is located at
   a. Computer-equipped classroom or lab
   b. Home
   c. Work
   d. Other (specify)_____

2. \_\_\_\_ The System Model you will use is a
   _____

3. \_\_\_\_ The monitor is
   a. Part of the Computer System Unit
   b. A separate unit

4. \_\_\_\_ There is a cable running directly from the back of the Macintosh to the printer.
   a. True
   b. False

5. \_\_\_\_ The available printer is a
   a. Dot Matrix (An ImageWriter, for example)
   b. Ink-jet (A StyleWriter, for example)
   c. Laser (A LaserWriter, for example)
   d. Other

6. \_\_\_\_ The keyboard is
   a. Standard
   b. Extended

If the Macintosh is not on and booted, do so now. Insert your System 7-Data disk in the floppy drive.

7. \_\_\_\_ What is the name of the disk icon in the top right corner of the desktop?
   _____

ASSIGNMENTS    47

8 \_\_\_\_    Deselect all icons on the desktop and examine the File menu. Which of the following commands in the File menu is available for execution?
   a. New Folder
   b. Open
   c. Put Away
   d. Duplicate
   e. None of the above.

9. \_\_\_\_   Select the Trash icon. Which one of the following commands on the File menu can not be executed?
   a. Open
   b. Close Window
   c. Get Info
   d. Page Setup
   e. All of these commands are available for execution.

10. \_\_\_\_  Select the System 7-Data disk icon. Drag it to the middle of the desktop. The disk icon should still be selected. Which one of the following commands on the Edit menu can not be executed?
   a. Cut
   b. Copy
   c. Select All
   d. Show Clipboard
   e. All of these commands are available for execution.

11. \_\_\_\_  Select all icons on the desktop. Which one of the following commands on the Edit menu can be executed?
   a. Cut
   b. Copy
   c. Paste
   d. Clear
   e. All of these commands are available for execution.

12.    Deselect all icons on the desktop. Write down the first command in the Special menu.

   _____

13.    Select the Trash icon. Write down the first command in the Special menu.

   _____

14. _____ Select the System 7-Data disk icon, examine the Edit menu and note which commands are available for execution. Select the Trash icon, examine the Edit menu and note which commands are available for execution. Was there any change in the list of available commands?
    a. Yes
    b. No

Turn on Balloon Help.

15. Deselect all icons. Point to the File menu title. The help balloon says:
    Use this menu to perform operations with _____, _____, _____, _____ and _____.

16. Display the File pull-down menu. Drag down the list of commands and stop on the Open command. The last sentence in the help balloon says:
    Not available because _____.

17. Point to the Label menu. The last sentence in the help balloon says:
    Not available because there is _____
    _____.

18. Select your System 7-Data disk icon. Point to the Label menu. The last sentence in the help balloon says:
    The labels you assign can be used _____.

# Handling Floppy Disks

## Learning Objectives

### After completing this Chapter you will be able to:

1. Explain why Macintosh users need floppy disk drives as well as a hard disk drive.
2. Explain how to properly insert a floppy disk.
3. List and explain the five ways to eject a floppy disk.
4. Explain why you would want to leave a dimmed floppy disk icon on the desktop after ejecting the disk.
5. Explain why disks need to be initialized or formatted.
6. List and explain the tasks performed during the initialization process.
7. Describe the purpose of the disk directory.
8. Compare and contrast dialog and status boxes.
9. Explain how buttons are used and the meaning of the bold button.
10. Explain how, why and when you would lock a floppy disk.
11. List and describe the three ways to copy the entire contents of one floppy disk to another.
12. Discuss why you need backup disks.
13. Explain why it's advisable to use the Erase Disk command from the Special menu to remove everything from a floppy disk.
14. List the steps necessary to rename an icon completely or partially.

## Introduction

A floppy disk drive is necessary even if your Macintosh has a hard drive. Why? If you go to a computer store to buy additional application programs, will they sell them to you on a hard drive or on a floppy disk? If your hard drive has a head crash (read/write heads touch the recording surface) wouldn't it be a good idea to have your important files backed up (copied) to floppy disks? If you want to share a document file with a co-worker, are you going to loan them your hard drive from your home computer system? Do you want to store unimportant data files on your hard drive? If you do, it will quickly fill up.

Floppy disks are a primary source of data storage. They are readily available in the stores, inexpensive, simple to use, and transportable. This chapter will discuss how to use floppy disks. We will discuss inserting the disk in the drive as well as copying and erasing the entire disk. In a later chapter, you will copy individual files from one floppy disk to another and erase selected files.

To do the exercises and assignments in this chapter, you will need the System 7-Data disk that came with the book, and one blank disk.

## Inserting Floppy Disks

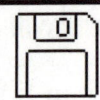

To insert a floppy disk in the disk drive, hold the floppy disk with the disk label facing up with your thumb on the label (opposite the shuttered end), insert the shutter end into the disk drive and push gently. If your disk does not have a label attached, the side with the write-protect tab and hub should face down. The directional arrow next to the shutter also indicates the side and end of the disk that should be inserted into the disk drive first.

## Ejecting Floppy Disks

You can eject a floppy disk in several ways. Which method you use will depend on whether you want the system to be aware of the disk after it has been ejected. If you leave the disk icon on the desktop, the Finder program will be aware of the disk's existence. This would be necessary if you wanted to copy files between disks.

There are several ways to eject a floppy disk from the desktop.
1. Drag the disk icon to the Trash. This is the best method if you do not plan on using the disk again soon. The icon disappears from the screen and the Finder forgets that the disk exists. This does not erase the disk!
2. Select the **Eject Disk** command from the Special menu. This leaves the dimmed disk icon on the desktop and the Finder will periodically ask you to insert the ejected disk.
3. The keyboard equivalent ( ⌘ E) ejects the disk and leaves a dimmed icon on the desktop.

4. You can eject the disk by holding down the ⌘ and shift keys, while pressing the number 1, 2, or 0 key. **Shift ⌘ 1** will eject the floppy in the internal drive (the top or left drive if you have more than one floppy drive). **Shift ⌘ 2** will eject the floppy in the external drive (the bottom or right drive if you have more than one floppy drive). If you have a third floppy drive **Shift ⌘ 0 (zero)** will eject the floppy. The dimmed disk icon remains on the desktop.
5. Use the Shut Down or Restart commands on the Special menu.

Figure 3.1 summarizes the available methods to eject a floppy disk.

*Figure 3.1—Ejecting Floppy Disks*

| Method | Results |
| --- | --- |
| Drag the disk icon to the Trash | Ejects floppy disk. Icon disappears from desktop. |
| Eject Disk command | Ejects active floppy disk. Icon remains on desktop. * |
| ⌘ E | Ejects active floppy disk. Icon remains on desktop. * |
| Shift ⌘ 1 | Ejects floppy disk in internal drive. Icon remains on desktop. * |
| Shift ⌘ 2 | Ejects floppy disk in external drive. Icon remains on desktop. * |
| Shift ⌘ 0 | Ejects floppy disk in third drive. Icon remains on desktop. * |
| Restart command | Ejects all floppy disks. System reboots. |
| Shut Down command | Ejects all floppy disks. System is ready to power down. |

\* Do not use this method to eject the disk if you are finished, and intend to leave the computer on and booted for the next person.

## Locking Floppy Disks

Locking your floppy disk is a way to **write-protect** the disk. It prevents you from writing additional information on the disk and from erasing information off the disk. You can view the files on the disk and you can examine the contents of data files, but you can not alter them. The floppy disk may be unlocked at any time by sliding the tab down.

**To lock a floppy disk:**
1. Find the sliding tab on the back corner of the disk, opposite the shuttered end.
2. Slide the tab up until you can see through the hole in the plastic cover.

Let's practice inserting and ejecting floppy disks.

### Activity 3.1—Booting, Inserting, and Ejecting a Floppy Disk

Step 1  If your Macintosh computer is not on and booted, do so now.

Step 2  Find the System 7-Data disk that came with the book. Lock the System 7-Data disk. Place your thumb on the label opposite the shuttered end. Insert the shuttered end of the disk into the drive and push gently.

*What's Happening*
Your Macintosh grabs the disk and pulls it into the disk drive. The System 7-Data disk icon appears on your desktop. (Figure 3.2)

*Figure 3.2—Disk Icon*

Step 3  Point to the System 7-Data disk icon and drag it to the Trash, so that the Trash icon turns dark. Release the mouse button.

*What's Happening*
An outline of the floppy disk icon moves with the arrow pointer. As the icon outline and the arrow pointer cover the Trash, the Trash icon turns dark. (Figure 3.3)

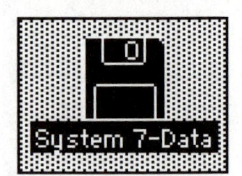

*Figure 3.3—Ejecting a Floppy Disk*

The floppy disk is ejected from the drive and you can now remove it. The floppy icon on the screen disappears. If the disk icon is still on your desktop or on top of the Trash, move it off the Trash and try again.

Step 4     Insert the System 7-Data disk in the drive again.

*What's Happening*
Your Macintosh grabs the disk and pulls it into the disk drive. A disk icon appears on your desktop.

Step 5     Click on the System 7-Data disk to select it. Point to the Special menu and select Eject Disk.

*Figure 3.4—Dimmed Icon*

*What's Happening*
Your data disk has been ejected but the dimmed disk icon is still on the desktop. The system still knows the disk exists. (Figure 3.4)

Step 6     Insert the System 7-Data disk in the drive again.

Step 7     Click on the System 7-Data disk to select it. Use the keyboard equivalent command to eject the disk (⌘ E).

*What's Happening*
Your data disk is ejected but the dimmed disk icon is still on the desktop. The system still knows the disk exists.

Step 8     Drag the System 7-Data disk icon to the Trash.

## Formatting Floppy Disks

Floppy disks are flexible plastic disks covered with a metal oxide coating capable of retaining magnetic bits of data. Each disk has two surfaces or sides, and each side is divided into concentric circles called **tracks**. Each track is further broken into sections called **sectors**. Most new 3.5 floppy disks are soft-sectored and can be used by either a Macintosh or IBM microcomputer. The sectors have not been defined because sector definition varies from one operating system to the next. Therefore, new floppy disks need to go through an **initialization** (also called **formatting**) process. Formatting erases all information that may have been previously stored on the disk.

You can purchase **pre-formatted disks** but generally they are more expensive than unformatted disks. Pre-formatted disks do not have to be initialized again. The manufacturer has already performed the initialization process. If you purchase pre-formatted disks, verify you are buying disks pre-formatted for the Macintosh and not the IBM computer.

During disk initialization, the system does the following:
- Divides the tracks into sectors that are usable by the system.
- Identifies any flawed or unusable sectors.
- Assigns an address mark to each sector.
- Creates a Directory (index) file for the disk.
- Erases the disk, if it has been used before.

The **directory** stores the names and locations of all files on the disk. The directory is located on several outside tracks of the disk. When the disk is first initialized, the directory is basically empty, but as you write files to the disk the directory fills up. The operating system uses the directory file to identify the exact location of files on the disk. If any flawed sectors are found, the directory file will identify those sectors as unusable. **Flawed sectors** are sectors on the disk that have been damaged or are considered unreliable by the system for storing information.

The Macintosh system will use dialog boxes to guide you through the initialization process every time you insert a new or unreadable disk. If you insert a floppy disk in the drive that has been used with a different operating system, the Macintosh will inform you that the disk is unreadable and give you the option to initialize or eject the disk. Occasionally you may get a false unreadable message. If you are confident that the disk should be readable, eject the disk and reinsert it. Remember, initializing a disk wipes out all information previously stored on the disk.

Floppy disk capacity will vary according to the disks you purchase, your disk drive, and how you format (initialize) them. A Double-Sided Double-Density (**DS-DD**) disk can store a maximum of 800 KB, and should be initialized with a two-sided format. If you initialize the disk with the one-sided format, it will only hold 400 KB and may be used in an old 400 KB disk drive. A Double-Sided High-Density (**DS-HD**) disk can store 1.4 MB. Which disk you buy and how you format it will be determined by your disk drive and any other drive you plan on using. For example, if you have a DS-HD disk drive on your Macintosh at home, but the computer at school or work can only access DS-DD disks, which disk would you purchase? If you intend to use the disk at both locations, you would buy DS-DD disks.

During the formatting process, dialog and status boxes will appear. A **dialog box** requires an action from you before the system can proceed with the task at hand. Frequently, the dialog box contains a question and one or more buttons. A **button** is a hot-spot on the screen. Clicking on a button tells the system what to do. A **bold button**, (one that is in a more pronounced oval), is the default answer. If you press the Return key on the keyboard, you select the **default button**. The System will not continue the process until you respond to the question(s).

Figure 3.5 contains three buttons. Pressing the Return key will select the Eject button. Clicking on any of the buttons will execute that action.

*Figure 3.5—Sample Buttons*

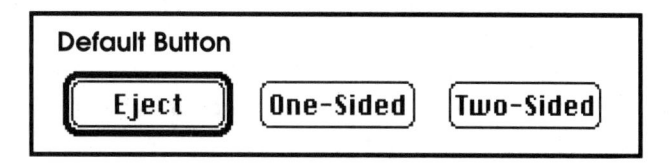

```
┌─────────────────────────────────────────────┐
│  Default Button                             │
│   ╔═══════╗  ┌──────────┐  ┌──────────┐    │
│   ║ Eject ║  │One-Sided │  │Two-Sided │    │
│   ╚═══════╝  └──────────┘  └──────────┘    │
└─────────────────────────────────────────────┘
```

A **status box** will inform you of the formatting progress. It provides you with information only. A status box does not need a response from you.

## Activity 3.2—Formatting a Floppy Disk

Step 1    Insert a *new* disk in your available floppy drive.

### What's Happening

The Macintosh will attempt to read the disk and will find it unreadable. One of the following messages will appear. (Figure 3.6 or 3.7)

If you are using a DS-DD disk, the message in Figure 3.6 will appear.

*Figure 3.6—DS-DD Disk Unreadable Message*

```
┌─────────────────────────────────────────────┐
│    ┌──┐   This disk is unreadable:          │
│    └──┘   Do you want to initialize it?     │
│                                             │
│   ╔═══════╗  ┌──────────┐  ┌──────────┐    │
│   ║ Eject ║  │One-Sided │  │Two-Sided │    │
│   ╚═══════╝  └──────────┘  └──────────┘    │
└─────────────────────────────────────────────┘
```

If you are using a DS-HD disk, the message in Figure 3.7 will appear.

*Figure 3.7—DS-HD Disk Unreadable Message*

```
┌─────────────────────────────────────────────┐
│    ┌──┐   This disk is unreadable:          │
│    └──┘   Do you want to initialize it?     │
│                                             │
│   ╔═══════╗                  ┌────────────┐│
│   ║ Eject ║                  │ Initialize ││
│   ╚═══════╝                  └────────────┘│
└─────────────────────────────────────────────┘
```

The **Eject button** is provided in case you want to stop the initialization process. Let's look at two examples where you would want to stop the initialization process.
1. If you insert an IBM-formatted disk in the drive that has files stored on it, the operating system displays the *disk unreadable* message. You would not want to initialize the disk because the disk would be erased.
2. If you insert a DS-HD disk in a DS-DD drive, you will get a *disk unreadable* message. A double-density drive can not read a high density disk.

Step 2   Click on the Two-Sided or Initialize button. (Figure 3.6 or 3.7)

*What's Happening* ⚠

The initialization process will begin and the **alert dialog box** in Figure 3.8 will appear. The dialog box is warning you that the initialization process will erase the disk. Any time you see a dialog box with this symbol, be alert and read the message carefully. Clicking on the Cancel button will stop the formatting process.

*Figure 3.8—Erase Warning/Alert*

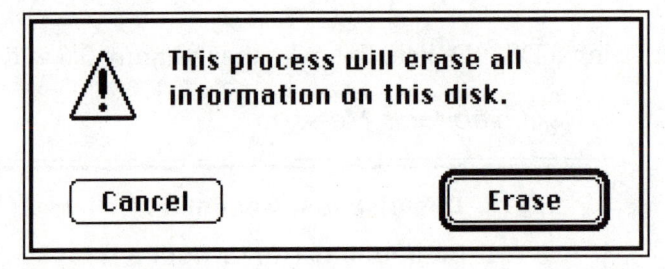

```
┌─────────────────────────────────────┐
│  ⚠   This process will erase all    │
│      information on this disk.      │
│                                     │
│  [ Cancel ]          [  Erase  ]    │
└─────────────────────────────────────┘
```

Step 3   Click on the Erase button.

*What's Happening*

A dialog box appears requesting the name to be assigned to the disk. (Figure 3.9)

*Figure 3.9—Disk Name-Untitled*

```
┌─────────────────────────────────┐
│   ⤒   Please name this disk:    │
│       ┌───────────────────────┐ │
│       │ Untitled              │ │
│       └───────────────────────┘ │
│                                 │
│            [   OK   ]           │
└─────────────────────────────────┘
```

Step 4   Type in Lastname-Sys 7 and click on the OK button. (Figure 3.10)

*Figure 3.10—Disk Name: Lastname-Sys 7*

```
Please name this disk:
Lastname-Sys 7
       OK
```

**What's Happening**
   Initialization continues and the following status boxes appear and disappear:
      Formatting Disk...
      Verifying Format...
      Creating Directory...
   When the initialization process is complete, a new floppy disk icon will appear on the desktop. (Figure 3.11)

Step 5   Drag the Lastname-Sys 7 disk icon to the Trash.

*Figure 3.11—New Data Disk*

**What's Happening**
   The floppy disk is ejected from the drive.

Step 6   Take the paper label and use a ink pen to write on it before attaching it to the disk cover. Write your Lastname-Sys 7 (for example, Sullivan-Sys 7) and the date.

## Copying Floppy Disks

You can copy all files from one floppy to another in three ways, depending on your hardware configuration. (Figures 3.12-3.14) You may have a dual floppy drive system, a single floppy drive system, a single floppy and a hard drive system, or a dual floppy drive system with a hard drive. The disk you want to make a copy of is called your **source disk** and the disk you will be copying to is your **destination disk.** The destination disk will be erased before the copy is performed. Always lock your source disk before copying it. You would not want to accidentally erase the wrong disk.

*Figure 3.12—Copying Disks Using Two Floppy Drives*

1. Insert the locked source disk in the top or left drive and the destination disk in the bottom or right drive.
2. Drag the icon of the source disk over the top of the destination disk icon.
3. Answer dialog boxes as they appear.
4. If you had to remove a floppy Startup disk from one of the drives to perform this copy, the Macintosh may request the Startup disk in order to complete the copy.

*Figure 3.13—Copying Disks Using a Single Floppy Drive*

Note: All Macintosh systems can use this method.
1. Place the locked source disk in the floppy drive.
2. Eject the disk with the Eject Disk command so that a dimmed disk icon is left on the desktop.
3. Insert the destination disk in the floppy drive. Both disk icons now appear on the desktop.
4. Drag the icon of the source disk over the top of the destination disk icon.
5. Answer dialog boxes as they appear.
6. Switch disks in the floppy drive as directed.

*Figure 3.14—Copying Disks Using a Single Floppy Drive and the Hard Drive*

1. Place the locked source disk in the floppy drive.
2. Drag the source disk's icon on to the hard drive's icon. This will not erase the hard drive.
3. Respond to the dialog box that appears informing you that the two disk are different types and that the source disk's data will be placed in a file folder on the hard drive.
4. Once the copy is complete, drag the source disk to the Trash.
5. Double-click on the hard disk icon to display the hard disk window.
6. Insert the floppy destination disk and drag the file folder from the hard drive to the floppy destination disk icon.
7. Remove the file folder from the hard drive by dragging it to the Trash.
8. Use the Empty Trash command on the Special menu to remove the folder from the Trash.

## Activity 3.3—Copying a Floppy Disk

In this exercise you will copy the contents of the System 7-Data disk (source disk) to your newly initialized Lastname-Sys 7 disk (destination disk). A **backup disk** is like insurance. If anything happens to your original data disk, you have another disk with the same contents. This is extremely important if you are transporting floppy disks between two locations, for instance between school and home. You will be using the single-floppy drive method to backup your data disk.

Step 1   Verify your System 7-Data disk is locked.

Step 2   Insert your source disk (System 7-Data) in the available floppy drive.

### What's Happening
The floppy disk icon appears on the screen.

Step 3   Click on the System 7-Data disk icon to select it.

### What's Happening
The icon turns dark.

Step 4   Point to the Special menu and select the Eject Disk command.

### What's Happening
The disk will be ejected from the drive, but the dimmed disk icon will remain on the desktop.

Step 5   Remove your source disk and insert your destination disk (Lastname-Sys 7) in the drive.

### What's Happening
This disk icon will appear on the desktop. (Figure 3.15) Notice the icon for the System 7-Data disk is shaded. This indicates the disk is no longer in the drive.

*Figure 3.15—Desktop with 3 Disk Icons*

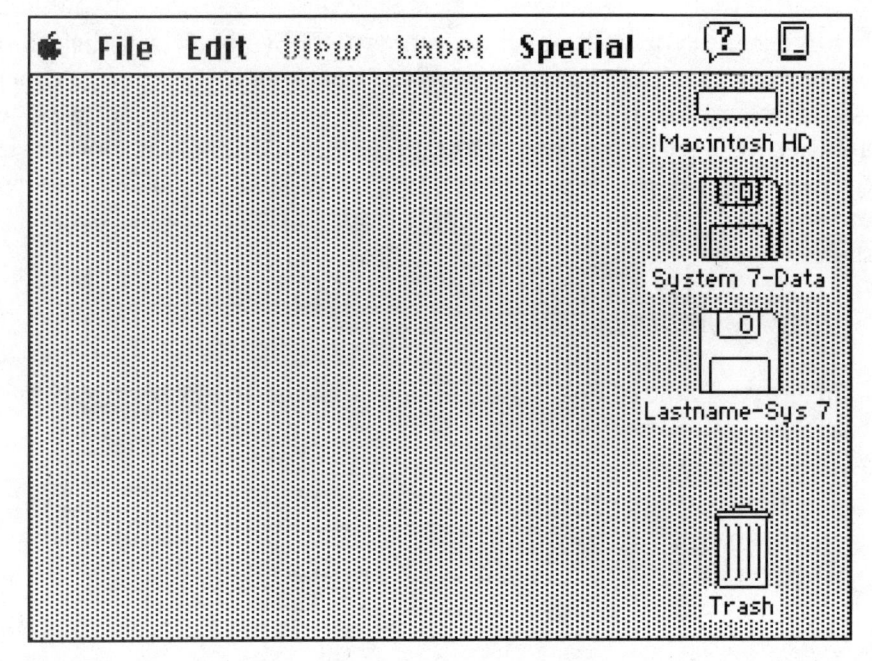

Step 6    Drag the source disk icon (System 7-Data) over the top of the destination disk icon (Lastname-Sys 7) until it is dark. (Figure 3.16) Release the mouse button.

*Figure 3.16—Copying System 7-Data Disk*

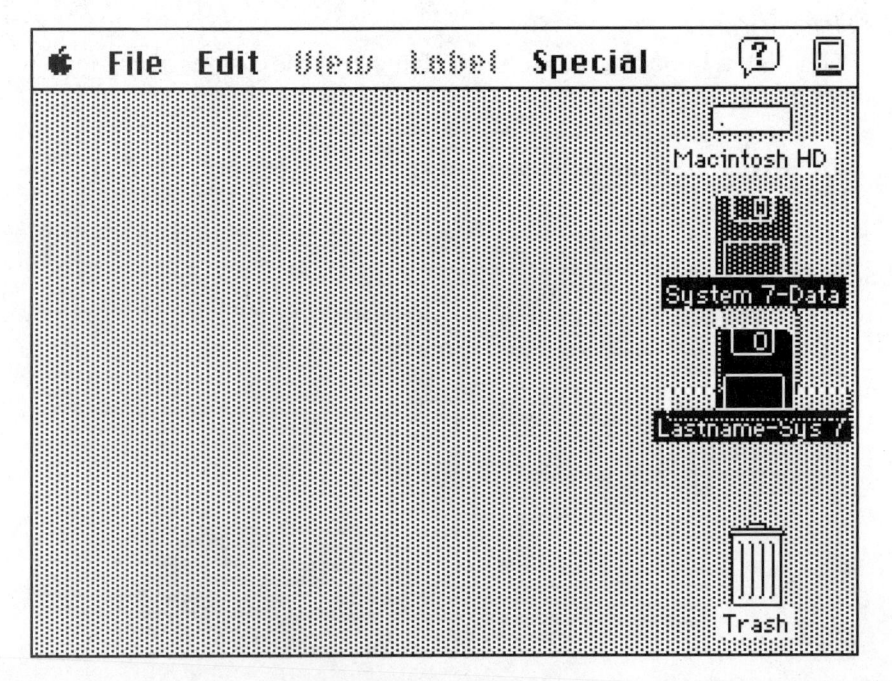

## What's Happening

The destination disk turns dark. If the system ejects the Lastname-Sys 7 disk and asks for the System 7-Data disk, insert it. (Figure 3.17)

*Figure 3.17—Message to Switch Disk*

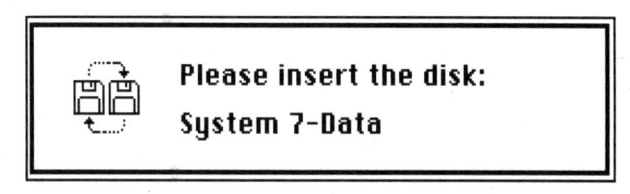

> Please insert the disk:
> System 7-Data

The system will present you with a dialog box verifying your intent to replace the contents of the destination disk with the contents of the source disk. (Figure 3.18)

*Figure 3.18—Diskcopy Alert Dialog Box*

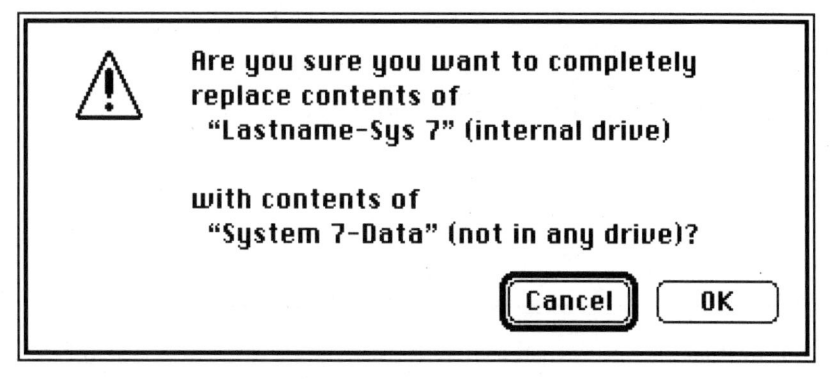

> ⚠ Are you sure you want to completely replace contents of
> "Lastname-Sys 7" (internal drive)
>
> with contents of
> "System 7-Data" (not in any drive)?
>
> [ Cancel ]  [ OK ]

Step 7    Click OK. Follow the instructions in the dialog boxes as they appear.

## What's Happening

The system uses memory as an intermediary (it reads from the source disk, asks you to switch disks as shown in Figure 3.19, writes to the destination disk, and so on). The System automatically ejects the disk and waits for the other one.

*Figure 3.19—Example of Swap Disk Messages*

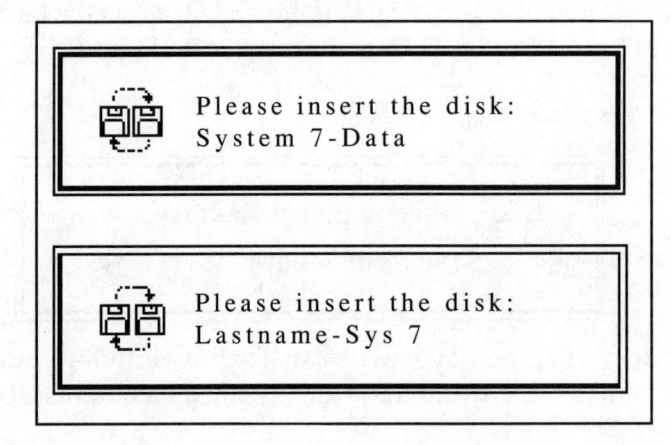

> Please insert the disk:
> System 7-Data

> Please insert the disk:
> Lastname-Sys 7

The system displays status boxes on the desktop telling you that it is preparing, reading, writing, and verifying disks. (Figure 3.20)

*Figure 3.20—Copy Status Box*

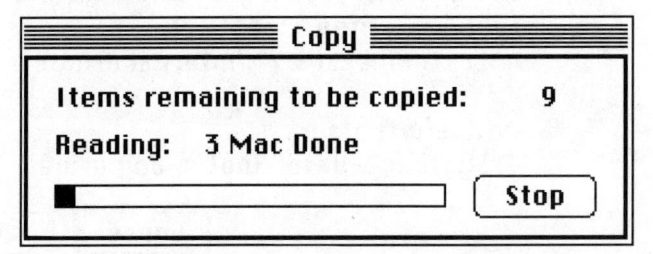

> **Copy**
> Items remaining to be copied: 9
> Reading: 3 Mac Done
> [ Stop ]

Step 8   When the copy is complete (the system does not inform you when it's done—the status boxes just disappear), drag the two floppy disk icons to the Trash.

## Erasing Floppy Disks

The process of wiping out the entire contents of a floppy disk is called erasing, or reinitializing a disk. There are two primary reasons to erase a floppy disk: either you no longer need the information stored on it, or the disk has become unreadable. The best method to erase a disk is to use the **Erase Disk** command on the Special menu. This process will erase the entire contents of the disk and reinitialize it. The other method is to Select All icons on the floppy disk and drag them to the Trash. You must then use the **Empty Trash** command. This will remove the file entries (names and icons) from the Directory file (identifies those sectors as empty) but will not erase the information from the disk and will not perform the initialization process to verify the quality of the disk. The information that was stored in the disk files will remain until they are written over by new files. Remember, once you begin the Erase Disk process you can't change your mind. The Erase Disk command will not work on your Startup disk (the disk you used when booting the Macintosh).

**To Erase a Disk:**
1. Click on the disk icon that you want to erase (the icon turns dark).
2. Choose the Erase Disk command of the Special menu.
3. Read the dialog box carefully and confirm the name of the disk to be erased.
4. Click on the appropriate button.
    Cancel—if you changed your mind.
    One-sided—if your system uses 400 KB floppy disks.
    Two-sided—if your system uses 800 KB floppy disks.
    Initialize—if your system uses 1.4 MB floppy disks.
5. Rename the disk.
6. Prepare a new paper label. Remove the old label and place the newlabel on the disk.

## Activity 3.4—Erasing the Lastname-Sys 7 Disk

In this exercise, you will erase the Lastname-Sys 7 disk you just created. It's fortunate you still have the original disk that came with the book (System 7-Data). Be sure to complete the assignments at the end of the chapter to recreate this Lastname-Sys 7 disk.

Step 1   Lock your Lastname-Sys 7 disk and insert it in the floppy drive.

Step 2   Click on the Lastname-Sys 7 disk icon, to make sure it is the selected, or active disk.

Step 3   Point to the Special menu and try to select the Erase Disk command.

*What's Happening*

The Erase Disk command may be dimmed. You can't select it or you will get an error message. If the command is not dimmed and you select it, the alert dialog box shown in Figure 3.21 will appear.

*Figure 3.21—Erase Disk Alert Dialog Box*

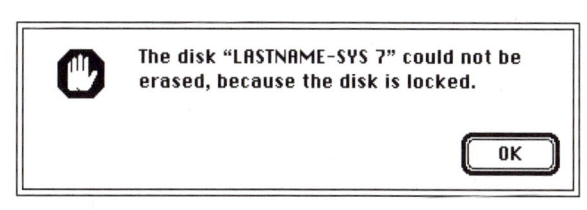

> The disk "LASTNAME-SYS 7" could not be erased, because the disk is locked.
>
> [ OK ]

You will be informed that you can't erase the disk because it is locked. Click on the OK button.

Step 4   Drag the Lastname-Sys 7 disk icon to the Trash, unlock the disk and insert it back in the drive.

Step 5   Click on the Lastname-Sys 7 disk icon, to make sure it is selected.

Step 6   Point to the Special menu and select the **Erase Disk** command.

## What's Happening

The dialog box in Figure 3.22 appears if you have a DS-DD disk.

*Figure 3.22—Erase DS-DD Disk Dialog Box*

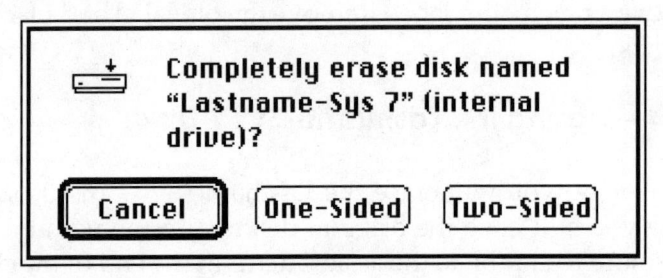

```
Completely erase disk named
"Lastname-Sys 7" (internal
drive)?

[ Cancel ]   [ One-Sided ]   [ Two-Sided ]
```

If you are using a DS-HD disk, the dialog box in Figure 3.23 will appear. Make sure that you read the message carefully. Verify the name of the disk you are about to erase. The initialize process will begin.

*Figure 3.23—Erase DS-HD Disk Dialog Box*

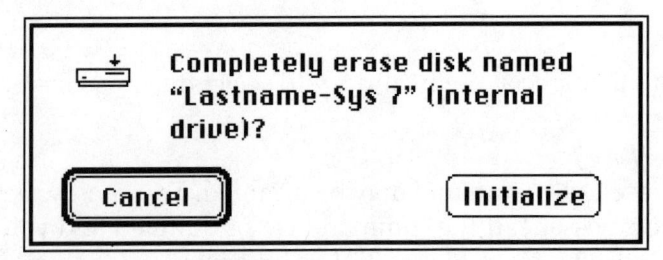

```
Completely erase disk named
"Lastname-Sys 7" (internal
drive)?

[ Cancel ]                   [ Initialize ]
```

Step 7   Click on the Initialize or Two-Sided button.

## What's Happening

You have just erased your Lastname-Sys 7 disk. You will make a new one in the Assignments at the end of the chapter.

Step 8   Drag your Lastname-Sys 7 disk to the Trash.

## Renaming Floppy Disks

Renaming a disk icon is a simple process. You can't rename locked disks. Disk names may be a maximum of 27 characters. The colon (:) character is not allowed.

**To completely rename a disk icon:**
1. Click on the *name* of the disk icon (not the icon) you want to rename, or click on the icon and then press the Return key. The icon name will appear in a white outline.
2. Type the new name.

**To partially change the name:**
1. Click on the name of the disk icon you want to rename.
2. Position the pointer on the name where the change is to be made (the pointer should change to an I-beam).
3. Click to identify insertion point.
4. Modify the name with one of the following methods.
   - Use the delete key to delete 1 character to the left of the I-beam.
   - Type the additional characters in at the insertion point.
   - Use the cut, copy, paste, clear commands, from the Edit menu (discussed later).

### Activity 3.5—Renaming a Floppy Disk

*Figure 3.24—Icon Name Highlighted*

Step 1   Insert your unlocked Lastname-Sys 7 disk in the drive. Click on the Lastname-Sys 7 name.

*What's Happening*
The disk icon will be highlighted. The icon name will have a white outline around it. (Figure 3.24)

*Figure 3.25—Renamed Icon*

Step 2   Type Data Disk. Click anywhere on the empty desktop to deselect the icon.

*What's Happening*
You have renamed your Lastname-Sys 7 disk. Look at the floppy icon on your desktop. The floppy icon on the desktop will reflect the new name. (Figure 3.25)

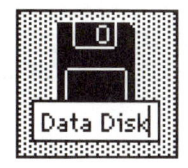

Step 3   Rename your disk icon one more time. Name it your lastname-Sys 7. (For example, Sullivan-Sys 7.) Click anywhere on the empty desktop to deselect the icon.

Step 4   Drag the Lastname-Sys 7 disk to the Trash.

## Key Terms

⌘ E
⌘ 0
⌘ 1
⌘ 2
Alert dialog box
Backup disk
Bold button
Button
Cancel button
Default answer
Destination disk
Dialog box
Directory
DS-DD

DS-HD
Eject button
Eject Disk
Empty Trash
Erase Disk
Flawed sectors
Formatting
Initialize
Pre-formatted disks
Sectors
Source disk
Status box
Tracks
Write protect

## Discussion Questions

1. Why do you need to initialize new floppy disks?
2. What happens during the initialization process?
3. Describe the difference between Status and Dialog boxes.
4. What will happen if you insert a new preformatted IBM disk in the Macintosh drive?
5. Why should you lock the source disk before performing a floppy-to-floppy disk copy?
6. Why should you make backup copies of floppy disks?
7. Explain the difference between dialog and status boxes.
8. What is meant by default button? How can you tell which button is the default button?

## True/False Questions

For each question, circle the letter T if the statement is true and the letter F if the statement is false.

T  F  1. Dragging a floppy disk to the Trash will erase the disk.
T  F  2. The number of disk icons on the desktop can never out number the number of disk drives on the Macintosh.

T  F   3. The Macintosh tries to assist you in your answers by displaying the *"correct"* answer (the answer used most), in a bold button on dialog boxes.
T  F   4. During a floppy-to-floppy disk copy, the destination disk will be erased before the copy is performed.
T  F   5. You can't rename locked floppy disks.
T  F   6. Floppy disk drives are not necessary if your Macintosh has a hard drive.
T  F   7. Unformatted new disks must be initialized before they can be used to store information.
T  F   8. Be careful not to use the Erase Disk command on your current boot disk, as it will bring your entire system down as it erases the disk.
T  F   9. Disk names may not be longer than 27 characters.
T  F  10. Initializing a disk will erase the disk.
T  F  11. During a floppy-to-floppy disk copy, both disk icons must be present on the desktop.
T  F  12. A dimmed floppy disk icon indicates that the disk is locked and can't be written to.

## Completion Questions

Write the correct answer in each blank space.

1. The Macintosh uses _____ boxes to inform you of its progress during the initialization process.
2. The Macintosh uses a _____ box to ask you questions during the initialization process, and waits for your response.
3. Choose the Eject Disk command from the ____ menu to remove a floppy disk from the drive.
4. The keyboard equivalent to eject a floppy disk is _____.
5. The Empty Trash command is available on the _____ menu.
6. _____ sectors are sectors on the disk that have been damaged and should not be used to store information.
7. During the copy routine the _____ disk is the floppy you are copying from, and the _____ disk is the floppy you are copying information to.
8. The _____ character is not allowed in disk names.
9. The Erase Disk command is available on the ____ menu.
10. Before copying a floppy disk, you should always ____ your source disk.
11. A _____ is a hot spot on the dialog box.
12. The _____ stores the name and locations of various files on the disk.

13. List five ways to eject a floppy disk. Identify which ones will leave a dimmed disk icon on the desktop.
    a.
    b.
    c.
    d.
    e.
14. A _____ disk is a type of insurance in case anything happens to the original disk.

## Assignments

In this exercise, you will recreate your Lastname-Sys 7 disk (Activity 3.3). Use your locked System 7-Data disk as the source disk and your Lastname-Sys 7 disk as your destination disk. When you are finished, put your original System 7-Data disk away and don't use it unless something happens to your copy (Lastname-Sys 7). If in the future, you accidentally erase your Lastname-Sys 7 disk you can use the original System-7 Data disk to create a new copy. Answer the two questions below as you go through the copy process.

_____ 1. During the copy process, the pointer changed shape. Which shape did not appear?
    a.        b.        c.

_____ 2. During the copy process, which two of the following steps are
_____    described incorrectly?
    a. Lock the System 7-Data disk.
    b. Insert the System 7-Data disk in the floppy drive.
    c. Eject the System 7-Data disk by dragging its icon to the Trash.
    d. Insert the Lastname-Sys 7 disk.
    e. Drag the Lastname-Sys 7 disk icon over the top of the System 7-Data disk icon.
    f. Swap floppy disks as instructed.

# 4 Windows

## Learning Objectives

**After completing this Chapter you will be able to:**

1. Describe what a window is and how it is used.
2. List and explain several ways to open an icon.
3. List and explain several ways to close an icon.
4. Describe the following common features of windows: Close Box, Title Bar, Information Bar, Zoom Box, Scroll Bars, Scroll Arrows, Scroll Boxes, Size Box.
5. Describe two ways to size a window.
6. Explain what is meant by scrolling a window and how to scroll slowly and quickly.
7. Explain how to move a window on your desktop.
8. Define an active window.
9. Describe how to make a window on your desktop the active window.
10. Explain how you can tell which open window is the active window.
11. Explain how to select icons on the active window.
12. Describe the difference between an icon and list view window.

## Introduction

If you had a filing cabinet, would you leave the drawers open so you could always see what's stored inside? If you had a file folder in the drawer or on your desk, would it be opened if you weren't using it? No, of course not. If you think of a disk as a place to store documents, it is very similar to a filing cabinet. A **file folder**, whether on disk or inside a filing cabinet, is for storing related documents. The file folder may be filled with letters to friends or documents relating to a specific customer. If you don't leave your filing cabinet drawers open, should you leave disk or computer folders open on the Macintosh desktop?

You can see what's inside a disk or folder by opening a window on the desktop. A **window** is a region on the desktop that is associated with a specific icon. When you open a disk, folder, application program, data file (document) or the Trash, the Macintosh opens a new desktop work area for that icon, called a window. Windows allow you to look inside the icon and see what's inside.

A window displaying the contents of a folder or disk is known as a Finder window. The Finder program is part of the operating system. It is loaded into memory during the boot process and remains in memory until you shut down. This program is responsible for managing the desktop. Every time you open, close, copy, delete, or rename an icon you are working with the Finder. Finder windows may be displayed in icon or list view.

In this chapter you will learn the parts of a window, common window operations, and keyboard shortcuts. Finder windows displayed in icon and list views are emphasized in this chapter. We will discuss document windows in Chapter 8.

## Opening an Icon

To find out what is inside a disk or folder icon, you must open it. Think of it as if you were opening the drawer of a filing cabinet to see what is inside.

Opening a document icon will load the application program that was used to create the document into memory and place the document in an open window. If the application program is not available, that is, not on an accessible disk, an alert box will appear. An **alert dialog box** is used to warn you that you may be trying to do something you did not want to do or can't do. For example, Figure 4.1 shows the Alert Box that appeared when an attempt was made to open the Employee DB icon. The application program that created the document, Microsoft Works, was not accessible.

*Figure 4.1—Sample Alert Box*

> 🖐 **The document "EMPLOYEE DB" could not be opened, because the application program that created it could not be found.**
>
> [ OK ]

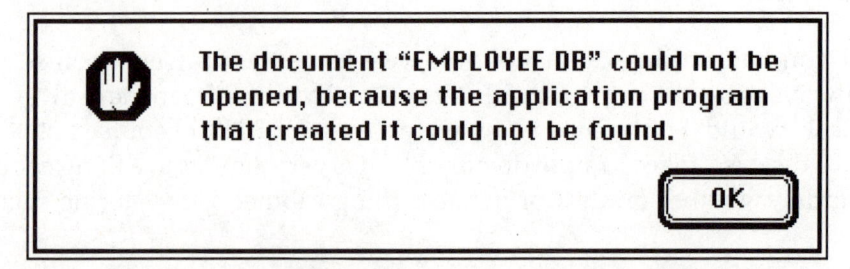

Figure 4.2 summarizes different techniques to open an icon.

*Figure 4.2—Opening an Icon*

| Method | Steps |
|---|---|
| File Menu Command | Click on the icon you want to open.<br>Choose the File menu command Open. |
| Mouse Shortcut | Double-click on the icon you want to open. |
| Keyboard Shortcut | Click on the icon you want to open and Press ⌘ O, or<br>Click on the icon you want to open and Press ⌘ down arrow. |

## Activity 4.1—Opening an Icon Using the Open Command

Step 1  If the Macintosh is not booted, do so now. Insert your locked Lastname-Sys 7 data disk in the floppy drive.

*What's Happening*

You should have a hard disk, floppy disk, and Trash icon on the desktop.

Step 2  Click on the Lastname-Sys 7 disk icon to select it.

Step 3  Position your arrow pointer on the File menu name and press and hold the mouse button.

*What's Happening*

The File menu appears.

Step 4  Drag the arrow pointer down the list of commands until **Open** is highlighted, then release the mouse button.

*What's Happening*

A new window should open on your screen allowing you to view some of the contents of the disk. Figure 4.3 shows the window in **icon view.** The icons on your disk window may appear in a different order. The icons may also vary in shape depending on the available (accessible) application programs. Every object on the window is represented by a name and an icon. Look at your desktop. The Lastname-Sys 7 disk icon (on the top right corner of the desktop) is dimmed, indicating it is open.

*Figure 4.3—Lastname-Sys 7 Disk Window*

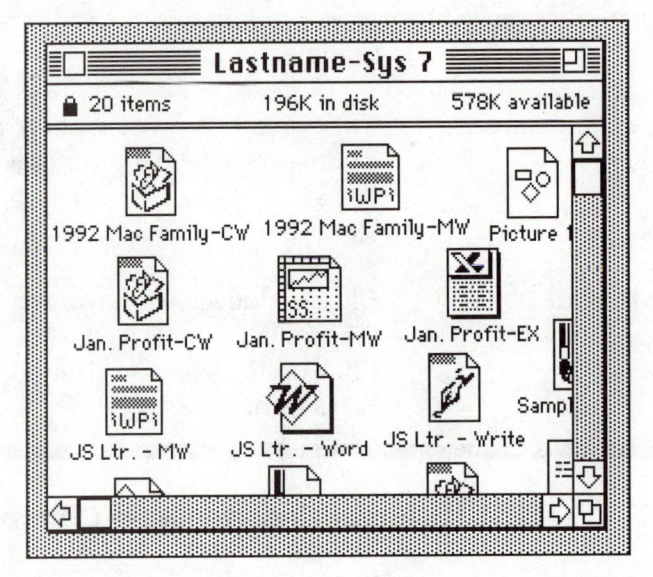

## Closing An Icon

When you are finished working with a window and you close it, the window disappears from your desktop. Figure 4.4 shows different techniques to close the active window. If you have multiple windows on the desktop, only one at a time can be active.

*Figure 4.4—Closing the Active Window*

| Method | Steps |
| --- | --- |
| File Menu Command | Choose the Close Window command from the File menu. |
| Mouse Shortcut | Click on the window's Close box. |
| Keyboard Shortcut | Press ⌘ W (This does not work in all application programs.) |

### Activity 4.2—Closing a Window using the Close Window Command

Step 1    Point to the File menu and press and hold down the mouse button.

*What's Happening*

    The File pull-down menu appears.

Step 2    Drag the arrow pointer down the list of commands until **Close Window** is highlighted, and release the mouse button.

*What's Happening*

    The Lastname-Sys 7 window disappears.

### Activity 4.3—Opening an Icon using the Mouse Shortcut

Step 1    Position the tip of the pointer arrow on your Lastname-Sys 7 disk icon and double-click.

*What's Happening*

    A new window should open on your screen allowing you to view some of the contents of the disk. If a window doesn't open, you didn't double-click quickly enough. Try again.

## Switching Between Icon and List Views

All Finder windows may be viewed in an icon (Figure 4.3) or list view (Figure 4.5). The **list view** provides more information than the icon view and may be sorted according to any column.

### Activity 4.4—Switching between Views

Step 1    Choose the by Name command in the View menu.

*What's Happening*

    You remember how to choose menu commands—point at the menu, press and hold the mouse button, drag the arrow down until the desired command is highlighted, and release the mouse button. The contents of the Lastname-Sys 7 window is now displayed in a list view alphabetically by name, as shown in Figure 4.5.

*Figure 4.5—List View Window*

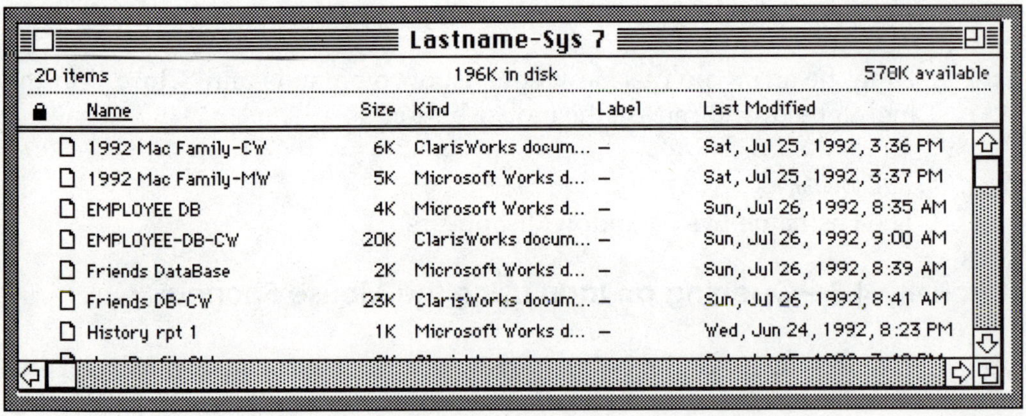

| 🔒 | Name | Size | Kind | Label | Last Modified |
|---|---|---|---|---|---|
| | 📄 1992 Mac Family-CW | 6K | ClarisWorks docum... | — | Sat, Jul 25, 1992, 3:36 PM |
| | 📄 1992 Mac Family-MW | 5K | Microsoft Works d... | — | Sat, Jul 25, 1992, 3:37 PM |
| | 📄 EMPLOYEE DB | 4K | Microsoft Works d... | — | Sun, Jul 26, 1992, 8:35 AM |
| | 📄 EMPLOYEE-DB-CW | 20K | ClarisWorks docum... | — | Sun, Jul 26, 1992, 9:00 AM |
| | 📄 Friends DataBase | 2K | Microsoft Works d... | — | Sun, Jul 26, 1992, 8:39 AM |
| | 📄 Friends DB-CW | 23K | ClarisWorks docum... | — | Sun, Jul 26, 1992, 8:41 AM |
| | 📄 History rpt 1 | 1K | Microsoft Works d... | — | Wed, Jun 24, 1992, 8:23 PM |

Window title: Lastname-Sys 7 — 20 items — 196K in disk — 578K available

The icon and name of each item on the window is displayed along with Size, Kind, Label, and Last Date and Time modified. If you have a locked file, a padlock will appear to the right of the last column. The information in your window may vary slightly from Figure 4.5. The application program that created a document must be on an available disk for the Kind column to display its name.

Step 2   Choose the **by Icon** command in the View menu.

## What's Happening

The window is now displayed in an icon view. (Figure 4.6)

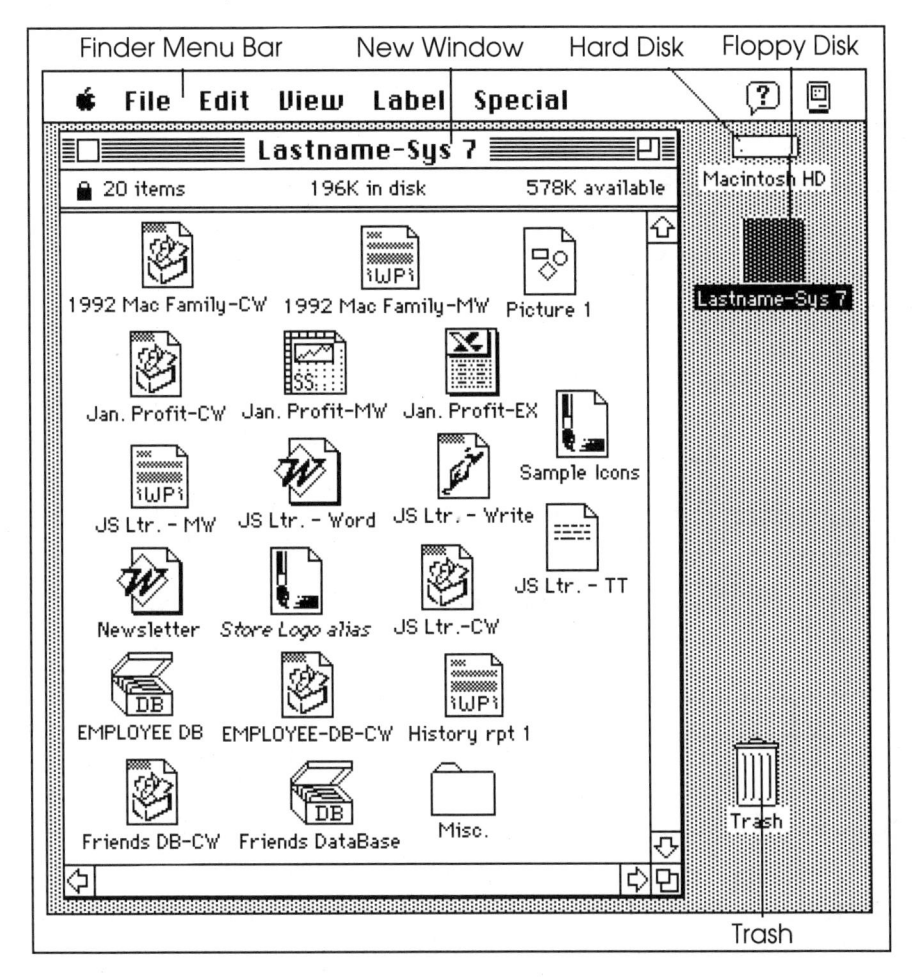

*Figure 4.6—The Desktop with an Open Window*

## Common Windows Features and Operations

All windows share common features and operations. Figure 4.6 shows the desktop containing the open Lastname-Sys 7 data disk. The desktop displays two disk icons, the Trash, the Finder menu bar and the window displaying part of the contents of the floppy disk. Let's identify and discuss the common features of windows shown in Figure 4.7.

*Figure 4.7—Parts of the Window*

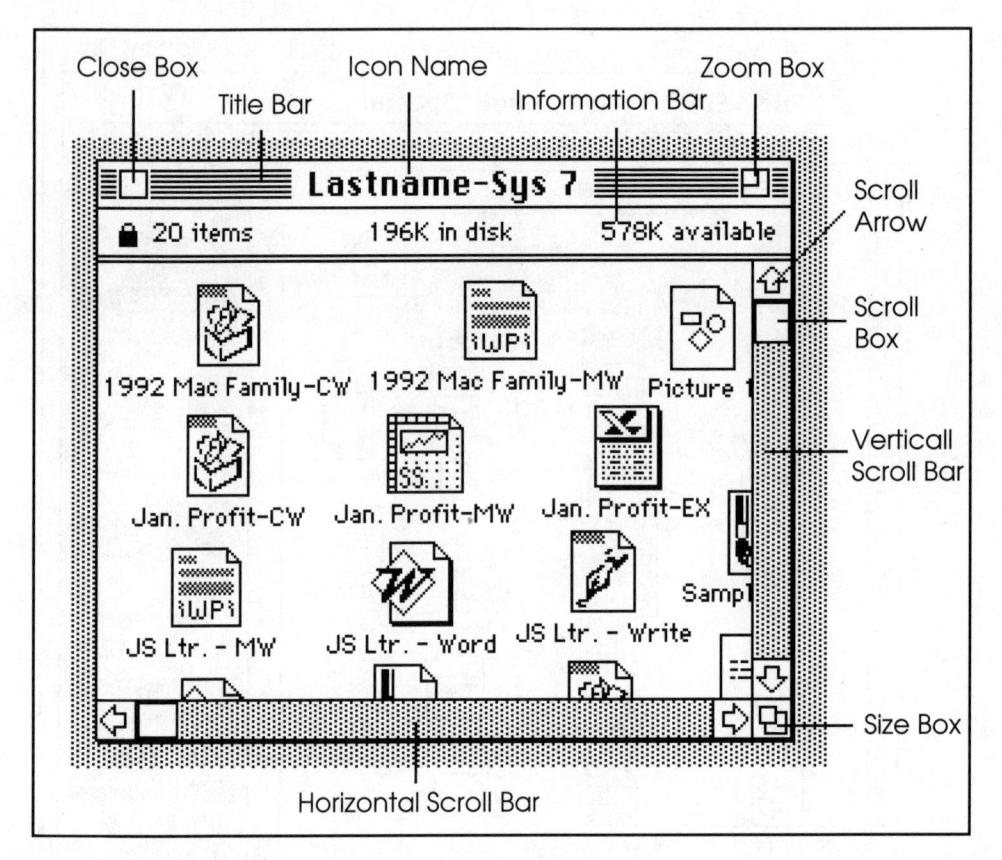

[Figure 4.7: A diagram of a Macintosh Finder window titled "Lastname-Sys 7" with labels pointing to: Close Box, Title Bar, Icon Name, Information Bar, Zoom Box, Scroll Arrow, Scroll Box, Verticall Scroll Bar, Size Box, and Horizontal Scroll Bar. The information bar shows "20 items", "196K in disk", "578K available". Icons shown include: 1992 Mac Family-CW, 1992 Mac Family-MW, Picture 1, Jan. Profit-CW, Jan. Profit-MW, Jan. Profit-EX, JS Ltr. - MW, JS Ltr. - Word, JS Ltr. - Write, Sampl...]

**Close Box.** The close box is used to close the window. If you click on the box, the window closes. As long as you are pressing the mouse button a "star" will appear in the close box. Once you let go of the button the window disappears. If you move the pointer off the close box and then release the mouse button, the window will not close.

**Title Bar.** The title bar at the top of the window contains the close box, the name of the icon, and the zoom box. The horizontal lines in the title bar indicates that this is the active window. **Inactive windows** will not have the lines.

**Information Bar.** The information bar may appear below the title bar. The information bar will not appear if you are working in an application program. If you are displaying a Finder window in list view, you have the option of displaying the information bar or not (refer to Chapter 11). The information bar informs you on the number of items in the window, the amount of used disk space and the amount of available disk space. If the disk is locked, the **Padlock** icon will appear on the left edge of the bar.

**Name of Open Object.** The name of the open file, disk, or folder icon will always be displayed in the title bar.

**Zoom Box.** The zoom box, located on the right of the title bar, is a quick way to switch from a small to a big window and back.

**Scroll Bars.** There are vertical and horizontal scroll bars on the window. The window is not always large enough to allow you to view the complete contents of the icon. The vertical scroll bar allows you to scroll the window up and down, and the horizontal bar scrolls left and right. A shaded scroll bar tells you that there is more to see and is referred to as an **active scroll bar**. **Inactive scroll bars** (not shaded) let you know that you are seeing the whole window in that direction.

**Scroll Arrows.** There are two scroll arrows on each scroll bar. They provide a means to scroll your window slowly. Clicking on an arrow or positioning the pointer on the arrow and holding down the mouse button will slowly scroll the window.

**Scroll Boxes.** There is a scroll box on each scroll bar. Each one shows the relative position of the window to the whole picture. For example, if you have created a 30-page report in a word processing program and your scroll box is in the middle of the vertical bar, your window will display the middle portion of the whole document. Dragging the scroll box is one way to move quickly through a document, disk, folder, or Trash window. Click anywhere in the scroll bar—above, below, to the left or to the right of the scroll box—to move one full screen at a time.

**Size Box.** The size box, located in the lower right corner of the window, is used to alter the size of the window to your specifications. To use the size box, point to it, press and hold the mouse button, drag the window to the desired size, and release the mouse button.

## Executing Window Operations

Let's perform some common window operations. Your Macintosh should be booted, and the Lastname-Sys 7 disk should be in the floppy drive. The Lastname-Sys 7 window should be open in icon view on the desktop.

*Figure 4.8—Small Window*

### Activity 4.5—Sizing Windows

**Using the Size Box**

Step 1   Point to the size box in the lower right corner of the window, press and hold the mouse button, and drag up and to the left. Release the button. (Figure 4.8)

### What's Happening

A dotted outline of the window follows the pointer as you drag it. When the outline is as small as it can be in any direction, it stops moving. When you release the mouse button, the window springs to its new size. The contents of the window do not change—you just can't see everything now.

*Figure 4.9—Dotted Outline*

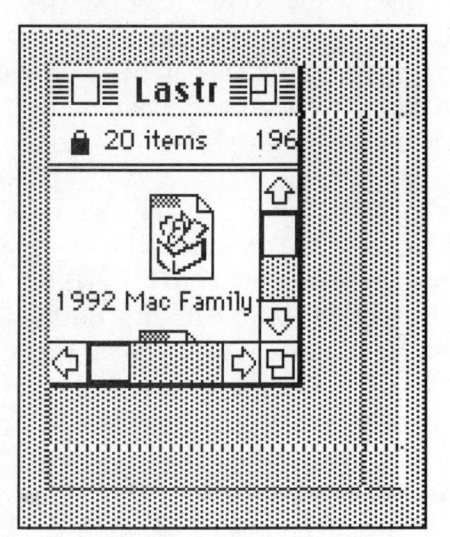

Step 2   Now, drag the window to make it a little bigger, but do not completely display all icons.

### What's Happening

The dotted outline of the window follows the pointer. (Figure 4.9) When you release the mouse button, the window springs to its new size.

The size box is used to alter the size of the window to your specifications. This is useful when you want to view multiple open windows on the desktop.

**Using the Zoom Box**

Step 3   Point to the zoom box in the top right corner and click once.

### What's Happening

The window becomes large enough to display all icons in the window. If there is too much information in the window to display everything, the window will almost fill the desktop in order to show as much as possible. The inactive scroll bars (not grey) indicate that you are viewing the entire picture.

Step 4   Point to the zoom box again and click once.

### What's Happening

The window returns to its previous size. With a single click in the zoom box, you can quickly switch back and forth from a small window to a large window.

Step 5   Point to the zoom box and hold the Option key down while clicking on the zoom box.

*What's Happening*

The window almost completely fills the desktop.

Step 6   Point to the zoom box again and click once.

*What's Happening*

The window shrinks, but not back to its previous size. The window is sized just large enough to display all the icons in this window. Figure 4.10 summarizes several techniques for sizing a window.

*Figure 4.10—Sizing Finder Windows*

| Method | Result |
| --- | --- |
| Size Box | Point to the size box and drag the window to any size. |
| Click on Zoom Box | Window gets just large enough to show contents. |
| Option Key + Zoom Box | Window almost completely fills the desktop. |

*Figure 4.11—Shaded Scroll Bars*

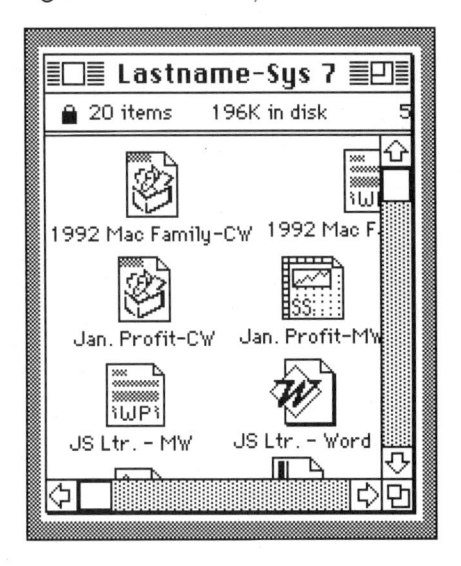

### Activity 4.6—Scrolling a Window

Step 1   Size the window until the vertical and horizontal scroll bars are both shaded.

*What's Happening*

Some of the icons will be hidden from view. (Figure 4.11)

**Using Scroll Arrows**

Step 2   Click several times on the down scroll arrow (arrow pointing down in bottom right corner) until the vertical scroll box is in the bottom right corner.

*What's Happening*
>The window begins to scroll up and will display different icons. Each click scrolls the window about one-half inch. Notice the icons at the top of the screen are scrolling out of view.

Step 3    Click several times on the right scroll arrow (arrow pointing right in bottom right corner) until the horizontal scroll box is in the bottom right corner of the window.

*What's Happening*
>The window will scroll to the left and the icons on the left hand side will scroll out of view.

Step 4    Position the mouse pointer (arrow) on the up scroll arrow. Hold the mouse button down until the scroll box is in the top corner of the scroll bar.

*What's Happening*
>The window slowly scrolls down. The icons on the top of the window are now visible.

**Using Scroll Boxes**

Step 5    Point to the vertical scroll box and drag it half way down the vertical scroll bar.

Step 6    Point to the horizontal scroll box and drag it to the opposite end of the horizontal scroll bar.

*What's Happening*
>This is a much quicker way to scroll your window vertically or horizontally.

Step 7    Choose **by Name** from the View menu. Size the window so that you can see about 4 files.

*What's Happening*
>The window is now displayed in a list view. (Figure 4.12) Everything we have been doing in the icon view will work in the list view.

*Figure 4.12—List View*

|  | Lastname-Sys 7 |  |  |  |
|---|---|---|---|---|
| 20 items |  | 196K in disk |  | 578K available |
| Name | Size | Kind | Label | Last Modified |
| 1992 Mac Family-CW | 6K | ClarisWorks docum... | — | Sat, Jul 25, 1992, 3:36 PM |
| 1992 Mac Family-MW | 5K | Microsoft Works d... | — | Sat, Jul 25, 1992, 3:37 PM |
| EMPLOYEE DB | 4K | Microsoft Works d... | — | Sun, Jul 26, 1992, 8:35 AM |
| EMPLOYEE-DB-CW | 20K | ClarisWorks docum... | — | Sun, Jul 26, 1992, 9:00 AM |

Step 8    Make sure the scroll box is at the top of the vertical scroll bar.

Step 9    Click on the scroll bar right below the scroll box.

## What's Happening

This is the fourth way to scroll the window. The next window full of information is displayed. For example, if you are viewing page five of a document on a full-page monitor, clicking below the scroll box will cause page six to be displayed. Clicking above the scroll box will display page four.

Figure 4.13 summarizes mouse and keyboard scrolling techniques.

*Figure 4.13—Scrolling Windows*

| Mouse Techniques | Result |
|---|---|
| Clicking scroll arrow | Window scrolls one-half inch per click. |
| Pointing and holding mouse button on scroll arrow | Window scrolls slowly until button is released. |
| Dragging scroll box | Window information is displayed relative to the scroll box position on the scroll bar. |
| Clicking on scroll bar next to the scroll box | Scrolls the window one window full in that direction. |

| Keyboard Techniques | Results |
| --- | --- |
| Pressing Home key | Top of window is displayed. Scroll box at the top of the scroll bar. |
| Pressing End key | Bottom portion of window is displayed. Scroll box at the bottom of scroll bar. |
| Pressing Page Down key | Contents of next window is displayed. |
| Pressing Page Up key | Contents of previous window is displayed. |

**Using Keyboard Techniques**

If you have an extended keyboard with the cursor control keys (Home, End, Page Up and Page Down) proceed with Steps 10 through 13. If you do not have an extended keyboard, proceed to Activity 4.7.

Step 10  Press the Home key.

*What's Happening*

The icons at the top of the window are visible. The scroll box is in the top corner of the vertical scroll bar.

Step 11  Press the End key.

*What's Happening*

The icons at the bottom of the window are visible. The scroll box is in the bottom corner of the vertical scroll bar.

Step 12  Press the Page Up key.

*What's Happening*

The window scrolls up one complete window.

Step 13  Press the Page Up key until the top of the window is displayed.

## Activity 4.7—Opening more than One Window at a Time

Step 1   Choose by Icon from the View menu to display the Lastname-Sys 7 window in an icon view.

Step 2   Double-click on the Trash.

### What's Happening

A new window opens, showing that the Trash is empty. This window may be overlapping your original window. (Figure 4.14)

*Figure 4.14—Active Window*

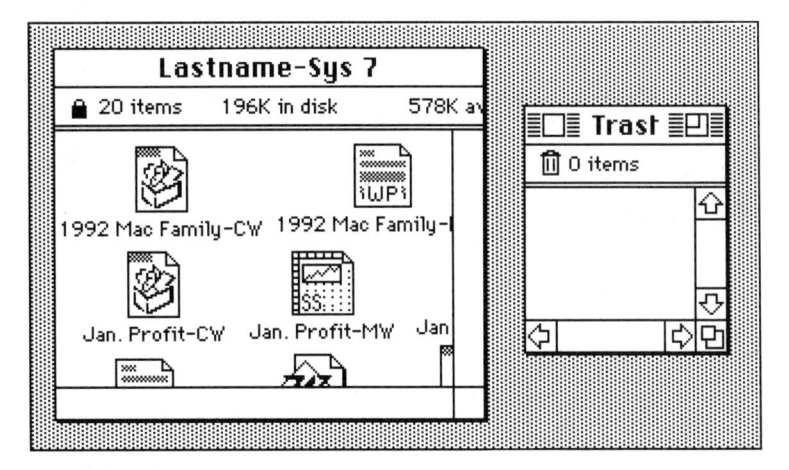

Notice that the title bar of the Trash window has horizontal lines in it. The lines tell us that this is the active or selected window. The scroll bars, close box, zoom box, and size box on the Lastname-Sys 7 window have disappeared. You can have many open windows on the desktop, but only one can be active at a time. A stack of windows on your desktop is similar to a stack of papers on your table top. You can have many papers on your table top but you can only read one at a time.

Look at the icons on the desktop. The Trash and Lastname-Sys 7 disk icons are dimmed, indicating they are open. The Trash icon is highlighted, indicating it is the **active window**.

## Activity 4.8—Activating a Window

Step 1   Click on an empty area of the Lastname-Sys 7 window.

## What's Happening

This window is now your active window—you should see the lines in the title bar, the scroll bar, and close, zoom, and size boxes. The floppy disk icon on the desktop is highlighted.

### Activity 4.9—Opening a Folder Icon

Step 1   Scroll the Lastname-Sys 7 window as necessary to locate the Misc. folder icon. Double click on the icon.

## What's Happening

A third window displaying the contents of the folder appears on your screen. It automatically becomes the active window.

### Activity 4.10—Moving and Arranging Windows

Step 1   Click on the Lastname-Sys 7 disk to activate the window. Size the window as small as possible.

Figure 4.15—Moving a Window

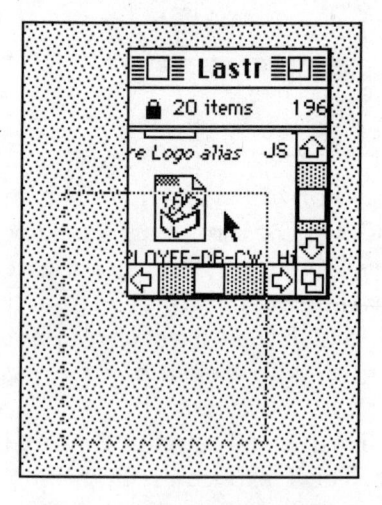

Step 2   Point anywhere in the title bar of the Lastname-Sys 7 window (except the zoom or close box). Press and hold the mouse button while dragging the window to the bottom left corner of your desktop. (Figure 4.15)

Step 3   Release the button.

## What's Happening

A dotted outline of your window follows your pointer until you release the button. The window moves to its new location.

Step 4   Activate the Misc. folder window. Size the window as small as possible. Drag this window next to the Lastname-Sys 7 window.

Step 5   Activate the Trash window. Size the Trash window as small as possible. Drag this window next to the Misc. window.

Step 6   Click on the open desktop.

## What's Happening

All your open windows are out of the way in a neat row along the bottom of the desktop. Clicking on the desktop deactivated all windows. (Figure 4.16)

*Figure 4.16—Three Windows on the Desktop*

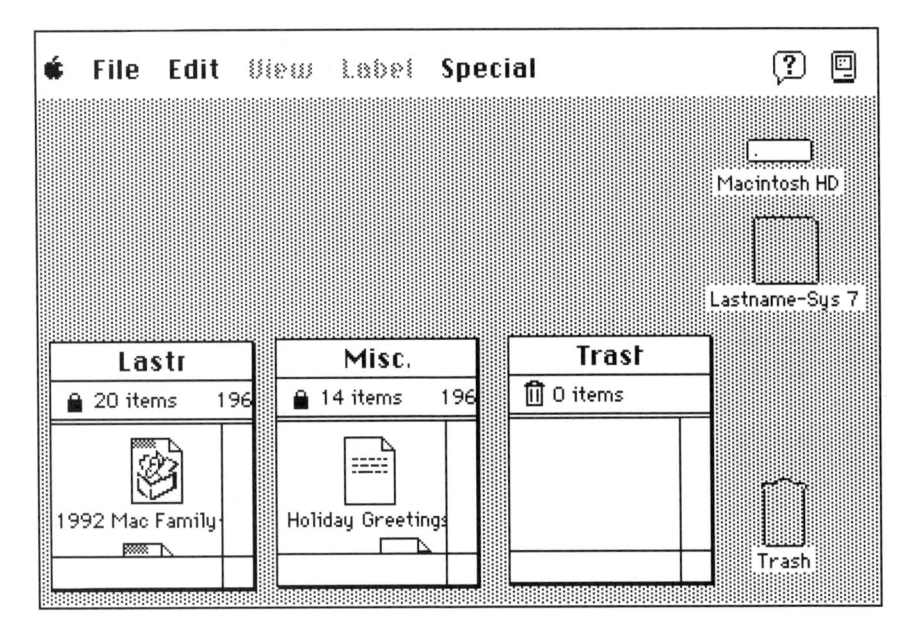

## Activity 4.11—Zooming and Shrinking Windows

Step 1  Click on the Lastname-Sys 7 window to activate the window. Click on the zoom box.

## What's Happening

The Lastname-Sys 7 window grows large enough to display the icons inside.

Step 2  Click on the zoom box in the Lastname-Sys 7 window to shrink the window.

## What's Happening

The window has been returned to its previous size and is at the bottom of the desktop (where it was before).

Step 3  Click on the Misc. folder window to activate the window. Click on the zoom box.

## What's Happening

The Misc. window grows large enough to display the icons inside.

Step 4    Click on the zoom box in the Misc. window to shrink the window.

*What's Happening*

All three windows are open and available, but are not in the way. Clicking on the zoom box makes the window large enough to work with and clicking the zoom box again makes the window resume its previous size and location on the desktop.

### Activity 4.12—Closing Windows

**Using the Close command**

Step 1    Activate the Trash window by clicking anywhere inside of it.

*What's Happening*

The Trash window becomes the active window—horizontal lines appear in the title bar.

Step 2    Point to the File menu, hold the mouse button down, and slowly move the pointer down until Close Window is highlighted. Let go of the button.

*What's Happening*

The Trash window should close and disappear from your desktop screen.

**Using the Close Box**

Step 3    Click on the Misc. window. Point to the close box of the Misc. window and click once.

*What's Happening*

The Misc. window will close.

**Using ⌘ W**

Step 4    If the Lastname-Sys 7 window is not active, click on the window. Use the keyboard shortcut ⌘ W to close the window.

*What's Happening*

The Lastname-Sys 7 window will close.

**Closing Multiple Windows in one step**

Step 5    Open the Lastname-Sys 7 disk.

Step 6    Locate and open the Misc. folder.

Step 7    Open the Trash.

*What's Happening*
> You now have three windows open on your desktop. Let's close all of them in one step.

Step 8    Hold down the Option key on your keyboard and click in the close box of your active window.

*What's Happening*
> All three windows close.

## Selecting Icons in the Active Window

There are several ways to select an icon(s) in the active window. You should remember these methods from our desktop discussion in Chapter 2. All methods work in both the icon and list view window. Figure 4.17 summarizes the methods to select icons. To deselect an icon, click on an empty area of the window or on another icon.

### Activity 4.13—Selecting Icons in the Active Window

Step 1    Open the Lastname-Sys 7 disk. If you can't see all the icons in the window, click once on the zoom box.

Step 2    Press the Tab key.

*What's Happening*
> The first icon in alphabetic order will be highlighted. Blank spaces and numbers proceed letters in the collating sequence.

Step 3    Press the Tab key a couple of times to see which icons are highlighted.

Step 4    Click once on the icon in the top left corner of the window. Press the right arrow key.

*What's Happening*
> The icon to the right of the current icon becomes active.

Step 5    Choose by Name from the View menu.

Step 6    Press the F key.

## What's Happening

The Lastname-Sys 7 window is in list view. The first icon beginning with an F is highlighted (Friend's Database).

Step 7    Choose by Icon from the View menu.

Step 8    Close the window.

*Figure 4.17—Selecting Icons*

### Selecting One Icon

| Method | Action |
| --- | --- |
| Click on the icon | That icon becomes active. |
| Press an arrow key | The next desktop icon in that direction becomes active. |
| Press the Tab key | The next desktop icon in alphabetic order becomes active. |
| Press a letter key | The first desktop icon whose name begins with that letter becomes active. |

### Selecting Multiple Icons

| Method | Group includes |
| --- | --- |
| Shift-Click | Each icon clicked on. |
| Box | Any icon in or touched by the box. |
| Menu command—Select All (⌘ A) | All icons on the desktop or active window. |

## Key Terms

⌘ O
⌘ W
Active scroll box
Active scroll bar
Active window
Alert dialog box
by Icon
by Name
Close box
Close Windows
File folders
Icon view
Inactive scroll bar

Inactive Window
Information bar
List view
Open
Padlock
Scroll arrows
Scroll bars
Scroll box
Size box
Title bar
Window
Zoom box

## Discussion Questions

1. Describe several ways to open and close an icon window.
2. What is a window?
3. Describe the common features of windows: close box, title bar, information bar, zoom box, scroll bars, scroll arrows, scroll boxes, and size box.
4. Describe these common window operations:
   - changing window sizes using the size box and the zoom box
   - scrolling windows using scroll arrows and box
   - working with multiple windows (opening, activating, arranging, closing)

## True/False Questions

For each question, circle the letter T if the statement is true and the letter F if the statement is false.

T  F  1. To close a single window, it must be the active window.
T  F  2. The disk window's information bar always contains the number of files on the entire disk.
T  F  3. The name of the open icon is always displayed in the title bar.
T  F  4. File folders are used on the Macintosh to store related documents.
T  F  5. ⌘ O is the keyboard shortcut to open an icon.
T  F  6. The commands to open and close an icon are available on the View menu.
T  F  7. If you have three windows open on the desktop when you execute the Close Window command, all three will close automatically.

T F  8. The close box is located in the window's top left corner.
T F  9. Multiple windows may be opened on the desktop, but only one can be active.
T F  10. A shaded scroll bar indicates that everything could not fit in the open window.
T F  11. Clicking on the scroll arrows is the fastest way to scroll a window.
T F  12. Clicking on the size box will cause the window to fill the screen. Clicking on it again will return the window to its original size.
T F  13. The booting disk icon must always remain in the desktop's top right corner.
T F  14. A padlock in the information bar indicates that the disk is locked.

## Completion Questions

Write the correct answer in each blank space.

1. A _____ is an enclosed region on the desktop that has a menu bar and is associated with a specific disk, folder or document icon.
2. To move a window, the arrow pointer must be touching the window's _____.
3. If the _____ _____ is half way down the scroll bar, it indicates you are viewing the middle of a document or window.
4. A window's title bar contains the _____ , _____ and _____.
5. The active window will have horizontal lines displayed in the _____.
6. You should use the _____ to size the window to any size.
7. A short-cut way to open an icon is to _____ on the icon.
8. Use the left scroll arrow to scroll the window's contents to the _____.
9. The _____ is used to size the window to your exact specifications.
10. _____ on the window to make it the active window.

## Matching Questions

For each question, place the letter of the correct answer on the line provided.

A. Close Box      B. Title Bar      C. Information Bar
D. Zoom Box       E. Size Box       F. Active Scroll Bar
G. Inactive Scroll Bar

\_\_\_1.  Scroll bar appears white, indicating you are seeing the entire picture in that direction.
\_\_\_2.  Appears in the window's top left corner.
\_\_\_3.  Appears in the window's top right corner.
\_\_\_4.  Appears in the window's bottom right corner.
\_\_\_5.  Scroll bar is shaded, indicating you are not seeing the entire picture in that direction.

___6. Contains the zoom and close boxes.
___7. If a disk is locked, the padlock will appear here.

## Assignments

1. Examine the sample Macintosh desktop picture. Next to each number, place the letter of the answer that best describes the item. Each letter is used once.

   1. _____  2. _____  3. _____  4. _____  5. _____
   6. _____  7. _____  8. _____  9. _____  10. _____
   11. _____  12. _____  13. _____  14. _____  15. _____

   a. Close box            b. File folder          c. Finder menu bar
   d. Floppy disk          e. Hard disk            f. Horizontal scroll bar
   g. Information bar      h. Name of open icon    i. Padlock
   j. Size box             k. System Folder        l. Title bar
   m. Trash can            n. Vertical scroll bar  o. Zoom box

**Sample Macintosh Desktop**

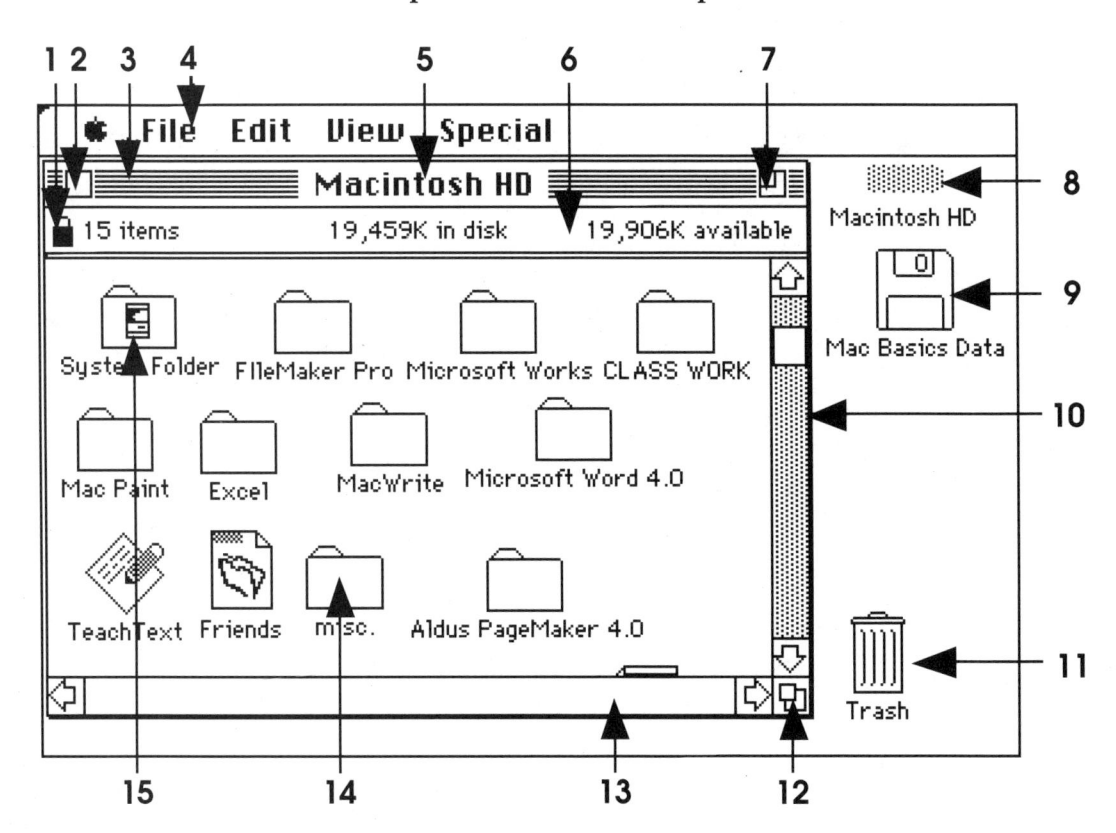

2. Look at the sample Macintosh desktop picture used in question 1. Which scroll bar is active? ___
   a. Horizontal
   b. Vertical

   If your Macintosh is not on and booted, do so now. Lock your Lastname-Sys 7 data disk. Insert your *locked* Lastname-Sys 7 data disk in the available floppy drive. Answer the following questions as they relate to that disk.

3. Open the Lastname-Sys 7 data disk. Click on the zoom box so that the window almost fills the desktop. Drag the Employee DB icon to the bottom right corner of the window. Drag the Store Logo icon to the bottom left.

3. Open the Lastname-Sys 7 data disk. Click on the zoom box so that the window almost fills the desktop. Drag the Employee DB icon to the bottom right corner of the window. Drag the Store Logo icon to the bottom left corner. Close the Lastname-Sys 7 data disk window. Now reopen the disk window. Answer the following questions.

   A. Is the window the zoomed size you left when you closed the window? ___
      a. Yes
      b. No
   B. Are the two icons you moved still in the bottom left and right corners? ___
      a. Yes
      b. No

4. Drag the Picture 1 icon on to the desktop. An alert dialog box will appear. Answer the following questions as they relate to this dialog box.
   a. The message in the box reads_____.
   b. The buttons in the box reads _____.
   c. The picture in the dialog box is in the shape of a _____.
   d. The two possible methods to respond to this dialog box are:
      _____.
      _____.

5. Open the Misc. folder. Display the window in a list view by name. What is the first entry in the window? _____

6. What's the name of the file folder inside the Misc. folder?

   _____

7. Open the file folder that is stored inside the Misc. folder. Answer the following questions as they pertain to this folder.
   a. What's the name of your active window?_____
   b. How many windows do you have open on your desktop? _____
   c. How many icons are stored inside this file folder? _____
   d. Use the scroll bars to display the icon in the top left corner of the folder. What is the name of the icon?_____
   e. Use the scroll bars to display the icon in the bottom left corner of the folder. What is the name of the icon? _____
   f. Use the scroll bars to display the icon in the top right corner of the folder. What is the name of the icon? _____
   g. Use the scroll bars to display the icon in the bottom right corner of the folder. What is the name of the icon?_____

8. Do not close any of the open windows to your Lastname-Sys 7 data disk. Drag the Lastname-Sys 7 data disk to the Trash. The disk will eject. Insert the disk back into the floppy drive. The windows are now ___
   a. Open
   b. Closed

9. Open the Lastname-Sys 7 data disk, the Misc. folder and the folder inside the Misc. folder. Size the windows so that they are all on the desktop and not overlapping. Eject the Lastname-Sys 7 data disk but leave its dimmed icon on the desktop. Unlock the disk and insert it back into the floppy drive. Leave the windows open and drag the disk icon to the Trash. Now reinsert the disk in the drive. The windows are now ___
   a. Open
   b. Closed

10. Can you close the Lastname-Sys 7 data disk window and the Misc. folder window but leave the other file folder window open?___
    a. Yes
    b. No

    Close all open windows.

# The Apple Menu and Desk Accessories

## Learning Objectives

**After completing this Chapter you will be able to:**

1. Define desk accessory.
2. Explain how to access and close a desk accessory.
3. Describe what information is available through the About This Macintosh option of the Apple menu.
4. Describe the tasks performed by the Finder program.
5. Explain the Alarm Clock DA; including how to display the computer's date and time, how to reset date and time, how to set the alarm and how to turn the alarm off.
6. Explain how to use the Calculator DA.
7. Describe how to use and the purpose of the Note Pad DA.
8. Describe the Puzzle DA.
9. Explain how to access and display different items pasted in the Scrapbook.
10. Describe how to use the Key Cap DA, and how to view different fonts.

## Introduction

This chapter will cover eight of the nine entries found in most **Apple menus**. When a Startup disk is created, the Apple System 7 Install program automatically places nine items on the Apple menu. (Figure 5.1)

*Figure 5.1—Apple Menu*

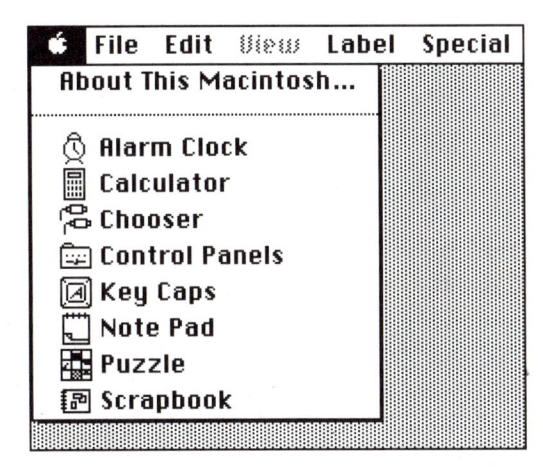

```
  File   Edit   View   Label   Special
  About This Macintosh...

  ⏰ Alarm Clock
  🖩 Calculator
  📇 Chooser
  🎛 Control Panels
  ⌨ Key Caps
  📝 Note Pad
  🧩 Puzzle
  📖 Scrapbook
```

The first entry in the menu will change depending on whether you are at the desktop level or within an application program. For example, at the desktop level the entry reads "**About This Macintosh...**" but from within the TeachText application program the entry will be "About TeachText...". Seven desk accessories are included in the menu: Alarm Clock, Calculator, Chooser, Key Caps, Note Pad, Puzzle, and Scrapbook. A **desk accessory** (DA) is a small application program that is accessible at any time from within any application program. You can have several desk accessories open at the same time. You should close all unnecessary DAs because they take up desktop space and memory. The **Control Panels** entry gives you access to a variety of programs that may be used to customize your Macintosh system. Control Panels are discussed in Chapter 11.

Your Apple menu may not look exactly like the one above—you may have additional entries. Some application packages will add entries to your Apple menu when they are installed on your disk. In Chapter 12 you will learn how to add and remove items in the Apple menu.

The following activities will introduce you to desk accessories and the information entry, About This Macintosh, in the Apple menu. Some of them are fairly simple and may need little explanation, while others provide many options and need more in-depth discussion.

If you are using a Macintosh in a computer-equipped classroom or lab, or you share your Macintosh, be sure to restore everything you change in this chapter to the way you found it. Remember, be courteous.

## Activating and Closing Desk Accessories

To select the entry you want, access the Apple pull-down menu on the far left of the menu bar. Point to the menu and hold down the mouse button to display the menu. Slowly move the mouse down the list of available entries until the one you want is highlighted. Let go of the mouse button and the entry will activate, opening a window for you. A window is a region on the screen that allows you access to that specific entry.

You close desk accessories by clicking on the close box or by choosing Close or Quit from the File menu. Some entries will automatically close as soon as you make a selection or when you move in or out of an application.

## About This Macintosh

When you choose the Apple menu entry **About This Macintosh** while on the desktop level, an information window displays the version number of the System software installed on your Startup disk. It also shows the size of RAM Memory, and how memory is divided between System software and application programs. Remember System software is loaded into RAM during booting and continues to operate as long as the computer is on. Later, when you are using application programs, you will find that this entry in the Apple menu provides information about the application program you are working in rather than the operating system.

You need to know the version number of your System software because application programs require options available in specific versions of the system. For example, an application program may require system version 6.0 or higher. You should be aware of the consequences of installing a different version of System software. Updated versions of these files may not run the older application programs. For example, System 7 will not work with some older versions of application programs. The programmers have had to modify the application programs to work with System 7 and to take advantage of the new features System 7 provides.

Remember our previous discussions on **version numbers** and how they are assigned—any time a software package is enhanced or upgraded (improved) it is assigned a higher number than the previous release. If the number before the decimal changes, there are major differences between this release and the previous one. If the number after the decimal changes, there are minor differences. For example, the change from 6.08 to 7.0 was a major upgrade in software, but 7.0 to 7.1 was a minor change.

### Activity 5.1—Using About This Macintosh

Step 1   Your Macintosh system should be on and booted, with all windows closed.

Step 2   Point to the  menu, hold the mouse button down, move the mouse so that the About This Macintosh entry is highlighted, and release the button.

## What's Happening

You have selected this entry from the pull-down menu, a window has opened, and you should see an information window similar to the one in Figure 5.2. It may not be exact—you may have a different Macintosh model, System Software version number or a different amount of RAM storage.

According to this window there is 5,120K, approximately 5 MB, of Total Memory (RAM) on this Macintosh IIsi. The system files are using 1,431K of RAM memory and application programs have access to 3,373K. Version 7.1 of the operating system is being used.

This DA can be used to double-check on the amount of memory installed on a new Macintosh, and when you have extra memory installed.

*Figure 5.2—About This Macintosh*

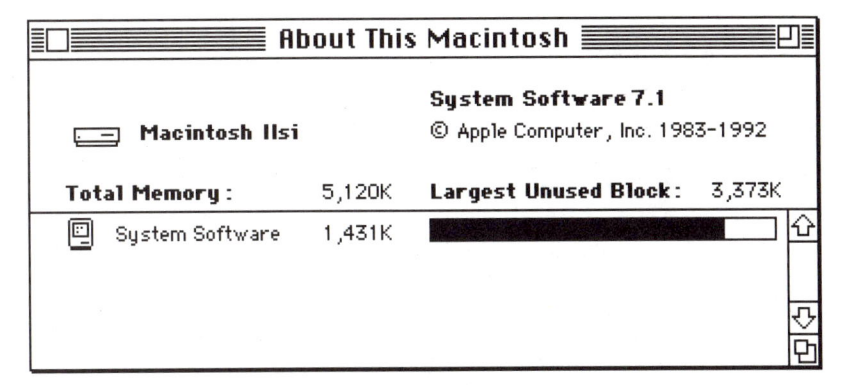

```
┌─────────────── About This Macintosh ───────────────┐
│                                                      │
│                      System Software 7.1             │
│       Macintosh IIsi   © Apple Computer, Inc. 1983-1992│
│                                                      │
│   Total Memory:      5,120K    Largest Unused Block:  3,373K │
│                                                      │
│       System Software   1,431K   [████████████      ]│
│                                                      │
└──────────────────────────────────────────────────────┘
```

Step 3    After reviewing the information, click on the close box to close the window.

---

## The Alarm Clock                    ⓧ Alarm Clock

The **alarm clock** is used to:
- See the computer's current time or date.
- Reset the current time or date stored in the computer.
- Set the alarm and turn it on or off.

It is extremely important to set the correct date and time on your Macintosh. When you create or modify document files or format disks, the computer date is given to that object. You can use this date to verify which copy of a file is the latest. Your Macintosh will not forget the date and time just because you power down the system. A battery maintains this information.

There are a variety of uses for the alarm feature. Some people tend to lose track of time when working on the Macintosh. Therefore, the alarm can be used to alert you to the current time. For instance, if you have a 1:30 PM class or meeting you must attend, you could set the alarm to go off at 12:30 PM. If you are working on the computer late in the evening, perhaps you should set the alarm to remind you to go to bed.

### Activity 5.2—Setting the Alarm Clock

Step 1   Point to the  menu, hold the mouse button down, move the mouse so that the Alarm Clock option is highlighted, and release the button.

*What's Happening*

You have just selected the Alarm Clock DA. It should activate and display a new window on your desktop. (Figure 5.3) You may see the expanded Alarm Clock instead, if it has been left open. (Figure 5.4) The Finder menu bar has been replaced with the Alarm Clock menu bar. The Alarm Clock icon appears on the far right end of the menu bar.

*Figure 5.3—The Alarm Clock*

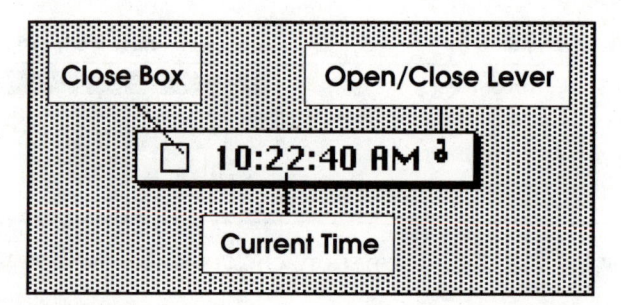

```
                Close Box              Open/Close Lever
                       ┌─────────────────────────┐
                       │  □  10:22:40 AM  ♪     │
                       └─────────────────────────┘
                              Current Time
```

Step 2   Click on the Open/Close Lever (Figure 5.3) to expose the expanded clock. (Figure 5.4)

*Figure 5.4—Expanded Alarm Clock*

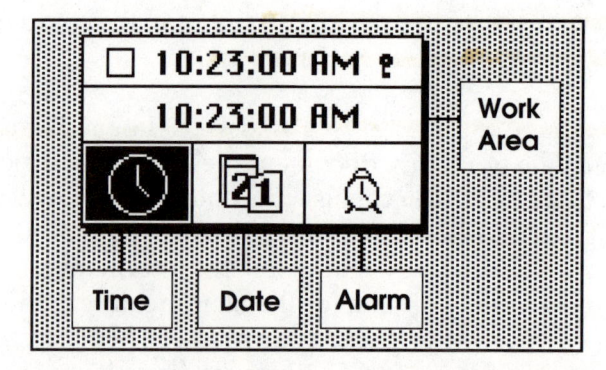

```
         ┌────────────────────────────┐
         │   □  10:23:00 AM  ♪        │
         │      10:23:00 AM      Work │
         │                       Area │
         │   [🕐]    [21]    [⏰]     │
         └────────────────────────────┘
            Time    Date    Alarm
```

## *What's Happening*

Two more panels appear. The top panel shows you the current date or time. The second panel is your work area. It will change with your selection—setting the time, date or alarm. The third panel is where you make your selection.

Step 3  Verify that the Time icon is dark—if not, click on it. Click on the hour in the middle panel. (Figure 5.5)

*Figure 5.5—Time*

## *What's Happening*

You are going to change the hour. Notice the hour is highlighted and double arrows appear on the right.

Step 4  Click on the up or down arrow until the hour number is 8.

## *What's Happening*

The arrows scroll the numbers up and down. You can also type the number you want. You can change the minutes, seconds, and AM/PM the same way—click on the one you want to change and scroll the arrows.

*Figure 5.6—Setting the Clock*

Step 5  Set the time to 8:15:36 AM. (Figure 5.6) Scroll through minutes, seconds and AM/PM. When you are done, click on the clock icon in the bottom left panel to set the new time. Click on the Date icon in the bottom panel.

*Figure 5.7—New Time*

## *What's Happening*

Once you have clicked on the Clock icon, the top panel will display the new time. Clicking on the Date icon causes the current date to be displayed in the work area. (Figure 5.7)

Step 6  Click on the numbers in the middle panel and change the date in the work area (the second panel) to 12/25/93. Scroll through months, days, and years. (Figure 5.8)

*Figure 5.8—Setting New Date*

[Clock showing 8:24:35 AM, date 12/**25**/93 with scroll arrows, date icon selected]

*Figure 5.9—New Date*

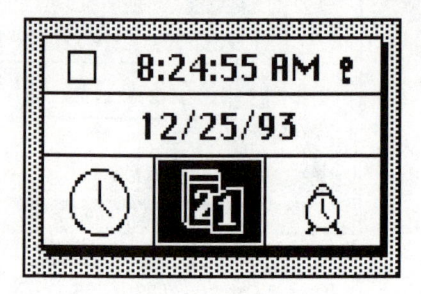

[Clock showing 8:24:55 AM, date 12/25/93, date icon selected]

*Figure 5.10—Entering the Alarm Time*

[Clock showing 10:33:47, alarm 10:39:30 AM with scroll arrows, alarm clock icon selected]

*Figure 5.11—Turning the Alarm Clock On*

[Clock showing 10:34:02 AM, alarm 10:39:30 AM, ringing alarm icon]

Step 7  Click on the date icon (bottom panel) to set the date. (Figure 5.9)

*What's Happening*
> Figure 5.9 displays the new date and time. The scroll arrows have disappeared.

☞ *Note: It is very important to set the clock to the correct date and time.*

Step 8  Repeat steps 3 through 7 to set the clock to the current date and time.

Step 9  Click on the Alarm Clock (bottom panel). Set the hour to your correct time and set the minutes five minutes ahead of the current time, as shown in Figure 5.10.

*What's Happening*
> You have entered the alarm time.

Step 10  Click on the Alarm Clock icon to set the alarm time. Turn the alarm on by clicking on the on/off button (middle panel, left side).

*What's Happening*
> The Alarm Clock icon becomes a ringing alarm. (Figure 5.11)

Step 11  Select the  menu entry **About Alarm Clock.**

*What's Happening*
> An information window will appear. (Figure 5.12)

*Figure 5.12—About Alarm Clock*

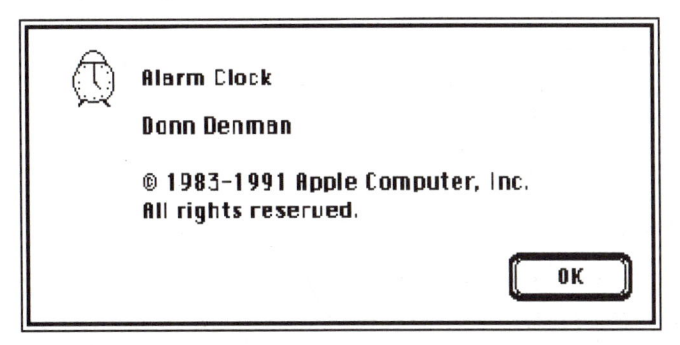

```
Alarm Clock
Donn Denman
© 1983-1991 Apple Computer, Inc.
All rights reserved.
                                    OK
```

Step 12  Click on the OK button to close the window.

Step 13  Close the expanded clock by clicking on the close lever in the top panel, right. (Figure 5.13) Close the alarm clock by clicking in the close box on the left side.

*Figure 5.13—Closing the Alarm DA*

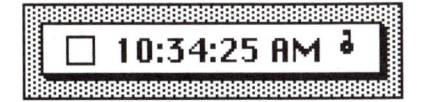

```
☐ 10:34:25 AM
```

## What's Happening

The alarm will go off in five minutes—an alert will sound and a flashing alarm clock icon will appear on the left end of the menu bar over the Apple. (Figure 5.14) It will continue to flash until you turn the alarm clock off. You will learn how to select a different alert sound and to control the volume in Chapter 11.

*Figure 5.14—Ringing Alarm*

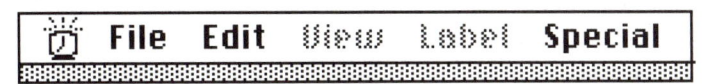

```
🔔  File   Edit   View   Label   Special
```

Step 14  To turn the alarm off:
Select the Alarm Clock DA.
Open to the expanded clock.
Click on the Alarm Clock (bottom row).
Click the on/off button (middle row).
Close the expanded clock.
Close the Alarm Clock DA window.

## The Calculator          🖩 Calculator

The computer **Calculator** works just like a hand-held model. You can use the mouse to click on each key (number), or you may use the numeric keypad on the extended keyboard. (Figure 5.15)

*Figure 5.15—The Calculator*

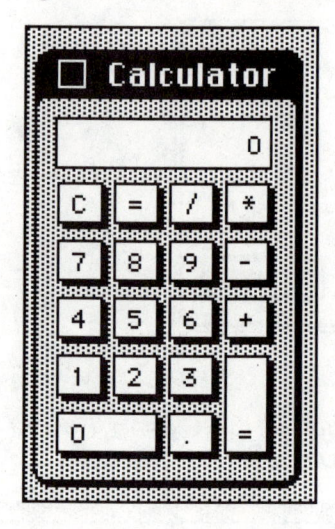

### Activity 5.3—Using The Calculator

Step 1    Select Calculator from the  menu.

*What's Happening*
> The Calculator menu bar is displayed and the calculator icon appears on the right edge of the menu bar.

Step 2    Click on the numbers and operation buttons with the mouse or use the numbers and operation keys on the numeric keypad.

Step 3    Close the Calculator window by clicking in the close box.

### Activity 5.4—Using About This Macintosh with open DAs

Step 1    Open the Alarm Clock DA.

Step 2    Open the Calculator DA.

Step 3    Make the desktop active by clicking on the open desktop.

*What's Happening*
> Both DA windows should be on the desktop. The Finder menu bar should be displayed.

Step 4    Select About This Macintosh from the  menu.

*What's Happening*
> An information window appears showing how memory is currently divided. Your window may not look exactly like Figure 5.16. You may have a different Macintosh model, and a different amount of memory. In Figure 5.16, the Alarm Clock and Calculator DAs are using 20K each, System Software is using 1,471K and the largest unused block is 3,294K. The amount of memory used by the System Software increases as you open additional application programs.

*Figure 5.16—About This Macintosh and Memory*

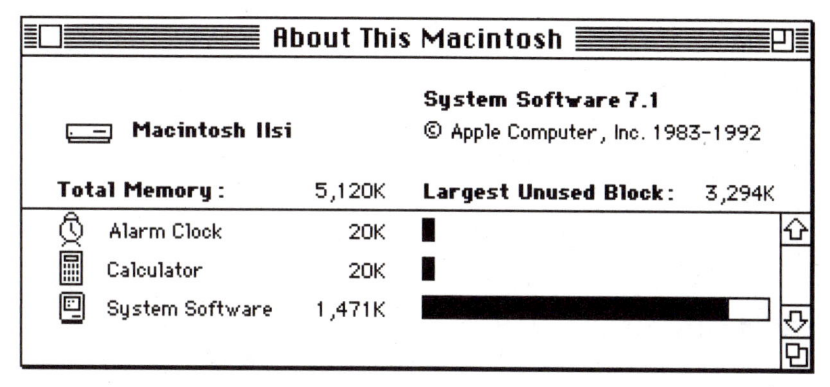

```
≡□≡≡≡≡≡≡≡≡ About This Macintosh ≡≡≡≡≡≡≡□≡
                              System Software 7.1
         Macintosh IIsi        © Apple Computer, Inc. 1983-1992

      Total Memory:    5,120K   Largest Unused Block:   3,294K
       Alarm Clock      20K    ▮
       Calculator       20K    ▮
       System Software  1,471K ▬▬▬▬▬▬▬▬▬▬▬▬▬▬
```

Step 5  Close the information window by clicking in the close box. Close the Alarm Clock and Calculator windows.

## The Chooser     🖧 Chooser

The primary purpose of the **Chooser** is to let you communicate with peripheral devices—a printer, for example. The window that opens when you select the Chooser DA will vary according to your system configuration. If you have a stand-alone Macintosh with one printer, you will use the Chooser once to tell the System which printer to use. You will probably not need to use it again unless you upgrade your system software or add an additional printer. If you are on a network (multiple computers linked together in order to share information and/or peripherals) or you have more than one printer, you will use the Chooser more frequently. This DA will be discussed in detail in Chapter 7.

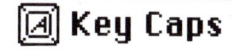

## Key Caps     🄰 Key Caps

The **Key Caps** desk accessory allows you to view the available fonts (type faces) on your system before you use them in a document. You can also view the optional characters produced when using the modifier keys—Option, Control and Shift. The optional characters will vary depending on the selected font.

### Activity 5.5—Using the Key Caps DA

Step 1  Select Key Caps from the  menu.

*What's Happening*

The Key Caps window appears showing a standard character set on a sample Macintosh keyboard. The Caps Lock key appears dark if it is activated. The Key Caps menu appears on the menu bar. (Figure 5.17)

104  CHAPTER 5  •  THE APPLE MENU AND DESK ACCESSORIES

*Figure 5.17—Key Caps DA*

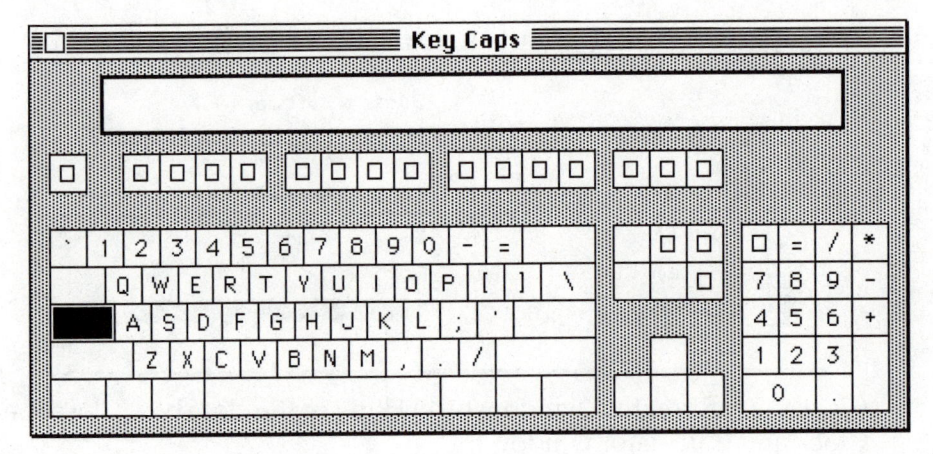

[Key Caps window showing a keyboard layout with a text display area at top and keys arranged in standard QWERTY layout with numeric keypad on the right]

*Figure 5.18—Key Caps Menu*

[Menu showing: File, Edit, Key Caps menu with items: Athens, Cairo, Chicago, Courier, ✓Geneva, Helvetica, London, Los Angeles, Mobile, Monaco, MT Extra, New York, Palatino, San Francisco, Symbol, Times, Venice]

Step 2    Display the Key Caps menu.

## What's Happening

The Key Caps menu displays a list of available fonts on your Macintosh. The entries in your menu may vary from the sample in Figure 5.18. The check-mark identifies the active font. A **Font** is a set of characters using the same typeface (Geneva, for example), style (**bold** or *italics*) and point size. A **point** is equal to 1/72 of an inch and measures character height. Different fonts may be used in the same document to improve its appearance. Fonts will be discussed further in Chapter 12.

Step 3    If Geneva is not the active font, drag the arrow pointer down the menu bar until Geneva is highlighted. Release the mouse button.

Step 4    Verify that the Caps Lock key is not activated and key in the following statement: This is an example of the Geneva font.

## What's Happening

The keys you press are highlighted on the sample keyboard and the statement appears in the text bar. (Figure 5.19)

*Figure 5.19—Text Entered in Geneva Font*

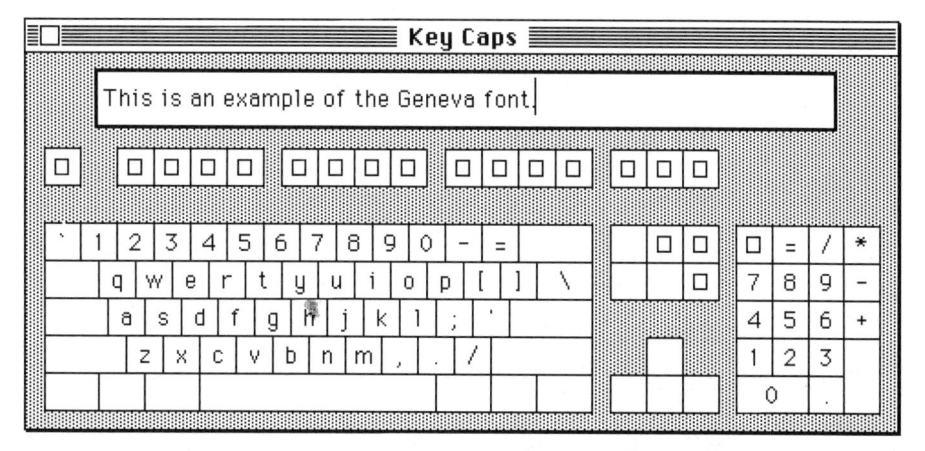

**Step 5** Press the Option, Shift, and Control keys individually. As you do, the keyboard changes to reveal different letters and characters. Try holding down the Option and Shift key together to see other possibilities. For example, in most fonts if you type the equal sign (=) while holding down the Option key, the not equal sign ( ) will appear. If you hold both the Option and Shift key while pressing the = key, a plus or minus sign (±) will appear.

## What's Happening

Notice that when you hold down the Option key, some keys on the Key Caps keyboard are enclosed in a shaded box (',e,u,i,n). These Option-key combinations produce an accent mark over the next character typed. To use accent marks, hold down the Option key while pressing the specified character, then type the character to be accented. Figure 5.20 describes the accent marks available and shows examples using the letter a.

*Figure 5.20—Accent Marks*

| Accent Mark | Example | Key Combinations |
|---|---|---|
| Acute accent | á | Option e |
| Circumflex | â | Option i |
| Grave accent | à | Option ' |
| Tilde | ã | Option n |
| Umlaut | ä | Option u |

Step 6   To see different available fonts, pull down the Key Caps menu and choose from the list of available fonts.

## What's Happening

When you select another font, the Key Caps keyboard displays the selected font and the sentence you previously typed is displayed in that font. For example, the Cairo font is shown in Figure 5.21 and the London font is displayed in Figure 5.22. Pressing the Option, Shift, Control or Option and Shift keys will cause different characters to be displayed.

*Figure 5.21—Cairo Font*

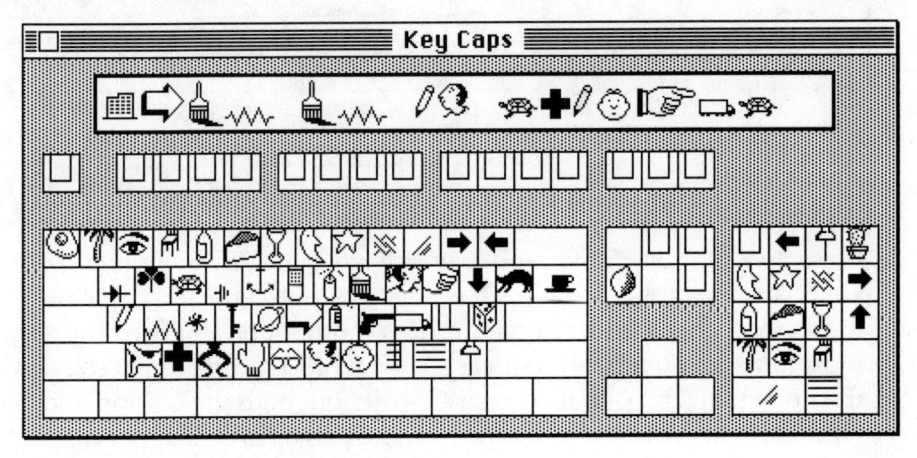

*Figure 5.22—London Font*

Step 7   Click on the close box.

## Note Pad

**Note Pad**

Use the **Note Pad** DA as you would a pad of paper. There are eight "sheets" in the note pad. You can see the next sheet by clicking on the folded corner. The pages will change from 1 to 2 to 3, and so on. Clicking on the unfolded corner will turn the pages back from 3 to 2 to 1.

### Activity 5.6—Using the Note Pad DA

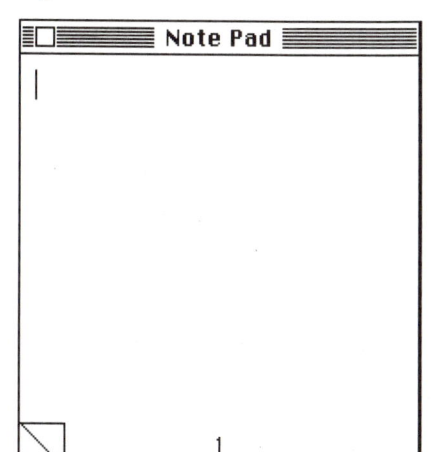

*Figure 5.23—The Note Pad DA*

Step 1   Select the Note Pad DA from the  menu.

*What's Happening*

A note pad will appear on the desktop. (Figure 5.23) Messages remain on the note pad until you erase them. Powering the system down does not erase messages.

Step 2   Close the Note Pad by clicking on the close box.

## Puzzle

### Activity 5.7—The Puzzle DA

*Figure 5.24—The Puzzle DA*

Step 1   Select the Puzzle DA from the  menu.

*What's Happening*

The puzzle in Figure 5.24 appears. This desk accessory is like a plastic puzzle cut into small squares. The squares can be moved around to create a picture.

Step 2   Click on any square above, below, to the left or right of the dotted square.

*What's Happening*

The two squares will change places.

Step 3   Continue to move squares around to solve the puzzle, if you like. Good Luck! When you are finished, close the Puzzle DA by clicking on the close box.

## Scrapbook          📄 **Scrapbook**

The Scrapbook is the seventh standard DA. It allows the user to paste frequently used text or pictures into the scrapbook and to retrieve them later to include in other documents. The Scrapbook is stored on the booting disk. The Scrapbook takes up disk space, so do not store unnecessary items in the Scrapbook. This DA will also be discussed in Chapter 8.

### Activity 5.8—Using the Scrapbook

Items in the Scrapbook will vary, but how you access and use the Scrapbook is always the same. Follow the steps below to see what is in your Scrapbook.

Step 1     Point to the  menu and select Scrapbook.

### What's Happening

A new window will open on your desktop and the last entry displayed in your Scrapbook will appear. The numbers on the bottom left corner of the window, tell you there are 7 pictures in the Scrapbook—you are viewing number 1. (Figure 5.25) The shaded scroll bar indicates there is more to see.

*Figure 5.25—The Scrapbook DA*

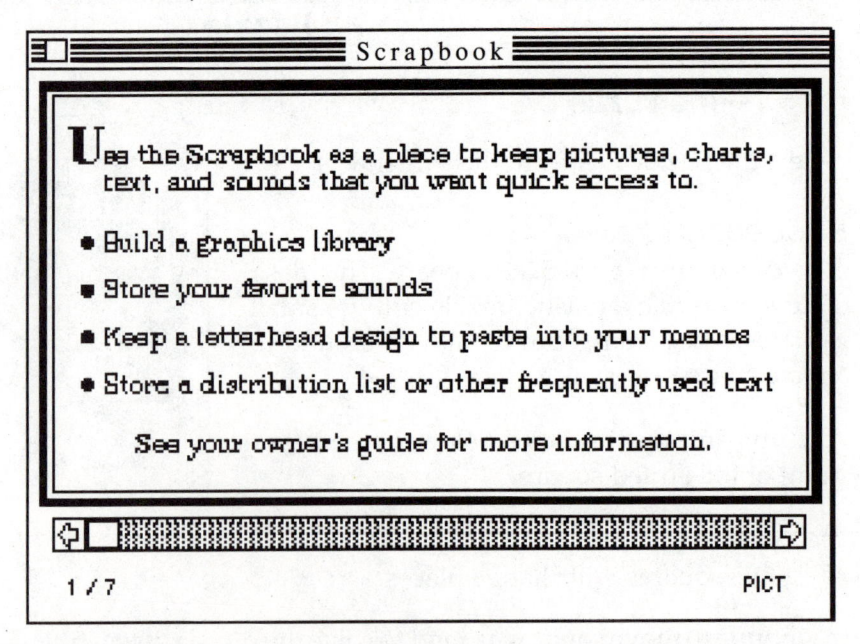

```
┌─────────────── Scrapbook ───────────────┐
│                                          │
│  Use the Scrapbook as a place to keep    │
│  pictures, charts, text, and sounds      │
│  that you want quick access to.          │
│                                          │
│  • Build a graphics library              │
│  • Store your favorite sounds            │
│  • Keep a letterhead design to paste     │
│    into your memos                       │
│  • Store a distribution list or other    │
│    frequently used text                  │
│                                          │
│  See your owner's guide for more         │
│  information.                            │
│                                          │
│  ◁ ▓▓▓▓▓▓▓▓▓▓▓▓▓▓▓▓▓▓▓▓▓▓▓▓▓▓ ▷        │
│  1 / 7                            PICT   │
└──────────────────────────────────────────┘
```

Step 2     Use the scroll bar at the bottom to scroll through your Scrapbook. (Figure 5.26)

*Figure 5.26—Scrolling through the Scrapbook*

**Step 3** Click on the close box.

*What's Happening*

In a later chapter, you will learn how to cut and paste items in your Scrapbook, and how to paste them into a document from the Scrapbook.

## Key Terms

| | |
|---|---|
| 🍎 | Desk accessory |
| About Alarm Clock | Fonts |
| About This Macintosh | Key Caps DA |
| Alarm Clock DA | List box |
| Apple menu | Note Pad DA |
| Calculator DA | Points |
| Chooser | Puzzle DA |
| Control Panels | Scrapbook |
| DAs | Version numbers |

## Discussion Questions

1. What does the Apple menu provide?
2. What is a desk accessory?

3. How do you select, activate, and close a DA?
4. Describe the seven DAs: Alarm Clock, Calculator, Chooser, Key Caps, Scrapbook, Note Pad, and Puzzle.
5. How do you set the alarm?
6. When must you access the Chooser?
7. Is it possible to add DAs to the  menu?

## True/False Questions

For each question, circle the letter T if the statement is true and the letter F if the statement is false.

T  F  1. The Macintosh Alarm Clock is used primarily by the lab personnel to inform you when your time is up.
T  F  2. System 6.0.7 is older than System 7.1.
T  F  3. Desk accessories are available on the Apple menu.
T  F  4. All messages on the Note Pad DA are erased when you Restart or Shut Down the Macintosh.
T  F  5. The Finder program is loaded into memory during the booting process.
T  F  6. You can add additional DAs to the Special menu.
T  F  7. If the word Apple does not appear on your menu bar, you can't access any desk accessories.
T  F  8. The graphical form of interaction between the Macintosh and the user was developed to allow users to feel less intimidated and more comfortable with the Macintosh.
T  F  9. It doesn't matter if your Macintosh does not know the correct date or time.
T  F  10. You must set the date and time every time you boot your Macintosh.

## Completion Questions

Write the correct answer in each blank space.

1. The Alarm Clock DA allows you to set the _____, _____ and_____.
2. Creating and maintaining the desktop is the responsibility of the _____.
3. Using the _____, _____, and/or _____ key in conjunction with another key will type a different character.
4. _____ are different typefaces available in a variety of sizes and styles.
5. The _____ is used to store words or pictures you want to retrieve later to include in another document.
6. The _____ DA allows you to see fonts before using them in your document.

# Assignments

Boot your Macintosh. The Macintosh desktop should be clean—no open windows.

## About This Macintosh

Access the About This Macintosh option of the Apple menu. Complete the following questions as they apply to your Macintosh system.
1. Use the information in the About This Macintosh window to fill in the blanks.
    a. System Software Version number_____
  Memory Usage
    b. Total Memory           _____
    c. Largest unused Block   _____
    d. System Software        _____

2. The About This Macintosh window is still open on the desktop. Open the following DAs in order: Puzzle, Note Pad, Calculator.

    ____ a. Which window is active?
          1. Note Pad
          2. Calculator
          3. Puzzle
          4. About This Macintosh

    ____ b. Which shape does the icon on the right end of the Finder menu bar resemble?

          1. ▣   2. ▦   3. ▭   4. ▢

Use the information in the About This Macintosh window to fill in the blanks. Move the other windows if necessary but do not close them.

3. Memory Usage
    a. Total Memory         _____
    b. Largest unused Block _____
    c. System               _____
    d. Calculator           _____
    e. Puzzle               _____
    f. Note Pad             _____

____4. How are the open windows listed in the About This Macintosh window?
   a. In the order that they were opened.
   b. Alphabetically.
   c. Other

Close all open windows.

## Alarm Clock

Access the Alarm Clock DA. Open the expanded Alarm Clock. Answer the following questions as they pertain to this DA.

____5. Try changing the date to 2/30/93 by keying in the numbers. What happened?
   a. The Macintosh accepted this new date.
   b. The Macintosh beeped and would not accept the number 30.
   c. An Alert/Warning dialog box appeared.
   d. The Macintosh assumed you wanted the date to be 2/3/93.
   e. Both B and D are true.

____6. Click on the Time icon in the third panel. Which one of the following statements is true?
   a. The Clock in the first panel stops ticking off the seconds.
   b. The Clock in the second panel stops ticking off the seconds.
   c. When you click on the hour in the second panel, both clocks stop ticking.
   d. When you click on the hour in the second panel, the second panel clock stops ticking.
   e. All are true.

____7. Click on the Alarm icon in the third panel and then click on the hour in the second panel. Which of the following statements is false?
   a. The scroll arrows are in the second panel.
   b. Clicking once on the on/off switch in the second panel causes the Alarm icon in the third panel to change.
   c. Pressing the Tab key on the keyboard highlights the minutes in the second panel.
   d. You can not key in the number to be used—you must use the scroll arrows.
   e. None, all statements are true.

☞ *Note: It is very important to restore the correct date and time.*

Make sure you have the date and time set correctly. If you turned the Alarm on, turn it off. Close the expanded Alarm Clock. Close the Alarm Clock DA.

## Key Caps

Access the Key Caps DA, select the Geneva Font, and answer the following questions.

___ 8. The letter v key changes to a   when you press the following key(s).
   a. Control
   b. Option
   c. Shift-Control
   d. Shift-Option

___ 9. The letter p key changes to a „ when you press the following key(s).
   a. Control
   b. Option
   c. Shift-Control
   d. Shift-Option

___ 10. The \ key changes to a » when you press the following key(s).
   a. Control
   b. Option
   c. Shift-Control
   d. Shift-Option

___ 11. The number 8 key changes to a ¥ when you press the following key(s).
   a. Control
   b. Option
   c. Shift-Control
   d. Shift-Option

___ 12. The number 4 key changes to a ¢ when you press the following key(s).
   a. Control
   b. Option
   c. Shift-Control
   d. Shift-Option

Close all open windows.

# 6 The Finder Menu Bar

## Learning Objectives

**After completing this Chapter you will be able to:**

1. Describe the commands available on the File, Edit, View, Label, Special, Help and Application menus on the Finder menu bar.
2. Use the Get Info command to view information on various icons.
3. Use the Comment Box in the Get Info window to write a note on the selected icon.
4. Explain how the Put Away command works.
5. Demonstrate how the Cut, Copy, Paste, and Clear commands in the Edit menu operate.
6. Explain how the Clipboard is used for temporary storage.
7. Use the Select All command.
8. Change the way you view the icons in the open window: small icon, icon, name, size, kind, label, and date.
9. Describe two ways you can tell which view you are using to display the list of files, folders, and application programs in your active window.
10. Explain how to use the Clean Up command of the Special menu.
11. Explain the importance of the Application menu and how to use it.

## Introduction

In this chapter, we will discuss the various commands available in the **Finder menu bar**. (Figure 6.1)

*Figure 6.1—Finder Menu Bar*

```
 🍎   File   Edit   View   Label   Special                    ⁉️  🖥
```

These menus **allow you to perform desktop-related tasks.** They may only be accessed when you are at the Finder desktop level, not from within an application program. Activities are provided in this chapter to execute only selected commands. You have used some of the commands in previous chapters (Open, Close Window, Select All, Shut Down, by Name, by Icon, Erase Disk, Eject Disk, About Balloon Help, and Show/Hide Balloons) and others commands (Find, Find Again, Duplicate, Empty Trash) will be executed in later chapters. Figure 6.2 provides a quick review of menu operations.

*Figure 6.2—Menu Operations*

| Operation | Steps |
| --- | --- |
| Access a Menu | Point at menu name. Press and hold mouse button. |
| Execute a command | Access the necessary menu. Drag arrow down menu bar to highlight command. Release mouse button. |
| Dimmed Commands | Not available for execution. |
| Ellipsis (...) after command | Additional information required. Dialog box will be provided. |
| ⌘ + a letter | Command keyboard shortcut. |
| ✓ in front of a command | Identifies current selection. |

# The File Menu

The File menu is shown in Figure 6.3.

*Figure 6.3—The File Menu*

```
┌─────────────────────────┐
│ File                    │
│   New Folder        ⌘N  │
│   Open              ⌘O  │
│   Print             ⌘P  │
│   Close Window      ⌘W  │
│                         │
│   Get Info          ⌘I  │
│   Sharing...           │
│   Duplicate        ⌘D  │
│   Make Alias            │
│   Put Away          ⌘Y  │
│                         │
│   Find...           ⌘F  │
│   Find Again        ⌘G  │
│                         │
│   Page Setup...         │
│   Print Desktop...      │
└─────────────────────────┘
```

1. **New Folder.** The New Folder command creates a new folder on your active window. You should name the folder.
2. **Open**. The Open command opens a window to the selected icon. If the icon represents a disk, a new window appears on the desktop displaying the contents of the disk. If the icon represents the Trash, a Trash window opens. If the icon represents a folder, a new window will appear displaying the contents of the folder. If the icon represents a document file (letter, report, graphic picture), the system tries to locate the related application program. If found, the document is loaded into memory. If the icon represents an application program, the program will be loaded into memory and, depending on the program, a greeting screen or new document window will appear on your desktop
3. **Print**. Normally you will print a document from within the application program you are using, but you may also be able to use the Print command in the File menu. The application program that was used to create the document must be on an available disk, the hard disk or the floppy disk

currently in the drive. This command does not work with all application programs. This command is useful when you are in a hurry and you just want to print a document. Click on the icon(s) representing the document(s) you want to print and select the Print command. Selecting the Finder Print command starts a chain reaction of events:
- The application program the document was created in is located and read into memory.
- The selected document is opened and read into memory.
- A Print dialog box appears on your desktop and waits for you to enter your selections.
- The document is printed.
- The document and the application program windows are closed.

4. **Close Window**. The Close Window command closes the active window.
5. **Get Info**. The Get Info command opens a window that displays information on the selected icon. The information displayed varies according to the type of item the icon represents, but it may include:
   - The kind of item (disk, folder, application, document, alias).
   - Which application program created it (if it is a document).
   - The size, date created, last date modified.
   - Where it is located—drive, disk, folder(s).
   - If it is an application—the version number, and the suggested, minimum, and preferred memory size.
   - A comment box for your remarks.
   - A locked check box for documents or applications. If the box is checked, that document or application cannot be easily thrown away, renamed, or modified.
6. **Sharing.** Use this command to share disks and folders with other network users. File sharing must be turned on in the Sharing Setup control panel. (Refer to Chapter 12)
7. **Duplicate**. The Duplicate command makes a copy of your selected icon files, and gives it the name of the original icon followed by the word copy. The duplicate icon is placed in the active window.
8. **Make Alias.** The Make Alias command creates a small file (1-2K in size), that represents the original file and directs the system to the location of the original file. This allows you to place the alias in an easily accessible location and to keep the original file where it belongs. Aliases may be created for application programs, documents, folders, DAs, disks, the Trash, and so on. Chapter 12 will provide additional information on alias files.
9. **Put Away.** The Put Away command will place any selected documents, folders, or applications (that you have left on the desktop or in the active Trash window) back where they came from.

10. **Find.** Use the Find command to locate files on any disk or shared folder. This command will help you locate files you can't find.
11. **Find Again.** Use the Find Again command to continue the search you started using the Find command.
12. **Print Desktop.** The Print Desktop command will print the contents of the entire active window.
13. **Page Setup**. The Page Setup command allows you to specify paper size, orientation, and other printer options.

Let's execute some of these commands.

### Activity 6.1—Using the Get Info Command

Step 1   Your Macintosh system should be on and booted. Insert your unlocked Lastname-Sys 7 data disk in the floppy drive. All windows should be closed.

**Get Info on the Lastname-Sys 7 floppy disk**

Step 2   If the Lastname-Sys 7 floppy icon is not highlighted, select it by clicking on it.

Step 3   Select the Get Info command on the File menu.

*Figure 6.4—Floppy Info Window*

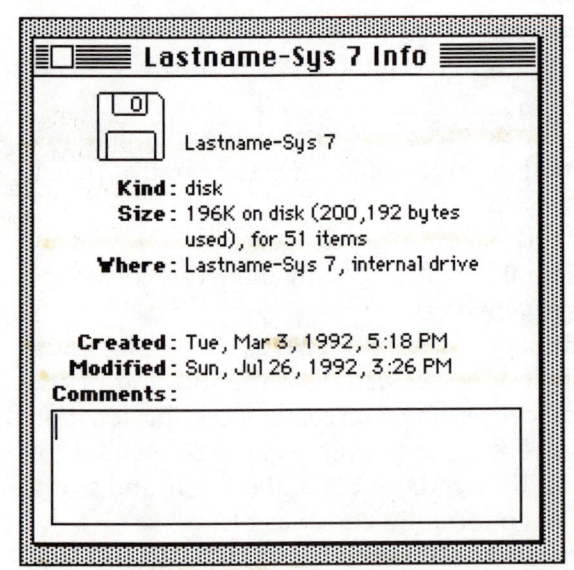

*What's Happening*

The Lastname-Sys 7 Info window will appear. The entries in your window may vary slightly from Figure 6.4. This information window contains useful information about the floppy disk: Kind, Size, Where, Created, Modified. The Size entry tells you the number of items stored on the entire disk. Remember, the status information bar only tells you how many items are in the open window. A Comment box is provided for additional remarks.

Step 4   Click the close box in the Info window to close the window.

**Get Info on the Trash icon**

Step 5   Click on the Trash icon to select it.

Step 6   Select the Get Info command on the File menu.

*What's Happening*

The Trash Info window will appear. The Info window in Figure 6.5 shows that the Trash is empty (Contents).

Notice the **Warn Before Emptying** checkbox at the bottom of the window. The X indicates that the system will warn you before erasing files or folders you have placed in the Trash. Clicking once on this box will direct the system not to warn you before emptying the Trash. Do not change this setting.

*Figure 6.5—Trash Info Window*

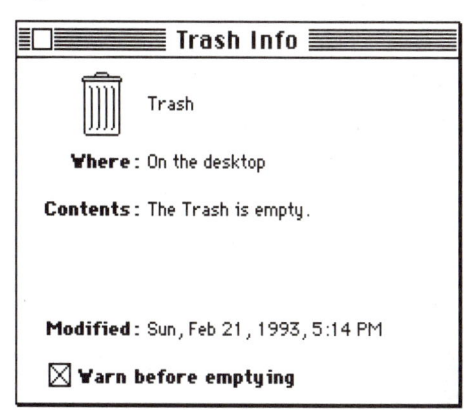

Step 7   Click the close box in the Info window to close the window.

### Get Info on a document icon

Step 8   Double-click on the Lastname-Sys 7 disk icon to open the disk window.

Step 9   Click once on the JS Ltr.-TT icon and select the Get Info command on the File menu.

*What's Happening*

The JS Ltr.-TT Info window will appear. In Figure 6.6 the document has been identified as a TeachText document (Kind). Two dates are displayed: the Created date identifies when the document was first created and the Modified date identifies the last time the document was changed. Two checkboxes are available along the bottom of the window: Locked and Stationary Pad. Clicking in the **Locked checkbox** will lock the document. If a document is locked, you can not modify or erase it. Clicking in the **Stationary Pad checkbox** will identify this document as a template. It can then be repeatedly opened and used as a master for other documents created by the same application program, TeachText.

*Figure 6.6—Document Info Window*

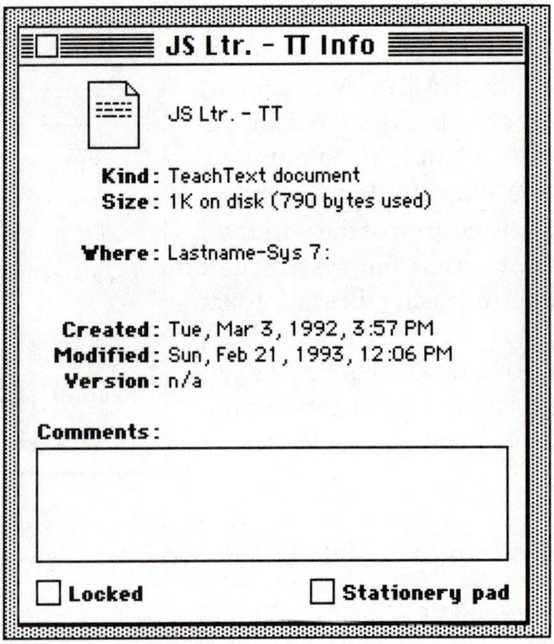

```
┌─────────────────────────────────────┐
│ ▣         JS Ltr. - TT Info         │
├─────────────────────────────────────┤
│      ▤   JS Ltr. - TT               │
│                                     │
│      Kind: TeachText document       │
│      Size: 1K on disk (790 bytes used)│
│                                     │
│     Where: Lastname-Sys 7:          │
│                                     │
│   Created: Tue, Mar 3, 1992, 3:57 PM│
│  Modified: Sun, Feb 21, 1993, 12:06 PM│
│   Version: n/a                      │
│                                     │
│  Comments:                          │
│  ┌───────────────────────────────┐  │
│  │                               │  │
│  │                               │  │
│  └───────────────────────────────┘  │
│  ☐ Locked          ☐ Stationery pad │
└─────────────────────────────────────┘
```

Step 10   Close the JS Ltr.-TT Info window.

**Get Info on an alias icon**

Step 11   Click once on the *Store Logo alias* icon and select the the Get Info command on the File menu.

## What's Happening

The *Store Logo alias* Info window will appear. (Figure 6.7) The standard information is available: Kind, Size, Where, Created, and Modified. Two additional items have been included in this info window: the **Original** entry and the **Find Original button.** The Original entry tells you the location of the original file. The Find Original button directs the system to locate the original file, open folders as necessary and select the original file on the desktop. The Locked checkbox locks this alias icon, but it does nothing to the original file.

*Figure 6.7—Alias Info Window*

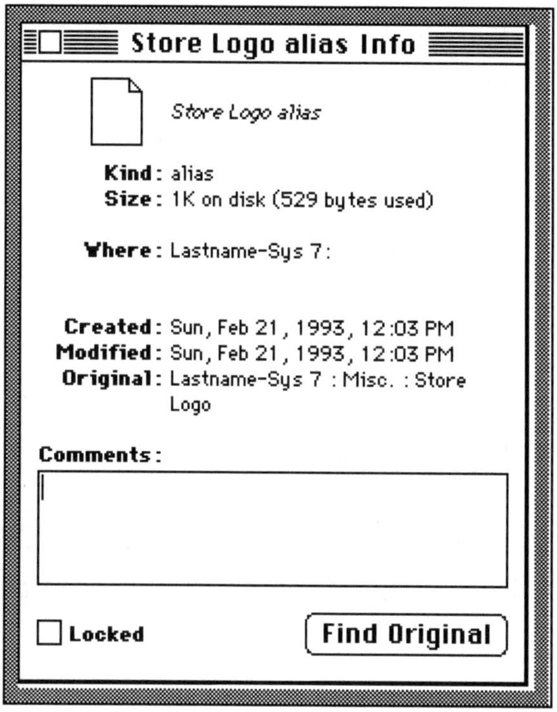

```
┌─────────────────────────────────────┐
│ ▣═══ Store Logo alias Info ═══      │
│                                      │
│    ▯   Store Logo alias             │
│                                      │
│      Kind: alias                    │
│      Size: 1K on disk (529 bytes used) │
│                                      │
│     Where: Lastname-Sys 7:          │
│                                      │
│   Created: Sun, Feb 21, 1993, 12:03 PM │
│  Modified: Sun, Feb 21, 1993, 12:03 PM │
│  Original: Lastname-Sys 7 : Misc. : Store │
│            Logo                     │
│                                      │
│  Comments:                          │
│   ┌─────────────────────────────┐  │
│   │                             │  │
│   │                             │  │
│   └─────────────────────────────┘  │
│                                      │
│   ☐ Locked          [ Find Original ] │
└─────────────────────────────────────┘
```

Step 12   Click on the Find Original button.

## What's Happening

The Misc. folder window will appear on your desktop. The original file, Store Logo, is highlighted.

Step 13   Close the Misc. window, close the *Store Logo alias* Info window.

### Get Info on a folder icon

Step 14   If the Lastname-Sys 7 window is not in icon view, select by Icon from the View menu.

Step 15   Click once on the Misc. folder icon and select the Get Info command of the File menu.

## What's Happening

The Misc. Info window will appear. (Figure 6.8) The Locked and Stationary Pad checkboxes are not available on folder icons. The Size entry specifies the number of items directly stored inside this folder and items within any folder within the Misc. folder.

*Figure 6.8—Misc. Folder Info Window*

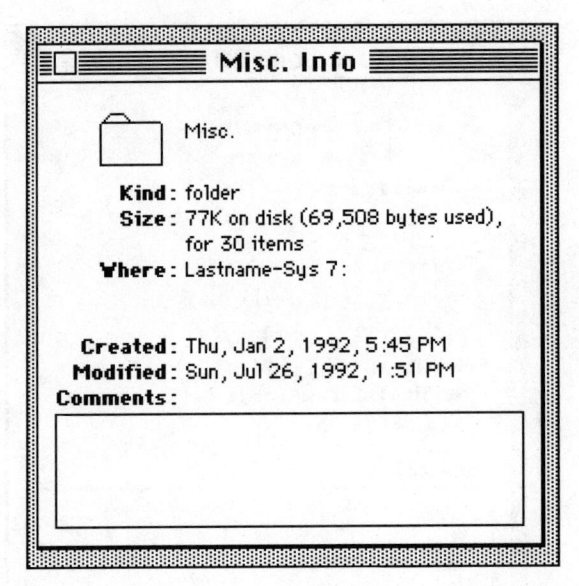

```
╔═══════════════════════════════╗
║ ▭        Misc. Info           ║
╠═══════════════════════════════╣
║                               ║
║    📁    Misc.                ║
║                               ║
║    Kind: folder               ║
║    Size: 77K on disk (69,508 bytes used), ║
║          for 30 items         ║
║    Where: Lastname-Sys 7:     ║
║                               ║
║    Created: Thu, Jan 2, 1992, 5:45 PM     ║
║    Modified: Sun, Jul 26, 1992, 1:51 PM   ║
║    Comments:                  ║
║    ┌─────────────────────┐    ║
║    │                     │    ║
║    │                     │    ║
║    └─────────────────────┘    ║
╚═══════════════════════════════╝
```

Step 16   Point to the title bar of the Misc. Info window and drag the window to the top left corner of the desktop.

Step 17   Activate the Lastname-Sys 7 window by clicking on it. Double-click on the Misc. folder icon in the Lastname-Sys 7 window.

### What's Happening
The Misc. folder window will appear. Count the number of items in this window or find the number in the information/status bar.

Step 18   Double-click on the Class Work folder on the Misc. window.

### What's Happening
The Class Work window will appear. Count the number of icons in this window or find the number in the information/status bar. The number of items in the Misc. folder (14), plus the number of items in the Class Work folder (16) should equal the Size entry in the Misc. Info window (30).

Step 19   Hold down the Option key while clicking in the active window's close box.

### What's Happening
All open windows on the desktop will close.

## Get Info on an application icon

Step 20  Double-click on the Startup disk icon.

*What's Happening*

The Startup disk window is open on the desktop.

Step 21  Choose by Name from the View menu.

Step 22  Scroll the window as necessary to locate the TeachText program. If you can't locate the program, it may be stored inside a folder. Ask your instructor. Click once on the TeachText icon. and select the Get Info command on the File menu.

*What's Happening*

The TeachText Info window will appear. (Figure 6.9) Since this icon represents an application program, the Version number of the program, 7.1 is provided. A Memory Requirements section is also provided. **Suggested Size** is the amount of memory (RAM) the program creators recommend in order to use the program.

**Minimum Size** represents the smallest amount of RAM memory that your Macintosh will use for the program. For standard program performance, the Minimum Size should not be smaller than the Suggested Size.

The **Preferred Size** entry is used to specify the amount of memory you would like the system to allocate for this program, if available (if not already allocated to other programs). The Preferred Size cannot be smaller than the Minimum Size.

*Figure 6.9—Application Info Window*

Step 23  Close the TeachText Info window. Close the Startup disk window.

## Activity 6.2—Using Select All and Put Away

Step 1  If the Lastname-Sys 7 window is not open on your desktop, open it. Open the Misc. folder. Open the Class Work folder.

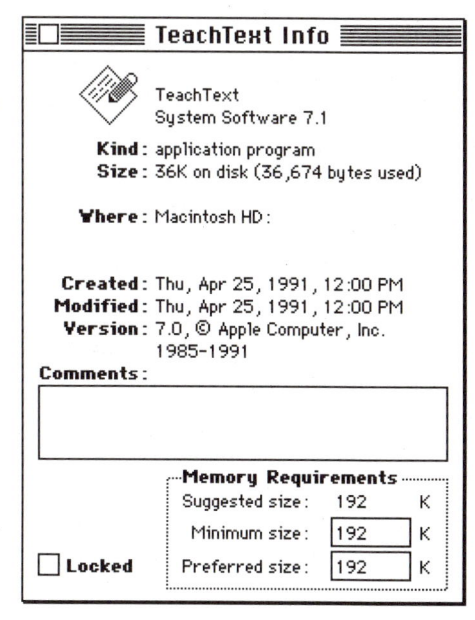

Step 2  Choose the Select All command on the Edit menu.

## What's Happening

All icons on the Class Work window are highlighted. (Figure 6.10)

*Figure 6.10—Select All*

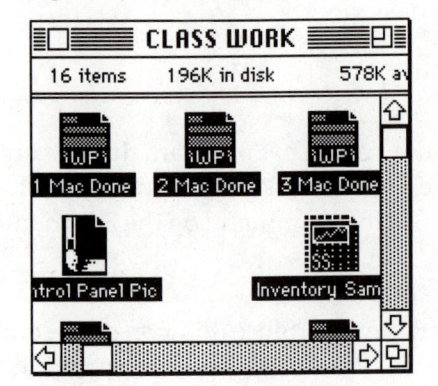

**Step 3** Drag the group to the Trash. When the Trash icon turns dark, release the mouse button. Close all open windows.

## What's Happening

The Trash icon bulges, indicating it is no longer empty. All icons on the Class Work window are now in the Trash. (Figure 6.11)

*Figure 6.11—Trash Window*

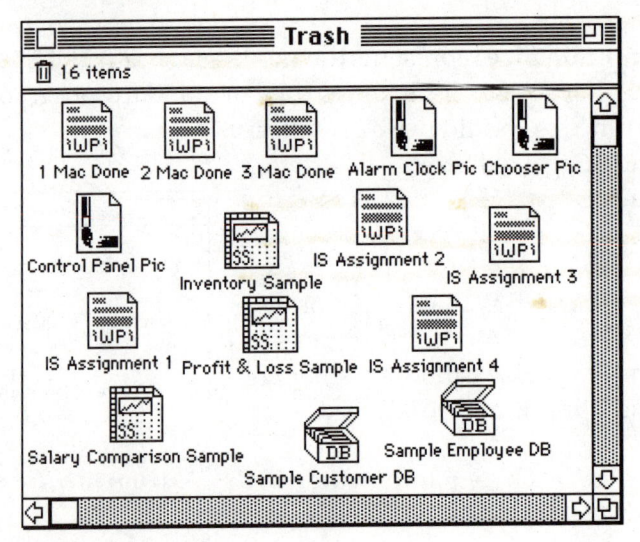

**Step 4** Open the Trash icon.

**Step 5** Use the Select All command of the Edit menu to highlight all icons in the Trash window

**Step 6** Choose the **Put Away** command of the File menu.

**Step 7** Open the Lastname-Sys 7 disk. Open the Misc. folder. Open the Class Work folder.

### What's Happening

All icons have been removed from the Trash and placed back where they came from. Items can be recovered from the Trash as long as you have not executed the Empty Trash command in the Special menu.

Step 8   Close all open windows.

## The Edit Menu

The Edit menu helps you edit the names of disks, documents, applications, and folders. It is also useful in editing your comments in the Note Pad or comment box of the Get Info command. These commands also appear and function the same way in most application programs. (Figure 6.12)

*Figure 6.12—The Edit Menu*

1. **Undo.** The Undo command reverses your last editing action.
2. **Cut.** Once you have selected material, the Cut command removes it and places it on the Clipboard.
3. **Copy.** Once you have selected material, the Copy command places a copy of it on the Clipboard. The original selected material remains where it was.
4. **Paste.** The Paste command places a copy of the contents of the Clipboard at your insertion point.
5. **Clear.** The Clear command removes the selected material but does not place it on the Clipboard.
6. **Select All.** The Select All command selects all the icons on the active window, if you have one. If not, all icons on the desktop will be selected.
7. **Show Clipboard.** The Show Clipboard command opens a window displaying the contents of the Clipboard (the last material you cut or copied there). The **Clipboard** is used for temporary storage. Each time you cut or copy a picture or text it is placed on the Clipboard, replacing the Clipboard's previous contents.

## Activity 6.3—Using Cut, Copy, Paste, Clear, Undo, and Show Clipboard

### Enter a comment in the Get Info Comment Box

Step 1  All windows should be closed on the desktop. The Lastname-Sys 7 data disk should be in the floppy drive. Open the Lastname-Sys 7 disk.

Step 2  Click on the *Store Logo alias* icon and select the Get Info command of the File menu.

## What's Happening

The *Store Logo alias* Info window will appear on the desktop. The flashing vertical line in the left corner of the comment box is the cursor. It identifies the insertion point. The next character you type will be placed here.

Step 3  Choose Show Clipboard from the Edit menu.

## What's Happening

The Clipboard window will appear on your desktop. The Edit menu commands will work without the Clipboard window open but it is interesting to watch how the contents of the Clipboard changes as you cut and copy text and graphics.

Step 4  If the Clipboard window is overlapping the *Store Logo alias* Info window, drag it to the side. Decrease the size of the Clipboard window if necessary. Both windows should be visible on the desktop. Click once on the Info window to activate it.

Step 5  Key in the comment:
```
        This Logo will be used in the PageMaker chapter.
```

Step 6  Press the Return key to advance to the next line.

### Use the Copy and Paste command

Note: As you move the arrow pointer on to the Comments box, it assumes the shape of an I-beam.

Step 7  Place the I-beam at the beginning of the sentence, hold the mouse button down, and drag the I-beam across the screen until the complete sentence is highlighted. (Figure 6.13) Release the mouse button.

*Figure 6.13—Comment Box*

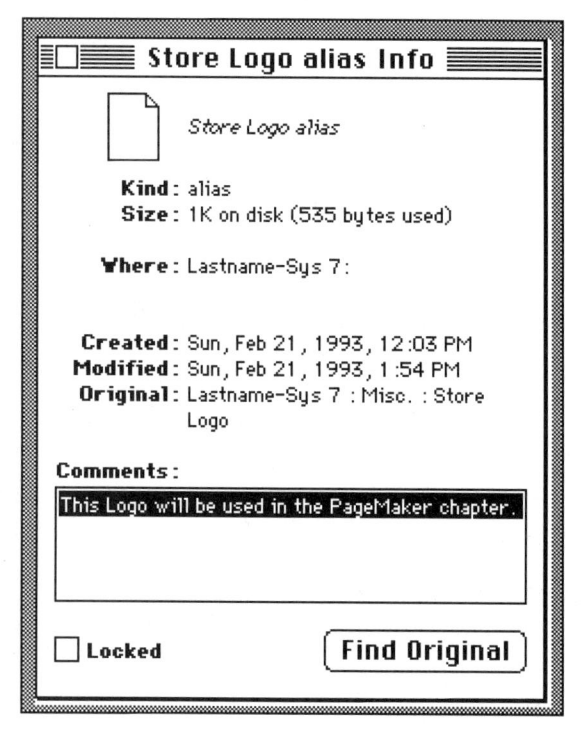

### What's Happening
The sentence has been selected for further action. If you make a mistake and don't highlight the entire sentence, just click anywhere in the Comments box to deselect the text and try again.

Step 8   Choose Copy from the Edit menu.

### What's Happening
The sentence you just copied has been placed on the Clipboard for temporary storage. The original sentence is still in the Comments box. (Figure 6.14)

Step 9   Position the I-beam at the beginning of the line following the first sentence and click.

*Figure 6.14—Clipboard with Sentence*

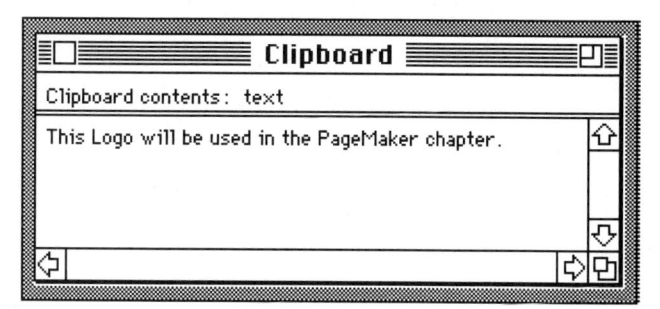

### What's Happening
This has deselected the statement and has identified the next insertion point.

Step 10    Choose Paste from the Edit menu. If the cursor is not on the third line, press the Return key.

## What's Happening

A copy of whatever was on your Clipboard has been pasted at your point of insertion. (Figure 6.15)

*Figure 6.15—Pasted Sentence*

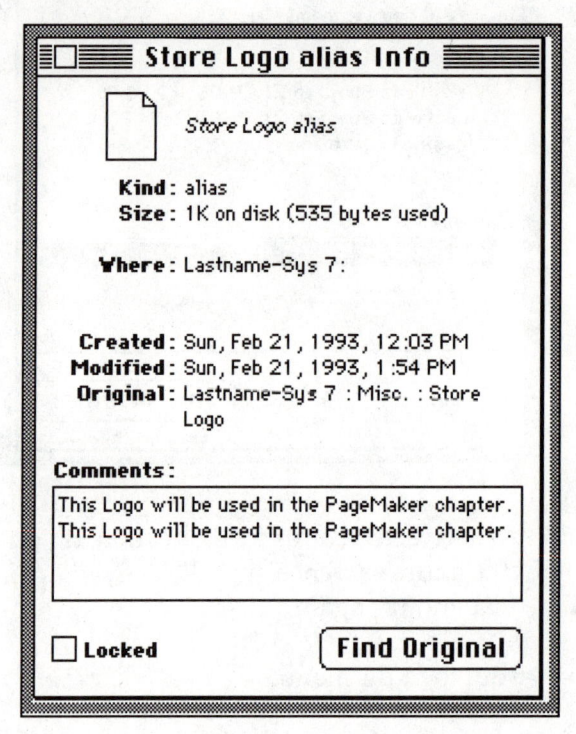

```
================ Store Logo alias Info ================
         [doc icon]   Store Logo alias

           Kind: alias
           Size: 1K on disk (535 bytes used)

          Where: Lastname-Sys 7:

        Created: Sun, Feb 21, 1993, 12:03 PM
       Modified: Sun, Feb 21, 1993, 1:54 PM
       Original: Lastname-Sys 7 : Misc. : Store
                 Logo

       Comments:
       ┌──────────────────────────────────────────┐
       │ This Logo will be used in the PageMaker  │
       │ chapter.                                 │
       │ This Logo will be used in the PageMaker  │
       │ chapter.                                 │
       └──────────────────────────────────────────┘

       ☐ Locked                    [ Find Original ]
```

Step 11    Use the keyboard equivalent to paste the sentence again: ⌘ V. Press the Return key to move to the next line.

## What's Happening

The sentence appears a third time in the Comments box. You can repeatedly paste the contents of the Clipboard.

Step 12    Highlight the word PageMaker by placing the I-beam on the word and double-clicking. Use the keyboard equivalent to copy it to the Clipboard: ⌘C.

## What's Happening

Notice the original sentence on the Clipboard has been replaced by the word PageMaker. (Figure 6.16)

Step 13    Position the I-beam at the beginning of the fourth line in the comment box. Click once to identify the insertion point.

*Figure 6.16—Clipboard with Word*

Step 14    Paste the word across the entire line. Use the keyboard equivalent to paste the word.

⌘ V, Press the Space Bar once
⌘ V, Press the Space Bar once
⌘ V, Press the Space Bar once
⌘ V, Press the Space Bar once.
(See Figure 6.17)

*Figure 6.17—Paste a Word*

**Use the Clear command**

Step 15    Position the I-beam at the beginning of the second line, and drag the I-beam down the comment box until the last three lines are highlighted. (Figure 6.18)

*Figure 6.18—Select three Lines*

Step 16    Choose Clear from the Edit menu.

*What's Happening*

The last three lines disappear from the Comments box. The Clear command does not place them on the Clipboard.

**Use the Cut command**

Step 17    Double-click on the word "This" in the first sentence.

*What's Happening*

The word "This" is highlighted.

Step 18    Choose Cut from the Edit menu.

*What's Happening*

The word disappears from the Comments box and a copy of it is placed on the Clipboard.

Step 19    The insertion point should still be at the beginning of the first line.
Key in: The Computer Store

*Figure 6.19—Inserting Text*

**Comments:**

```
The Computer Store Logo will be used in the
PageMaker chapter.
```

## What's Happening

As you enter the new phrase, the rest of the line moves over and even overflows on to the next line. This word-processing feature is called **wordwrap**. (Figure 6.19)

**Use the Select All command and the Delete key to remove the comments**

Step 20    Choose the Select All command from the Edit menu. Press the Delete key on the keyboard.

## What's Happening

The Select All command highlights all text in the comment box. The Delete key removes all selected text. A copy of the text was not placed on the Clipboard.

Step 21    Close all open windows.

Figure 6.20 summarizes the editing commands.

*Figure 6.20—Edit Menu Commands*

| Command | Action |
| --- | --- |
| Cut | Removes selected text or graphics. Pastes copy on the Clipboard. |
| Copy | Pastes copy of selected text or graphics on the Clipboard. |
| Paste | Pastes a copy of whatever is on the Clipboard at the current insertion point. |
| Clear | Removes selected text or graphics. Does not paste a copy on the Clipboard. |
| Select All | Selects entire document for further action. |

# The View Menu

The View menu is shown in Figure 6.21. The View menu allows you to modify how you view the list of files, folders, and applications in your active window. You may switch back and forth between an icon and a list window.

The command with a check mark next to it is your current view selection. The Views control panel (discussed in Chapter 11) is used to specify what to include in a list view, the font and point size to use, and how icons are to be arranged on the window.

*Figure 6.21—The View Menu*

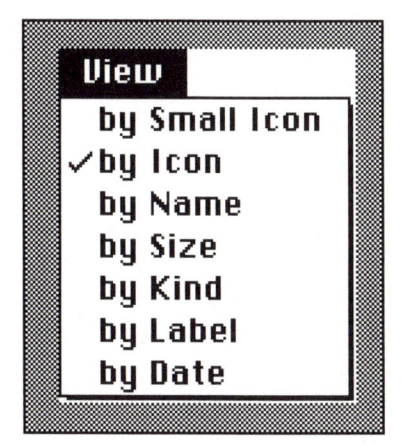

1. **by Small Icon.** The by Small Icon command places small icons to the left of the icon names. Use this view when you're trying to squeeze more icons into the disk window.
2. **by Icon.** The by Icon command is the large icon view you have been seeing. This is a graphically-oriented view of your disk or folder contents. The icon views are useful. Frequently, you can tell the the type of document an icon represents by the shape of the icon (word processing, graphics, database, spreadsheet) and which application program was used to create the document.
3. **by Name.** The by Name command displays a list view of the window sorted alphabetically by name. This view is useful when you want to locate a specific file by name.
4. **by Size.** The by Size command displays a list view of the window sorted according to size, with the largest one first. This option is useful when you are running out of disk space and need to look for files you can erase or move to another disk.
5. **by Kind.** The by Kind command displays a list view of the window sorted according to whether the file is a document, application, alias, or folder. If your Startup disk contains the application program that was used to create the document, its name will appear in the Kind column. This is useful when you remember creating a document using a specific application program but you do not remember the name you assigned to the file.
6. **by Label.** The by Label command displays a list view of the window sorted by label. This view is useful if you have grouped files by assigning labels.
7. **by Date.** The by Date command displays a list view of the window sorted chronologically by modification date, with the most recent file listed first. Use this view when you need to find your most recently created or modified documents.

## Activity 6.4—Using View Options

Step 1   If the Lastname-Sys 7 disk is in the drive, eject the disk and lock the disk. Otherwise, insert the locked Lastname-Sys 7 disk in the floppy drive.

Step 2    Open the Lastname-Sys 7 disk window.

Step 3    Choose by Small Icon from the View menu.

### What's Happening

Your open Lastname-Sys 7 data disk window now displays smaller icons with the names on the right side instead of underneath the icons. You may have to scroll the window to view all icons. If you had a very full window, this is one way to squeeze more objects into view. (Figure 6.22)

*Figure 6.22—View by Small Icon*

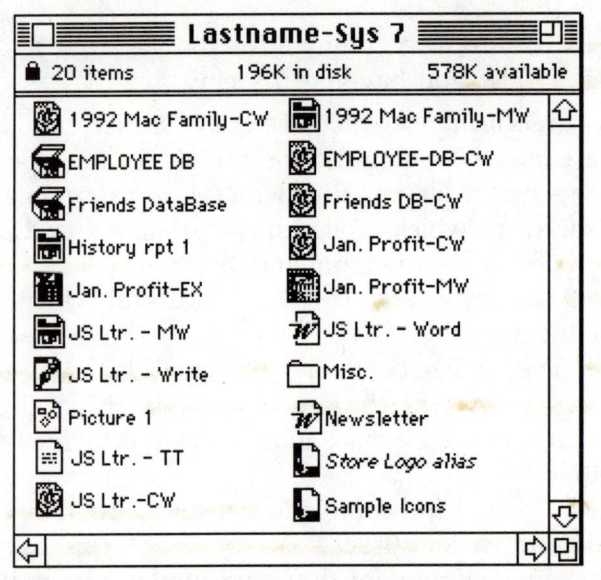

```
┌─────────────────────────────────────────┐
│ ≡≡≡≡≡≡ Lastname-Sys 7 ≡≡≡≡≡≡           │
│ 🔒 20 items      196K in disk    578K available │
│                                         │
│  💾 1992 Mac Family-CW   📄 1992 Mac Family-MW │
│  📦 EMPLOYEE DB          💾 EMPLOYEE-DB-CW    │
│  📦 Friends DataBase     💾 Friends DB-CW     │
│  📄 History rpt 1        💾 Jan. Profit-CW    │
│  📊 Jan. Profit-EX       📊 Jan. Profit-MW    │
│  📄 JS Ltr. - MW         📝 JS Ltr. - Word    │
│  📄 JS Ltr. - Write      📁 Misc.            │
│  🖼 Picture 1            📝 Newsletter        │
│  📄 JS Ltr. - TT         🖼 Store Logo alias  │
│  💾 JS Ltr.-CW           📄 Sample Icons      │
└─────────────────────────────────────────┘
```

Step 4    Choose by Name from the View menu to display the contents of the window in a list view alphabetically by name. (Figure 6.23)

*Figure 6.23—List View by Name*

```
┌─────────────────────────────────────────────┐
│ ≡≡≡≡≡≡ Lastname-Sys 7 ≡≡≡≡≡≡               │
│ 🔒 20 items      196K in disk    578K available │
│    Name                  Size  Kind        Lab│
│  📄 1992 Mac Family-CW   6K   ClarisWorks docum... │
│  📄 1992 Mac Family-MW   5K   Microsoft Works d... │
│  📄 EMPLOYEE DB          4K   Microsoft Works d... │
│  📄 EMPLOYEE-DB-CW       20K  ClarisWorks docum... │
│  📄 Friends DataBase     2K   Microsoft Works d... │
└─────────────────────────────────────────────┘
```

### Sorting The List View

Step 5    Click on the column heading Last Modified.

*What's Happening*

This is a short-cut method to display the list view sorted on a different column. Your window now displays the objects by Last Modified data and time, from the most recent to the oldest. The column heading, Last Modified, is underlined to indicate the selected view. Choosing the by Date command of the View menu would have accomplished the same task. (Figure 6.24)

*Figure 6.24—List View by Date*

| Name | Size | Kind | Label | Last Modified |
|---|---|---|---|---|
| Store Logo alias | 1K | alias | — | Sun, Feb 21, 1993, 1:54 |
| JS Ltr. - TT | 1K | TeachText document | — | Sun, Feb 21, 1993, 12:0 |
| ▷ Misc. | — | folder | — | Sun, Feb 21, 1993, 11:5 |
| Jan. Profit-EX | 4K | Microsoft Excel do... | — | Sun, Jul 26, 1992, 1:01 |
| Sample Icons | 5K | MacPaint document | — | Sun, Jul 26, 1992, 12:4 |

20 items    196K in disk    578K available

### Outline Views

Step 6    Click on the triangle to the left of the Misc. folder icon.

*What's Happening*

Clicking on the triangle to the left of a folder displays the contents of the folder in an outline view. (Figure 6.25) It does not open a new window to the folder. The triangle points down indicating an outline view of the folder's contents is displayed.

*Figure 6.25—Misc. Folder Outline List View*

| Name | Size | Kind |
|---|---|---|
| *Store Logo alias* | 1K | alias |
| JS Ltr. - TT | 1K | TeachText |
| ▽ Misc. | — | folder |
|   Sample Teach Text Doc | 1K | TeachText |
|   Poem 2 | 5K | Microsoft |
|   Short Story | 4K | Microsoft |
|   Poem 1 | 4K | Microsoft |
| ▷ CLASS WORK | — | folder |
| Home Expenses-CW | 8K | ClarisWor |
| Home Expenses-EX | 3K | Microsoft |
| Store Logo | 5K | MacPaint |
| Explanation of Benefits | 1K | TeachText |
| History Rpt 2 | 1K | Microsoft |
| Home Expenses-MW | 3K | Microsoft |
| Chris Friends | 2K | Microsoft |
| Holiday Greetings | 1K | TeachText |
| New Employee Letter | 1K | TeachText |
| Jan. Profit-EX | 4K | Microsoft |
| Sample Icons | 5K | MacPaint |

(Lastname-Sys 7 — 34 items, 196K in disk, 578K available)

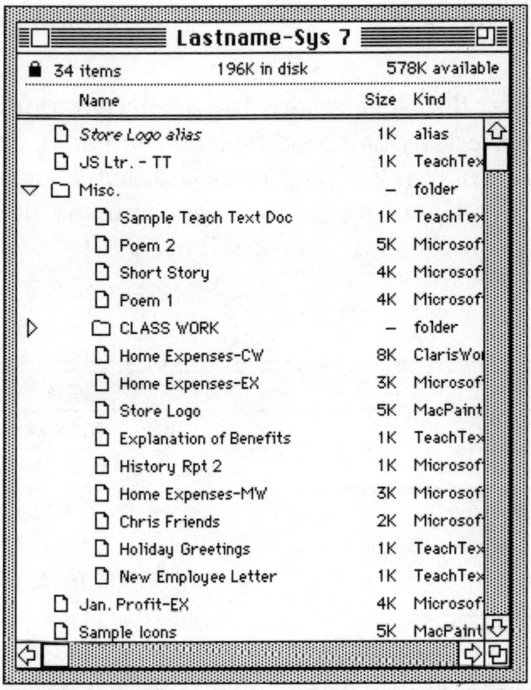

**Step 7** Click on the triangle to the left of the Class Work folder icon.

## What's Happening

An outlined view of this folder is displayed. (Figure 6.26)

**Step 8** Click on the triangle to the left of the Class Work folder icon. Click on the triangle to the left of the Misc. folder icon.
Close the Lastname-Sys 7 window.

## What's Happening

The outline views of the folders disappear and the disk window closes.

*Figure 6.26—Class Work Folder Outline List View*

(Lastname-Sys 7 — 50 items, 196K in disk, 578K available)

| Name | Size | Kind |
|---|---|---|
| *Store Logo alias* | 1K | alias |
| JS Ltr. - TT | 1K | Teac |
| ▽ Misc. | — | fold |
|   Sample Teach Text Doc | 1K | Teac |
|   Poem 2 | 5K | Micr |
|   Short Story | 4K | Micr |
|   Poem 1 | 4K | Micr |
| ▽ CLASS WORK | — | fold |
|   Chooser Pic | 10K | Mac |
|   Control Panel Pic | 7K | Mac |
|   Alarm Clock Pic | 11K | Mac |
|   3 Mac Done | 1K | Micr |
|   2 Mac Done | 1K | Micr |
|   1 Mac Done | 1K | Micr |
|   Inventory Sample | 2K | Micr |
|   Profit & Loss Sample | 2K | Micr |
|   Salary Comparison Sample | 2K | Micr |
|   Sample Salary Comparison | 2K | Micr |
|   Sample Customer DB | 2K | Micr |

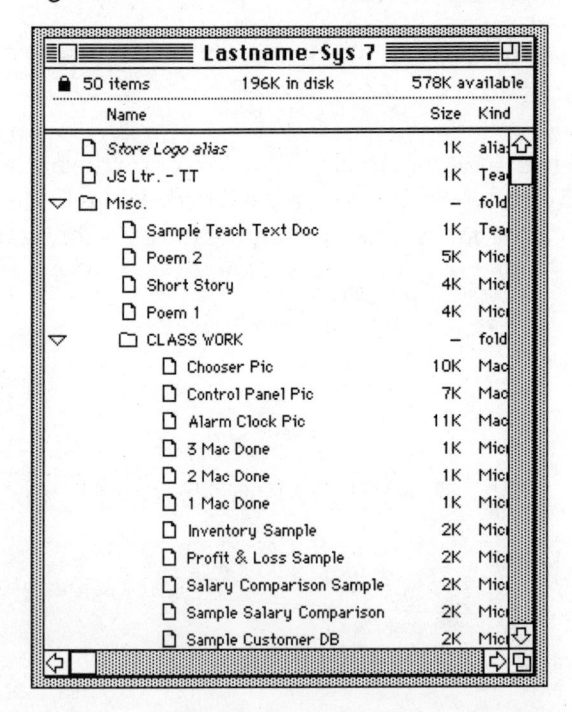

## The Label Menu

The Label menu is shown in Figure 6.27. Labels may be assigned to documents, folders, or programs, for quick recognition. Labels are used to group related files together. For instance, if you have several document files relating to a single project, you could assign the label, Project 1, to each of the files. Then when you request a list view of the window by Label, the files would be listed together.

Seven labels are available on the Label menu. The None entry indicates the active icon has not been assigned a label. The Labels control panel (discussed in Chapter 11) can be used to change label names and colors (if you have a color monitor). You will assign labels to files in Chapter 10.

*Figure 6.27—The Label Menu*

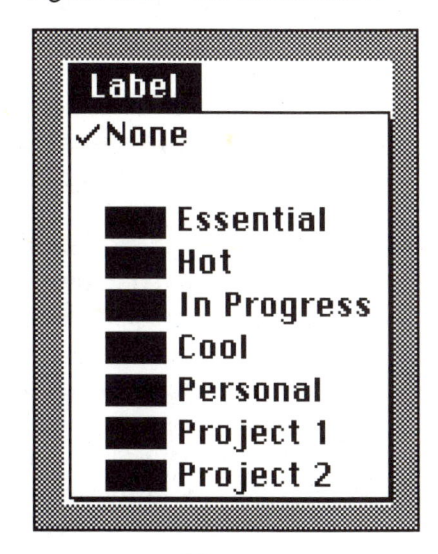

## The Special Menu

The Special menu is shown in Figure 6.28.

*Figure 6.28—The Special Menu*

1. **Clean Up.** The Clean Up command only works when your directory is displayed by icon or on the Finder desktop. It does not work on list view windows. The Clean Up command changes depending on what you have selected, whether you are using it in conjunction with the Option or Shift keys and how the last list view was sorted.
   - **Clean Up Desktop.** This command appears if the desktop is active. Upon executing the command all desktop icons will be moved to the next available space on the invisible grid. The Views control panel is used to specify a straight or staggered grid. (Discussed further in Chapter 11)

- **Clean Up All**. If you hold down the Option key while the desktop is active, with no active windows, the command changes to Clean Up All. The Startup disk icon will be placed in the top right corner of the desktop and all other desktop icons (other than the Trash) will be placed in a column under it. The Trash icon will be placed in the lower right corner of the desktop.
- **Clean Up Selection.** If you hold down the Shift key while you have icon(s) active on your desktop or in a window, the command changes to Clean Up Selection. Executing this command will cause only the selected icon(s) to move to the next available spot along the invisible grid.
- **Clean Up Window.** If you have an active window all icons will be arranged in neat rows and columns along an invisible grid.
- **Clean Up by Name/Size/Kind/Label/Date.** If you hold down the Option key while a window or icon in a window is selected, the Clean Up command will change. The command will vary depending on which column your last list view was sorted on. If your last sorted list view was displayed by Name, then the command will be "Clean Up by Name." All icons in the window will be arranged in alphabetical order by name along the invisible grid.

2. **Empty Trash.** The Empty Trash command will permanently throw away items in the Trash and identify their space on the disk as available. Remember, the Trash is only emptied upon your direction, either by your executing the Empty Trash command or by responding to a dialog box requesting your permission. An alert dialog box will appear to verify your request. The alert box can be temporarily turned off by holding down the Option key while executing the Empty Trash command. You can also turn off the warning indefinitely by using the Warn Before Emptying checkbox in the Trash Get Info window.
3. **Eject Disk.** The Eject Disk command ejects the selected disk or the disk of the active window and leaves its dimmed icon on the desktop.
4. **Erase Disk**. The Erase Disk command erases the disk and initializes it. You can't erase the current Startup disk.
5. **Restart.** The Restart command ejects floppies, erases RAM, and restarts the Macintosh. This is useful if you want to use a different Startup disk. A keyboard equivalent for this command is also available in case your Macintosh freezes-up and the keyboard and/or mouse don't work. Hold down the Control and ⌘ keys while pressing the Power On key. You could turn off the power and then turn it back on but Restart is easier on the hardware and software.
6. **Shut Down.** The Shut Down command ejects floppies, and (on some Macintosh systems) turns the computer off.

## Activity 6.5—Clean Up command

Step 1   The Lastname-Sys 7 disk should be in the floppy drive. All windows should be closed.

Step 2   Drag the Startup disk icon to the middle of the desktop. (If you are unable to move this icon, do not be concerned. Disk security software may prevent you from moving the hard disk icon.) Place the Lastname-Sys 7 disk icon in the middle of the desktop. Place the Trash icon below the disk icon(s), as shown in Figure 6. 29.

Step 3   Choose the Clean Up Desktop command from the Special menu.

*Figure 6.29—Three Icons*

*What's Happening*
The icons will be moved to the first available spot along the invisible grid.

Step 4   Hold down the Option key while selecting the Clean Up All command from the Special menu.

*What's Happening*
The disk icons are placed in the top right corner of the desktop and the Trash icon is in the bottom right corner.

Step 5   Open the Lastname-Sys 7 disk icon.

Step 6   Display the window in a list view by Date. Display the window in an icon view.

Step 7   Display the Special menu. Do not select a command.

*What's Happening*
The available Clean Up command is Clean Up Window.

Step 8   Release the mouse button. Hold down the Option key while displaying the Special menu. Do not select a command.

*What's Happening*
The available Clean Up command is Clean Up by Date. The last list view of the window was by Date (step 6). Therefore, the system automatically assumes you wish to Clean up by Date.

Step 9    Drag a box around two or three icons in the bottom row of the window—the icons turn dark. Drag the group of icons on top of the row above.

## What's Happening

The group of icons have partially covered the other icons. (Figure 6.30) The selected group of icons are still highlighted.

*Figure 6.30—Overlapping Icons*

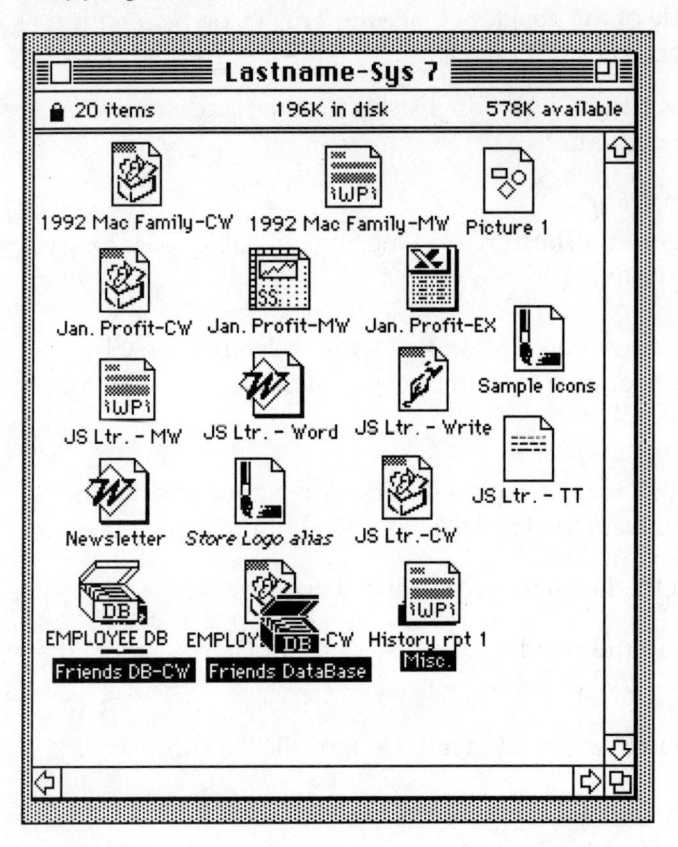

Step 10    Hold down the Shift key while selecting the Clean Up Selection command of the Special menu.

## What's Happening

The group of icons are moved off the other icons and are placed along the invisible grid.

Step 11    Close all open windows. Drag the Lastname-Sys 7 disk icon to the Trash.

## The Help Menu

The Help menu is shown in Figure 6.31. You experimented with the first two commands in Chapter 2.

*Figure 6.31—The Help Menu*

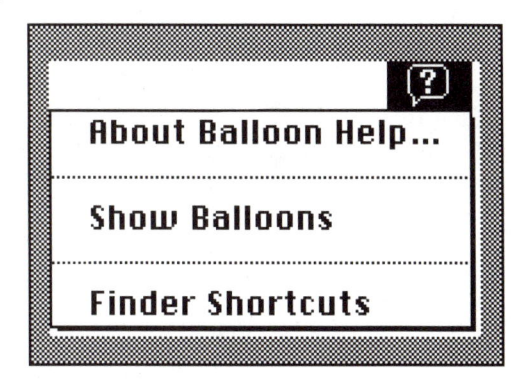

1. **About Balloon Help.** This command simply displays a dialog box explaining how to use Balloon Help.
2. **Show Balloons / Hide Balloons.** This command toggles back and forth between Show Balloons and Hide Balloons. Use this command to turn Balloon help on and off.
3. **Finder Shortcuts.** The Finder Shortcuts command displays a dialog box describing keyboard shortcuts on working with icons, selecting icons, working with windows, working with outline views, and miscellaneous options.

### Activity 6.6—Using the Finder Shortcuts Command

Step 1   Make sure that all windows are closed on the desktop.

Step 2   Choose the Finder Shortcuts command from the Help menu.

*What's Happening*

The Finder Shortcuts window appears. (Figure 6.32) A list of available keyboard shortcuts is available on five windows.

*Figure 6.32—Finder Shortcuts Window*

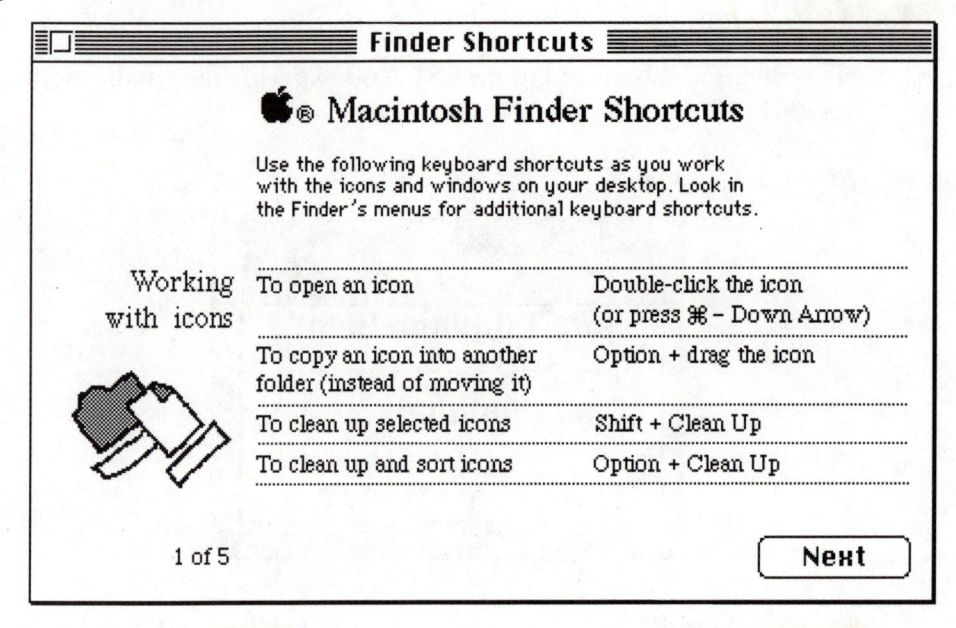

```
┌─────────────────────────────────────────────────┐
│ ≣□         ≣ Finder Shortcuts ≣                 │
├─────────────────────────────────────────────────┤
│                                                 │
│         🍎® Macintosh Finder Shortcuts          │
│                                                 │
│   Use the following keyboard shortcuts as you work
│   with the icons and windows on your desktop. Look in
│   the Finder's menus for additional keyboard shortcuts.
│                                                 │
│  Working   To open an icon      Double-click the icon
│  with icons                     (or press ⌘ – Down Arrow)
│                                                 │
│            To copy an icon into another   Option + drag the icon
│            folder (instead of moving it)
│                                                 │
│            To clean up selected icons   Shift + Clean Up
│                                                 │
│            To clean up and sort icons   Option + Clean Up
│                                                 │
│         1 of 5                      [ Next ]    │
└─────────────────────────────────────────────────┘
```

Step 3   Click on the Next and the Previous buttons to move through the five windows.

Step 4   Close the Finder Shortcuts window.

## The Application Menu

In System 7 you can have multiple application programs open on the desktop but only one can be active at a time.

The Application menu is split into two sections: the top section controls which open application windows are visible, and the bottom section displays a list of open programs. The check mark indicates the active program. In Figure 6.33, the Finder icon is displayed on the menu bar, and there is only one open program—the Finder.

*Figure 6.33—The Application Menu*

```
┌──────────────────────┐
│                  🖥   │
├──────────────────────┤
│  Hide Finder         │
│  Hide Others         │
│  Show All            │
├──────────────────────┤
│ ✓ 🖥 Finder          │
└──────────────────────┘
```

1. **Hide Finder.** This command changes to display the name of the active program.

In Figure 6.34, the active program is Microsoft Word. Notice the check mark next to the name and the Application menu icon.

Selecting the Hide Microsoft Word command will cause the program's menu bar and all Word document windows to be hidden from view.

2. **Hide Others.** Selecting this command will cause all open program windows (other than the active program), to be hidden from view.
3. **Show All.** Reverses the Hide command. All open windows will be displayed on the desktop.

*Figure 6.34—Active Program-Word*

## Activity 6.7—Using the Application Menu

Step 1   All windows on the desktop should be closed.

Step 2   Open the Alarm Clock, Calculator and Note Pad DAs.

*What's Happening*

All three windows are open on the desktop.

Step 3   Display the Application menu.

*Figure 6.35—Active Program: Note Pad*

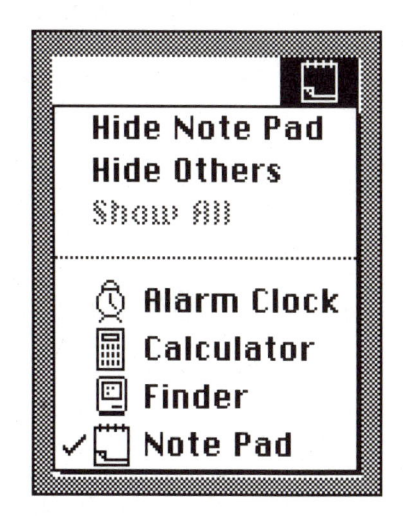

*What's Happening*

There are several ways to tell which program is active. The icon for the Application menu is in the shape of a note pad. The check mark next to the Note Pad icon and name in the Application menu indicates it is the active program. (Figure 6.35) The horizontal lines in the Note Pad title bar indicates that this is the active program/window. The Note Pad's menu bar is displayed across the top of the desktop. About This Notepad is the first entry in the  menu.

Step 4   Place the three open windows next to each other on the desktop. (Figure 6.36)

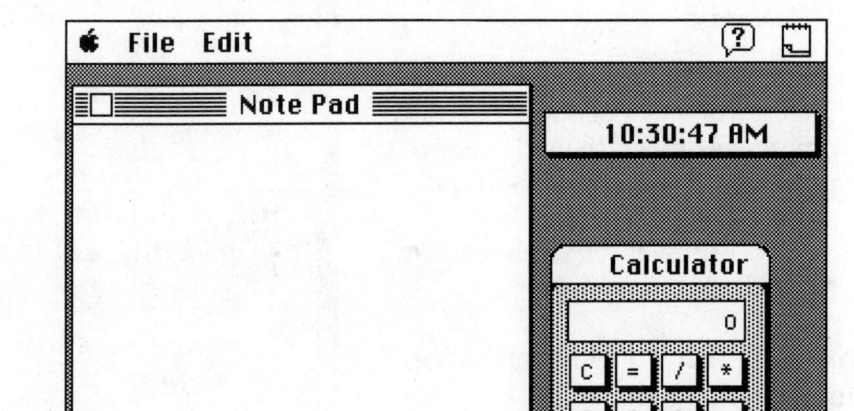

*Figure 6.36—Three Open Application Windows*

Step 5      Click on the Calculator.

## What's Happening

The Calculator is now the active program. When you look at the Application menu, the icon has changed to a calculator. In the list of open programs, the Calculator program icon now has the check mark.

Step 6      Display the Application menu and highlight Alarm Clock in the list of available programs.

## What's Happening

The Alarm Clock program is now active.

Step 7      Choose the Hide Others command in the Application menu.

## What's Happening

The Calculator and Note Pad windows disappear from view. The windows have not been closed—just hidden.

Step 8      Choose Note Pad from the Application menu.

*What's Happening*

        The Note Pad window reappears.

Step 9     Choose Show All to display all open windows.

Step 10    Close all open windows.

Figure 6.37 summarizes how you can tell which program is active. Figure 6.38 summarizes how to activate a different program.

*Figure 6.37—How to Tell Which Open Program is Active*

- Program window appears active on the desktop.
- Program menu bar appears on the desktop.
- The Application menu icon displays the program's icon at the right edge of the menu bar.
- The program name has a check mark next to it in the Application menu.
- The program name is the first entry in the  menu.

*Figure 6.38—Activating an Open Program*

- Click on the program's open window.
- Choose the program name from the Application menu.

## Key Terms

| | |
|---|---|
| About Balloon Help | by Small Icon |
| Application menu | Clear |
| by Date | Clean up All |
| by Icon | Clean up Desktop |
| by Kind | Clean up by Name/Size/Kind/Label/Date |
| by Label | Clean up Selection |
| by Name | Clean up Window |
| by Size | Clipboard |

Close Windows ⌘ W
Copy ⌘ C
Cut ⌘ X
Duplicate ⌘ D
Edit menu
Eject Disk ⌘ E
Empty Trash
Erase Disk
File menu
Find ⌘ F
Find Again ⌘ G
Find Original Button
Finder menu bar
Finder Shortcuts
Get Info ⌘ I
Help menu
Hide Balloons
Hide Finder
Hide Others
Label menu
Locked checkbox
Make Alias
Memory Current Size

Memory Preferred Size
Memory Suggested Size
New Folder ⌘ N
Open ⌘ O
Page Setup
Paste ⌘ V
Print ⌘ P
Print Desktop
Put Away ⌘ Y
Restart
Select All ⌘ A
Sharing
Show Balloons
Show All
Shut Down
Show Clipboard
Special menu
Stationary Pad checkbox
Undo ⌘ Z
View menu
Warn Before Emptying Checkbox
Wordwrap

## Discussion Questions

1. How do you access a menu, select a command, and execute it?
2. How do you get out of the menu without executing a command?
3. What does the ellipsis character (...) following a command mean?
4. What are keyboard equivalents?
5. Explain the Get Info command.
6. Explain the Put Away command.
7. Explain how Cut, Copy, and Clear differ.
8. What and where is an object pasted if you select the Paste command?
9. What is the Clipboard?
10. Explain the different options of the View menu. When would one option be better than the other?
11. Discuss the advantages and disadvantages of the Balloon option in the Help menu.
12. Why would you use the Restart command?
13. Why should you use the Shut Down command?
14. Do all menu bars look alike?

## True/False Questions

For each question, circle the letter T if the statement is true and the letter F if the statement is false.

T   F   1. A Get Info command is available for all icons whether they are disks, folders, or files.
T   F   2. Since file names are limited in size, a Comments box is provided through the Get Info command.
T   F   3. The Put Away command will close all windows in preparation for Shut Down.
T   F   4. The I-beam will appear as you move the arrow pointer on to the Comments box of the Get Info window.
T   F   5. You can lock disks and files from within the Get Info window.
T   F   6. ⌘ C will clear information out of the Clipboard.
T   F   7. Shutting down the computer properly will allow the Macintosh to save the contents of the Clipboard to disk.
T   F   8. Viewing files by Icon is not as useful as listing the files by Name, especially if you are looking for a specific file.
T   F   9. The selected command in the View menu will have a check-mark next to it.
T   F   10. You can see what is on the Clipboard by selecting the Show Clipboard command from the Special menu.

## Completion Questions

Write the correct answer in each blank space.

1. If you display a list of your disk files by Name, you will see additional information about each file, including _____, _____, _____, _____, and _____.
2. The _____ or the _____ command of the View menu will always display the number of files in the window and the amount of disk space in use and available.
3. You can immediately tell by examining the window's information bar if the list of files is displayed by name, size, date, or kind because_____
4. To select text, position the _____ at the beginning of the text and drag the _____ over the desired text.
5. Selected text appears _____.
6. The flashing _____ identifies where the next character you type will appear.
7. The _____ command of the Edit menu will remove the selected text and place a copy of it on the Clipboard.

8. To copy information from the Clipboard to your current document use the _____ command in the Edit menu.
9. _____ is a word-processing technique that eliminates the need for you to press the Return key at the end of every line.
10. The quickest way to find a file you created yesterday is to display your list of files by _____.

## Matching Questions

Match the name of the Menu with each command. Place the letter of the correct answer on the line provided. Menu names will be used more than once.

A. File Menu     B. Edit Menu     C. View Menu
D. Label Menu     E. Special Menu     F. Help Menu
G. Application Menu

___ 1. Eject Disk     ___ 8. by Name     ___15. Erase Disk
___ 2. Shut Down     ___ 9. Empty Trash     ___16. by Date
___ 3. Show Balloons     ___10. Select All     ___17. Show All
___ 4. Close Window     ___11. Paste     ___18. Cut
___ 5. Get Info     ___12. Put Away     ___19. Finder Shortcuts
___ 6. Show Clipboard     ___13. by Icon     ___20. Hide Finder
___ 7. Restart     ___14. Open

## Assignments

Boot your Macintosh. The Macintosh desktop should be clean, with no windows open. Insert the locked Lastname-Sys 7 disk in the available floppy drive.

### Part 1

Fill in the blanks by accessing the Get Info command for each of the following icons. Open disk and folder windows as necessary to locate the icons. Click once on each of the specified icons.

1. Trash
   a. Where _____
   b. Contents _____

2. Misc. (located on the Lastname-Sys 7 disk).
   a. Kind _____
   b. Size _____
   c. Where _____

3. Newsletter (located on the Lastname-Sys 7 disk).
    a. Kind     _____
    b. Size     _____
    c. Where    _____
    d. Created  _____
    e. Modified _____
    f. Comments _____
                _____
    g. Locked   _____

4. Holiday Greetings (located on the Lastname-Sys 7 disk inside the Misc. folder).
    a. Kind     _____
    b. Size     _____
    c. Where    _____
    d. Created  _____
    e. Modified _____
    f. Comments _____
                _____
    g. Locked   _____
    h. The Created and Modified dates look unusual. Explain why and how this could have happened.
    
    _____
    
    _____
    
    _____

5. Inventory Sample (located inside the Class Work folder which is inside the Misc. folder on the Lastname-Sys 7 disk).
    a. Kind     _____
    b. Size     _____
    c. Where    _____
    d. Created  _____
    e. Modified _____
    f. Comments _____
                _____
    g. Locked   _____

    Close all disk and folder windows.

## Part 2

Use the View menu commands to answer the following questions.

6. Open the Lastname-Sys 7 disk window. Place the icons in alphabetic order by name.
   a. The first icon listed is _____
   b. The last icon listed is _____
   c. The number of locked icons is _____

7. Open the Misc. folder.
   a. The current view for this window is _____

   Choose the by Kind view.
   b. How many documents are there? _____
   c. How many folders are there? _____
   d. How many locked icons are there? _____

   Choose the by Date view.
   e. The first icon listed is _____
   f. The last icon listed is _____

8. Open the Class Work folder.
   a. The current view for this window is _____

   Choose the by Size view. Examine the Inventory Sample icon and answer the following questions.
   b. Size _____
   c. Kind _____
   d. Last Modified (date and time) _____

   Close all open windows.

## Part 3

Choose Finder Shortcuts from the Help menu and answer the following questions.

9. The title for page 2 is _____

10. Review the entries on page 2 and complete the following statement.
    To make the desktop active _____

11. The title for page 3 is _____

12. Review the entries on page 3 and complete the following statement.
    To move a window without making it active _____

13. The title for page 4 is _____

14. Review the entries on page 4 and complete the following statement.
    To change the view _____

15. The title for page 5 is _____

16. Review the entries on page 5 and complete the following statement.
    To take a snapshot of the screen _____
    _____

Close all open windows.

## Part 4

Open four DAs in the following order: Alarm Clock, Calculator, Puzzle, Note Pad. Leave all four DA windows open and answer questions 17 through 22.

17. View the Application menu and answer the following questions.
    a. The first entry in the menu is _____
    b. The second entry in the menu is _____
    c. Which entry in the menu has a check mark next to it? _____
    d. How many open programs are listed in the menu? _____
    e. The Application menu icon is in the shape of a _____

18. Select the second entry in the Application menu.
    a. What happened? _____
    _____

    b. The first available entry (not dimmed) in the Application menu is
    _____

19. View the Apple menu and answer the following questions.
    a. The first entry in the Apple menu is _____
    b. Select the first entry in the Apple menu. Who wrote this program?
    _____

    Close this information window.

20. Choose Puzzle from the Application menu. View the Application menu and answer the following questions.
    a. The first entry in the menu is _____
    b. Which entry in the menu has a check mark next to it? _____
    c. The Application menu icon is in the shape of a _____
    d. How many open windows are on the desktop? _____

21. View the Apple menu and answer the following questions.
    a. The first entry in the Apple menu is _____

22. Close the Puzzle and Note Pad windows. Which window became active?
    _____

Choose Show All in the Application menu. Close all open windows.

## Part 5

Examine the Microsoft Works 3.0 information window provided to answer the questions.

23. ___ If there is plenty of memory available when you start the Microsoft Works program, how much memory will be allocated to the program?

    a. 1024K
    b. 675K
    c. 1536K
    d. None of the above.

24. ___ If the program performs poorly, unexpectedly quits, or performs below expected standards, you should increase the memory allocated in which entry?
    a. Suggested size
    b. Minimum size
    c. Preferred size
    d. All of the above.

# 7 Printing

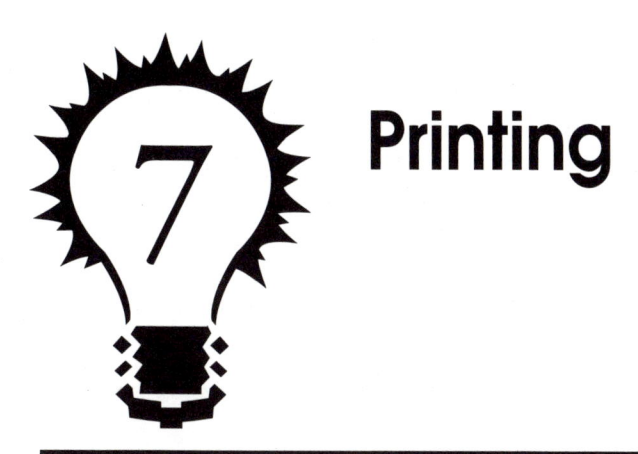

## Learning Objectives

**After completing this Chapter you will be able to:**

1. Describe how to use the buttons on the ImageWriter printer.
2. Explain the Chooser Desk Accessory (DA).
3. Briefly explain the difference between a networked and a stand-alone printer.
4. Explain and select the correct options in the ImageWriter, StyleWriter and LaserWriter Page Setup windows.
5. Explain and select the correct options in the Print window.
6. Print directories.
7. Load the TeachText application program and a TeachText document into RAM.
8. Make minor editing changes to a TeachText document.
9. Save and print a TeachText document.

## Introduction

How can you be a productive Macintosh user if you don't know how to print? It's unreasonable to create a document on the computer if you can't print it. It's hard to imagine using a draw and paint program to create a great picture, only to discover that you can't print it. You can write a research paper and save it to disk, but most instructors are not willing to accept a term paper on disk. The Macintosh has several ways to print documents from within an application program or from the desktop.

In this chapter, you will be printing directories of the Lastname-Sys 7 data disk and the Startup disk. You will also learn how to print from within an application program. The windows described in this activity are for the Apple Computer, Inc. line of printers: ImageWriter, StyleWriter or LaserWriter. Several third-party manufacturers (Kodak, Hewlett-Packard, Epson, Okidata, NEC, Panasonic) have printers that will work with the Macintosh. Note: If you do not have an ImageWriter, StyleWriter or LaserWriter, the windows that appear may be slightly different from the ones presented here.

## Printers

The **ImageWriter II is a dot matrix printer**. This impact printer uses a strike-on method to press a fabric ribbon against the paper, leaving a mark. A collection of individual pins are used to form characters. If you look closely at a document created by a dot matrix printer you can see that each character consists of tiny dots. Although the ImageWriter's print quality is not as good as the other two types of printers, it does have some advantages. It is relatively inexpensive to buy and maintain, it handles continuous-form computer paper or single-sheets, it accepts multiple part forms (up to four), and it prints in color (with color software and color ribbon).

The **StyleWriter** printer is a non-impact, **ink-jet printer.** Characters are formed by shooting tiny jets of ink on to the paper. As the tiny dots of ink are shot on to the paper, they turn in to ink splotches and blend together more than the dots created by the ImageWriter. The StyleWriter's print quality, weight (under seven and a half pounds) and small size makes this printer a good investment for traveling Macintosh users.

Laser printers, called **LaserWriters**, use a process similar to a photocopying machine. Lasers beam complete pages on to a metal drum and dry powder is electrostatically attracted to the drum, which is picked up by the paper as it passes over it. Macintosh users who need great print quality and print speed should consider buying a laser printer.

Figure 7.1 shows the quality, speed, and paper handling capabilities of Apple printers. Print quality is measured in dots per inch (**dpi**) and print speed is measured in characters per second (**cps**) or pages per minute (**ppm**).

*Figure 7.1—Apple Printers*

| Printer | Quality | Speed | Paper |
|---|---|---|---|
| ImageWriter II | 160dpi | 1/2 ppm | Single Sheet or Tractor Feed |
| Style Writer | 360 dpi | 1/2 ppm | 50 page Sheet Feeder |
| Personal LaserWriter LS | 300dpi | 4 ppm | 70 sheet tray or 250-sheet cassette |
| Personal LaserWriter NTR | 300dpi | 4 ppm | 70 sheet tray or 250-sheet cassette |
| LaserWriter IIf | 300dpi | 8 ppm | 200 sheet cassette |
| LaserWriter IIg | 300dpi | 8 ppm | 200 sheet cassette |

## ImageWriter

If you are using an ImageWriter, you need to understand the printer's control panel which is located on top of the printer. Examine the control panel as you read the following descriptions to help you understand the three indicator lights and five buttons.

1. **ON/OFF Button and Light.** Turn the printer on by pressing this button. The indicator light next to it is green when the printer is on.
   - A red error light will light up according to the error.
   - A continuous light means the printer has run out of paper. Turn the printer off and load paper.
   - A blinking light means that the front cover is not on correctly or the paper (or print mechanism) is jammed.
   - Irregular blinking indicates a dip switch is set incorrectly (inside under ribbon). Check the user manual that came with the printer for help.

2. **Select Button and Light.** The select button places the printer on-line or off-line. If the indicator light is on, it means the printer is on-line and can receive and print data. When the select light is off (off-line), you can't print. The

printer must be off-line for the other ImageWriter II buttons (print quality, line feed, form feed) to work.

The following three buttons will only work if the printer is turned on (on/off light is green) and the select light is off.

3. **Print Quality Button and Light**. There are three levels of print quality.
   - **Draft**—Left side of light is lit. High speed (250 characters per second at 10 characters per inch), will mean lowest quality.
   - **Standard**—Right side of light is lit. Medium speed (180 characters per second 2 pages per minute), produces good dot matrix quality.
   - **Near letter quality**—Both sides of light are lit. Slow speed (45 characters per second, 1/2 page per minute), produces the best dot matrix quality.

   Note: If you use the Print command dialog box and set the print quality to anything other than draft, it will override the Print Quality button selection.

4. **Line Feed Button**. Each time you press this button the paper will advance a line. If you hold the button down, the printer will repeat up to four line advances.

5. **Form Feed Button**. This button has three functions.
   - **Form Feed**—Pressing the button will advance the paper one full page length.
   - **Paper Load**—When loading paper, pressing the button causes the paper to be loaded with the print head 1/6 inch from top edge of the paper.
   - **Paper Eject**—When a print job ends mid-page, pressing the button will advance the paper to the beginning of the next page.

## The Chooser Desk Accessory

Special programs called print drivers have been installed in the **Extension folder** inside the System Folder of your Startup disk. Each **print driver** program contains the codes and commands to properly operate a specific printer. So, if your Macintosh has access to an ImageWriter, StyleWriter, and a LaserWriter you need three different print driver programs on your Startup disk. The print driver programs interact with application programs, thereby eliminating the need for each application program to include printer instructions.

The first step in printing a directory or document is to select a printer. The **Chooser Desk Accessory,** available on the Apple () menu, is used to specify which printer to use. The contents of the Chooser window will vary according to your system configuration and which print drivers are installed in the Startup disk's Extension folder. If you have a stand-alone Macintosh with one printer, you will use the Chooser once to tell the System which printer to use. You will probably not need to use it again unless you upgrade your system software or install a different printer. If your Macintosh is on a network or you have more than one printer, you will use the Chooser more frequently.

A **Computer Network** is a configuration of multiple computers, printers, disk drives, CD-ROM disks and other devices that are interconnected, making it possible for the devices to communicate with each other. Networks can be useful. For example, if you have 20 Macintoshes in an office or computer-equipped classroom, do you want to buy a Laser printer and a dot matrix printer for each one? It would be a waste of money. If all the Macintoshes are on a network with two Laser printers and two dot matrix printers, you can save money. There are some drawbacks—someone may have to wait to print, for example. If printing becomes a problem, a computer could be set up to act as a print server. All print files would be sent to the **print server**, and stored there until a printer was available. This would eliminate the need for your Macintosh and you to wait until a printer is available—you could return to work knowing that your document would print as soon as possible.

The network can also include a file server. A **file server** allows all computers on the network to access the directories and files stored on its hard drive. Any Macintosh with a hard drive can be a file server. A file server is used to store application programs and data files you wish to share with others. **Network versions** of some application programs can be purchased. A network version of a program allows more than one Macintosh user access to the program at a time.

*Figure 7.2—A Sample Computer Network*

There are many possible system configurations and networks available. **AppleTalk** is a common Macintosh network. It is a relatively low-cost network, and is simple to install and maintain.

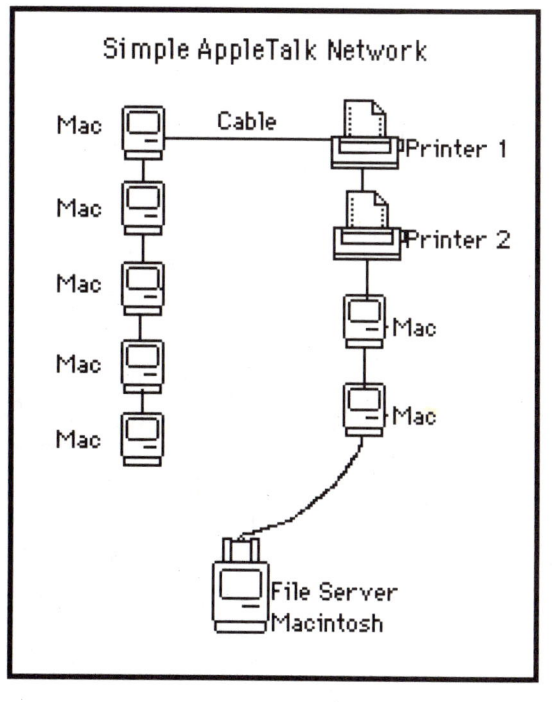

Figure 7.2 shows an example of a simple AppleTalk Network. It has 7 Macintoshes, 2 printers, and a file server connected by cables.

Activity 7.1 and 7.2 present two different Chooser windows. Which activity you perform will depend on whether you are planning to print to a network printer or to a stand-alone printer. The ImageWriter and StyleWriter can operate as stand-alone printers or as network devices but LaserWriter printers require AppleTalk software.

If you are using a LaserWriter printer or if your Macintosh is connected to an AppleTalk network, skip Activity 7.1 and proceed to Activity 7.2—The Chooser Using an AppleTalk Network.

If you do not have a LaserWriter printer (or other laser printer) and your printer is directly cabled to your Macintosh perform Activity 7.1.

### Activity 7.1—The Chooser Using a Stand-alone Printer

Step 1   Boot your Macintosh.

Step 2   If you are using a printer with continuous computer paper (ImageWriter), align the paper in the printer. Place the top edge of the paper under the paper bail—the metal bar with 2 rollers. Turn the printer on. If you have an ink-jet printer (StyleWriter), verify there is paper in the paper tray before you turn the printer on.

Step 3   Select Chooser from the  menu.

### What's Happening

The Chooser window appears. (Figure 7.3)

Step 4   If the printer icon representing the printer you wish to use is not highlighted, click on it, and the other icons will appear.

### What's Happening

The window is divided into two list boxes. A **list box** provides you with a list of options to choose from. The list box on the left lists all available print drivers in your Startup disk's Extension folder. This does not necessarily mean your Macintosh has access to all these printers. The list box on the right lists the ports where the printer may be attached. In Figure 7.3, the ImageWriter and printer port icons are highlighted, indicating they have been selected. The AppleTalk option is identified as inactive. This Macintosh is not on an AppleTalk network.

THE CHOOSER DESK ACCESSORY    157

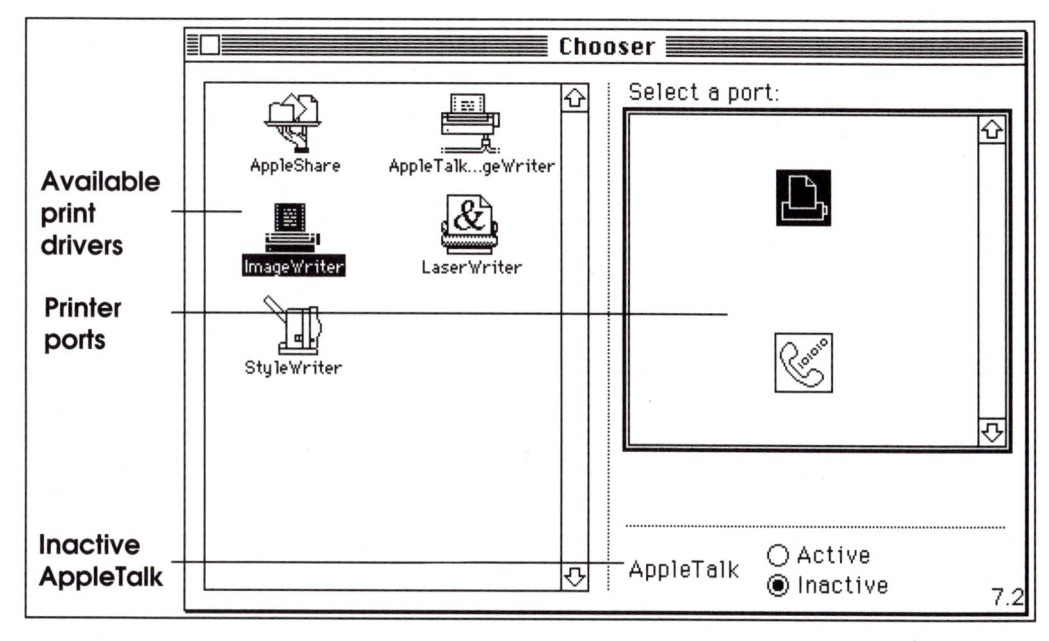

*Figure 7.3—Using the Chooser with a Stand-Alone Printer*

**Available print drivers** — AppleShare, AppleTalk...geWriter, ImageWriter, LaserWriter

**Printer ports** — StyleWriter

**Inactive AppleTalk**

Chooser — Select a port: — AppleTalk ○ Active ● Inactive

On the back of the Macintosh system unit you will find two serial ports: the printer and modem ports. A **port** is a socket where you can plug in a cable to connect to a printer, another computer, a modem, and so on. A **serial port** transmits information from the computer to the printer in a single file, one bit at a time. A **bit** (short for binary digit) is the smallest unit a computer will recognize. It is either in the "on" state, represented by the binary digit 1, or in the "off" state, represented by the binary digit 0. Every number, letter or character is represented in a coded binary form. Almost all microcomputers use an 8-bit coding scheme called **ASCII**—an acronym for **American Standard Code for Information Interchange**. Remember, 8 bits make a byte (a character).

An icon is located above each port for easy identification. The printer port has a small printer icon located above it.

The modem port has a small phone handset located above it. **Modem** (pronounced "mow-dum") is short for **Modulator-Demodulator.** This device allows you to send information stored on your computer (or receive information) through phone lines to other computers. Printers may be attached to either port via a cable but most Macintosh users prefer to use the printer port, leaving the modem port available for an external modem.

Step 5    Examine the back of your system unit to verify which port the printer is using. Click on the port icon that represents how your printer is attached. Click on the AppleTalk Inactive button.

### What's Happening
All three icons must be highlighted: Printer icon, Printer Port icon, and the Inactive button. A dialog box may appear confirming your selection. Read it, click on OK, and continue.

Step 6    Close the Chooser window.

## Activity 7.2—The Chooser Using an AppleTalk Network Printer

If your Macintosh is on an AppleTalk Network, follow these instructions. (If you are using a laser printer, you probably need AppleTalk.) Dialog boxes may appear—read them and click on the OK buttons to continue. If you are using a stand-alone printer, you have already selected the printer in Activity 7.1. Skip this Activity and proceed to the section called Print a Directory on the Macintosh.

Step 1    Boot your Macintosh.

Step 2    If you are using a printer with continuous computer paper (ImageWriter), align the paper in the printer. Place the top edge of the paper under the paper bail—the metal bar with 2 rollers. Turn the printer on.

If you have an individual sheet-feed printer (LaserWriter or StyleWriter), verify there is paper in the paper tray. Turn the printer on. The printer may generate a test page before it is ready.

Step 3    Select Chooser from the  menu. If the print driver icon representing the printer you wish to use is not highlighted (top left box), click on it, and the other information will appear.

### What's Happening
The Chooser window appears. (Figure 7.4) Two or three list boxes will appear. A **list box** provides you with a list of options to choose from. The list box on the top left displays icons for the available print drivers in the Extension folder on the Startup disk. The **AppleTalk Zones** list box will only be displayed if you are on a network that has established zones. The **Select a LaserWriter:** list box will list the names of all available printers matching the device type you have selected. **Background Printing** buttons will only be provided if you have selected the LaserWriter or StyleWriter printer icon. **Background printing**

allows you to continue working without waiting for your document to finish printing. (Refer to Chapter 12 for more detail on Background printing.) The **AppleTalk** Active button must be selected.

*Figure 7.4—Using the Chooser with a Network Printer*

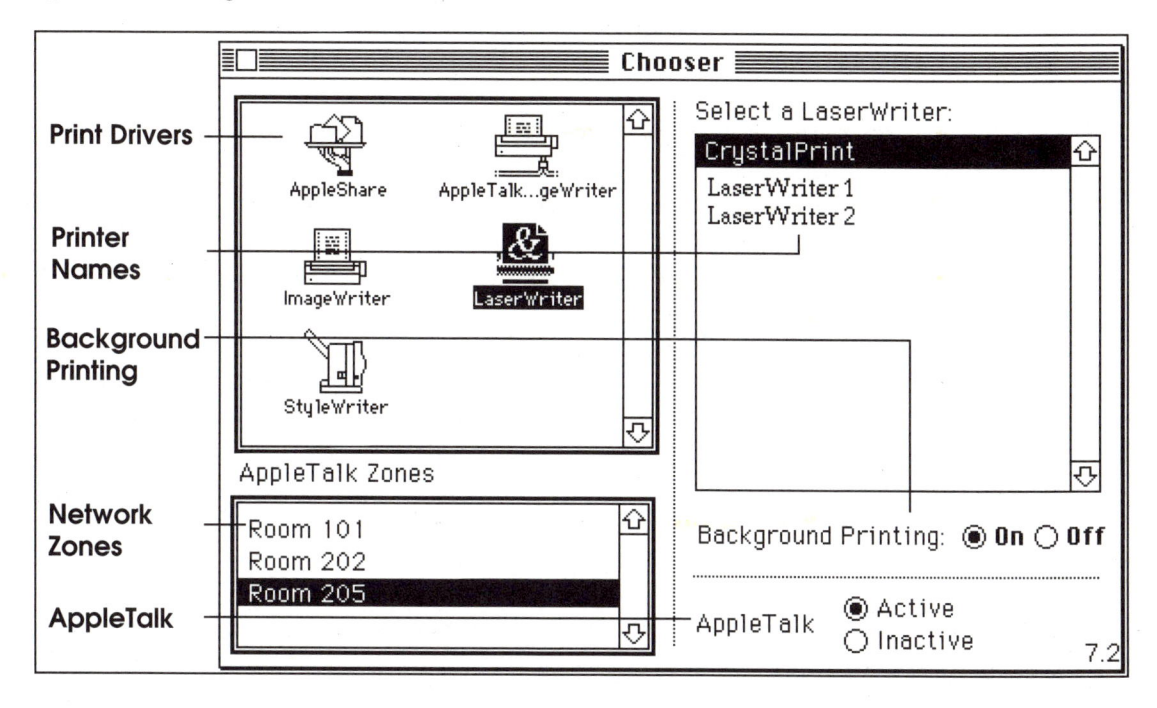

[Figure: Chooser window showing Print Drivers (AppleShare, AppleTalk...geWriter), Printer Names (ImageWriter, LaserWriter, StyleWriter), Background Printing, Network Zones (Room 101, Room 202, Room 205), AppleTalk Zones, Select a LaserWriter list (CrystalPrint, LaserWriter 1, LaserWriter 2), Background Printing: On/Off, AppleTalk: Active/Inactive]

Step 4  Click on the appropriate zone (if necessary) and printer name. Verify the Background Printing On button and the AppleTalk Active button are selected.

Step 5  Close the Chooser window.

## Printing a Directory on the Macintosh

You can print a directory (a list of the window's contents) by using the **Print Window** command. Activity 7.3, 7.4, and 7.5 will provide steps to execute this command using either an ImageWriter, a LaserWriter, or a StyleWriter printer. Pay careful attention to the instructions. The windows that appear on your desktop may vary from the ones presented here. The Chooser, Page Setup, and Print windows vary according to the hardware and network software your system is using.

160    CHAPTER 7  •  PRINTING

## Activity 7.3—Printing a Directory on an ImageWriter

Use the following instructions if you are printing on an ImageWriter dot-matrix printer. If you are printing on a LaserWriter, skip this activity and proceed to Activity 7.4—Printing a Directory on a LaserWriter. If you are using a StyleWriter, skip this activity and proceed to Activity 7.5—Printing a Directory on a StyleWriter.

Step 1    Insert your unlocked Lastname-Sys 7 disk in the available floppy drive.

Step 2    Open your Lastname-Sys 7 disk. The window appears on the screen.

Step 3    Check the View menu and verify that there is a check mark next to the by Icon command.

Step 4    If the scroll bars are active, click on the zoom box. Verify that the icons are not overlapping. If they are, drag the overlapping icons to new locations in the disk window.

Step 5    Select the **Page Setup** command of the File menu.

*Figure 7.5—ImageWriter Page Setup Dialog Box*

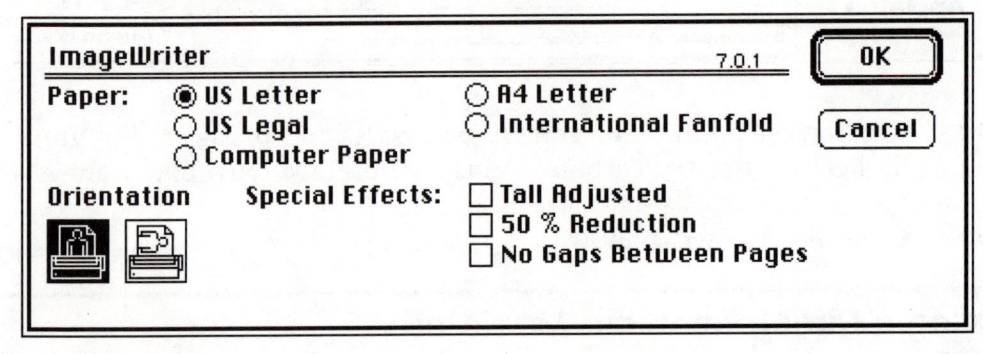

```
ImageWriter                                    7.0.1      [  OK  ]
Paper:    ⦿ US Letter        ○ A4 Letter
          ○ US Legal         ○ International Fanfold    [ Cancel ]
          ○ Computer Paper
Orientation    Special Effects:  ☐ Tall Adjusted
                                 ☐ 50 % Reduction
                                 ☐ No Gaps Between Pages
```

*What's Happening*

The Page Setup dialog box appears. (Figure 7.5) You must choose from the following options.

**Paper** (inches)
| | | |
|---|---|---|
| US Letter | = | 8.5 by 11 |
| US Legal | = | 8.5 by 14 |
| Computer Paper | = | 14 by 11 |
| A4 Letter | = | 8.25 by 11.6667 |
| International Fanfold | = | 8.25 by 12 |

**Orientation**
    Portrait                      =         Vertical
    Landscape            =         Horizontal

**Special Effects**
    **Tall Adjusted**        =         Prints portrait mode and scales graphics correctly. For example, circles frequently will print out jagged and warped if this button is not selected.
    **50% Reduction**       =        Prints document half the original size.
    **No Gaps Between Pages**   =        Use to print up to the paper's perforation without a break.

Step 6     Your Page Setup dialog box should look like the one in Figure 7.5. If necessary, make changes in the Page Setup dialog box by clicking on the appropriate button. The Tall Adjusted check box should have an X in it. Click OK to close the dialog box.

Step 7     Select the Print Window command of the File menu.

*Figure 7.6—ImageWriter Print Dialog Box*

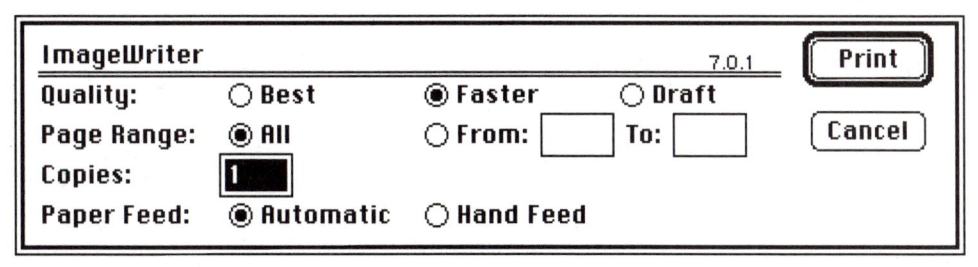

```
ImageWriter                                            7.0.1    [ Print  ]
Quality:       ○ Best        ● Faster       ○ Draft
Page Range:    ● All         ○ From: [   ] To: [   ]    [ Cancel ]
Copies:        [1]
Paper Feed:    ● Automatic   ○ Hand Feed
```

*What's Happening*
    The ImageWriter Print dialog box appears. (Figure 7.6) You must choose from the following options.

    **Quality**
        Click on the print quality you want the document to be printed in.
        Best     =    45 char/second, 160 dpi
        Faster   =    180 char/second, 72 dpi
        Draft    =    250 char/second, poor

**Page Range**
Click on All or type in the number of the first page number and the last page number to print.
All      =   Print all pages of document
From     =   First page to print
To       =   Last page to print

**Copies**
How many copies of the document do you want? 1.

**Paper feed**
**Automatic** means you are using continuous feed paper.
**Hand feed** may be used if you are feeding individual sheets of paper to the printer.

Step 8  Your Print dialog box should look like the one in Figure 7.6. Make changes if necessary. Click Print.

Step 9  Go to the printer and retrieve your **hard copy** (paper copy) of the directory. Press the Select button (light goes out) and press the Form Feed button to advance the paper. Tear the page off carefully.

Step 10  Proceed to Activity 7.6—Printing a Directory of the System Folder.

## Activity 7.4—Printing a Directory on the LaserWriter

Use the following instructions if you are printing on a LaserWriter printer. If you are printing on an StyleWriter, proceed to Activity 7.5. If you are working on an ImageWriter, proceed to Activity 7.6.

Step 1  Insert your unlocked Lastname-Sys 7 disk in the available floppy drive.

Step 2  Open your Lastname-Sys 7 disk. The window appears on the screen.

Step 3  Check the View menu and verify that there is a check mark next to the by Icon command.

Step 4  If the scroll bars are active, click on the zoom box. Verify that the icons are not overlapping. If they are, drag the overlapping icons to new locations in the disk window.

Step 5  Select the Page Setup command of the File menu.

## What's Happening

The Page Setup dialog box appears. (Figure 7.7) You must choose from the following options.

*Figure 7.7—LaserWriter Page Setup Dialog Box*

```
┌─────────────────────────────────────────────────────────┐
│ LaserWriter Page Setup              7.1.2    ┌────OK────┐│
│ Paper: ◉ US Letter  ○ A4 Letter              └──────────┘│
│        ○ US Legal   ○ B5 Letter  ○ [Tabloid ▼] ┌─Cancel─┐│
│                                                └────────┘│
│        Reduce or [100]%   Printer Effects:   ┌─Options─┐ │
│        Enlarge:           ☒ Font Substitution?└────────┘│
│        Orientation        ☒ Text Smoothing?              │
│        [👤][👤]           ☒ Graphics Smoothing?          │
│                           ☒ Faster Bitmap Printing?      │
└─────────────────────────────────────────────────────────┘
```

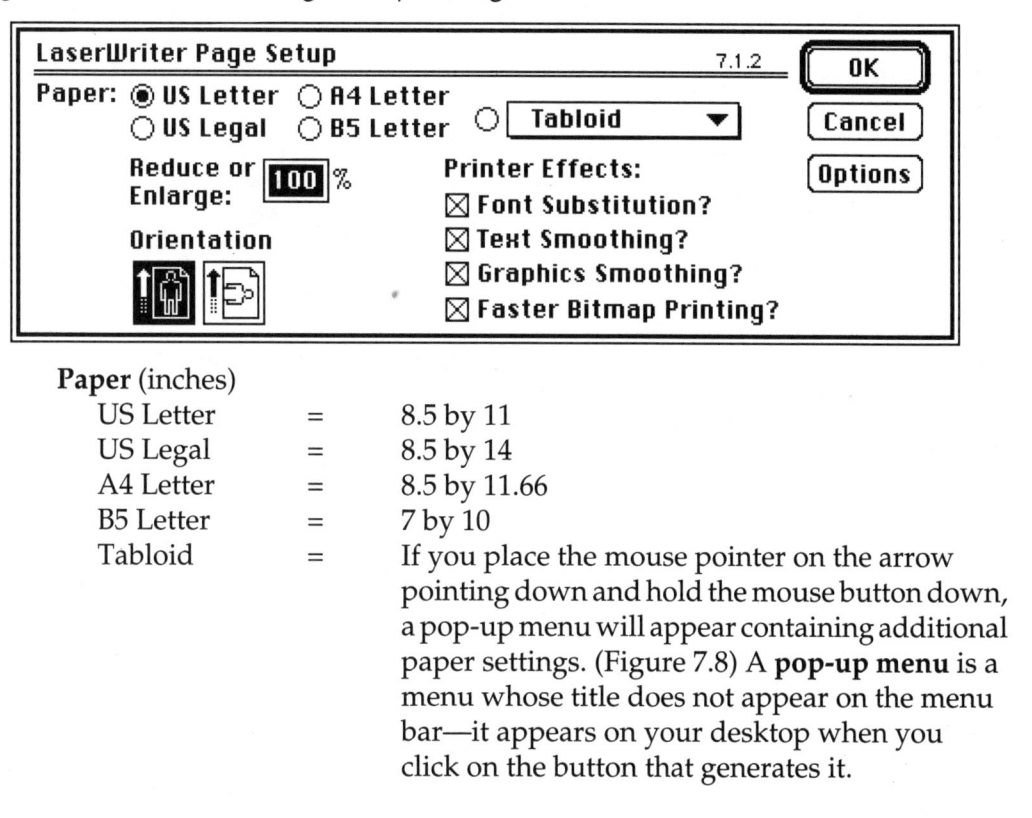

**Paper** (inches)
| | | |
|---|---|---|
| US Letter | = | 8.5 by 11 |
| US Legal | = | 8.5 by 14 |
| A4 Letter | = | 8.5 by 11.66 |
| B5 Letter | = | 7 by 10 |
| Tabloid | = | If you place the mouse pointer on the arrow pointing down and hold the mouse button down, a pop-up menu will appear containing additional paper settings. (Figure 7.8) A **pop-up menu** is a menu whose title does not appear on the menu bar—it appears on your desktop when you click on the button that generates it. |

*Figure 7.8—Additional LaserWriter Paper Sizes*

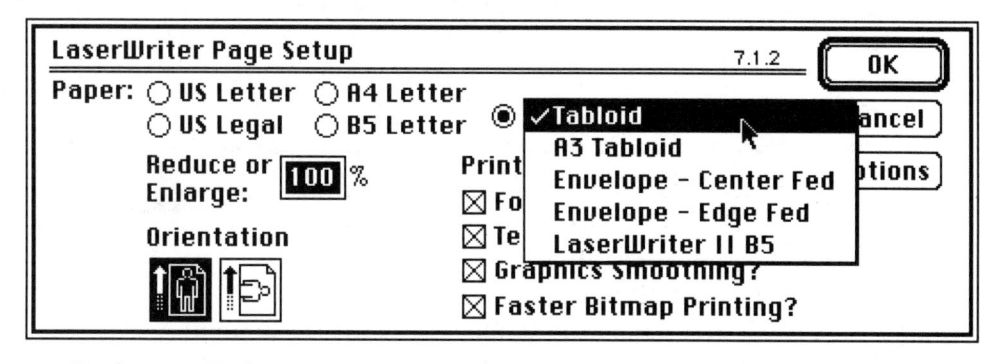

```
┌─────────────────────────────────────────────────────────┐
│ LaserWriter Page Setup              7.1.2    ┌────OK────┐│
│ Paper: ○ US Letter  ○ A4 Letter                          │
│        ○ US Legal   ○ B5 Letter  ◉ ┌──✓Tabloid──┐ ancel │
│                                    │ A3 Tabloid  │       │
│        Reduce or [100]%   Print    │ Envelope - Center Fed│ ptions│
│        Enlarge:           ☒ Fo     │ Envelope - Edge Fed │      │
│        Orientation        ☒ Te     │ LaserWriter II B5  │       │
│        [👤][👤]           ☒ Graphics Smoothing?          │
│                           ☒ Faster Bitmap Printing?      │
└─────────────────────────────────────────────────────────┘
```

**Reduce or Enlarge**

100% means print the document at 100%.

You can type in a percentage of reduction or enlargement. For example, 50% would print the document at half its original size.

**Orientation**
Portrait     =     Vertical
Landscape    =     Horizontal

**Printer Effects**
**Font Substitution**
If Font Substitution is selected, three built in fonts will be substituted for certain ones you specify on the screen. Helvetica will be substituted for Geneva, Times for New York and Courier for Monaco.
**Text Smoothing**
Improves the appearance of certain fonts, eliminates the rough edges.
**Graphics Smoothing**
The jagged edges of graphic images will be smoothed.
**Faster Bitmap Printing**
Text and graphics that use bitmaps will print faster.

**Three Buttons**
**OK** accepts the answers in the window and closes the window.
**Cancel** indicates that you have changed your mind; it cancels the command. The window will close and any changes you typed in will be ignored.
**Options** opens an additional window of LaserWriter option.

Step 6     Click on the Options button.

## What's Happening

The Options button causes the Options dialog box in Figure 7.9 to appear. As you select each option, the sample document on the left will demonstrate it.

*Figure 7.9—LaserWriter Options Dialog Box*

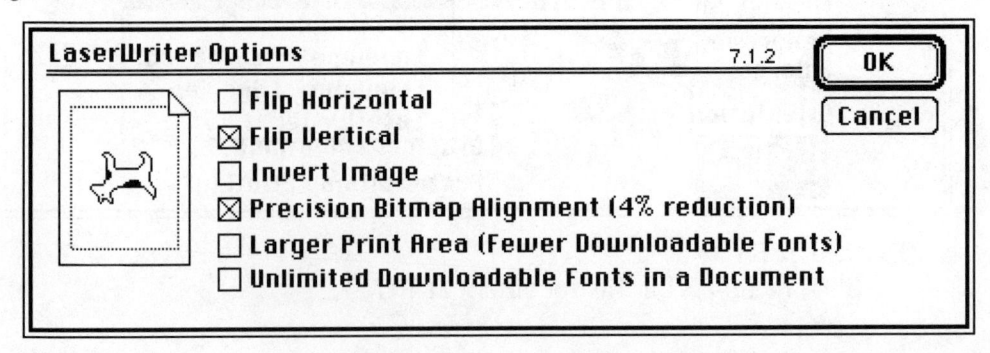

Six options are available in the Options dialog box. There is **checkbox** associated with each option. An X will appear in the checkbox if the associated option is on.

**Flip Horizontal** and **Flip Vertical** changes the image along a vertical and horizontal axis. Notice the X in the Flip Vertical box. The dog in the sample document has been flipped.
**Invert Image** prints a negative image of your document.
**Precision Bitmap Alignment** prints bitmap images at 4 times the resolution of the Macintosh screen. Images you create in paint and draw programs are often bitmap images and may be distorted if you do not select this option. The printed image will be reduced by 4%.
**Larger Print Area** allows you to print on more of the total page area.
**Unlimited Downloadable Fonts in a Document** allows you to use more fonts in your document. Normally only two or three fonts are used for each document. If this option is selected, the document may print slower.

Step 7   Click on the different checkboxes in the Options dialog box to see what happens. Before closing this dialog box, make sure there is not an X in any of the checkboxes. Click on the OK button.

*What's Happening*

The Options dialog box closes.

Step 8   Click on the OK button in the Page Setup dialog box.

*What's Happening*

Your selections have been accepted and the dialog box closes.

Step 9   Select the Print Window command of the File menu.

*What's Happening*

The LaserWriter Print dialog box will appear. (Figure 7.10) You must choose from the following options.

*Figure 7.10—LaserWriter Print Dialog Box*

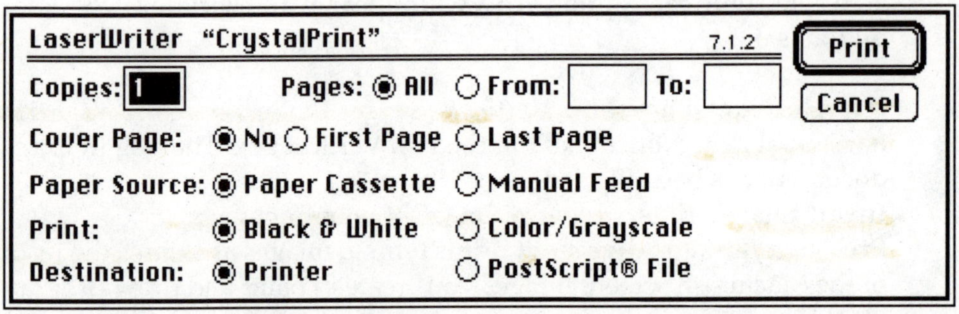

```
┌─────────────────────────────────────────────────────────────────┐
│ LaserWriter  "CrystalPrint"                    7.1.2   [ Print ]│
│ Copies: [1]        Pages: ⦿ All  ○ From: [   ] To: [   ]        │
│                                                        [Cancel] │
│ Cover Page:     ⦿ No  ○ First Page  ○ Last Page                 │
│ Paper Source: ⦿ Paper Cassette  ○ Manual Feed                   │
│ Print:           ⦿ Black & White    ○ Color/Grayscale           │
│ Destination:  ⦿ Printer             ○ PostScript® File          │
└─────────────────────────────────────────────────────────────────┘
```

**Copies**
How many copies of the document do you want? 1.

**Pages**
Click on All, or type in the number of the first page number and the last page number to print.
- All   =   Print all pages of document
- From  =   First page to print
- To    =   Last page to print

**Cover Page**
A cover page is recommended only if the printer is located in a separate area. A report containing your User Name, active program, document name, date, time, and printer name may be printed as the last or first page.

**Paper Source**
You need to specify whether a paper cassette (tray) is installed in your printer or whether you will be manually feeding paper.

**Print**
If you are using a color printer you will need to specify Black and White or Color/Grayscale.

**Destination**
Graphic document files may print better if they are first saved as a PostScript file. If you select this option the Print button changes to Save.

Step 10   If necessary make changes in the Page Setup dialog box. Click Print to accept the settings.

Step 11   Go to the printer and retrieve your hard-copy (paper copy) of the directory.

Step 12   Proceed to Activity 7.6—Printing a Directory of the System Folder.

## Activity 7.5—Printing a Directory on the StyleWriter

Use the following instructions if you are printing on a StyleWriter printer. If you are printing on an ImageWriter or LaserWriter proceed to Activity 7.6.

Step 1   Insert your unlocked Lastname-Sys 7 data disk in the available floppy drive.

Step 2   Open your Lastname-Sys 7 data disk. The window appears on the screen.

Step 3   Check the View menu and verify that there is a check mark next to the by Icon command.

Step 4   If the scroll bars are active, click on the zoom box. Verify that the icons are not overlapping. If they are, drag the overlapping icons to new locations in the disk window.

Step 5   Select the Page Setup command of the File menu.

*Figure 7.11—StyleWriter Page Setup Dialog Box*

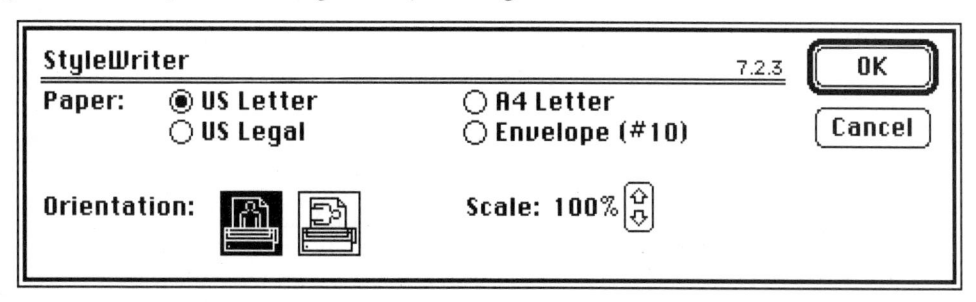

```
┌─────────────────────────────────────────────────────────┐
│ StyleWriter                              7.2.3   [ OK ] │
│ Paper:   ● US Letter        ○ A4 Letter                 │
│          ○ US Legal         ○ Envelope (#10)  [Cancel]  │
│                                                         │
│ Orientation:  [📄] [📄]     Scale: 100% ⇅              │
└─────────────────────────────────────────────────────────┘
```

### What's Happening

The Page Setup dialog box appears. (Figure 7.11) You must choose from the following options.

**Paper** (inches)
| | | |
|---|---|---|
| US Letter | = | 8.5 by 11 |
| US Legal | = | 8.5 by 14 |
| A4 Letter | = | 8.5 by 11.66 |
| Envelope | = | Standard number 10 business envelope |

**Orientation**
| | | |
|---|---|---|
| Portrait | = | Vertical |
| Landscape | = | Horizontal |

**Scale**
Use this option to set the size of the printed document. For example, you can use the down arrow to print the document at 80% of its original size.

Step 6    Your Page Setup dialog box should look like the one in Figure 7.11. If necessary, make changes in the Page Setup dialog box by clicking on the appropriate button. Click OK to close the dialog box.

Step 7    Select the Print Window command of the File menu.

## What's Happening

The StyleWriter's Print dialog box will appear. (Figure 7.12) You must choose between the following options.

*Figure 7.12—StyleWriter Print Dialog Box*

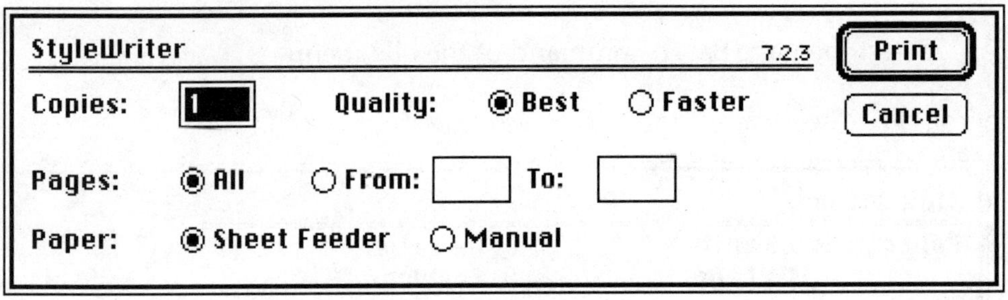

```
StyleWriter                                    7.2.3   [ Print  ]
Copies:  [1]    Quality:  ● Best    ○ Faster   [ Cancel ]
Pages:   ● All  ○ From: [   ]  To: [   ]
Paper:   ● Sheet Feeder    ○ Manual
```

**Copies**
How many copies of the document do you want? 1.

**Quality**
Best    =    Prints at 360 dpi
Faster  =    Prints at 180 dpi

**Pages**
Click on All or type in the number of the first page number and the last page number to print.
All     =    Print all pages of document
From    =    First page to print
To      =    Last page to print

**Paper feed**
Sheet Feeder  =    A paper cassette tray is attached
Manual        =    Sheets are individually fed

Step 8   Your Print dialog box should look like the one in Figure 7.12. Make changes if necessary. Click Print.

Step 9   Go to the printer and retrieve your **hard copy** (paper copy) of the directory.

Step 10  Proceed to Activity 7.6—Printing a Directory of the System Folder.

### Activity 7.6—Printing a Directory of the System Folder

Step 1   Close your Lastname-Sys 7 data window. Open your Startup disk window.

Step 2   Locate the System Folder icon on your Startup disk window.

Step 3   Double-click on the System Folder icon to show the files inside.

*What's Happening*
A new window will appear on your desktop, showing the files stored in this folder.

Step 4   Choose the by Name command of the View menu.

*What's Happening*
The names of the files in the System Folder should now be listed alphabetically. You previously selected the printer (Chooser) and defined the page-setup (Page Setup). You do not have to do this again unless you wish to change your answers in one of the dialog boxes.

Step 5   Select the Print Window command of the File menu.

Step 6   Click on the Print button in the Print dialog box.

Step 7   Go to the printer and retrieve your hard copy (paper copy) of the directory.

Step 8   Close your System Folder window.

Step 9   Close your Startup disk window.

## Printing from within an Application Program

The application program TeachText comes with System 7. TeachText is a simple word processing program. The TeachText program should be on your Startup disk. In this Activity you will open a TeachText document on your Lastname-Sys 7 data disk, make one minor correction to the document, write the modified document back to disk, and print the document.

### Activity 7.7—Printing a Document in TeachText

Step 1    Open your Lastname-Sys 7 disk.

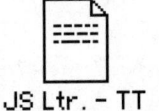

Step 2    Double-click on the JS Ltr. - TT document icon.

*What's Happening*

The application program, TeachText, that originally created the document will be opened automatically and loaded into RAM. The document will then be loaded into RAM and will appear in a window on your desktop. (Figure 7.13)

*Figure 7.13—TeachText Window*

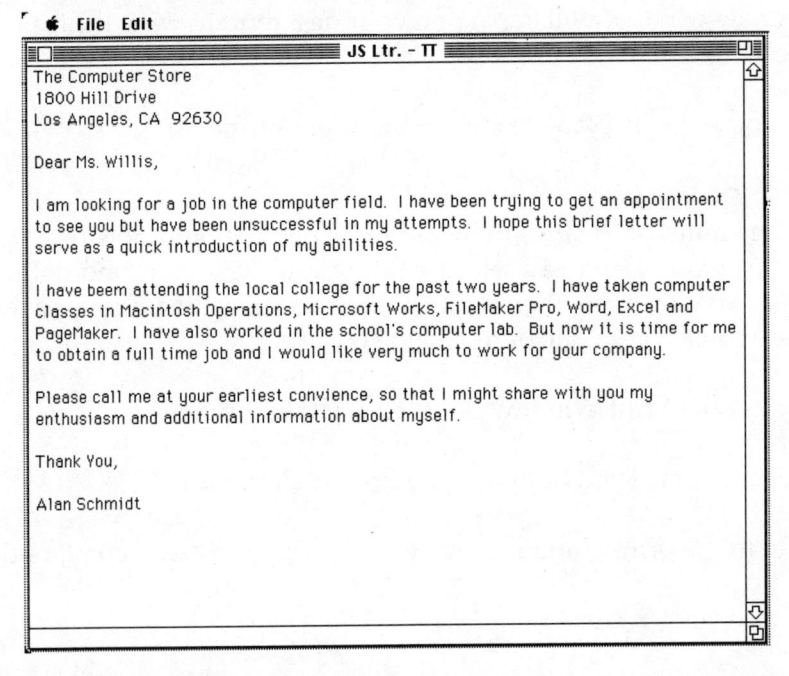

```
 File Edit
===================== JS Ltr. - TT =====================
The Computer Store
1800 Hill Drive
Los Angeles, CA  92630

Dear Ms. Willis,

I am looking for a job in the computer field.  I have been trying to get an appointment
to see you but have been unsuccessful in my attempts.  I hope this brief letter will
serve as a quick introduction of my abilities.

I have beem attending the local college for the past two years.  I have taken computer
classes in Macintosh Operations, Microsoft Works, FileMaker Pro, Word, Excel and
PageMaker.  I have also worked in the school's computer lab.  But now it is time for me
to obtain a full time job and I would like very much to work for your company.

Please call me at your earliest convience, so that I might share with you my
enthusiasm and additional information about myself.

Thank You,

Alan Schmidt
```

Examine your desktop. The Finder menu bar along the top of the desktop has been replaced with the TeachText menu bar. The Trash and disk icons may be partially or completed covered by the new window. The Application menu icon now displays the TeachText icon.

Step 3    Display the Apple  menu. Notice the first entry, About This Macintosh, has been replaced with **About TeachText.** Select this entry.

*Figure 7.14—TeachText Information Box*

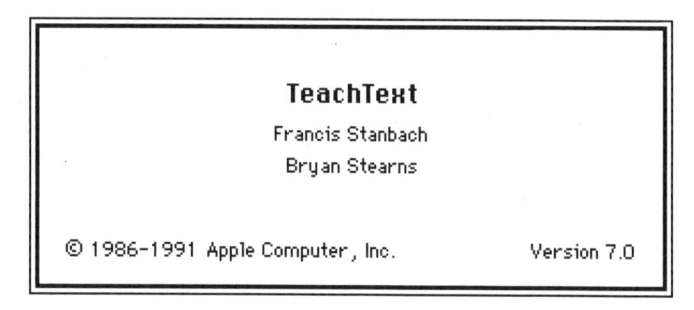

```
                    TeachText
                  Francis Stanbach
                  Bryan Stearns


     © 1986-1991 Apple Computer, Inc.        Version 7.0
```

## What's Happening

A new information box appears giving you a little information about the TeachText program. (Figure 7.14)

Step 4    Click on the information box to close it.

Step 5    Display the File and Edit menus. (Figure 7.15) Many of the commands should look familiar. Do not choose any of the commands.

*Figure 7.15—TeachText Menus*

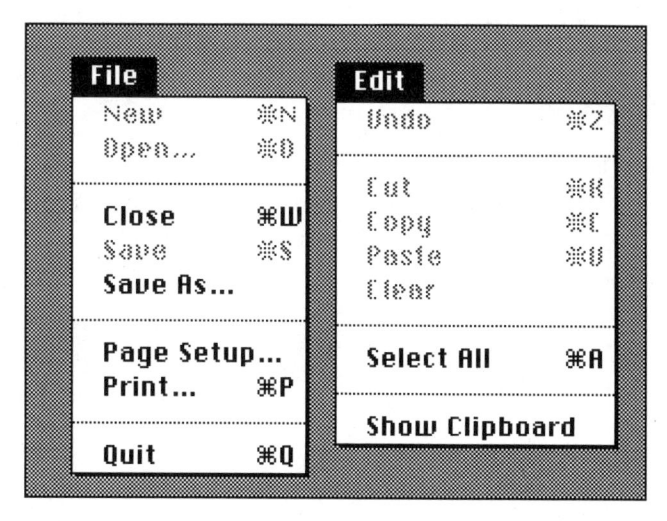

| File | | Edit | |
|---|---|---|---|
| New | ⌘N | Undo | ⌘Z |
| Open... | ⌘O | | |
| | | Cut | ⌘X |
| Close | ⌘W | Copy | ⌘C |
| Save | ⌘S | Paste | ⌘V |
| Save As... | | Clear | |
| | | | |
| Page Setup... | | Select All | ⌘A |
| Print... | ⌘P | | |
| | | Show Clipboard | |
| Quit | ⌘Q | | |

**Editing, Saving and Printing the Document**

Look at the document. The third word in the second paragraph (beem) is incorrect.

Step 6   Use the Edit techniques you learned previously to change beem to been.

Step 7   Choose **Save** from the File menu.

*What's Happening*
> The corrected document has been written to the disk, replacing the incorrect document. If a dialog box appears informing you that the disk is locked, eject the disk (⌘ E). Unlock the disk and reinsert the disk in the drive. Repeat step 7.

Step 8   Choose **Print** from the File menu.

*What's Happening*
> The Print dialog box for your printer will open. (Figure 7.6, 7.10, or 7.12)

Step 9   Check the settings and then click on the Print button.

*What's Happening*
> Retrieve your printed document from the printer.

Step 10   Close the JS Ltr. - TT document window.

*What's Happening*
> Examine the menu bar. The TeachText menu is still displayed because the TeachText program is still active. You just don't have an open TeachText document on the desktop.

Step 11   Choose **Quit** from the File menu.

*What's Happening*
> You have closed the TeachText program and are back at the desktop level with the Finder menu bar displayed. Any time you are finished working with an application program, you need to execute the Quit command. This command will close program files in an orderly way.

Step 12   Close all open windows.

Congratulations, you have had your first encounter with an application program. You will have the opportunity to experiment more in the next chapter.

# Key Terms

50% Reduction
About TeachText
AppleTalk
AppleTalk Zones
ASCII
Automatic feed paper
Background printing
Binary digit
Bit
Byte
Characters Per Second
Checkbox
Chooser DA
Computer network
Cover page
CPS
Dot matrix Printer
DPI
Dots Per Inch
Draft
Extension Folder
Faster Bitmap Printing
File server
Flip Horizontal
Flip Vertical
Font Substitution
Form Feed
Graphics Smoothing
Hand feed paper
Hard copy
ImageWriter II
Ink jet printer
Invert Image
Landscape Orientation

Larger Print Area
LaserWriter printers
Line Feed
List box
Modem
Near Letter Quality
Network versions
No gaps between Pages
Orientation
Page Per Minute
Page Range
Page Setup
Paper feed
Pop-up menu
Port
Portrait Orientation
PPM
Precision Bit map Alignment
Print ⌘ P
Print drivers
Print servers
Print Window
Printer Effects
Print Quality
Quit ⌘ Q
Reduce/Enlarge
Save ⌘ S
Serial port
Special Effects
StyleWriter printer
Tall Adjusted
Text Smoothing
Unlimited Downloadable Fonts

## Discussion Questions

1. Discuss the printers available in your work environment and which one(s) should be used. Discuss the buttons and indicator lights on the printers in your work environment.
2. List the steps necessary for printing in your work environment. They may differ slightly from the text.
3. Is it necessary to access the Chooser DA every time you print?
4. Discuss the advantages and possible disadvantages of computer networks.

## True/False Questions

For each question, circle the letter T if the statement is true and the letter F if the statement is false.

T F 1. The AppleTalk button on the Chooser window must be selected if you are not working on a network.
T F 2. A LaserWriter allows you to reduce or enlarge the printed document.
T F 3. US Letter size paper is 8.5 by 11 inches.
T F 4. Each time you access the Print Window command, you can only print one copy of the document.
T F 5. The Automatic or Continuous button on the Paper Feed entry in the Print dialog box should be selected if you have a paper cassette tray feeding individual sheets to the printer.
T F 6. You must always access the Chooser before you print.
T F 7. If you print a directory by icon, only the icons in view on your active window will print.
T F 8. If you print a directory by name, a list of all files in the open active window will print whether they are showing in the window or not.
T F 9. Use the Page Setup dialog box to specify the paper size on which you will print.
T F 10. The appearance of the Page Setup window will vary according to the printer you have selected from the Chooser.

## Completion Questions

Write the correct answer in each blank space.

1. If you print your document in landscape orientation, you are printing your document _____ on the page.
2. A _____ menu is a menu whose title does not appear on the menu bar—it appears on your desktop when you click on the button that generates it.
3. The best print quality available on the ImageWriter is called_____.
4. The Print Window command is available on the _____ menu.
5. Legal size paper is _____ inches by _____ inches.
6. _____ is a term used to describe a computer system where multiple computers, printers, disk drives or other devices are interconnected making it possible for the devices to communicate with each other.

## Assignments

Boot your Macintosh. The Macintosh desktop should be clean—no open windows. Insert the locked Lastname-Sys 7 disk in the available floppy drive.

### Part 1—Printing Directories

1. Print a directory of your Startup disk by Kind.
2. Print a directory of your Lastname-Sys 7 disk by Name.
3. Open the Misc. folder on the Lastname-Sys 7 disk and print a directory by Date.
4. Print a directory of the Misc. folder by Name.
5. Close the Misc. folder window. Display the Lastname-Sys 7 disk by name. Click on the triangles next to the Misc. and Class Work folder to display their contents in an outline view. Print this directory.

### Part 2—TeachText

6. Follow the instructions in Activity 7.7 to reopen the JS Ltr.-TeachText document. Use the cut, copy, and paste editing techniques you learned in Chapter 6 to modify the document as follows.

a. In the second paragraph, cut "Lastname-Sys 7 data Operations, Microsoft Works, FileMaker Pro, Word, Excel and PageMaker". Insert names of computer courses you have completed. ("I have taken computer classes in ...")
b. In paragraph three, correct the spelling of the word convience, to convenience.

c. In paragraph three, insert your home phone number.
"Please call me at your earliest convenience, (222) 888-1233, so that..."

d. Change the name at the end of the document from Alan Schmidt to your name.

7. Print the document.

8. Quit the Program. A dialog box will appear to inform you that you have not saved the modified document. Do not save the modified document to disk.

Close all open windows.

# Working with TeachText and the Finder

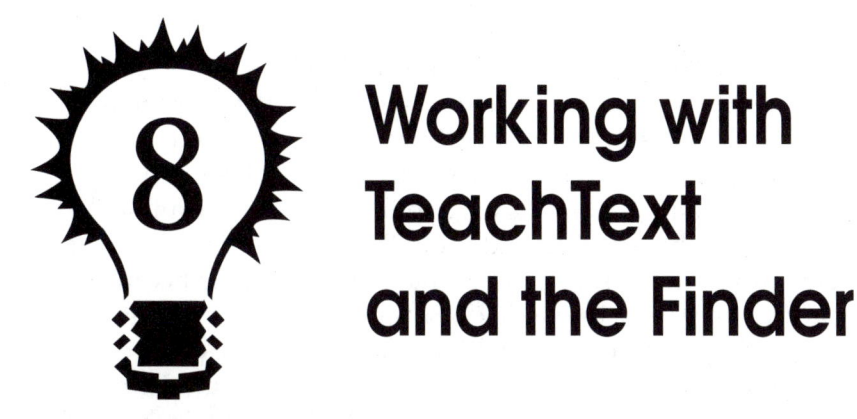

## Learning Objectives

**After completing this Chapter you will be able to:**

1. Create a document using TeachText.
2. Explain the commands available in the File and Edit menus of the TeachText program.
3. Describe and use editing techniques to erase a few characters, an entire word, and a line of text.
4. Describe the parts of the Directory dialog box.
5. Describe how to save a file on disk and in a specific folder.
6. Retrieve a file from a specific folder in TeachText.
7. Paste text or pictures in the Scrapbook.
8. Copy text or pictures from the Scrapbook to paste in a TeachText document.
9. Print documents from within an application program.
10. Remove entries from the Scrapbook.

## Introduction

The primary focus of this book is Macintosh Operating System 7.1. All Macintosh users need to understand the power of the operating system and how to use it effectively, but until you experiment with application programs, it's hard to appreciate the Macintosh. Therefore, application programs are briefly introduced in this chapter and Chapters 14 through 17. Remember, application software is the group of programs you would use to create letters, spreadsheets, graphs, pictures, and so on.

In this chapter, you will use the TeachText application program. This simple word-processing program is included with your system when you purchase a Macintosh. TeachText is not a complex word-processing program—it lacks many capabilities. It does not provide you with a choice of fonts or styles (underline, bold words, italics), it can't check your document for misspelled words, it does not allow double-spacing, and so on. Then *why* are we going to use this program? This program is used for demonstration purposes because all Macintosh users have access to it and it does provide the document (file) management procedures you need to know. You will learn how to open, create, save, close, and print documents. You will learn your way around Directory dialog boxes. You will learn how to use the Clipboard and Scrapbook. You will also learn how to open and quit application programs.

## Before you start this chapter:

### 1. Verify that the TeachText program is on your Startup disk.

If you are not working on your own computer, check with the person in charge to verify that the program is on the disk and how to access the program. If you are working on your own Macintosh, check to see if the program is on your Startup disk. If it is not, you will need to locate the program on the original system disks and copy it to the Macintosh hard drive.

### 2. Obtain a new floppy disk.

You will be creating several documents in this chapter. They will be written to (saved) on a new disk titled, Lastname-Data.

# Creating a New Document in TeachText

In this activity, you will format your new disk, open the TeachText application program, key in a short letter, save the letter to disk, close the letter window, and quit the TeachText program.

### Activity 8.1—Creating a document in TeachText

Step 1    Boot your Macintosh.

Step 2    Place your new disk in the floppy drive.

## What's Happening

A dialog box will appear informing you that the disk is unreadable and asking if you wish to initialize the disk.

CREATING A NEW DOCUMENT IN TEACHTEXT    179

Step 3    Initialize your new disk. Name it Lastname-Data (for example, Sullivan-Data).

TeachText

Step 4    Open the Startup disk. Locate the TeachText icon and double-click on it.

## What's Happening

The TeachText program is loaded into RAM. A new window named Untitled appears on the desktop. The Finder menu bar is replaced by the TeachText menu bar. The TeachText icon replaces the Finder icon. (Figure 8.1) The  menu is available on all menu bars.

*Figure 8.1—TeachText Desktop*

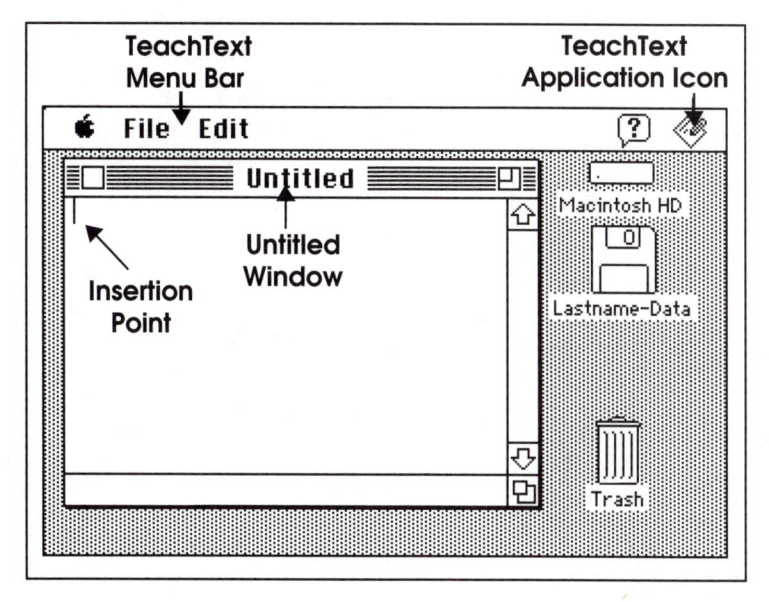

The Finder program has not disappeared. It continues to maintain the desktop and to control disk resources. It simply works in the **background** while the application program works in the **foreground.**

Anytime you open a new program, examine the menu bars. You will be encouraged by the number of commands you already know and will have an idea of what you must learn. You will even find that many of the commands are stored under the same menu names.

Step 5    Point to the File menu and hold the mouse button. Release the mouse button when you finish viewing the menu.

*Figure 8.2—TeachText File Menu*

```
┌─────────────────────┐
│ File                │
│ New          ⌘N     │
│ Open...      ⌘O     │
│                     │
│ Close        ⌘W     │
│ Save         ⌘S     │
│ Save As...          │
│                     │
│ Page Setup...       │
│ Print...     ⌘P     │
│                     │
│ Quit         ⌘Q     │
└─────────────────────┘
```

*Figure 8.3—TeachText Edit Menu*

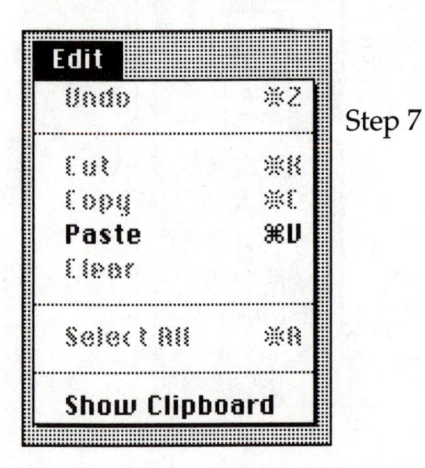

```
┌─────────────────────┐
│ Edit                │
│ Undo         ⌘Z     │
│                     │
│ Cut          ⌘X     │
│ Copy         ⌘C     │
│ Paste        ⌘V     │
│ Clear               │
│                     │
│ Select All   ⌘A     │
│                     │
│ Show Clipboard      │
└─────────────────────┘
```

## What's Happening

The File pull-down menu is displayed. (Figure 8.2) Some of the commands on this menu should look familiar: Open, Close, Page Setup, Print. We will discuss the other commands in this chapter.

**Step 6** Point to the Edit menu and hold the mouse button. Release the mouse button when you finish viewing the menu.

## What's Happening

The Edit pull-down menu is displayed. (Figure 8.3) Most of the commands on this menu should look familiar: Cut, Copy, Paste, Clear, Select All, Show Clipboard. The **Undo** command will sometimes reverse the last operation you performed. (It is not always available.) For example, if you accidentally cut a paragraph from your document, you can retrieve it if you immediately select Undo.

**Step 7** Review the hints on entering text in Figure 8.4 and text editing techniques in Figure 8.5. Then key in the letter in Figure 8.6. Your document will not look exactly the same as Figure 8.6. For instance, the lines within your document may not end on the same word. Do not press the Return key at the end of lines within a paragraph.

*Figure 8.4—Helpful Hints on Entering Text*

---

### Helpful Hints on Entering Text

- The flashing vertical line in the top left corner of the window identifies your current insertion point. As you start typing, the characters will appear here.

- Do not press the Return key at the end of the line within a paragraph. You will be using the word-wrap technique, which allows the program to automatically move to the next line. Your line breaks may not appear in the same locations as the example.

- You *do* need to press the Return key when you are on a sentence that does not fill the line and yet you need to advance to the next line (at the end of each address line, at the end of the greeting, at the end of the paragraph, and so on).

- Pressing the Return key twice at the end of a line creates a blank line.

---

*Figure 8.5—Text Editing Techniques*

---

### Text Editing Techniques

- **To erase a few characters:** Use the mouse to position the I-beam immediately after the characters you want to erase. Click once, move the mouse off to the side, and the cursor (flashing vertical line) will remain where you placed it. Press the Delete or Backspace key one time for each character you want to erase. Key in new characters if desired.

- **To erase an entire word:** Double click on the word (the word turns dark). Press the Delete key.

- **To erase an entire line:** Position the I-beam at one end of the text you wish to erase. Hold the mouse button down and drag the I-beam across the text—the text turns dark. Release the mouse button and press the Delete key.

- **To enter additional text:** Position the I-beam where the new text is to be inserted and click once. Key in your text.

- **To deselect text:** Click anywhere on the document.

*Figure 8.6—TeachText Document*

> MAC COMPUTERS
> 10 Orange Street
> Downtown, CA. 92999
>
> Dear Mr. Moore,
>
> Thank you for stopping by on Saturday to discuss your interest in purchasing a new Macintosh computer. I hope I answered all your questions satisfactorily. I truly feel the Macintosh is a great computer and that you would be pleased with the model we discussed. The Macintosh Performa 600 with 4MB of RAM and a 80MB hard drive should meet your immediate needs. It can be upgraded as your small company grows. For the price you can't beat it.
>
> Our company has been in business for eleven years and will be here to service your needs for years to come. The Macintosh comes with a warranty from Apple and you can purchase the Extended Warranty Service for a reasonable price. Any repairs you need will be handled at our store. We do not send your Macintosh across town for repairs.
>
> I look forward to doing business with you.
>
> Sincerely,
>
> Your Name

Step 8   Look at the document you just keyed in and correct errors as necessary. Verify that you have entered your name in the closing (last line).

Step 9   Choose the Save command from the File menu.

## What's Happening

The document you keyed in is currently being stored in RAM. A copy of it is not written to disk until you execute the Save command. That means if the power goes off or someone accidentally knocks the power cord loose, you have lost the entire document. You would have to enter the document again.

A Directory dialog box has appeared on your desktop. (Figure 8.7) You must direct the system where to save the document (disk and folder) and name the document.

CREATING A NEW DOCUMENT IN TEACHTEXT    183

*Figure 8.7—Directory Dialog Box*

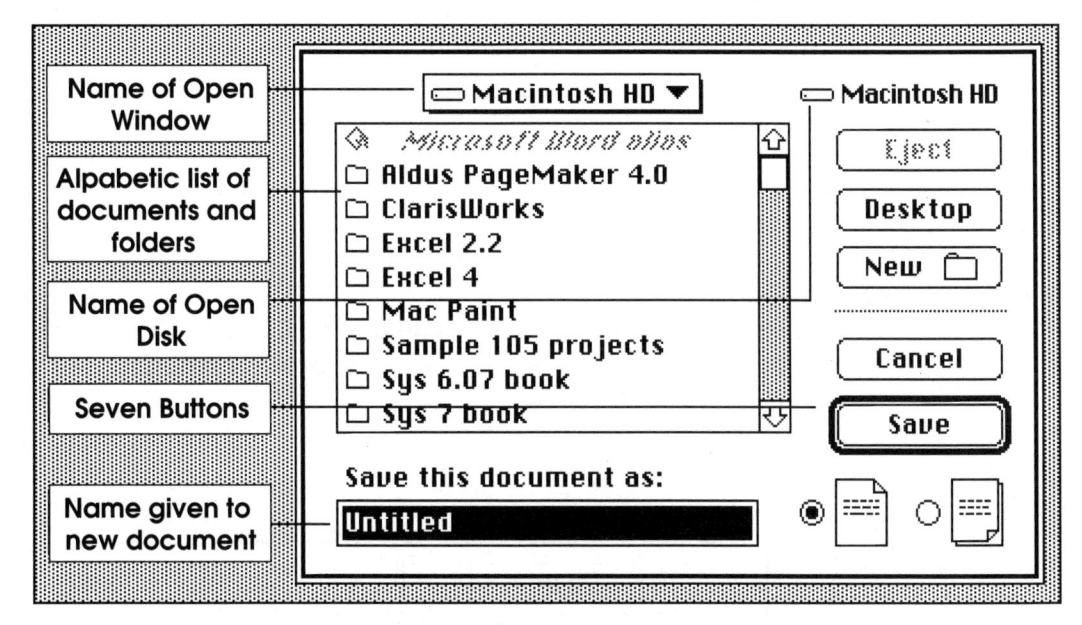

```
Name of Open Window ────────┐
                            │   ┌─ Macintosh HD ▼        ⌐ Macintosh HD
Alphabetic list of           │   Microsoft Word alias          [ Eject ]
documents and folders ──────┤   ▫ Aldus PageMaker 4.0
                            │   ▫ ClarisWorks                 [ Desktop ]
                            │   ▫ Excel 2.2
                            │   ▫ Excel 4                     [ New   ]
Name of Open Disk ──────────┤   ▫ Mac Paint
                            │   ▫ Sample 105 projects         [ Cancel ]
                            │   ▫ Sys 6.07 book
Seven Buttons ──────────────┤   ▫ Sys 7 book                  [ Save  ]
                            │
                            │   Save this document as:
Name given to               │   [ Untitled              ]    ● 📄  ○ 📄
new document ───────────────┘
```

Let's examine the contents of the Directory dialog box.
1. The name of the open window or desktop appears in the top left corner.
2. The list box contains an alphabetic list of files and folders in the open window.
3. The **Save this document as**: entry is available for you to enter the name of the new document.
4. The name of the active disk appears in the top right corner.
5. Seven buttons, some of which are dimmed and cannot be executed.
   - **Eject**—This button can be used to eject a floppy disk. It is only available if a floppy disk is the active disk.
   - **Desktop**—This button makes the desktop active and provides you access to icons on the desktop.
   - **New**—Use this button to create a new file folder on the active window or the desktop.
   - **Cancel**—Clicking on this button will close the Directory dialog box. It cancels your command.
   - **Save**—Click on this button to write your document to the active disk and window.
   - **TeachText Document**
   - **Stationary Pad Document**—The two icons in the bottom right corner are used to specify how the document is to be saved. If the icon on the left is selected, the document will be saved as a TeachText document. If the icon on the right is selected, the document will be saved as a stationary pad—a template to be used for future documents.

When you attempt to open a stationary document, a copy of the document is created and opened. The original stationary document does not change.

The Directory dialog box in Figure 8.7 shows the open window as the Startup disk—Macintosh HD. The current document is named Untitled. If you click on the Save button, the document will be saved on the Macintosh HD and called Untitled.

Step 10   Click on the Desktop button.

### What's Happening

You do not want to save your document on the Startup disk. Clicking on the Desktop button makes the desktop active and provides a list of icons on the desktop. (Figure 8.8)

*Figure 8.8—Active Desktop*

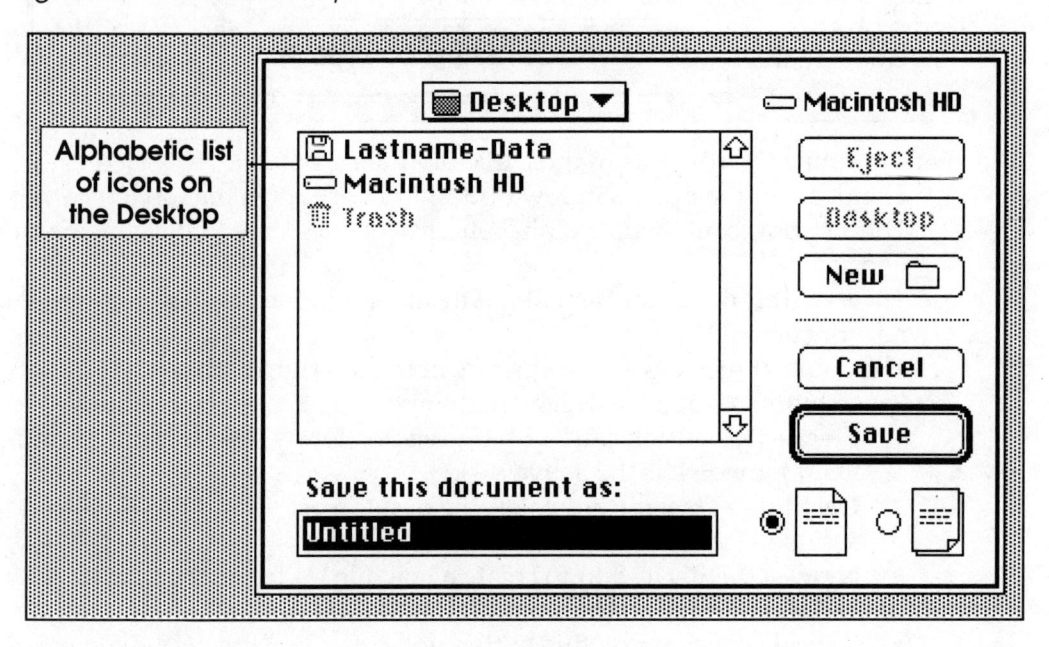

```
┌─────────────────────────────────────────────────┐
│                  Desktop ▼        ▭ Macintosh HD│
│ Alphabetic list  💾 Lastname-Data      [ Eject ]│
│   of icons on    ▭ Macintosh HD                 │
│   the Desktop    🗑 Trash              [Desktop]│
│                                        [ New 📁]│
│                                        [Cancel ]│
│                                        [ Save  ]│
│                  Save this document as:         │
│                  [Untitled          ]  ⦿📄 ○📄  │
└─────────────────────────────────────────────────┘
```

Step 11   Click once on the Lastname-Data icon to select it. Then click on the Open button.

### What's Happening

The Lastname-Data disk is activated. Its name appears in the top right corner of the Directory dialog box and on top of the list box.

Step 12   Click on the New button.

## What's Happening

Let's file all business letters in a file folder. Remember, file folders on the Macintosh are used to file related documents, just like paper file folders. Clicking on the New button will create a new file folder. A pop-up dialog box appears asking for the new folder's name.

Step 13   Key in the folder name—Business Ltrs. (Figure 8.9)

*Figure 8.9—Creating a New File Folder*

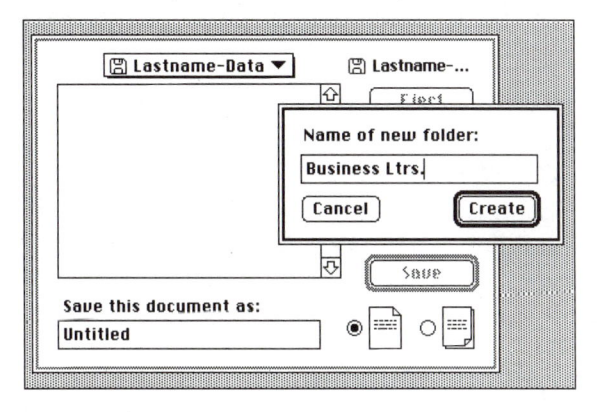

Step 14   Click on the Create button.

## What's Happening

The file folder, Business Ltrs., is created and becomes the active window.

Step 15   Press the Tab key until the entry Save this document as is highlighted. Key in the document name—Moore-Sales Ltr. Click on the Save button.

## What's Happening

The document is saved on disk as a file called Moore-Sales Ltr. The Directory dialog box disappears. (Figure 8.10) If you were to make any modifications to the document now, the changes would not be written out to disk until you issue the Save command again.

*Figure 8.10—Naming the Document*

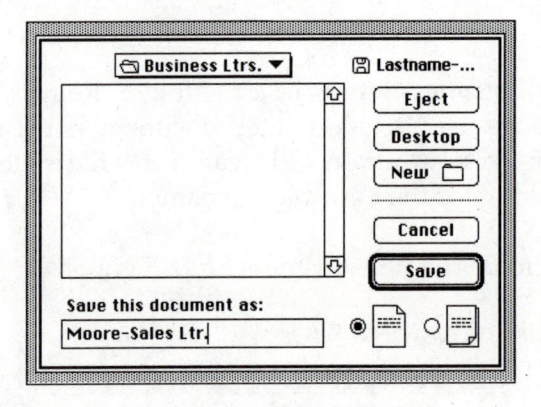

**Step 16** Choose the Close command from the File menu.

*What's Happening*

The Moore-Sales Ltr. window disappears from your desktop. The TeachText menu bar is still on top of your desktop.

**Step 17** Choose Quit from the File menu.

*What's Happening*

You have directed the system to close the application program TeachText. You are back at the Finder level. The Finder menu bar is displayed across the top of the desktop.

## Opening an Existing Document, Modifying it, and Saving it as a New Document

In this exercise, you will open the document you just created and saved, Moore-Sales Ltr. You will modify the document by erasing the customer name Mr. Moore and inserting a different customer's name, Ms. Taylor. Since you want to keep the original letter on your disk to Mr. Moore, you will use the Save As command to write this document to disk as Taylor-Sales Ltr. The **Save As** command allows you to rename a document and to specify a different folder or disk to save the document on. The **Save** command simply writes the modified document to the same location as the original document under the same name.

In order to modify an existing document, the application program must be read into RAM and then the document must be read into RAM. Some application programs have the ability to open documents that were created by a different application program. Figure 8.11 describes three methods to open documents.

*Figure 8.11—Three ways to Open a Document*

- Double-click on the application program icon. Use the program's Open command to open the document.

- Double-click on the document icon. The application program that created the document will automatically be loaded into memory and the document window will appear.

- Drag the document icon over the top of any application program icon that can open it. The application program will be read into memory and the document window will appear.

Note: Not all methods will work at all times. Some methods may not work on a network server.

## Activity 8.2—Modifying the Original Document

Step 1　Your computer should be booted. The Lastname-Data disk should be in the floppy drive. The Startup disk window should be open on the desktop.

Step 2　Double-click on the TeachText icon.

### What's Happening

The TeachText application program is loaded into RAM. The TeachText menu bar appears across the top to the desktop. A new window named Untitled appears on the desktop. You do not want to create a new document, you want to modify an existing document. The Untitled window must be closed.

Step 3　Click on the Close box to close the Untitled window.

Step 4　Choose the Open command from the TeachText File menu.

### What's Happening

The Directory dialog box appears displaying the name of your Startup disk.

Step 5　Click on the Desktop button to display a list of icons on the desktop.

Step 6　Double-click on the Lastname-Data icon in the list box.

## What's Happening

The Directory dialog box displays your Lastname-Data disk as the active disk. A list of folders and files on this disk is displayed in the list box.

Step 7   Double-click on the Business Ltrs. folder icon in the list box to open the folder.

Step 8   Double-click on the Moore-Sales Ltr. icon (in the list box).

## What's Happening

The Moore-Sales Ltr. document appears on your desktop.

Step 9   Position the I-beam after the salutation—Mr. Moore. Hold the mouse button down and drag the I-beam over Mr. Moore. Press the delete key and the name disappears. Type in the new name—Ms. Taylor.

## What's Happening

This letter is to be mailed to a second customer. There is no need to create the document from scratch if you can use an existing document and make minor changes to it. You have changed the name on the letter.

Step 10   Choose the Save As command from the File menu.

## What's Happening

The Save command would save the modified document in RAM as Moore-Sales Ltr. The original letter to Mr. Moore would be overwritten on disk by this modified document. To save this document to disk and leave the original document alone, you need to use the Save As command. The Save As command will provide a Directory dialog box to enable you to direct the system where to save this new file and to give it a new name.

Figure 8.12—Save this Document as

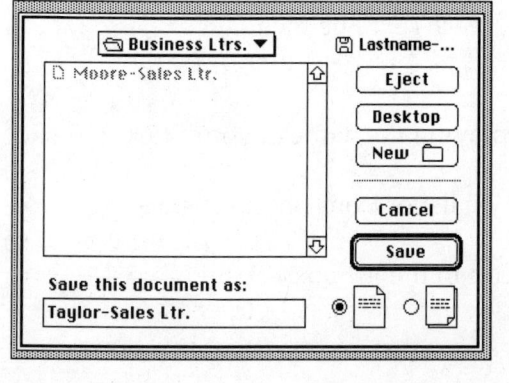

Step 11   Examine the Directory dialog box to verify the Lastname-Data disk is the active disk and that Business Ltrs. is the open window.

Step 12   The Save this document as: entry should be highlighted. Over the top of the old name (Moore-Sales Ltr.) key in the name of the new document—Taylor-Sales Ltr. (Figure 8.12)

Step 13   Click on the Save button.

## Pasting In The Scrapbook

In this exercise, you will paste the company's name to the Scrapbook. The Scrapbook, unlike the Clipboard, stores information until you instruct the system to remove it. Pictures, text, numbers—anything you want—can be copied to the Scrapbook. Weeks and months later you can copy information from the Scrapbook into a document.

### Activity 8.3—Coping Information and Pasting it in the Scrapbook

Step 1    Your computer is booted and the TeachText document, Taylor-Sales Ltr., is open on the desktop.

Step 2    Position the I-beam before the word MAC in the address, hold the mouse button down and drag down to highlight the three address lines. Release the mouse button.

*What's Happening*

You have selected three lines of text for further action.
MAC COMPUTERS
10 Orange Street
Downtown, CA 92999

Step 3    Choose Copy from the Edit menu.

*What's Happening*

A copy of the company's name and address has been placed on the Clipboard for temporary storage.

Step 4    Click anywhere on the document to deselect the text (text is no longer highlighted).

Step 5    Choose Scrapbook from the  menu (Scrapbook window appears).

Step 6    Choose Paste from the Edit menu.

*What's Happening*

A copy of the information stored in the Clipboard has been pasted into the Scrapbook. You will see it in the Scrapbook window. (Figure 8.13) The numbers in the bottom left corner tell you the number of the picture you are looking at and the number of pictures currently stored in the Scrapbook.

*Figure 8.13—Pasting in the Scrapbook*

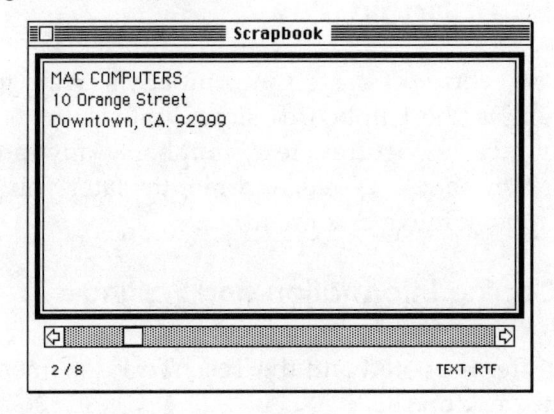

```
┌─────────────── Scrapbook ───────────────┐
│ ┌─────────────────────────────────────┐ │
│ │ MAC COMPUTERS                       │ │
│ │ 10 Orange Street                    │ │
│ │ Downtown, CA. 92999                 │ │
│ │                                     │ │
│ │                                     │ │
│ │                                     │ │
│ │                                     │ │
│ └─────────────────────────────────────┘ │
│  2/8                          TEXT, RTF │
└─────────────────────────────────────────┘
```

Step 7    Close the Scrapbook window.

Step 8    Close the Taylor-Sales Ltr. window.

## Copying from the Scrapbook

In Activity 8.3, you saved the name and address of the company in the Scrapbook. You will now create a new letter to the employees using the information in the Scrapbook.

### Activity 8.4—Creating a New Letter and Copying Information from the Scrapbook

Step 1    Verify your computer is booted, the TeachText program has been started and the TeachText menu bar is across the top of the desktop.

Step 2    Choose **New** from the File menu to open a new Untitled document window.

Step 3    Choose Scrapbook from the  menu. The Scrapbook window appears.

Step 4    If the Company name and address is not the current picture in the Scrapbook, scroll until you see it on the Scrapbook window.

Step 5    Choose Copy from the Edit menu.

*What's Happening*

A copy of the current picture in the Scrapbook is copied to the Clipboard.

Step 6   Close the Scrapbook.

Step 7   Choose Paste from the Edit menu.

*What's Happening*

Whatever is on the Clipboard is automatically inserted in your current document at the point of insertion. The company name and address should now appear in the Untitled document window.

Step 8   Key in the rest of the letter. (Figure 8.14)

*Figure 8.14—Employee Letter*

---

Dear Employees,

This company has had a great year. Sales have increased by twenty percent. We have opened two new stores and plan on opening a third one next year.

You are responsible for a large portion of our success. Without you the company could not succeed. Your friendliness and expertise keeps the customers coming back for more.

Effective next month your paychecks will reflect a ten percent increase in salary. Thanks for your hard work and loyalty.

Sincerely,

Pat Smith

---

Step 9   Choose Save from the File menu.

*What's Happening*

The Directory dialog box appears. You are to save this document as Employee Letter in the Lastname-Data window, not in the Business Ltr. folder.

Step 10  Position the mouse on the triangle next to the name of the open window. Press and hold the mouse button.

## What's Happening

A pop-up menu appears. (Figure 8.15) It shows that you are currently in the Business Ltrs. folder, which is stored on the Lastname-Data disk, and the Lastname-Data disk is located on the desktop.

*Figure 8.15—Displaying the Pop-up Menu*

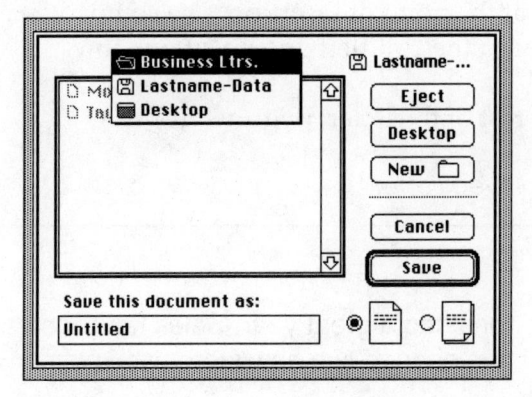

Step 11  Drag the arrow down the list until Lastname-Data is highlighted. Release the mouse button.

## What's Happening

The Directory dialog box now displays Lastname-Data as the active window.

Step 12  Press the Tab key to highlight the entry Save this document as.

Step 13  Key in the new name, Employee Letter. (Figure 8.16)

*Figure 8.16—Saving Employee Letter*

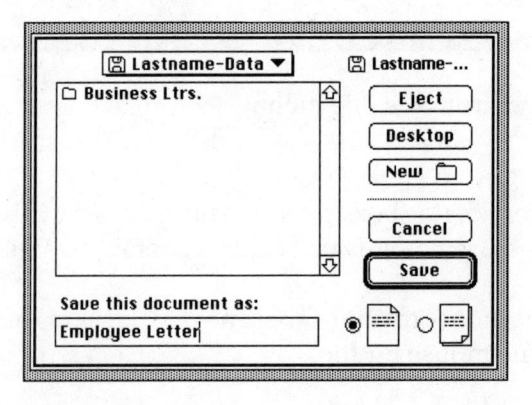

Step 14  Click on the Save button.

## Printing the Letters

What good would it be to create letters if you never print them? In this exercise, you will print the Employee Letter and the Moore-Sales Ltr. Refer to Chapter 7 Printing, if you need more explanation on the Chooser, Page Setup, and Print windows.

### Activity 8.5—Printing Two Letters

Step 1  The Employee Letter should still be on your desktop.

Step 2  Turn the printer on.

Step 3  Choose the Chooser DA from the Apple menu. If necessary, enter the correct entries in the Chooser window.

Step 4  Choose Page Setup from the File menu, verify the settings are correct, and close the window.

Step 5  Choose Print from the File menu, verify settings, and click on the Print, or OK button.

*What's Happening*

Status boxes may appear on your desktop as the document is printed.

Step 6  Close the Employee Letter window.

*What's Happening*

The letter disappears from the desktop.

Step 7  Choose **Open** from the TeachText File menu.

*What's Happening*

The Directory dialog box appears. Lastname-Data is the open window. The Moore-Sales Ltr. is in the Business Ltrs. folder.

Step 8  Double-click on the Business Ltrs. icon in the list box of the Directory dialog box. Double-click on the Moore-Sales Ltr. icon in the list box.

## *What's Happening*

The Moore-Sales Ltr. document is loaded into RAM and appears on your desktop.

Step 9  Choose Page Setup from the File menu, verify the settings are correct, and close the window.

Step 10  Choose Print from the File menu, verify settings, and click on the Print, or OK button.

Step 11  Close the Moore-Sales Ltr window.

Step 12  Choose Quit from the File menu.

## Removing The Entry From Your Scrapbook

You do not want to leave unnecessary entries in your Scrapbook. They take up disk space.

### Activity 8.6—Cutting an Entry from the Scrapbook

Step 1  Choose Scrapbook from the  menu.

Step 2  If the Company's name and address is not the current picture in your Scrapbook, use the scroll bar to find it.

Step 3  Choose Cut from the Edit menu.

### *What's Happening*

The picture containing the company name and address has been removed from the Scrapbook.

Step 4  Close all open windows.

## Key Terms

| | |
|---|---|
| Background | Open ⌘ O |
| Directory dialog box | Save ⌘ S |
| Foreground | Save As |
| New button | TeachText |
| New ⌘ N | Undo |

## Discussion Questions

1. What happens to the Finder program while you are working with TeachText?
2. What should you store in the Scrapbook?
3. Describe the difference between the Clipboard and the Scrapbook.
4. Describe the difference between Save and Save As.

## True/False Questions

For each question, circle the letter T if the statement is true and the letter F if the statement is false.

T  F   1. When you execute (start) an application program, the Finder program is no longer needed or in control.
T  F   2. As you create a document in TeachText, it is automatically written to disk.
T  F   3. TeachText is a great word processor—there is no need to buy a better one.
T  F   4. TeachText comes with your Macintosh operating system.
T  F   5. As you start the TeachText program, a new Untitled document window will appear on your desktop.
T  F   6. The first time you save the document to disk, the Macintosh will request a file name.
T  F   7. Commands available on application menu bars vary from the Finder menu bar.
T  F   8. The Scrapbook is volatile. In other words, when you turn the Macintosh off, the Scrapbook is wiped out.
T  F   9. The number in the left corner of the Scrapbook scroll bar tells you how many "pictures" you have pasted in the Scrapbook.
T  F  10. You can't access the desk accessories while working in TeachText.
T  F  11. You can't directly access the Finder menu bar while you are inside an application program.
T  F  12. The keyboard equivalents for the following commands are the same in TeachText as they are for the Finder: Open, Close, Cut, Copy, Paste, Undo.

## Completion Questions

Write the correct answer in each blank space.

1. As you create a document in TeachText, it is stored in _____.
2. To execute an application program, _____ on its icon.
3. Use the ____ command available on the ____ menu to reverse the last step you took.

4. To select an entire word, _____ on the word.
5. To insert characters on a line, position the _____ where you want to type and click the mouse button.
6. The keyboard equivalent to the Save command is _____.
7. If you wish to save your modified document under a different name than the original document, use the _____ _____ command.
8. The application program you are using works in the _____ while the Macintosh operating system continues to work in the _____.
9. The _____ available on the _____ menu allows you to paste text and pictures in it for copying to other documents at a later time.
10. The Scrapbook is stored on your _____ disk.
11. Choose the _____ command of the _____ menu when you are finished working with TeachText and wish to return to the Finder level.
12. To remove pictures from the Scrapbook use the _____ or _____ commands on the _____ menu.

## Assignments

Boot your Macintosh. The Macintosh desktop should be clean—no open windows. Insert your Lastname-Sys 7 disk in the available floppy drive. The TeachText application program should be on your Startup disk.

### Part 1

Practice opening, modifying, and printing a document created in TeachText.

1. Load the TeachText program into RAM. Open the Sample Teach Text Doc file. It is stored in the Misc. folder on your Lastname-Sys 7 disk.
   This document obviously needs work.

   > Teach Text is a simplistic wrod processing program that comes with the MAC OS. WHY? Sometimes the OS's documentation (manuals) are written, printed and ready to go, and then one of the programmers decides to add an additional option to the OS. How do you get the news out? By creating a file using Teach Text, naming the file READ ME and putting it on one of the disks included in the package.
   >
   > This program is not a full word processing program, it is missing many options.

Missing Options:
> Spell Checker
> Fonts
> Point Size
> Style (bold, shadowed)
> Ruler line, including tab stops
> Spacing
> Justification

2. Make the following modifications to this document. The underlined words identify changes or additions to the original document.

<u>Name:</u> <u>Your Name</u>
<u>Date:</u>   <u>Current Date</u>
<u>Class:</u>  <u>Meeting Day and time</u>

Teach Text is a <u>simple word</u> processing program that comes with the MAC OS. WHY? Sometimes the OS's documentation (manuals) are written, printed and ready to go, <u>when</u> one of the programmers decides to <u>include</u> an additional option <u>or modification</u> to the OS <u>programs</u>. <u>Obviously, Apple does not want to reprint all the manuals but</u> how do <u>they</u> <u>share</u> the news? By creating a <u>TeachText</u> file <u>named</u> <u>READ ME</u> and <u>placing</u> it on one of the disks included in the <u>software</u> package.

<u>Other software manufacturers know that all Mac users have access to the TeachText program. Last minute Read Me files are frequently found on their disks.</u>

<u>The TeachText</u> program is not a full word processing program, it is missing many options.

> Missing Options <u>include</u>:
> Spell Checker
> Fonts
> Point Size
> Style (bold, shadowed)
> Ruler line, including tab stops
> Spacing
> Justification

3. Choose the Save command from the File menu. The old document will be written over by this new one. A dialog box will not appear on your desktop.

4. Print the document. Close this document.

5. If you wish to exit the TeachText program, choose Quit from the File menu. If you wish to continue with Part 2, choose New from the File menu. A new Untitled document window will open.

## Part 2

Create and print a new TeachText document. If the TeachText program is not open, locate the TeachText program and double-click on its icon.

1. Write 2 short paragraphs describing your observations and feelings about this course.
   Paragraph 1 should list 3 reasons why you liked this course.
   Paragraph 2 should list 3 ways the course could be improved.
   Be sure to include your name, the date, and when this class meets (day and time) on the top of the document.

2. Choose the Save command of the File menu. Click on the Eject button to remove the Lastname-Sys 7 disk from the drive. Insert the Lastname-Data disk in the drive. Examine the Directory dialog box to verify the Lastname-Data disk is your active disk. Save this document on your Lastname-Data disk. Name the document, System 7 Class Observations.

3. Print the document. Close this document. Quit TeachText.

   Close all open windows.

# 9 File Manipulation:
## Duplicating, Copying, Renaming, Locking, Erasing, and Customizing Files

## Learning Objectives

**After completing this Chapter you will be able to:**

1. Duplicate a single file or a group of files.
2. Copy one or more files from one disk to another.
3. Rename a file using one of several methods.
4. Remove one or more files from the disk.
5. Describe when and how the Trash is emptied.
6. Retrieve one or more files from the Trash.
7. Explain how, why, and when to lock and unlock files.
8. Describe how to customize an icon.

## Introduction

This chapter will discuss how to manipulate files and the associated commands. Remember, a file is a collection of information stored on the disk. A file may be an application program or a document created within an application program—a letter, for example. Some commands have been discussed in earlier chapters but others will be new. You will learn how to lock, unlock, duplicate, copy, rename, and erase files. You will also look at several ways to customize icons. Icons represent objects and files on the desktop and in windows: documents, application programs, folders, disks, Trash. As you perform the activities within this chapter keep in mind that when you copy an icon from one disk to another you are copying the object the icon represents. When you make a duplicate copy of an icon, you are making a duplicate copy of the object the icon represents.

To complete the exercises in this chapter you will need three disks: Startup, Lastname-Sys 7, and Lastname-Data.

## Locking and Unlocking Files

An entire floppy disk may be write-protected by moving the write-protect tab on the back of the disk so that a hole appears in the floppy cover. An individual file may be write-protected (**locked**) by using the Get Info command. Do not lock application programs or System files. Many of these files will not work if they are locked.

If you choose to lock a file you may not rename the file, modify its contents, or erase the file, unless you first unlock the file. You may, however, duplicate the file or copy it to another disk. The duplicate file will not be locked. When you copy a file to another disk, the write-protection goes with the file. The file on the destination disk will be locked. Let's try this out by locking a file and then duplicating and copying it.

### Activity 9.1—Locking a File

Step 1  Boot your Macintosh. Place your unlocked Lastname-Sys 7 disk in the floppy drive.

Step 2  Open the Lastname-Sys 7 disk window. Display the contents of the window in a list view by name. Click on the zoom box to display the entire contents of the window.

Step 3  Examine the Picture 1 entry: name, size, kind, label, last modified.

Step 4  Click once on Picture 1 file icon to select it.

Step 5  Choose Get Info from the File menu.

Step 6  Click once in the Locked checkbox.

*What's Happening*

An **X** should appear in the checkbox. This indicates the file is now locked. (Figure 9.1)

*Figure 9.1—Locking a File*

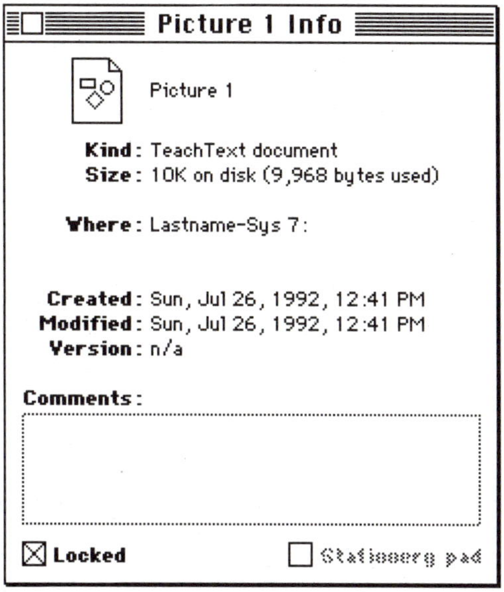

**Step 7**  Close the Picture 1 Info window.

**Step 8**  Examine the Picture 1 entry in the list window. A padlock now appears to the right of the last column. The padlock indicates the file is locked.

## Duplicate Command

Selecting the **Duplicate** command from the File menu will create a copy of the selected icon(s). If the selected icon is an application program, you create a copy of that application program. If the selected icon is a document file, you create a copy of that document file. If the selected icon is a folder, you create a copy of that folder and everything that is stored inside. The copies are automatically placed on the same disk and window as the original and are named the original file name followed by the word "copy." You may duplicate a file while in an icon or list view window. Frequently, Macintosh users will create duplicate files in order to modify them, leaving the original intact.

### Activity 9.2—Duplicating a File

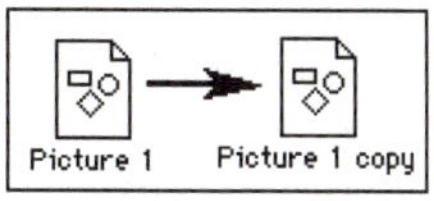

**Step 1**  Your Macintosh is on and booted. The unlocked Lastname-Sys 7 disk is in the floppy drive. The disk window is open. Display the window in an icon view.

**Step 2**  Click once on the Picture 1 file icon to select it.

Step 3   Choose **Duplicate** from the File menu.

*Figure 9.2—Duplicating a File*

**What's Happening**

A status box will appear to inform you of the copy progress. (Figure 9.2) A copy of the icon (file) will appear on your Lastname-Sys 7 window. It has been named Picture 1 copy.

Step 4   Display the Lastname-Sys 7 window in a list view by name.

**What's Happening**

Examine the Picture 1 copy entry. It contains the same information as the original file (size, kind, label, last modified) but the padlock does not appear to the right of the last column. The duplicate of a locked file is not locked.

Step 5   Select the Picture 1 copy icon. Choose Get Info from the File menu. Lock the file and close the Info window.

**What's Happening**

The padlock now appears on the Picture 1 copy entry.

### Activity 9.3—Duplicating a Group of Files

Step 1   The Lastname-Sys 7 window is displayed in a list view by name.

Step 2   Hold down the Shift key while clicking on three icons: EMPLOYEE-DB-CW, Friends-DB-CW, Jan. Profit-CW.

**What's Happening**

All three icons are highlighted, indicating that these objects have been selected for further action.

Step 3   Choose Duplicate from the File menu.

**What's Happening**

A status box will appear to inform you of the system's progress in duplicating the three files. Three new file names will then appear in the window: EMPLOYEE-DB-CW copy, Friends-DB-CW copy, Jan. Profit-CW copy. Notice the file names have been copied exactly (upper/lower case) and the word copy has been added to the names. The three new files are the active objects.

*Figure 9.3—New files appear in List Window*

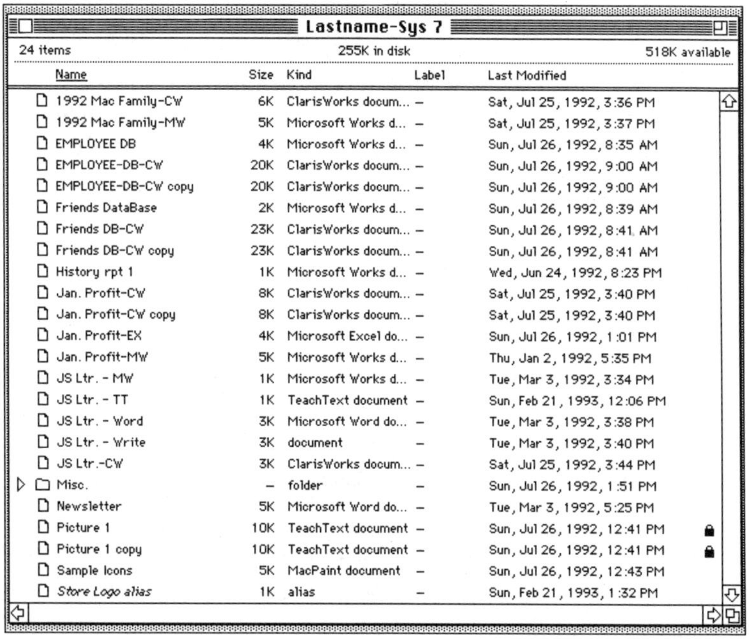

```
┌─────────────────────── Lastname-Sys 7 ───────────────────────┐
│ 24 items              255K in disk              518K available│
│   Name                     Size  Kind            Label  Last Modified      │
│   □ 1992 Mac Family-CW     6K    ClarisWorks docum...  –    Sat, Jul 25, 1992, 3:36 PM │
│   □ 1992 Mac Family-MW     5K    Microsoft Works d...  –    Sat, Jul 25, 1992, 3:37 PM │
│   □ EMPLOYEE DB            4K    Microsoft Works d...  –    Sun, Jul 26, 1992, 8:35 AM │
│   □ EMPLOYEE-DB-CW         20K   ClarisWorks docum...  –    Sun, Jul 26, 1992, 9:00 AM │
│   □ EMPLOYEE-DB-CW copy    20K   ClarisWorks docum...  –    Sun, Jul 26, 1992, 9:00 AM │
│   □ Friends DataBase       2K    Microsoft Works d...  –    Sun, Jul 26, 1992, 8:39 AM │
│   □ Friends DB-CW          23K   ClarisWorks docum...  –    Sun, Jul 26, 1992, 8:41 AM │
│   □ Friends DB-CW copy     23K   ClarisWorks docum...  –    Sun, Jul 26, 1992, 8:41 AM │
│   □ History rpt 1          1K    Microsoft Works d...  –    Wed, Jun 24, 1992, 8:23 PM │
│   □ Jan. Profit-CW         8K    ClarisWorks docum...  –    Sat, Jul 25, 1992, 3:40 PM │
│   □ Jan. Profit-CW copy    8K    ClarisWorks docum...  –    Sat, Jul 25, 1992, 3:40 PM │
│   □ Jan. Profit-EX         4K    Microsoft Excel do... –    Sun, Jul 26, 1992, 1:01 PM │
│   □ Jan. Profit-MW         5K    Microsoft Works d...  –    Thu, Jan 2, 1992, 5:35 PM  │
│   □ JS Ltr. - MW           1K    Microsoft Works d...  –    Tue, Mar 3, 1992, 3:34 PM  │
│   □ JS Ltr. - TT           1K    TeachText document    –    Sun, Feb 21, 1993, 12:06 PM│
│   □ JS Ltr. - Word         3K    Microsoft Word do...  –    Tue, Mar 3, 1992, 3:38 PM  │
│   □ JS Ltr. - Write        3K    document              –    Tue, Mar 3, 1992, 3:40 PM  │
│   □ JS Ltr.-CW             3K    ClarisWorks docum...  –    Sat, Jul 25, 1992, 3:44 PM │
│ ▷ □ Misc.                  –     folder               –    Sun, Jul 26, 1992, 1:51 PM │
│   □ Newsletter             5K    Microsoft Word do...  –    Tue, Mar 3, 1992, 5:25 PM  │
│   □ Picture 1              10K   TeachText document    –    Sun, Jul 26, 1992, 12:41 PM│
│   □ Picture 1 copy         10K   TeachText document    –    Sun, Jul 26, 1992, 12:41 PM│
│   □ Sample Icons           5K    MacPaint document     –    Sun, Jul 26, 1992, 12:43 PM│
│   □ *Store Logo alias*     1K    alias                 –    Sun, Feb 21, 1993, 1:32 PM │
└──────────────────────────────────────────────────────────────┘
```

Step 4   Click on an empty spot on the window to deselect all icons. (Figure 9.3)

At this point, you could safely open an application program and modify these three duplicate files. The original files would remain the same.

## Copying Files From One Disk to Another

In this activity, you will copy four files from the Lastname-Sys 7 disk to the Lastname-Data disk. The four files will exist on both disks. In Chapter 3 you learned how to copy the entire contents of one floppy disk (source) to another floppy disk (destination); drag the source disk icon over the top of the destination disk icon. There are two reasons why that method will not work this time.

- You do not want to copy all the files on the source disk to the destination disk.
- The destination disk already has files stored on it. The floppy to floppy copy process removes all files from the destination disk prior to copying the new files.

Both floppy disk icons must be on the Macintosh desktop during the copy process. You will be using one floppy drive and swapping source and destination disks to accomplish this task. Files will be read into RAM from the source disk. You will be directed to swap disks and the files will be read from RAM and written to the destination disk. Figure 9.4 diagrams this process.

*Figure 9.4—Copying Files between Disks*

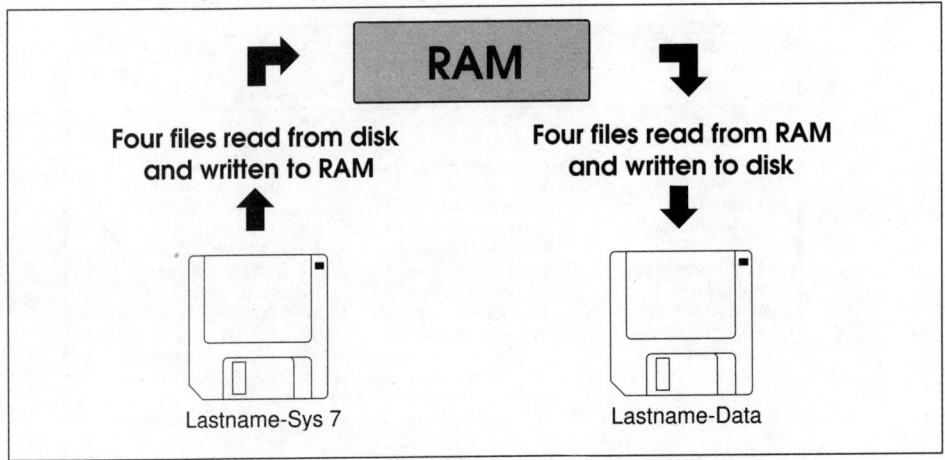

**RAM**

Four files read from disk and written to RAM

Four files read from RAM and written to disk

Lastname-Sys 7

Lastname-Data

## Activity 9.4—Copying Files from One Floppy to Another

Step 1   Your Macintosh is on and booted. The unlocked Lastname-Sys 7 disk is in the floppy drive. The disk window is open and is displayed in a list view by name.

Step 2   Click on the Lastname-Sys 7 disk icon to select it.

*What's Happening*

The disk icon becomes the active object on the desktop. The horizontal lines in the title bar of the Lastname-Sys 7 window disappear.

Step 3   Choose Eject Disk from the Special menu.

*What's Happening*

The floppy disk is ejected from the drive. The Macintosh will occasionally request that you reinsert the disk you just ejected. If this happens, place the disk back in the drive and eject it again.

Step 4   Insert your Lastname-Data disk in the drive.

*What's Happening*

You now have three disk icons on the desktop: Startup (Macintosh HD), Lastname-Sys 7 and Lastname-Data.

Step 5   Hold down the Shift key while clicking on the four files to copy from the Lastname-Sys 7 window: Picture 1 copy, EMPLOYEE-DB-CW copy, Friends-DB-CW copy, Jan. Profit-CW copy.

## What's Happening

All 4 files have been selected and are highlighted.

Step 6    Position the arrow pointer on one of the four files, hold down the mouse button and drag the group to the Lastname-Data disk icon (the disk icon turns dark). Release the mouse button. (Figure 9.5)

## What's Happening

The disk is ejected from the drive. A dialog box appears requesting the source disk. (Figure 9.6)

*Figure 9.6—Switching Disks*

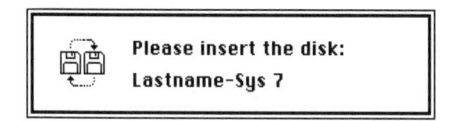

Step 7    Insert the Lastname-Sys 7 disk in the drive.

## What's Happening

Two status boxes will appear. The first one informs you that the system is preparing to copy 1-2-3-4 files. The second status indicates the system is reading 4 files into RAM. (Figure 9.7)

Once the files have been read into RAM, the Lastname-Sys 7 disk will be ejected and you will be asked to insert the Lastname-Data disk. (Figure 9.8)

Step 8    Insert the Lastname-Data disk.

*Figure 9.5—Copying 4 Files from One Floppy Disk to Another*

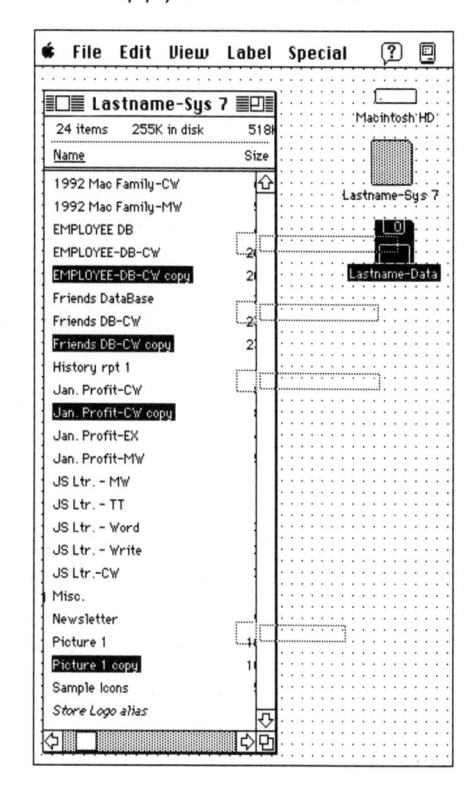

*Figure 9.7—Verifying and Reading*

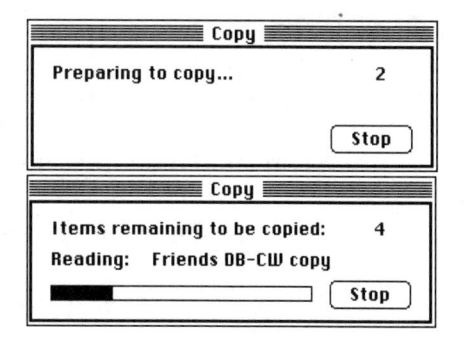

*Figure 9.8—Inserting Destination Disk*

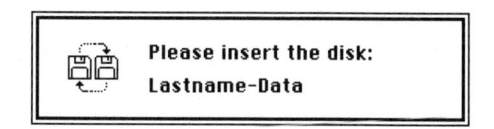

*Figure 9.9—Writing and Verifying*

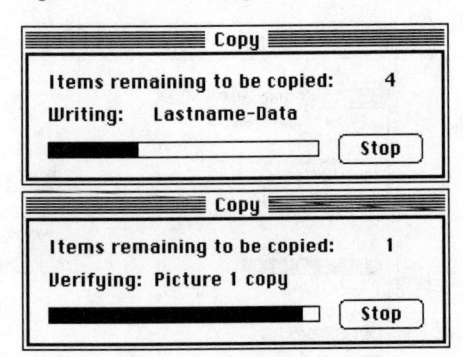

```
┌─────────── Copy ───────────┐
│ Items remaining to be copied:   4    │
│ Writing:   Lastname-Data             │
│ ▇▇▇▇▇▇▇▇▇▇▇▇▇▇▇▇▇▇▇ [ Stop ]        │
└──────────────────────────────┘

┌─────────── Copy ───────────┐
│ Items remaining to be copied:   1    │
│ Verifying: Picture 1 copy            │
│ ▇▇▇▇▇▇▇▇▇▇▇▇▇▇▇▇▇▇▇ [ Stop ]        │
└──────────────────────────────┘
```

*What's Happening*

Two status boxes will appear to inform you of the system progress: Writing, Verifying. When the copy process is done, the status boxes will disappear. Switch disks as directed. (Figure 9.9)

Step 9  Double-click on the Lastname-Data disk icon to open the disk window. Display the disk window in list view by name.

*What's Happening*

Examine the disk window to verify the 4 files have been copied. Look at the Picture 1 copy entry. This file was locked on the source disk and is therefore locked on the destination disk. The disk also contains the Business Ltrs. folder that you created in Chapter 8.

Step 10  Click on the close box of the Lastname-Data window and drag the disk icon to the Trash.

Step 11  Insert the Lastname-Sys 7 disk, close the disk window, and drag the disk icon to the Trash.

---

# Renaming Files

Occasionally you may wish to **rename** an icon (file, folder, disk). This is a simple process which can be done in a list or icon view window. You can't rename the System and Finder files, locked documents, application icons, or locked disks.

### Activity 9.5—Renaming Files

**Change the name of Jan. Profit-CW copy to Mac Store Profit-Jan**

Step 1  Your Macintosh is on and booted. Insert your unlocked Lastname-Data disk in the floppy drive. Open the disk window and display the window by icon.

Step 2  Place the mouse pointer on the icon name Jan. Profit-CW copy, and click once. Do not move the pointer off the icon name.

*What's Happening*
>Wait a couple of seconds and the name will appear in an outlined box. The pointer arrow will change to an I-beam.

Step 3    Key in the new name—Mac Store Profit-Jan.

Step 4    Click an empty spot of the window to deselect the icon.

*What's Happening*
>You have completely replaced the original name.

**Change the name of EMPLOYEE-DB-CW copy to Employee-Mac Store**

Step 5    Click once on the icon EMPLOYEE-DB-CW copy.

*What's Happening*
>The icon turns dark but the name does not appear in an outlined box. Since you did not click on the icon's name, the system simply selected the icon for further action.

Step 6    Press the Return or Enter key.

*What's Happening*
>The icon name appears in an outlined box and is ready to be edited.

Step 7    Key in the new name—Employee-Mac Store.

Step 8    Click an empty spot of the window to deselect the icon.

*What's Happening*
>You have completely replaced the original name.

**Change the name of Friends-DB-CW copy to Personal Friends**

Step 9    Display the Lastname-Data disk window in a list view window by name.

Step 10   Click on the icon name Friends-DB-CW copy.

Step 11   Position the I-beam immediately following the word "Friends." Hold the mouse button down and drag the I-beam to the right until -DB-CW copy is highlighted. Release the mouse button.

*What's Happening*
>You have selected text for further action.

*Figure 9.10—Renaming Files*

```
┌─────────────────────────┐
│ ▣≡  Lastname-Data  ≡▣  │
├─────────────────────────┤
│ 5 items   96K in disk 68│
├─────────────────────────┤
│    Name                 │
│ ▷ 📁 Business Ltrs.    ⇧│
│   📄 Employee-Mac Store │
│   📄 Mac Store Profit-Jan.│
│   📄 Personal Friends   │
│   📄 Picture 1 copy    ⇩│
│ ⇦                     ⇨ │
└─────────────────────────┘
```

Step 12  Press the Delete key to remove the selected text.

Step 13  Position the I-beam immediately in front of the word Friends. Click once to identify your point of insertion. Type Personal and press the space bar once.

*What's Happening*

You have renamed the Personal Friends file. (Figure 9.10)

Step 14  Click on an empty spot of the window to deselect the icon.

**Try to rename the Picture 1 copy file**

Step 15  Click on the Picture 1 copy icon's name.

*What's Happening*

Because the icon is locked, the name will not appear in an outlined box. You cannot rename a locked file.

Usually icon names are so short, it is faster to select the icon name and simply key in the new name. You can also use normal text editing techniques to modify icon names.

## Customizing Icons

In Chapter 11 you will learn how to specify the font and point size to be used for icon names. You will also learn how to change the size of icons through the Views Control Panel. This activity will explain how to assign a label and a different icon to a file.

### Using Labels

Seven label names are available on the Label menu. Each label is assigned a color or shade of gray (if your Macintosh monitor can display at least 16 colors or shades of gray and it has been set to do so). You can customize your Macintosh system by modifying the label names and associated colors found on this menu by using the Labels Control Panel (discussed in Chapter 11).

You may assign labels to icons by using the Labels Finder menu. This feature of the operating system allows you to group related items by color and/or label name. For instance, you can assign the same label to a group of files that are related to a specific project. The icons will be displayed in the color assigned to the label (depending on your monitor) and the label name will appear in the list view window. When you sort by Label, the files will be grouped together in the list view window.

### Activity 9.6—Assigning a Label to an Icon

Step 1   Your Macintosh is on and booted. Your unlocked Lastname-Data disk is in the floppy drive, and the disk window is displayed in a list view by name.

Step 2   Click on the Employee-Mac Store icon to select the icon.

Step 3   Display your Label menu. Look at the available labels.

*What's Happening*

The Label names and colors may vary from the ones displayed in Figure 9.11. The label menu on the left shows the label menu for a Macintosh system with a color or gray-scale monitor. The menu on the right is for a monochrome monitor.

*Figure 9.11—Label Menu*

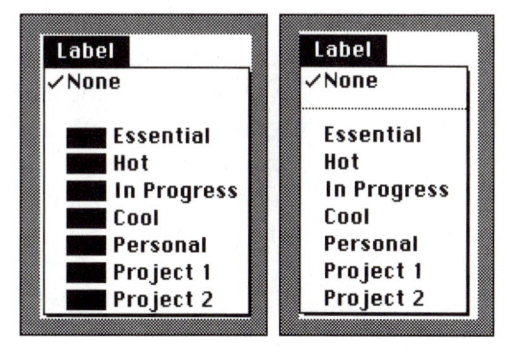

Step 4   Choose the first label (below None) in your Label menu.

*What's Happening*

This label name has been assigned to the Employee-Mac Store icon. Look at the Label column in the Lastname-Data list window. The label name should appear in this column.

Step 5   Assign the icon, Mac Store Profit-Jan., the same label.

*What's Happening*

Figure 9.12 shows that both files have been assigned the label Essential.

*Figure 9.12—Assigning Labels*

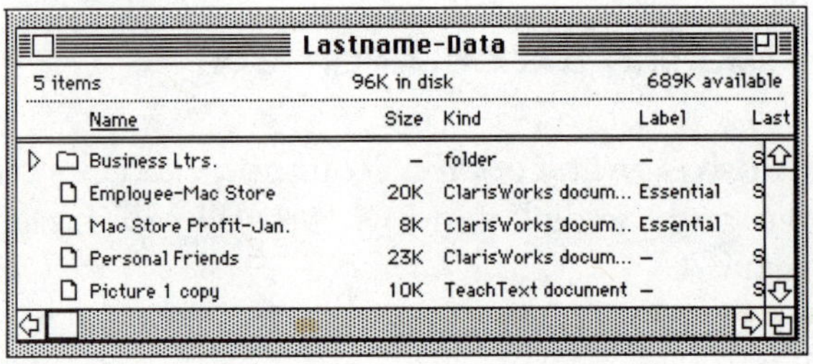

```
┌─────────────────── Lastname-Data ───────────────────┐
│ 5 items              96K in disk         689K available│
│   Name                    Size  Kind         Label     │
│ ▷ 🗀 Business Ltrs.         —    folder        —        │
│   🗋 Employee-Mac Store    20K   ClarisWorks docum... Essential │
│   🗋 Mac Store Profit-Jan.  8K   ClarisWorks docum... Essential │
│   🗋 Personal Friends      23K   ClarisWorks docum... — │
│   🗋 Picture 1 copy        10K   TeachText document —   │
└─────────────────────────────────────────────────────┘
```

### Removing Labels

Step 6    Click on the Employee-Mac Store icon. Choose None from the Label menu to remove the Essential label.

If you plan on using the labeling feature of System 7, you should use the Labels Control Panel to create label names and colors that reflect your icon grouping needs.

### Changing Icons

Application programs assign icons to the document files you create. The icon can help to identify which application program created the file and sometimes what type of file it represents. Claris Works assigns the same icon to all files. On the other hand, Microsoft Works assigns different icons to files according to the type of file it represents: a database, text, spreadsheet, or communication file. If you don't like the icon that was assigned to a file, System 7 allows you to change it. You may create a new icon picture in a paint or draw program or copy it from another source.

Two files on the Lastname-Data disk are database files. Let's assign a new icon to both files.

### Activity 9.7—Changing Icons

Step 1    Your Macintosh is on and booted. Your unlocked Lastname-Data disk is in the floppy drive. Display the disk window by icon.

Step 2    Double-click on the Picture 1 copy icon.

*What's Happening*

This file is locked. A warning dialog box will appear. (Figure 9.13)

CUSTOMIZING ICONS   211

Step 3   Click on the OK button.

*Figure 9.13—Locked File Warning*

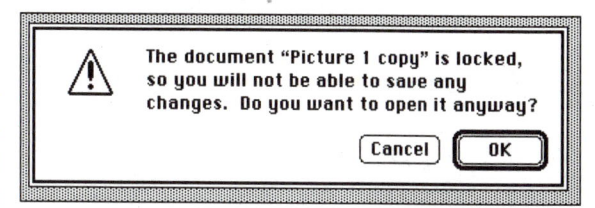

*What's Happening*

This file is a TeachText picture file. The TeachText program will be loaded into RAM and the Picture 1 copy window will appear on your desktop. This file contains sample icons. The arrow pointer has changed to cross-beams. ✛ You are going to select the icon in the top row, right corner.

Step 4   Position the cross-beam just above the left corner of the icon, hold the mouse button down and drag diagonally to **create a box around the icon.** (Figure 9.14) Release the mouse button.

*Figure 9.14—Selecting a Picture*

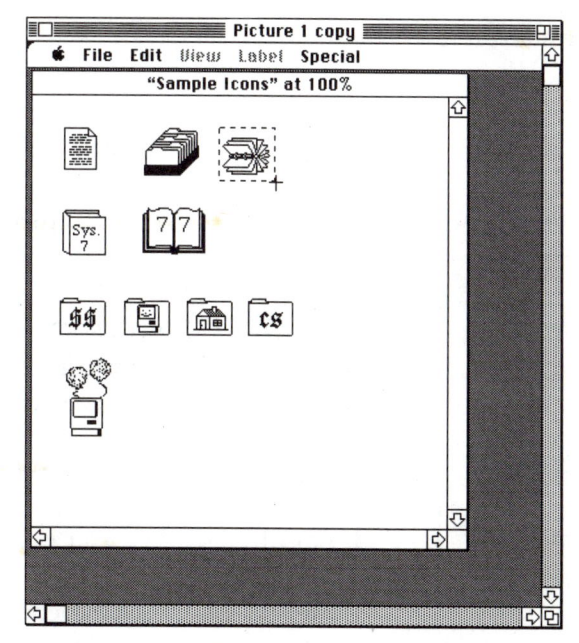

*What's Happening*

You have selected this picture for further action. If the box does not include the entire picture or the box does not tightly enclose the picture, click anywhere on the window to deselect the picture and try again.

Step 5   Choose **Copy from the Edit menu.**

212   CHAPTER 9 • FILE MANIPULATION

Step 6   Choose Show Clipboard from the Edit menu to verify a copy of the picture has been placed on the Clipboard. Close the Clipboard window.

Step 7   Choose Quit from the File menu.

*What's Happening*
The Picture 1 copy window and the TeachText program closes.

Step 8   Click on the Employee-Mac Store icon in the Lastname-Data disk window.

Step 9   Choose Get Info from the File menu.

Step 10   Click on the icon in the Employee-Mac Store Info window.

*What's Happening*
A box will appear around the icon.

Step 11   Choose Paste from the Edit menu.

*What's Happening*
The old icon picture has been replaced with the new picture. (Figure 9.15)

*Figure 9.15—Replacing Icons*

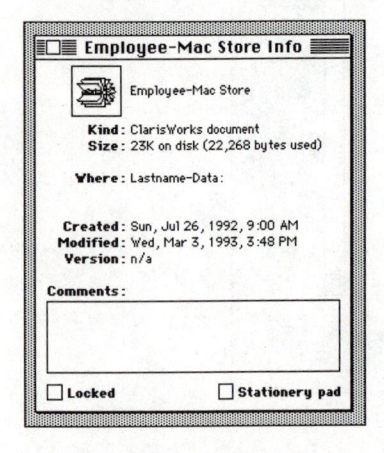

Step 12   Close the Employee-Mac Store Info window.

*What's Happening*
The new icon appears in the Lastname-Data window.

Step 13   Click on the Personal Friends icon.

Step 14   Choose Get Info from the File menu.

Step 15   Click on the icon in the Personal Friends Info window.

*What's Happening*
A box will appear around the icon.

Step 16   Choose Paste from the Edit menu.

*What's Happening*

The old icon picture has been replaced with the new picture.

*Figure 9.16—New Icons*

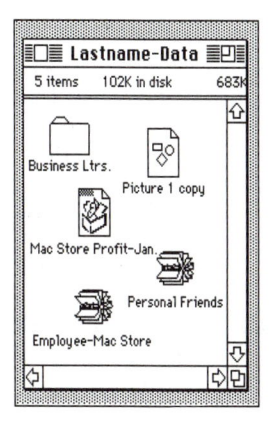

Step 17   Close the Personal Friends Info window. Examine the Lastname-Data window. Both files display the new icon. (Figure 9.16) Close the Lastname-Data disk window and drag the disk icon to the Trash.

If you change your mind, you can always change the icon back to the original. To remove the pasted icon picture and return to the original icon:

Click on the file to select it.
Choose Get Info from the File menu.
Click on the icon in the Info window.
Press the Delete key.

## Erasing Files

As your disks fill up, you will find it necessary to delete (erase, or throw away) files you no longer need. It is easy to collect unnecessary files on your hard disk or even on a floppy disk. Erasing a file removes the file entry in the disk's directory file and marks that area of the disk as available to be written to. The actual contents of the file stays on the disk until a new file writes over it. Some third-party vendors have created programs (Norton Utilities, for example) that can recover an erased file, unless it has been overwritten by a new file. The Macintosh Operating System does not provide a means to recover a file once the Trash has been emptied, so be careful when you throw files away.

The Trash provides you with a familiar method to throw away unwanted documents, applications and folder—simply place them in the Trash. Items in the Trash are not removed from your disk until you execute the **Empty Trash** command. Let's erase the four duplicate files on the Lastname-Sys 7 disk.

### Activity 9.8—Erasing a Group of Files

Step 1   Your Macintosh is on and booted. Place the unlocked Lastname-Sys 7 disk in the floppy drive. Display the disk window in a list view by name.

Step 2    Select and drag the four copy files to the Trash (Trash icon is highlighted): Picture 1 copy, EMPLOYEE-DB-CW copy, Friends-DB-CW copy, Jan. Profit-CW copy.

### What's Happening
The four files will disappear from the Lastname-Sys 7 disk window. The Trash icon now resembles a bulging trash can.

Step 3    Choose Empty Trash from the Special menu.

### What's Happening
The Empty Trash Warning dialog box will appear to inform you of the number of files you are about to erase. (Figure 9.17)

*Figure 9.17—Trash Warning*

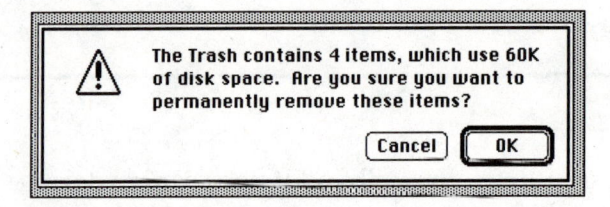

> ⚠ The Trash contains 4 items, which use 60K of disk space. Are you sure you want to permanently remove these items?
>
> [ Cancel ]  [ OK ]

Step 4    Click on the OK button.

### What's Happening
Another dialog warning box appears. (Figure 9.18) Remember the Picture 1 copy file was locked. You cannot erase a locked file.

*Figure 9.18—Locked File Warning*

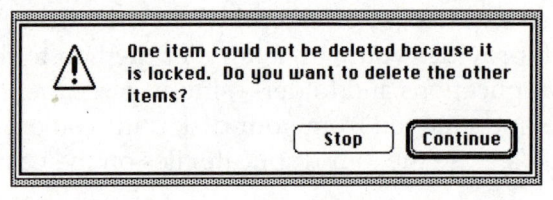

> ⚠ One item could not be deleted because it is locked. Do you want to delete the other items?
>
> [ Stop ]  [ Continue ]

Step 5    Click on the Continue button to erase the other 3 files.

**Unlocking a file**

Step 6    Double-click on the Trash icon to open it.

Step 7    Click once on the *Picture 1 copy* icon.

Step 8    Choose Get Info from the File menu.

Step 9  Click on the Locked checkbox (X disappears) in the Picture 1 copy Info window. Close the Picture 1 copy Info window.

**Erasing an unlocked file**

Step 10  Hold down the Option key while choosing Empty Trash from the File menu.

*What's Happening*

The Picture 1 copy file is erased. Holding down the Option key while selecting the Empty Trash command prevented the Empty Trash Warning dialog box from appearing. This option should be used cautiously. The Empty Trash Warning is meant to prevent you from accidentally erasing items.

Step 11  Close the Trash window.

Step 12  Close all open windows.

## Summary

We have covered many file handling operations in this chapter. Figures 9.19, 9.20, and 9.21 summarize the information you have learned.

*Figure 9.19—File Manipulation Techniques*

---

Manipulating Files and Folders

**To Duplicate a file or folder:**
1. Select the icon(s).
2. Choose Duplicate from the File menu.
3. Rename the duplicate icon.

**To Copy a file or folder from one floppy disk to another floppy:**
*Single floppy drive system configuration*
1. Insert the destination disk in the drive.
2. Open the destination disk and folders as necessary.
3. Select the destination disk icon and choose Eject Disk from the Special menu.
4. Insert the source disk in the drive.
5. Open the source disk and folders as necessary.
6. Select the desired icon(s) and drag them to the destination disk, folder or window.
7. Swap disks as directed.

*Dual floppy drive system configuration*
1. Insert the destination disk in one drive and the source disk in the other.
2. Open the source disk and folders as necessary.
3. Open the destination disk and folders as necessary.
4. Select the desired icon(s) and drag them to the destination disk, folder or window.

**To Lock or Unlock a file or folder:**
1. Select the icon(s).
2. Choose Get Info from the File menu.
3. Click in the Locked checkbox.
4. Close the Info window.

**To Erase a file or folder:**
1. Drag the icon(s) to the Trash.
2. Choose Empty Trash from the Special menu.

**To Rename a file or folder:**
1. Click on the icon's name.
2. Key in the new name or use editing techniques to modify the current name.

Figure 9.20—Customizing Icons

Customizing Icons

**To Change an icon:**
1. Create or locate the new icon and copy it to Clipboard.
2. Select the icon to be changed.
3. Choose Get Info from the File menu.
4. Click on the existing icon in the Info window (top left corner).
5. Choose Paste from the Edit menu.
6. Close the Info window.

**To Assign a Label to an icon:**
1. Select the icon(s).
2. Choose the appropriate label from the Label menu.

*The next two processes will be discussed in Chapter 11.*

**To Size an icon—Effects all icons in all windows:**
1. Choose Control Panels from the Apple menu.
2. Double-click on the Views icon.
3. Click on the desired icon size.
4. Close the Views and Control Panels windows.

**To Change Font and/ or Point Size—Effects all icons in all windows:**
1. Choose Control Panels from the Apple menu.
2. Double-click on the Views icon.
3. Select the desired font or point size from the pop-up menus.
4. Close the Views and Control Panels windows.

Figure 9.21—The Trash

### Trash Hints

**To throw away items:**
1. Select the icon(s) to remove and drag it to the Trash icon.

**To recover items from the Trash:**
1. Open the Trash window.
2. Drag the selected icons out of the Trash window to the desired window or disk, or select the items to be removed from the Trash and use the Put Away command to place the items back where they came from.

**Emptying the Trash:**
1. Trashed items remain on the disk and in the Trash until you execute the Empty Trash command (Special menu). Therefore, the disk space the files are using is not available to store other files until you empty the Trash.
2. The Empty Trash Warning dialog box appears whenever you empty the Trash.
3. The Empty Trash Warning may be temporarily avoided by holding down the Option key while executing the Empty Trash command.
4. The Empty Trash Warning can be turned off by using the Warn Before Emptying checkbox in the Trash Info window (Get Info command).

## Key Terms

Duplicate command ⌘ D
Empty Trash
Erase Trash
Labels
Locked files
Rename

## Discussion Questions

1. Why would you want a duplicate of a file on the same disk?
2. Why would you want a copy of a file on a second disk?
3. Should you lock all your files?
4. Should you rename system and application files?
5. Why would you want to erase a file?
6. Should you change the icon assigned to a file?
7. Discuss how and when the Trash is emptied.

## True/False Questions

For each question, circle the letter T if the statement is true and the letter F if the statement is false.

T F 1. If you duplicate a locked file, the new file will be locked.
T F 2. If you copy a locked file from one floppy disk to another, the file on the second disk will be locked.
T F 3. You can duplicate, copy, and erase a group of selected files.
T F 4. To copy a file from one floppy disk to another, both disk icons must be present on the desktop.
T F 5. Some third-party vendors have programs available that will recover erased files.
T F 6. If you duplicate a file, a dialog box will appear asking you where you want to place the new file.
T F 7. Your Macintosh must have two floppy disk drives to copy a file from one floppy to another.
T F 8. You must erase a disk in order to change its name.
T F 9. To rename a file, simply click on its icon and start typing.
T F 10. To remove a file from your disk, drag the file icon to the Trash.
T F 11. Once a file has been placed in the Trash, it is gone forever.

T  F  12. You can't duplicate a file in the by Icon view.
T  F  13. The label names in the Label menu can not be changed.
T  F  14. Use the Get Info command to lock, change icons, and rename files.
T  F  15. You can sometimes tell what kind of document is stored in a file by the icon assigned to the file.

## Completion Questions

Write the correct answer in each blank space.

1. To unlock a file use the _____ command on the _____ menu.
2. Locked files can not be _____, _____ or _____.
3. You can tell when the Trash has something stored inside because it _____.
4. If you duplicate a file called Friends, the copy will be called _____.
5. Use the _____ command to remove a floppy from the drive and leave a dimmed disk icon on the desktop.
6. The keyboard equivalent to duplicate a file is _____.
7. Pressing the _____ key will delete one character to the left of the _____.
8. To partially rename a file, _____ the portion of the name to remove, press the _____ key, and type the new name.
9. List three types of icons or files you can not rename: _____, _____ and _____.
10. You should not lock _____ or _____ files.
11. Use the _____ _____ _____ to change the available label names.
12. Icons are assigned to files by _____ _____.

## Assignments

Boot your Macintosh. The Macintosh desktop should be clean—no open windows. For this assignment, you will use your locked Lastname-Sys 7 disk and your Lastname-Data disk.

1. Print a directory by Name of your Lastname-Data disk. It should contain 4 files and 1 folder.

2. Print a directory by Icon of your Lastname-Data disk.

3. Copy 4 additional files from the locked Lastname-Sys 7 disk to the Lastname-Data disk.

1992 Mac Family-CW
History rpt 1
JS Ltr.-CW
Newsletter

Drag the Lastname-Sys 7 disk icon to the Trash. Use the Lastname-Data disk for questions 4 through 15.

4. Use the Duplicate command to make copies of the following files.
   1992 Mac Family-CW
   History rpt 1

5. Use the Duplicate command to make a copy of the file, 1992 Mac Family-CW copy. Notice the new name.

6. Rename History rpt 1 to History Report 1. Rename History rpt 1 copy to History Report 1 Copy.

7. Look at the label name that has been assigned to the Mac Store Profit Jan. file. Assign the same label to History Report 1.

8. Lock History Report 1.

9. Assign this icon picture to the Newsletter file. The new icon is in the Picture 1 copy file you used in Activity 9.7.

10. Assign this icon picture to the Business Ltrs. folder. The new icon is in the Picture 1 copy file you used in Activity 9.7.

11. Remove the pasted icon picture on the Personal Friends file.

12. Print a directory in list view by Name.

13. Print a directory by Icon.

14. Erase all but the original 4 files and the folder from the Lastname-Data disk Do not erase Business Ltrs., Employee-Mac-Store, Mac Store Profit-Jan., Personal Friends, Picture 1 copy.
    Note: You may have to unlock a file in order to erase it.

15. Print a directory of the Lastname-Data disk by Name.

Close all open windows.

# 10 File and Disk Management

## Learning Objectives

**After completing this Chapter you will be able to:**

1. Explain how to use the Hierarchical Filing System.
2. Draw and explain Hierarchical Filing System diagrams.
3. Explain the advantages of creating a HFS on your disk.
4. Create and name file folders.
5. Place documents, folders, and application programs inside folders.
6. Copy a HFS from one floppy disk to another floppy disk.
7. Dismantle a HFS.
8. Explain why you should open a folder before throwing it away.
9. Describe how to recover items from the Trash and how and when the Trash is emptied.
10. Explain why you shouldn't create too many levels in your HFS.
11. Describe available keyboard shortcuts to use when working with a hierarchical filing system.
12. Use the Find command to locate documents, programs, and folders.

## Introduction

Do you file your paper documents in stacks on the floor? Of course not—you place them in file cabinets. Are your paper documents loose in the bottom of the filing cabinet drawer? No, related documents are filed in labeled folders for quick and easy retrieval. Naturally you want to store your computer documents (files) in an organized fashion, as well.

The Macintosh System uses a **Hierarchical Filing System (HFS)** to help you keep track of your files. Many computer systems use a HFS to organize disks, including systems that use **UNIX** and **MS-DOS** (the operating systems used by IBM-PC and compatibles). The HFS concepts you will learn in this chapter are also applicable in those systems. The Macintosh HFS is easier to understand because of the direct analogy to file cabinets and folders provided by the graphical user interface. UNIX and DOS users refer to folders in the Hierarchical Filing System as **Subdirectories**.

This chapter will discuss the Macintosh hierarchical filing system. You will learn how to create file folders, how to place files and folders within folders, and how to dismantle your HFS. By using the HFS, you will build a hierarchy of files and folders, much like the process used in non-computerized offices. You will also use the Find and Find Again commands to locate filed documents, and folders.

You will need three disks for this chapter: Startup, Lastname-Sys 7, and Lastname-Data. The Lastname-Data disk will be erased and renamed Backup.

## Hierarchical File System

The top level of the hierarchy is the disk. On each disk you may place files and folders. Folders may hold additional files and folders. **Nesting of folders**—placing folders inside folders—may be many levels deep, but more than four levels can be tedious if you are searching for a file.

The following example describes the hierarchical filing system stored on a correspondence disk. A diagram of this is shown in Figure 10.1.

Level 1  At the disk level (level 1) two file folders, School and Personal, are used to separate the personal correspondence from school correspondence.

Level 2  The School folder has two folders inside. One folder contains faculty correspondence and the other one holds senate correspondence. The personal folder contains letters to Mom, Nancy, and Jim.

Level 3  The Faculty folder has three files in it: Agenda, Greeting, and Faculty. The Senate folder has two files stored inside: Rpt. 1 and Analysis.

This disk contains four file folders and eight files. You may feel it is a little more organized than necessary, but you should plan ahead. The contents of the disk will grow, and you have places prepared to store files as they are created.

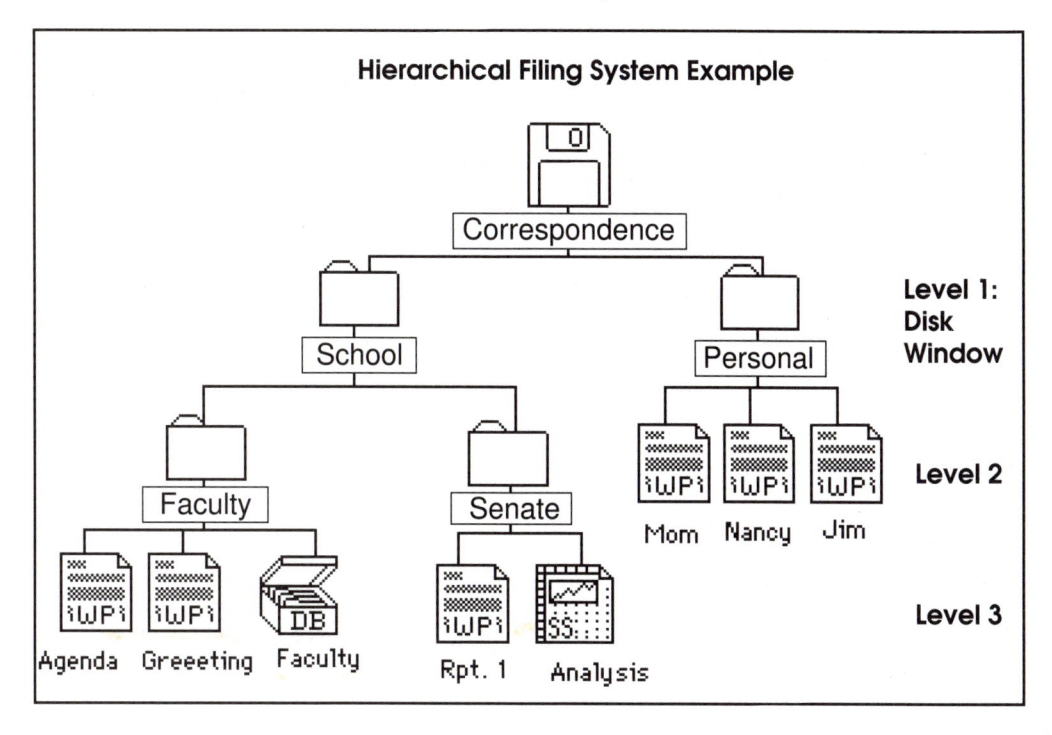

*Figure 10.1—An Example of a Hierarchical Filing System*

```
                    Hierarchical Filing System Example

                              [disk]
                          Correspondence

                    ┌────────────┴────────────┐
                 [folder]                  [folder]              Level 1:
                  School                    Personal             Disk
                                                                 Window
            ┌───────┴───────┐         ┌───────┼───────┐
         [folder]        [folder]   [WP]    [WP]    [WP]         Level 2
         Faculty          Senate    Mom    Nancy    Jim

       ┌────┼────┐          ┌───┴───┐
     [WP][WP][DB]         [WP]   [SS]                            Level 3
    Agenda Greeeting Faculty  Rpt. 1 Analysis
```

## Moving through the HFS

Once your HFS is created, you will want to move quickly and smoothly between levels. You already know three ways to open a folder/icon: double-click on the icon, Open command, ⌘ O. You also know three ways to close a window/folder: Close Box, Close Window command, ⌘ W. Several additional methods are available to open and close folders and to move from one level of the disk to another: pop-up menu, keyboard shortcuts.

### Using the Pop-up Menu

You may use the pop-up menu to move quickly to a higher level in your HFS. The pop-up menu is available in the active window on your desktop and in application program's directory dialog boxes. (Figure 10.2) Figure 10.3 summarizes how to use the pop-up menu.

*Figure 10.2—Pop-up Menu*

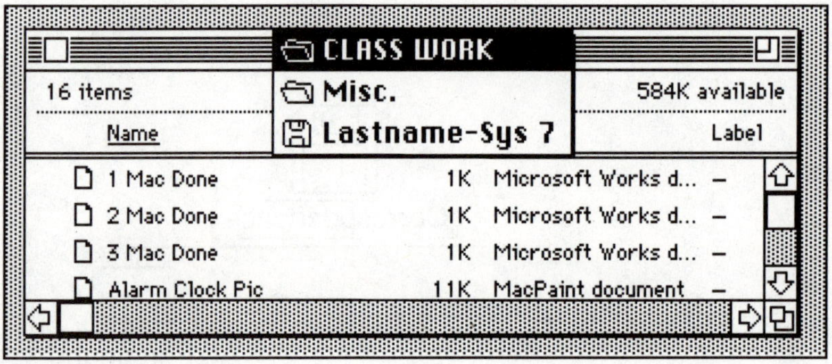

```
┌─────────────────────────────────────────────┐
│ ▢      📁 CLASS WORK                       │
├─────────────────────────────────────────────┤
│ 16 items    📁 Misc.           584K available│
│   Name      💾 Lastname-Sys 7        Label  │
│  ▯ 1 Mac Done      1K  Microsoft Works d... — │
│  ▯ 2 Mac Done      1K  Microsoft Works d... — │
│  ▯ 3 Mac Done      1K  Microsoft Works d... — │
│  ▯ Alarm Clock Pic 11K MacPaint document  — │
└─────────────────────────────────────────────┘
```

*Figure 10.3—HFS Pop-up Menu*

### HFS Pop-up Menus

| | **Process** | **Results** |
|---|---|---|
| ⌘ + | Position pointer on window title and press the mouse button. | Displays the window's hierarchy. |
| ⌘ + | Position pointer on window title, press the mouse button, drag the pointer to highlight desired folder or disk, and release button. | Opens highlighted folder or disk. |
| ⌘ + | Option key + Position pointer on window title, press the mouse button, drag the pointer to highlight desired folder or disk, release button. | Opens highlighted folder or disk and closes the window that was active. |

## Using Keyboard Shortcuts

Keyboard shortcuts can be used to move quickly from one level in the HFS to another. Each keyboard shortcut requires you to hold down the ⌘ key, a directional arrow key and sometimes the Option Key. Figure 10.4 summarizes these shortcuts. The directional arrow keys are listed as you see them on your keyboard. For example, ➜ means press the Right Arrow key.

*Figure 10.4—HFS Keyboard Shortcuts*

### HFS Keyboard Shortcuts

**Displaying Outline Views**

| Key(s) | Action |
|---|---|
| ⌘ → | Displays an outline view of the selected folder. * |
| ⌘ ← | Closes/hides the outline view of only the selected folder. * |
| ⌘ Option key → | Displays an outline view of the selected folder and all folders stored within the selected folder. * |
| ⌘ Option key ← | Closes/hides the outline view of the selected folder and all folders stored within the selected folder. * |

\* Window must be displayed in a list view by Name, Size, Kind, Label or Date.

**Opening, Closing, and Activating Windows**

| Key(s) | Action |
|---|---|
| ⌘ ↓ | Opens the selected icon. |
| ⌘ Option key ↓ | Opens the selected icon and closes the active folder/window. |
| ⌘ ↑ | Opens the folder that contains the active folder. |
| ⌘ Option key ↑ | Opens the folder that contains the active folder and closes the active folder. |

## Activity 10.1—Navigating the HFS

In this activity, you will examine the HFS on the Lastname-Sys 7 disk and experiment with the pop-up menu and some keyboard shortcuts. Some of the techniques you have previously used but many will be new.

Step 1   Boot your Macintosh. Place the Lastname-Sys 7 disk in the floppy drive.

Step 2   Double-click on the Lastname-Sys 7 disk icon. Display the disk window in an icon view. Double-click on the Misc. folder. Display the Misc. window in an icon view. Double-click on the Class Work folder. Display the Class Work window in an icon view.

*Figure 10.5—The HFS on the Lastname-Sys 7 Disk*

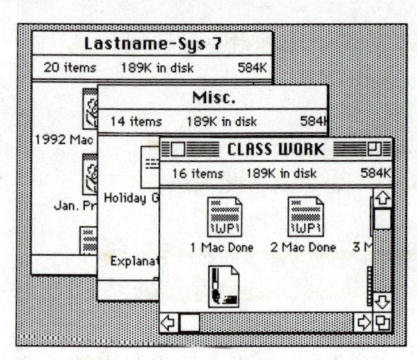

### What's Happening

Double-clicking on an icon opens a window to the icon. The new window automatically becomes the active window (horizontal lines in the title bar). You now have three levels exposed on the disk. Level 1, the Lastname-Sys 7 disk window, contains 20 items (19 documents and 1 file folder). Level 2, Misc. folder window, contains 14 items (13 documents and 1 file folder). Level 3, the Class Work folder window, contains 16 documents. (Figure 10.5)

Step 3   Click once on the 1 Mac Done icon in the Class Work window. Choose Get Info from the File menu.

### What's Happening

The 1 Mac Done Info window appears. You have used this command several times but let's examine the "Where" entry in this window: Where: Lastname-Sys 7: Misc.: CLASS WORK:. This entry tells you exactly where this document is stored on the disk. The document is stored in the Class Work folder, which is stored in the Misc. folder, which is stored on the Lastname-Sys 7 disk. The colon (:) is used to separate storage locations. (Figure 10.6)

*Figure 10.6—1 Mac Done Info Window*

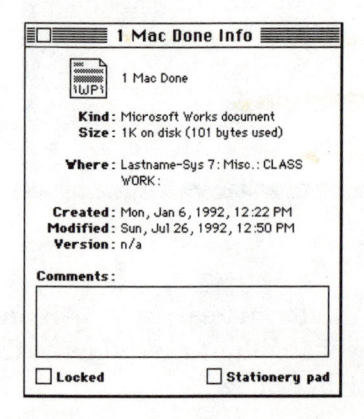

Step 4   Close the Info window.

**Pop-up Menu**

Step 5   Position the mouse pointer on the window title, Class Work. Hold down the ⌘ key while pressing the mouse button.

## What's Happening

The HFS Pop-up menu appears displaying the **directory path**. It visually describes the location of this folder on the disk. The Class Work folder is inside the Misc. folder on the Lastname-Sys 7 disk, as shown in Figure 10.7.

Figure 10.7—Class Work Pop-up Menu

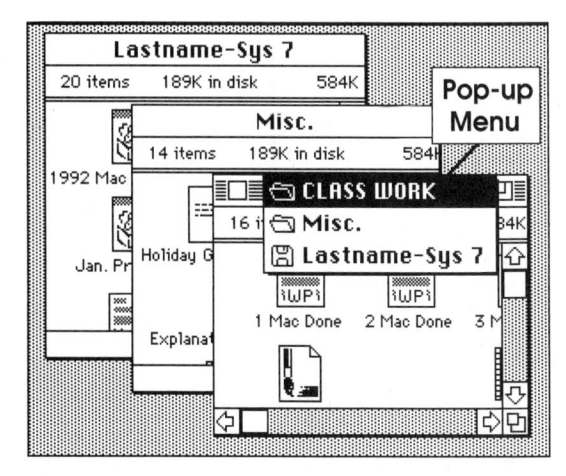

Step 6   Drag the pointer down the pop-up menu. Release the mouse button when Lastname-Sys 7 is highlighted.

## What's Happening

The horizontal lines in the title bar indicate the Lastname-Sys 7 window is the active window. (Figure 10.8)

Step 7   Click anywhere on the Misc. folder window.

Figure 10.8—Active Window-Lastname-Sys 7

## What's Happening

The Misc. folder window is now the active window. Clicking on a window activates the window. If you can see any part of a window, you can activate it simply by clicking on it.

Step 8   Close the Misc. and Class Work windows.

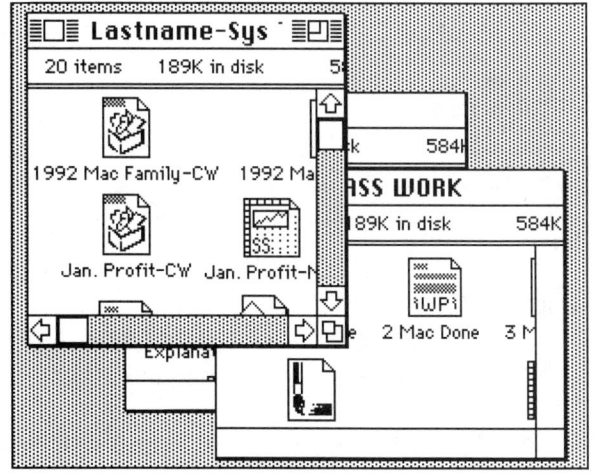

Step 9   Display the Lastname-Sys 7 window in a list view by date. Click on the zoom box to display most of the window.

### Displaying Outline Views

Step 10   Click once on the triangle next to the Misc. icon and name. Click once on the triangle next to the Class Work icon and name.

*Figure 10.9—Outline View*

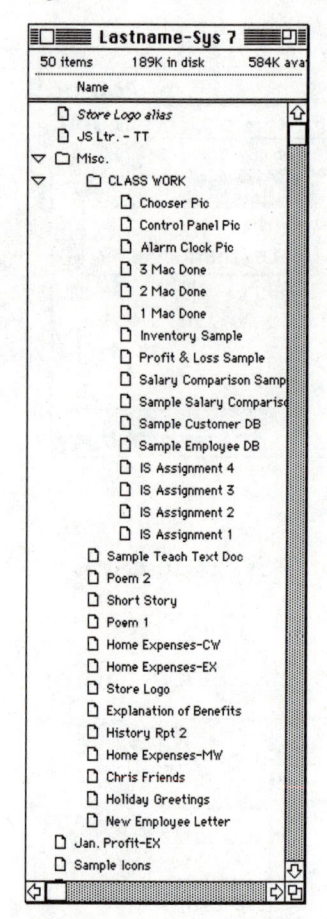

```
┌─────── Lastname-Sys 7 ───────┐
│ 50 items     189K in disk    584K ava│
│ Name                                 │
│  □ Store Logo alias                  │
│  □ JS Ltr. - TT                      │
│  ▽ □ Misc.                           │
│     ▽ □ CLASS WORK                   │
│         □ Chooser Pic                │
│         □ Control Panel Pic          │
│         □ Alarm Clock Pic            │
│         □ 3 Mac Done                 │
│         □ 2 Mac Done                 │
│         □ 1 Mac Done                 │
│         □ Inventory Sample           │
│         □ Profit & Loss Sample       │
│         □ Salary Comparison Samp     │
│         □ Sample Salary Comparis     │
│         □ Sample Customer DB         │
│         □ Sample Employee DB         │
│         □ IS Assignment 4            │
│         □ IS Assignment 3            │
│         □ IS Assignment 2            │
│         □ IS Assignment 1            │
│       □ Sample Teach Text Doc        │
│       □ Poem 2                       │
│       □ Short Story                  │
│       □ Poem 1                       │
│       □ Home Expenses-CW             │
│       □ Home Expenses-EX             │
│       □ Store Logo                   │
│       □ Explanation of Benefits      │
│       □ History Rpt 2                │
│       □ Home Expenses-MW             │
│       □ Chris Friends                │
│       □ Holiday Greetings            │
│       □ New Employee Letter          │
│  □ Jan. Profit-EX                    │
│  □ Sample Icons                      │
└──────────────────────────────────────┘
```

*What's Happening*

As you click on each triangle, the triangle points down and exposes the contents of the folder. This is called an **outline view**. (Figure 10.9) If the information bar is visible, it shows that there are 50 items in the window. This disk contains 48 documents and 2 file folders. If the information bar is not displayed, don't worry. It is not automatically displayed in list view windows. The View control panel can be used to direct the Macintosh to display this bar in list windows. (Refer to Chapter 11 to do this.)

Step 11   Click once on the triangle next to the Class Work icon and name. Click once on the triangle next to the Misc. icon and name.

*What's Happening*

As you click on each triangle, the outline view of the folder is hidden from view and the triangle points towards the right. To hide all outline views, start with the folder stored at the deepest level.

Step 12   Click once on the Misc. icon name to select the icon (turns dark).

Step 13   Hold down the ⌘ key while pressing the ➡ key.

*What's Happening*

The outline view of the Misc. folder appears. The Class Work folder is not displayed in an outline view.

Step 14   The Misc. folder icon should still be selected. Hold down the ⌘ key while pressing the ⬅ key to hide the outline view.

Step 15   The Misc. folder icon should still be selected. Hold down the Option key and the ⌘ key while pressing the ➡ key.

*What's Happening*

The Misc. folder and all folders inside the Misc. folder are displayed in an outline view.

Step 16   The Misc. folder icon should still be selected. Hold down the Option key and the ⌘ key while pressing the ← key.

*What's Happening*

This hides the outline view of all folders inside the Misc. folder and the Misc. folder.

**Using keyboard shortcuts to open, close and activate windows**

Step 17   Click once on the Misc. icon. Hold down the ⌘ key while pressing the ↓ key.

*What's Happening*

The Misc. window opens and appears on the desktop. The Lastname-Sys 7 window is still open on the desktop.

Step 18   Click once on the Class Work folder icon to select it. Hold down the ⌘ key and the Option key while pressing the ↓ key.

*What's Happening*

The Class Work window opens and the Misc. window (the previously active window) is closed.

Step 19   Hold down the ⌘ key and the Option key while pressing the ↑ key.

*What's Happening*

The Misc. folder that contains the Class Work folder opens and appears on the desktop and the Class Work window closes.

Step 20   Experiment with any of the other keyboard shortcuts or pop-up menu techniques. When you are done, hide all outline views and close all open windows.

Step 21   Drag the Lastname-Sys 7 disk to the Trash.

# Copying the HFS to Another Floppy Disk

You can copy a file(s), a file folder(s) (including everything stored inside), or an entire filing structure from one disk to another. In this exercise you will copy your Lastname-Sys 7 disk filing structure to the Backup disk.

## Activity 10.2—Erasing and Renaming a Floppy Disk

Erase your Lastname-Data disk and rename it Backup. Copy the Lastname-Sys 7 disk to the Backup disk.

Step 1    The Macintosh is on and booted.

Step 2    Insert your Lastname-Data disk in the floppy drive.

Step 3    Choose Erase Disk from the Special menu. Respond to dialog boxes as necessary.

Step 4    Rename the Lastname-Data disk. Name it Backup.

Step 5    Drag the Backup disk icon to the Trash. Change the name of the disk on the paper label.

## Activity 10.3—Copying the Lastname-Sys 7 Disk

### Copying a disk displayed in an outline view

Step 1    Insert the locked Lastname-Sys 7 disk in the floppy drive.

Step 2    Open the Lastname-Sys 7 disk. Display the Lastname-Sys 7 window in a list view by name.

Step 3    Display an outline view of the contents of the Misc. and Class Work folders.

*What's Happening*

The information bar (if available) should say there are 50 items in the window.

Step 4    Click once on the Lastname-Sys 7 disk icon to activate it. Choose Eject Disk from the Special menu.

Step 5    Insert your Backup disk in the drive.

Step 6    Drag the Lastname-Sys 7 disk icon over the top of the Backup disk icon.

*What's Happening*

A dialog box will appear to confirm your desire to replace the contents of the Backup disk with the contents of the Lastname-Sys 7 disk.

Step 7    Click on the OK button in the dialog box. Switch disks as directed. When the copy is complete, drag the Lastname-Sys 7 disk icon to the Trash.

Step 8    Open the Backup disk.

*What's Happening*

Examine the Backup disk window. It contains 50 items. The entire contents of the Lastname-Sys 7 disk has been copied to level 1 of the Backup disk. Look a little further and you will notice that you also have the Misc. and Class Work folders.

Step 9    Display the Backup window in a list view by name. Display an outline view of all folders.

*What's Happening*

*Oops!* There are 96 items on the Backup disk. The original disk only had 50 items on the entire disk. There is a copy of the Class Work folder at the disk level and another copy within the Misc. folder. This was not the proper way to copy the disk. You must make sure that the disk window is not displayed in an outline view when copying the entire contents of one disk to another.

**Erasing the Backup disk**

Step 10   Click on the Backup disk icon to activate it. Choose Erase Disk from the Special menu. Make sure you are erasing the Backup disk. Respond to dialog boxes as necessary.

**Copying the contents of the Lastname-Sys 7 disk to the Backup disk**

Step 11   Choose Eject Disk from the Special menu. Insert the Lastname-Sys 7 disk.

Step 12   If necessary, close all outline views. Close the Class Work folder outline view. Close the Misc. folder outline view. The Lastname-Sys 7 window is open and contains 20 items. Drag the Lastname-Sys 7 disk icon over the Backup disk icon and respond to dialog boxes as necessary.

Step 13   When the copying process is complete, close the Lastname-Sys 7 disk window and drag the Lastname-Sys 7 disk icon to the Trash.

Step 14   Open the Backup disk window.

*What's Happening*

The Backup disk window contains 20 items. You could display the contents of each folder (Misc. and Class Work) to verify the copy process.

## Dismantling the HFS

Now that you know how to copy the HFS from one floppy disk to another, let's dismantle it and create a different HFS on the Backup disk. In this activity you will take all the files out of the folders on the Backup disk and place them at the disk level (level 1). When the folders are empty, you will drag them to the Trash.

### Trashing File Folders

Be careful when throwing folders away. Look inside first and verify what is there. If folders are nested (a folder within a folder) look inside each one. If you throw a folder away at the top level, all folders and files inside are also trashed.

**To throw away file folders:**
- Open the file folder.
- Remove any files you wish to keep by dragging them out of the folder.
- If there are folders within the folder, open them and remove any files you wish to keep.
- Close the file folder(s).
- Drag the folder to the Trash.
- Empty the Trash.

### Activity 10.4—Dismantling the HFS

**Emptying and throwing away the Misc. Folder**

Step 1  The Macintosh is on and booted. The unlocked Backup disk should be in the floppy drive.

Step 2  Display the Backup window in an icon view.

Step 3  Open the Misc. folder and display this window in an icon view.

Step 4  With the Misc. folder window active, choose the Select All command of the Edit menu.

*What's Happening*
All icons in the Misc. window are selected (highlighted).

Step 5  Point to one of the selected icons and drag the group out of the Misc. window to an empty spot on the Backup disk window.

## What's Happening
The Misc. folder should be empty. Examine the information bar of the Backup window to verify that it now contains 34 items.

Step 6   Close the Misc. window.

Step 7   Drag the Misc. folder to the Trash.

**Emptying and throwing away the Class Work Folder**

Step 8   Open the Class Work folder and display the window in an icon view. Select all items in the Class Work window and drag them to the Backup disk window.

## What's Happening
The Class Work window should be empty. 49 items should now appear in the Backup disk window.

Step 9   Close the Class Work window.

Step 10  Drag the Class Work folder to the Trash. You now have 48 items in the Backup disk window.

Step 11  Open the Trash window.

*Figure 10.10—Two Items in the Trash*

## What's Happening
You should have two file folders in the Trash: Misc. and Class Work. (Figure 10.10)

Step 12  Close the Trash window. Choose Empty Trash from the Special menu.

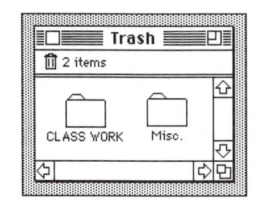

## What's Happening
The Alert Trash dialog box appears. Read the message and verify that you are about to erase two items containing zero K of disk space. If anything were stored inside the folders, they would not be taking up zero K disk space. (Figure 10.11)

*Figure 10.11—Trash Alert Box*

Step 13  Click on the OK button to remove the items from your disk (empty the Trash).

## Creating A Hierarchical Filing System

The Finder provides you with the necessary tools (the New Folder command of the File menu, the Hierarchical File System, Mac dragging techniques, and keyboard shortcuts) to maintain a neat and organized desktop and disk(s).

### Creating File Folders

There is an endless supply of empty folders available through the New Folder command of the File menu. When a new folder is created, a directory is automatically created for that folder. The name *untitled folder* is given to the new folder, so be sure to immediately name the folder on the desktop. The folder is placed in your active window.

**To create a new folder:**
- Open the disk and any folders to reach the desired level.
- Choose the New Folder command of the File menu or use the keyboard equivalent, ⌘ N.
- Type the name of the folder.

You can also create file folders while working with application programs. Any time you save a new document or use the Save As command, a directory dialog box appears. You must specify where to save the document (disk and folder) and name the document. Many application programs provide a New Folder button in this dialog box.

### Placing icons within folders

A document, application or another folder may be placed inside a file folder by dragging the icon on to the folder.

**To place documents, folders, or applications inside a folder:**
- The icon(s) to be moved and the folder must be on the desktop.
- Drag the icon(s) to the folder icon (folder is highlighted).
- Release the mouse button.

The item is no longer on the original window. It is now stored inside the file folder.

**To place a copy of a document, folder, or application program inside a folder:**
- The icon(s) to be moved and the folder must be on the desktop.

- Hold down the Option key while dragging the icon(s) to the folder icon (folder is highlighted).
- Release the mouse button and Option key.

The item is still in the original window and a copy of it has been placed in the file folder. Documents may also be placed directly into a file folder from within an application program.

## Activity 10.5—Creating an HFS

In this exercise you will create an HFS on your Backup disk. When you are done the HFS will look like the one in Figure 10.12

Level 1   The disk level contains three folders: (Family, Mac Store, School Work) and one file (Store Logo alias).

Level 2   Family folder contains two folders: Chris, Parents. Mac Store folder contains eleven files. School Work folder contains twenty-four files.

Level 3   Chris folder contains seven files. Parents folder contains five files.

Figure 10.12—Creating an HFS

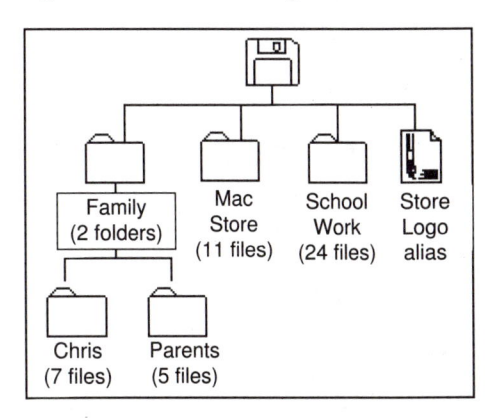

```
                    [disk]
        ┌─────────┬─────────┬─────────┐
     Family      Mac      School    Store
    (2 folders)  Store     Work     Logo
                (11 files) (24 files) alias
     ┌────┬────┐
   Chris  Parents
  (7 files) (5 files)
```

**Creating the Family folder and placing related files in it**

Step 1   The Macintosh is on and booted. The Backup window is active and displayed in a list view by name. Choose New Folder from the File menu.

*What's Happening*

A new folder, called untitled folder, will appear in the Backup window. The folder will be selected (highlighted).

Step 2   Type the new name of the folder—Family. Click on an empty space in the Backup window to deselect the folder.

*What's Happening*

You now have an empty Family folder in the Backup window. You can now file related documents in this folder.

Step 3   Drag the twelve related files, listed below, over the top of the Family folder.

        Chris Friends               Friends DataBase
        Friends DB-CW           History rpt 1
        History Rpt 2               Holiday Greetings
        Home Expenses-CW      Home Expenses-EX
        Home Expenses-MW      Poem 1
        Poem 2                     Short Story

*What's Happening*

As you drag the file(s) to the Family folder, the folder icon is highlighted. When you release the mouse button, the file(s) disappear from the Backup window as it is filed in the Family folder.

Step 4   To see if the files are in the folder, open the Family folder.

*Figure 10.13—The Family Folder*

*What's Happening*

Verify the Family window contains twelve files. If not, locate the missing files and drag them to this window. (Figure 10.13)

**Creating the Chris and Family file folders and Placing related documents in them**

Step 5   The Family window is active. Press ⌘ N to create a new folder. Type the new name of the folder—Chris. Click on an empty spot in the Family window to deselect all icons.

Step 6   Place the seven related documents, listed below, in the Chris folder.

        Chris Friends               Friends DataBase
        History rpt 1               History Rpt 2
        Poem 1                     Poem 2
        Short Story

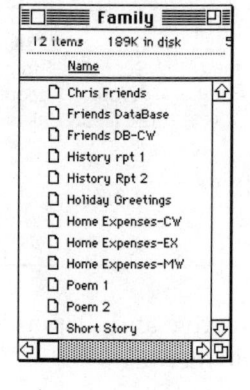

*Figure 10.14—The Chris Folder*

Step 7   Open the Chris folder and verify that seven items are stored in the folder. (Figure 10.14) If this folder does not contain the correct items, locate the missing items and drag them to this window before proceeding. Close the Chris folder.

CREATING A HIERARCHICAL FILING SYSTEM    237

Step 8   Verify the Family window is active. Press ⌘ N to create a new folder. Type the new name of the folder—Parents. Click on an empty spot in the Family window to deselect all icons.

Step 9   Place the five related documents, listed below, in the Parents folder.
Friends DB-CW          Holiday Greetings
Home Expenses-CW       Home Expenses-EX
Home Expenses-MW

*Figure 10.15—The Parents Folder*

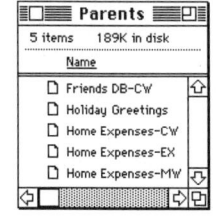

Step 10  Open the Parents folder and verify that five items are stored inside the folder. (Figure 10.15) If this folder does not contain the correct items, locate the missing items and drag them to this window before proceeding. Close the Parents folder.

## What's Happening

Look at the Family window. It now contains only two file folders. (Figure 10.16)

*Figure 10.16—Two Folders in the Family Folder*

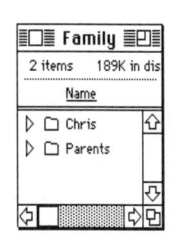

Step 11  Close the Family window. The Backup window is the only open window and is now active.

**Creating the Mac Store folder and placing related documents in it**

Step 12  Press ⌘ N to create a new folder in the Backup window.

Step 13  Type the new name of the folder—Mac Store. Click on an empty space in the Backup window to deselect the folder.

Step 14  Drag the 11 related files, listed below, to the Mac Store folder.
1992 Mac Family-CW        1992 Mac Family-MW
EMPLOYEE DB               EMPLOYEE-DB-CW
Explanation of Benefits   Inventory Sample
New Employee Letter       Newsletter
Profit & Loss Sample      Salary Comparison Sample
Store Logo

Step 15  Open the Mac Store folder.

*Figure 10.17—The Mac Store Folder*

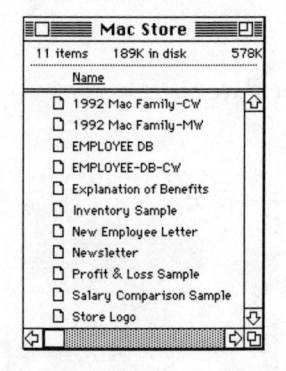

```
┌─────── Mac Store ═══════┐
│ 11 items    189K in disk    578K │
│   Name                           │
│ □ 1992 Mac Family-CW            │
│ □ 1992 Mac Family-MW            │
│ □ EMPLOYEE DB                   │
│ □ EMPLOYEE-DB-CW                │
│ □ Explanation of Benefits       │
│ □ Inventory Sample              │
│ □ New Employee Letter           │
│ □ Newsletter                    │
│ □ Profit & Loss Sample          │
│ □ Salary Comparison Sample      │
│ □ Store Logo                    │
└──────────────────────────────────┘
```

## What's Happening

Verify the Mac Store folder window contains eleven files. (Figure 10.17) If this folder does not contain the correct items, locate the missing items and drag them to this window before proceeding.

Step 16    Close the Mac Store folder window. The Backup window is the only open window.

**Creating the School Work folder and placing related files in it**

Step 17    Verify the Backup window is active. Press ⌘ N to create a new folder.

Step 18    Type the new name of the folder—School Work.

Step 19    Click on an empty space in the Backup window to deselect all icons.

*Figure 10.18—The School Work folder*

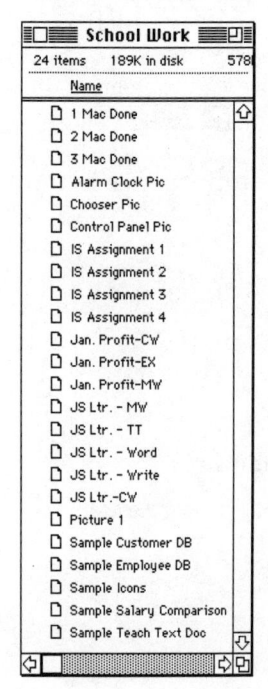

```
┌─────── School Work ═══════┐
│ 24 items    189K in disk    578 │
│   Name                          │
│ □ 1 Mac Done                    │
│ □ 2 Mac Done                    │
│ □ 3 Mac Done                    │
│ □ Alarm Clock Pic               │
│ □ Chooser Pic                   │
│ □ Control Panel Pic             │
│ □ IS Assignment 1               │
│ □ IS Assignment 2               │
│ □ IS Assignment 3               │
│ □ IS Assignment 4               │
│ □ Jan. Profit-CW                │
│ □ Jan. Profit-EX                │
│ □ Jan. Profit-MW                │
│ □ JS Ltr. - MW                  │
│ □ JS Ltr. - TT                  │
│ □ JS Ltr. - Word                │
│ □ JS Ltr. - Write               │
│ □ JS Ltr.-CW                    │
│ □ Picture 1                     │
│ □ Sample Customer DB            │
│ □ Sample Employee DB            │
│ □ Sample Icons                  │
│ □ Sample Salary Comparison      │
│ □ Sample Teach Text Doc         │
└─────────────────────────────────┘
```

Step 20    Do not place the Store Logo Alias file in the School Work folder. Drag the other 24 related files to the School Work folder.

Step 21    Open the School Work folder and verify that twenty-four items are stored inside. Close the School Work folder. (Figure 10.18)

## What's Happening

Level 1 of the Backup disk contains 3 file folders and 1 alias file. (Figure 10.19) The alias file should remain on the disk level for a later activity.

*Figure 10.19—Backup Disk-Level 1*

```
┌─────── Backup ═══════┐
│ 4 items    189K in disk │
│   Name                  │
│ ▷ □ Family              │
│ ▷ □ Mac Store           │
│ ▷ □ School Work         │
│   □ Store Logo alias    │
└─────────────────────────┘
```

## Duplicating a File Folder

You already know how to duplicate a file(s). Let's duplicate the Family folder. The Family folder contains two folders: Chris and Parents. When you duplicate a folder, the entire contents of the folder is copied. The contents of the new folder will be an exact copy of the original folder. However, the duplicate files will be unlocked, even if the original files are locked.

### Activity 10.6—Duplicating the Family Folder

#### Locking Two Files in the Family Folder

Step 1   The Macintosh is on and booted. Display the Backup disk window in a list view by name.

*What's Happening*

The Backup window contains three folders and one file.

Step 2   Click once on the triangle to the left of the Family folder to display an outline view of the folder.

Step 3   Display an outline view of the Chris folder.

Step 4   Click once on the Chris Friends file (in the Chris folder). Choose Get Info from the File menu. Click in the Locked checkbox, an X appears. Close the Info window.

Step 5   Close/hide the outline view of the Chris folder.

Step 6   Display an outline view of the Parents folder.

Step 7   Click once on the Holiday Greetings file (stored in the Parents folder). Choose Get Info from the File menu. If there is not an X in the Locked checkbox, click on it. Close the Info window.

Step 8   Close/hide the outline view of the Parents folder. Close/hide the outline view of the Family folder.

#### Duplicating the Family Folder

Step 9   Click once on the Family folder. Choose Duplicate from the File menu.

*What's Happening*

Status boxes will keep you informed during the duplicating process. A folder called Family copy will appear on the Backup window when the copy is complete.

Step 10   Display the Family copy folder in an outline view. Display the folders inside the Family copy folder in an outline view.

*What's Happening*

The Family copy folder contains the same folders and files that the original folder contained. The folders and files inside the Family copy folder maintained the original names. Examine the file entries Chris Friends and Holiday Greetings. The padlock does not appear on the right of the entries for these files, they are not locked.

Step 11   Close/hide the outline views of the Chris, Parents, and Family copy folders.

### Activity 10.7—Trashing the Family Folder

Let's remove the Family folder from the Backup disk. In Activity 10.6, you should have created a duplicate copy of this folder. If you did not, go back and do Activity 10.6 now.

Step 1   The Macintosh should be on and booted. Display the Backup disk window in a list view by Name.

Step 2   Drag the Family folder to the Trash. Choose Empty Trash from the Special menu.

*What's Happening*

The Trash dialog box in Figure 10.20 will appear to verify your desire to remove 15 items from the disk. The entire contents of the Family folder is in the Trash.

Figure 10.20—Trash Dialog Box

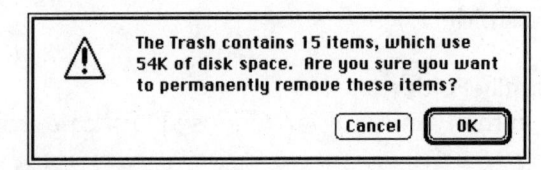

> ⚠  The Trash contains 15 items, which use 54K of disk space. Are you sure you want to permanently remove these items?
> 
> [ Cancel ]  [ OK ]

Step 3   Click on the OK button.

DUPLICATING A FILE FOLDER   241

*What's Happening*

Another Trash dialog box will appear. (Figure 10.21) It informs you that locked items can not be deleted, and asks if you wish to delete the other (unlocked) items.

*Figure 10.21—Locked Items in the Trash*

```
⚠  Some items could not be deleted because
   they are locked. Do you want to delete
   the other items?
              [ Stop ]  [[ Continue ]]
```

Step 4   Click on the Continue button.

*What's Happening*

A Trash Alert dialog box will appear for every folder that can not be deleted. The Chris and Parents folders can not be deleted because each folder contains a locked file. The Family folder can not be deleted because it still contains the Chris and Parents folders. (Figure 10.22)

*Figure 10.22—Trash Alert Boxes*

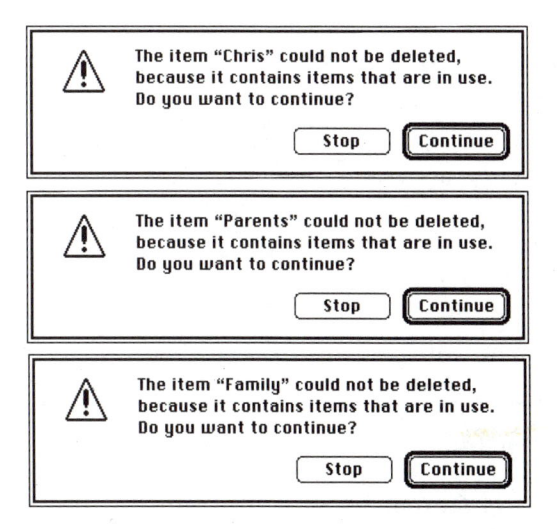

```
⚠  The item "Chris" could not be deleted,
   because it contains items that are in use.
   Do you want to continue?
              [ Stop ]  [[ Continue ]]

⚠  The item "Parents" could not be deleted,
   because it contains items that are in use.
   Do you want to continue?
              [ Stop ]  [[ Continue ]]

⚠  The item "Family" could not be deleted,
   because it contains items that are in use.
   Do you want to continue?
              [ Stop ]  [[ Continue ]]
```

Step 5   Click on the Continue button in each dialog box.

Step 6   Open the Trash icon. Open the Family, Chris, and Parents folder to double-check which files are locked.

*What's Happening*

You locked two files, Chris Friends and Holiday Greetings, previously in this chapter. Locked files and the folders they are stored in are not erased when you issue the Empty Trash command. If you trash the wrong item, you can remove it from the Trash by simply dragging the item out of the Trash to a disk or folder window.

Step 7   Close the Family, Chris, Parents, and Trash windows.

Step 8   Choose Empty Trash from the Special menu.

*What's Happening*

The Trash Warning dialog box in Figure 10.23 will appear. The Trash contains all locked items and can not be emptied. You could unlock each file one by one by using the Get Info command. The dialog box does provide you with a tip: a short cut. To delete locked items, hold down the Option key while you choose Empty Trash.

Figure 10.23—Trash Warning

Step 9   Click on the OK button to close the Trash dialog box.

Step 10  Hold down the Option key while selecting the Empty Trash command from the Special menu.

*What's Happening*

The Trash is emptied.

Step 11  Change the name of the Family copy folder to Family.

## The Find Command

The Macintosh Hierarchical Filing System allows the user to store a large number of files in an organized fashion within file folders. Sometimes a challenge may arise—in which folder or folders did you place a specific document, and what is its name? The Find and Find Again commands help you with this challenge. The **Find** command lets you specify the search criteria (what you are looking for), and where to look (on the desktop, on all disks, on a specific disk, in a specific folder). The **Find Again** command locates and displays the next item that matches your search criteria.

## Activity 10.8—Using the Find Command

### Locating the Holiday Greeting file on your Backup disk

Step 1   The Macintosh is on and booted. The Backup disk should be in the floppy drive. Close all open windows.

Step 2   Choose Find from the File menu.

*Figure 10.24—The Find Dialog Box*

### What's Happening

The Find dialog box will appear. (Figure 10.24) It contains an area to key in the partial or full name of the item you are searching for and three buttons: More Choices, Cancel, Find. You use the text box to key in the full name or any number of consecutive characters in the name. The Find command is not **case sensitive**; you do not need to specify uppercase or lowercase characters. It is to your advantage to be as specific as possible. The system will search all available disks and display the first item it finds containing the specified characters.

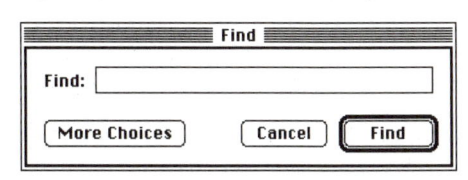

The expanded Find dialog box (Figure 10.26) may appear, if the previous user forgot to close it. If the expanded Find dialog box is on your desktop, click on the Fewer Choices button.

Step 3   Key in *holiday greet* and click on the Find button.

*Figure 10.25—Item Located*

### What's Happening

The system will search and display the first item it finds containing the characters holiday greet. A window (disk, folder, or Trash) will open displaying the highlighted item. Figure 10.25 displays the highlighted Holiday Greeting file in the Parents window. You may have a different window open on your desktop. The first item alphabetically located containing holiday greet will be on your desktop.

Step 4   Close the window displaying the highlighted item. Choose the Find Again command of the File menu. Click on the Find button.

### What's Happening

The Find Again command directs the system to locate and display the next item matching your request. The system will display the next item containing the specified characters, or it will beep, indicating that the system has been unsuccessful in locating additional items.

Step 5   If another item was located, close the window displaying the highlighted item.

### Using the Expanded Find Dialog Box

Step 6   Choose Find from the File menu. Press the Delete key to remove the highlighted text, *holiday greet*, in the Find text box. If the expanded Find dialog box (Figure 10.26) is not open, click on the More Choices button.

*Figure 10.26—Expanded Find Dialog Box*

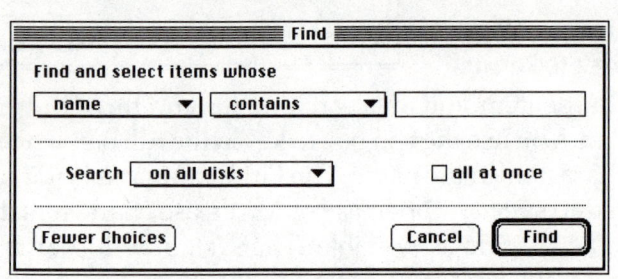

*What's Happening*

The expanded Find dialog box appears. This dialog box contains three sections: Find and Select, Search, and buttons.

The **Find and Select** section is used to specify the item(s) to locate. Two pop-up menus are used to set the search criteria. Nine choices are available on the **name pop-up** menu and the **contains pop-up** menu changes depending on the choice you make in the name pop-up menu. A **text box** is provided for you to enter the characters to search for. This entry changes from a text box to a pop-up menu depending on the choices you make in the other two pop-up menus.

The **Search** section allows you to specify where to look. Select the **all at once** checkbox to find all items on a disk or folder that match your request. The button section contains three buttons. The **Fewer Choices** button will close the expanded Find dialog box and display the original Find dialog box. You can stop the search operation by clicking on the Cancel button. Clicking on the Find button instructs the system to locate the next item that meets the required criteria.

Step 7   Point at the triangle on the *name* pop-up menu, and press and hold the mouse button to display the first pop-up menu.

*Figure 10.27—The First Pop-up Menu*

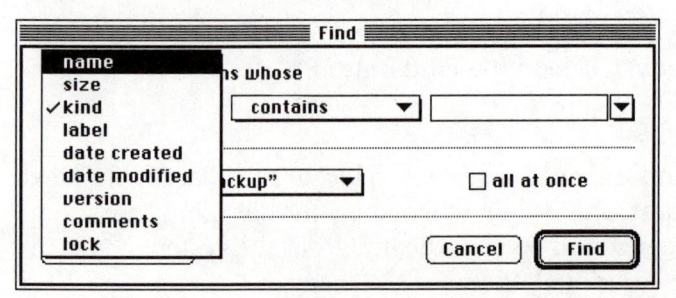

*What's Happening*

The check mark indicates the active option. To select an option, drag down the menu to highlight the desired option and release the mouse button, as shown in Figure 10.27.

Figure 10.28 summarizes your search options and offers suggestions on when to use each option.

*Figure 10.28—The Find Command*

| Search Criteria and Possible Uses for Each | |
|---|---|
| **Search Criteria** | **Use this Option when:** |
| Name | You know the file's exact name or only remember a portion of the name. You want to locate a group of files that contain the same characters. |
| Size | You are running out of disk space and wish to locate the largest files to copy to another disk or to compress before removing them from the disk. |
| Kind | You wish to locate all aliases, applications, documents, folders, or stationary pad files. |
| Label | You use labels to group related files and/or folders, and you want to find a group of files. |
| Date Created and/or Date Modified | You need to locate older files to remove from the disk or newer files to backup. |
| Version | You wish to locate an item by version number. |
| Comments | You remember the comment you entered in the Get Info's comment box. |
| Lock | You wish to locate locked files in order to unlock them. |

Step 8    Display the entries in the contains pop-up menu. (Figure 10.29)

*Figure 10.29—The Second Pop-up Menu*

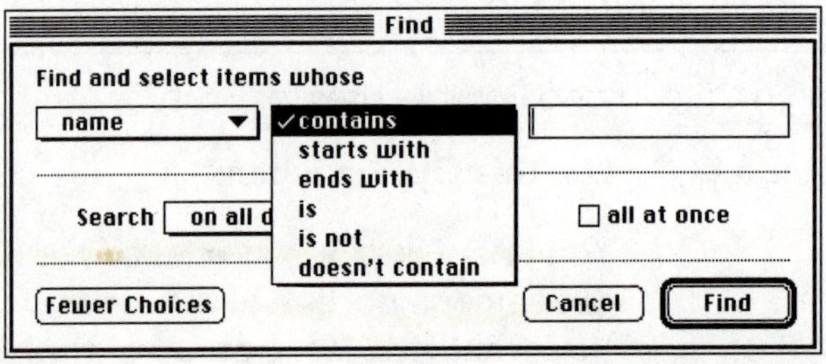

Step 9    Select different entries in the first pop-up menu and then display the second pop-up menu to see how its contents changes. Also, pay attention to how the text box changes.

**Locating all the items on the Backup disk that are larger than 10K**

Step 10   Choose *Size* from the first pop-up menu. Choose is greater than from the second pop-up menu. Key in 10 in the text box. Select on "Backup" in the Search pop-up menu. If an **X** does not appear in the all at once checkbox, click on the checkbox. (Figure 10.30) Click on the Find button.

*Figure 10.30—Using the Size Criteria*

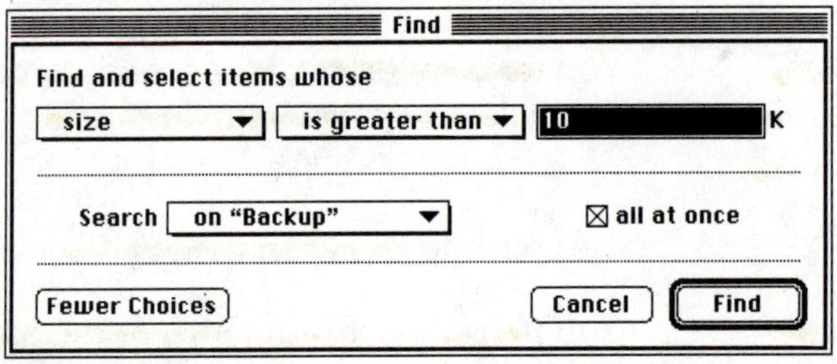

## What's Happening

Two Find Status boxes will briefly appear. The first one keeps you up to date on the search process and informs you how many items it finds. (Figure 10.31)

*Figure 10.31—Items Found*

The second Find status box counts down as it prepares to display the located items. (Figure 10.32)

*Figure 10.32—Displaying Found Items*

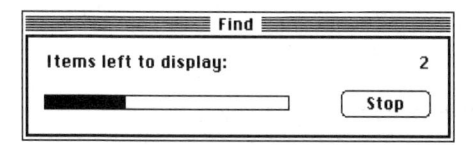

*Figure 10.33—Three Located Items*

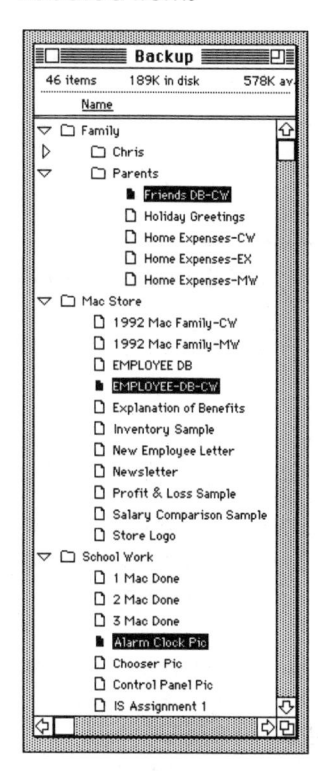

When the search has been completed, the Backup disk window will open in an expanded outline view. Matched items are highlighted. (Figure 10.33)

Step 11  Close the outline view of the School Work, Mac Store, Parents, and Family folders. Close the Backup disk window.

## Key Terms

All at once
   (Find Command)
Case sensitive
Contains pop-up menu
   (Find Command)
Directory path
Fewer Choices button
   (Find Command)
Find ⌘ F
Find Again ⌘ G
HFS pop-up menu
Hierarchical File System
HFS

MS-DOS
More Choices button
   (Find Command)
Name pop-up menu
   (Find Command)
Nesting folders
Outline view
Search pop-up menu
   (Find Command)
Subdirectories
Text box
   (Find Command)
UNIX

## Discussion Questions

1. Describe what is meant by a Hierarchical File System. Why should you use one?
2. Is a HFS necessary on all disks?
3. Discuss the precautions you should take as you dismantle your HFS.
4. Explain the Find and Find Again commands.

## True/False Questions

For each question, circle the letter T if the statement is true and the letter F if the statement is false.

T   F   1. The Macintosh will alert you if you place a folder containing files in the Trash.
T   F   2. A new folder is always placed in the active window.
T   F   3. When you create a new folder, a dialog box will appear requesting the folder's name.
T   F   4. To place a file inside a folder, drag the file icon over the top of the folder.
T   F   5. You should immediately name a new folder.
T   F   6. Before throwing a folder away, you should open it to see what's stored inside.
T   F   7. You can have multiple icons with the same name as long as they are in different folders on the disk.
T   F   8. If you copy a file folder from one disk to another, everything in the folder will be copied.
T   F   9. All new folders are given the name Empty Folder.
T   F   10. You can only nest folders 2 levels deep.
T   F   11. When copying a disk, the disk window should be open and displayed in a complete outline list view.
T   F   12. The Find Again command does not allow you to specify where to look for an item(s).

## Completion Questions

Write the correct answer in each blank space.

1. An endless supply of file folders are available from the _____ menu.
2. The keyboard equivalent for the New Folder command is_____.
3. It is recommended that you not nest folders more than _____ levels deep.

4. When you open the floppy disk window and all file folders are closed, you are on level _____.
5. DOS users refer to a file folder as a _____.
6. Positioning the arrow pointer on the window's name, while holding down the _____ key will display a a pop-up menu containing the window's _____.
7. In a list view window, a downward pointing triangle next to a folder's name indicates _____.
8. Holding down the _____ key while pressing the _____ _____ will display an outline view of the selected folder.
9. The _____ command lets you specify the _____ _____, and where to look for the item(s).
10. Because the Find command is not _____ _____, you do not need to specify upper or lower case characters.

## Assignments

Boot your Macintosh. The Macintosh desktop should be clean—no open windows. Place the Backup disk in the floppy drive. Open the Backup disk window.

### Part 1

Do all activities within this chapter prior to completing the following assignments.

1. Display the Backup disk window by Name. Display all folders in an outline view.
   Print the Backup disk window. Close the outline view of all folders.

2. Organize the School Work folder by course.
   Open the School Work folder. Create two new folders: Integrated Software Course and Introduction Course.

   Examine the outline view of the School Work folder in Figure 10.34. Place all files in the School Work folder in the Integrated Software Course folder or in the Introduction Course folder according to Figure 10.34.
   Display the School Work window in an outline list view by Name. Print the window. (Figure 10.34)

*Figure 10.34—School Work Folder: Outline View*

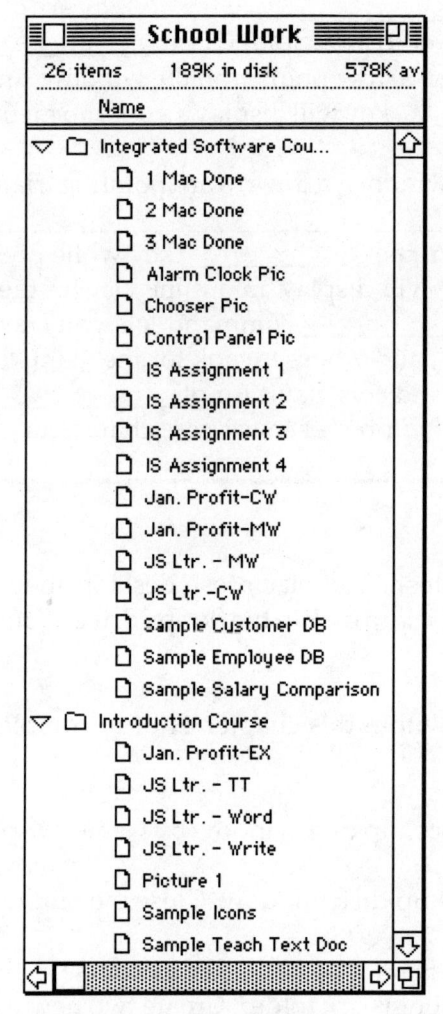

```
┌──────────────── School Work ────────────────┐
│ 26 items          189K in disk      578K av.│
├─────────────────────────────────────────────┤
│                   Name                      │
│  ▽  □ Integrated Software Cou...            │
│         □ 1 Mac Done                        │
│         □ 2 Mac Done                        │
│         □ 3 Mac Done                        │
│         □ Alarm Clock Pic                   │
│         □ Chooser Pic                       │
│         □ Control Panel Pic                 │
│         □ IS Assignment 1                   │
│         □ IS Assignment 2                   │
│         □ IS Assignment 3                   │
│         □ IS Assignment 4                   │
│         □ Jan. Profit-CW                    │
│         □ Jan. Profit-MW                    │
│         □ JS Ltr. - MW                      │
│         □ JS Ltr.-CW                        │
│         □ Sample Customer DB                │
│         □ Sample Employee DB                │
│         □ Sample Salary Comparison          │
│  ▽  □ Introduction Course                   │
│         □ Jan. Profit-EX                    │
│         □ JS Ltr. - TT                      │
│         □ JS Ltr. - Word                    │
│         □ JS Ltr. - Write                   │
│         □ Picture 1                         │
│         □ Sample Icons                      │
│         □ Sample Teach Text Doc             │
└─────────────────────────────────────────────┘
```

3. Tear down the HFS you created on the Backup disk. Place all files on the Backup disk level. Trash all empty file folders.

   Print the Backup disk window.

**Part 2**

There are numerous ways to create a HFS on a disk. This time you will file documents according to the application programs that were used to create them.

4. Create a new HFS.
   a. View the documents on the Backup disk by Kind.

b. Carefully examine the list of files. If your Startup disk has application programs stored on it, you may be able to tell which program was used to create each document (Kind column): Claris Works, Mac Paint, Mac Write, Microsoft Excel, Microsoft Word, Microsoft Works, and TeachText.

c. Create 7 new file folders on the Backup disk window.
        Claris Works Doc
        Mac Paint Doc
        Mac Write Doc
        Microsoft Excel Doc
        Microsoft Word Doc
        Microsoft Works Doc
        TeachText Doc

d. Leave the *Store Logo Alias* file on the disk window. Place all other files in their respective file folder according to figures below.

**Microsoft Works Doc** — 22 items, 189K in disk, 578K av

| Name | Size |
|---|---|
| 1 Mac Done | |
| 1992 Mac Family-MW | |
| 2 Mac Done | |
| 3 Mac Done | |
| Chris Friends | |
| EMPLOYEE DB | |
| Friends DataBase | |
| History rpt 1 | |
| History Rpt 2 | |
| Home Expenses-MW | |
| Inventory Sample | |
| IS Assignment 1 | |
| IS Assignment 2 | |
| IS Assignment 3 | |
| IS Assignment 4 | |
| Jan. Profit-MW | |
| JS Ltr. - MW | |
| Profit & Loss Sample | |
| Salary Comparison Sample | |
| Sample Customer DB | |
| Sample Employee DB | |
| Sample Salary Comparison | |

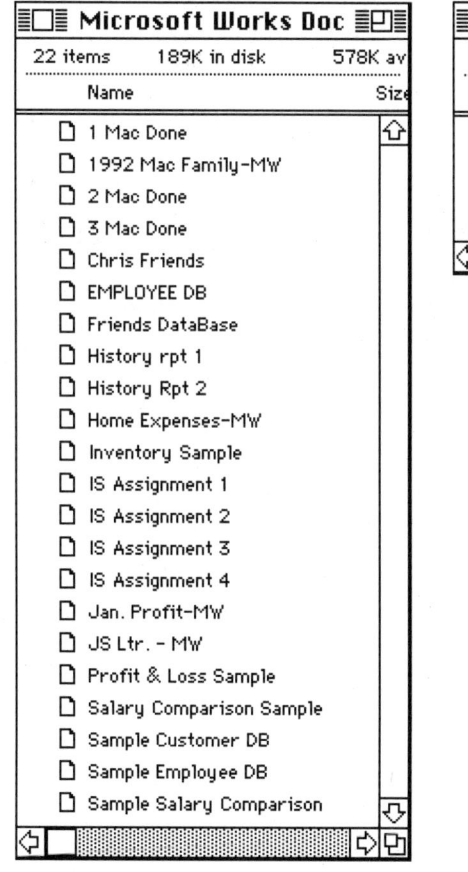

**Microsoft Excel Doc** — 2 items, 189K in disk, 578K availa

| Name | Size | Kin |
|---|---|---|
| Home Expenses-EX | 3K | |
| Jan. Profit-EX | 4K | |

**Mac Write Doc** — 1 item, 189K in disk, 578

| Name |
|---|
| JS Ltr. - Write |

**Microsoft Word Doc** — 5 items, 189K in disk, 578K a

| Name | Si |
|---|---|
| JS Ltr. - Word | |
| Newsletter | |
| Poem 1 | |
| Poem 2 | |
| Short Story | |

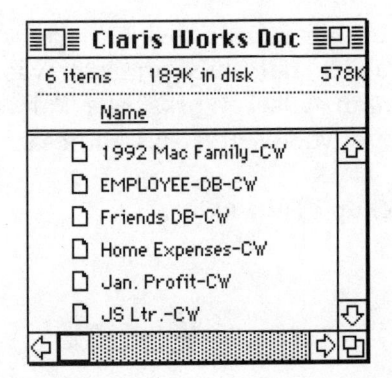

## Claris Works Doc
6 items    189K in disk    578K

**Name**
- 1992 Mac Family-CW
- EMPLOYEE-DB-CW
- Friends DB-CW
- Home Expenses-CW
- Jan. Profit-CW
- JS Ltr.-CW

## Mac Paint Doc
5 items    189K in disk

**Name**
- Alarm Clock Pic
- Chooser Pic
- Control Panel Pic
- Sample Icons
- Store Logo

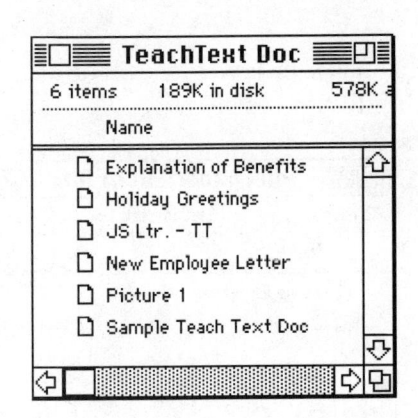

## TeachText Doc
6 items    189K in disk    578K

**Name**
- Explanation of Benefits
- Holiday Greetings
- JS Ltr. - TT
- New Employee Letter
- Picture 1
- Sample Teach Text Doc

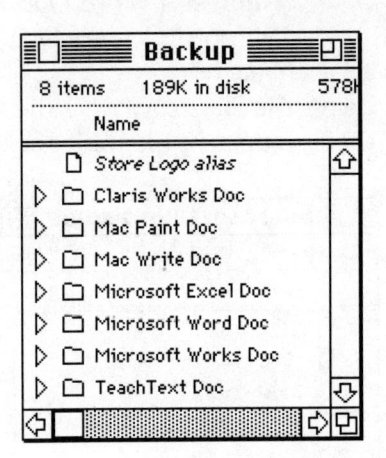

## Backup
8 items    189K in disk    578K

**Name**
- *Store Logo alias*
- ▷ 📁 Claris Works Doc
- ▷ 📁 Mac Paint Doc
- ▷ 📁 Mac Write Doc
- ▷ 📁 Microsoft Excel Doc
- ▷ 📁 Microsoft Word Doc
- ▷ 📁 Microsoft Works Doc
- ▷ 📁 TeachText Doc

e. Display the Backup window in an outline list view by Name. Print the window.

Close all open windows.

# The Control Panels

## Learning Objectives

**After completing this Chapter you will be able to:**

1. Set your preferences on the General Control Panel: Desktop Pattern, Rate of Insertion Point Blinking, Menu Blinking, Date, and Time.
2. Configure your Macintosh environment to meet your needs by using the other control panels: Startup Device, Keyboard, Mouse, Sound, Monitors, Color, Memory, Views, Labels, Numbers, and Date & Time.
3. Briefly explain the networking control panels: File Sharing Monitor, Sharing Setup, and User & Groups.

## Introduction

The **Control Panels** entry in the Apple menu allows you to access at least fifteen control panel programs: General Controls, Startup Disk, Keyboard, Mouse, Sound, Monitors, Color, Memory, Views, Labels, Numbers, Date & Time, File Sharing Monitor, Sharing Setup, User & Group. These programs are stored in the **Control Panels folder** inside the **System Folder** on your Startup disk. Each control panel program allows you to modify/customize one part of your Macintosh. Any changes you make are saved, even when you power down the computer.

☞ *Very Important*

Anytime you see this symbol, carefully read and perform the next step(s). The activities in this chapter tell you how to customize your Macintosh system. If you are working on a Macintosh you own, a customized system is exactly what you want. On the other hand, if you are working on a Macintosh shared with other computer users, you must be careful and considerate. It is important to restore all settings to the way you found them before leaving the Macintosh.

### Optional Activity

This symbol will be used to identify optional activities. Your Macintosh hardware may prevent you from trying all activities within this chapter. For example, you can not change the colors/gray displayed on your desktop if you don't have a color or gray-scale monitor.

## Activity 11.1—Accessing the Control Panels

Step 1   Your Macintosh should be on and booted. All windows should be closed. Select Control Panels from the  menu.

### What's Happening

The file folder containing the control panel programs appears on your desktop. (Figure 11.1) You may have additional entries in this folder.

*Figure 11.1—Control Panels Folder*

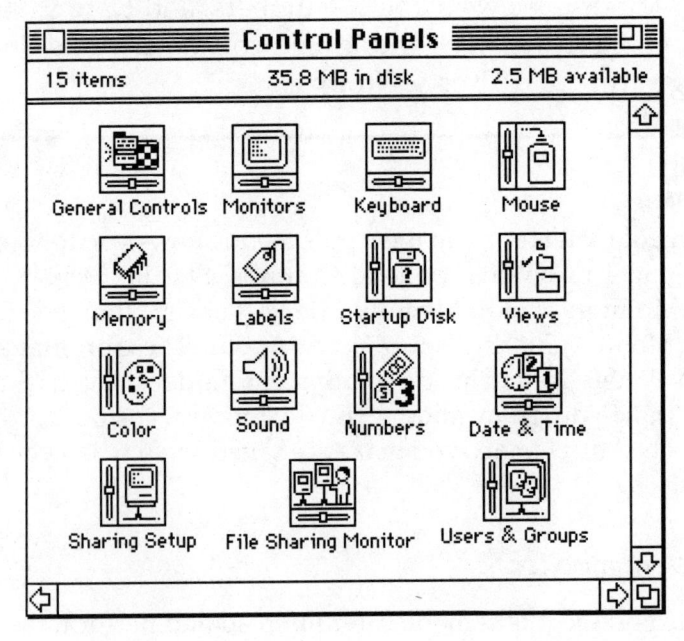

## Monitors

There are a variety of monitors available for the Macintosh Computer. The **Monitor control panel** can be used to specify the number of gray shades or colors to be displayed by your monitor. Your monitor and the adapter card must be capable of displaying that many colors. Generally, the more colors your monitor is set to display, the slower your system performs. Set the monitor to black and white for the fastest system performance.

This control panel may also be used to inform the system that you are using multiple monitors—their relative position to each other and which one is the main monitor. You would use the bottom portion of the Monitor control panel window to describe the monitors.

### Activity 11.2—Using the Monitors Control Panel

Step 1   The Control Panels window should still be on your desktop. If not, select Control Panels from the  menu.

Step 2   Double-click on the Monitors icon.

*Figure 11.2—Monitors Controls*

*What's Happening*

The Monitors control panel window appears. (Figure 11.2)

Step 3   Examine the Monitors window but do *not* change the entries.

*What's Happening*

The Grays or Colors button is used to direct the monitor to display Grays or Colors. The list box is used to specify the number of colors or grays to display: Black & White, 4, 16, 256. The color bar along the bottom of the window shows the range of colors you have directed the monitor to display. Clicking on the Options button will display a dialog box listing the type of video card being used by the selected monitor. Depending on your hardware, you may also be able to specify the amount of memory to reserve for your Macintosh's built-in video ability.

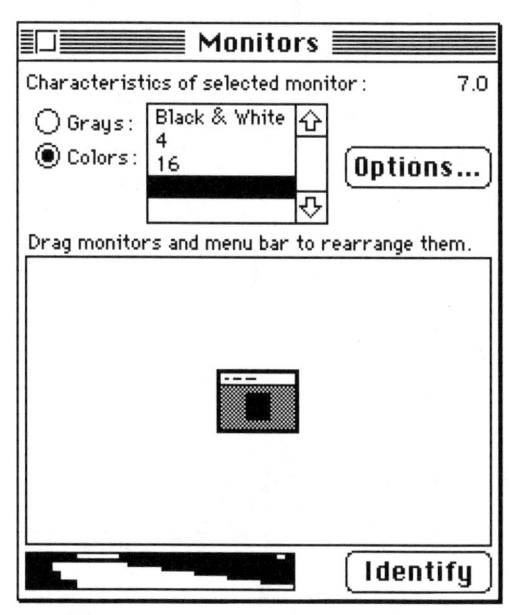

The box labeled *Drag Monitors and menu bar to rearrange them* will contain a separate monitor icon for each monitor you have attached to your system. You must specify their relative position to each other so the mouse pointer can move from one monitor to the next. Each monitor is assigned an ID number. Pressing the Identify button displays each monitor's ID number on the screen.

Step 4    Click on the close box to close the Monitors window.

## General Controls

### Activity 11.3 —Accessing the General Control Panels

Figure 11.3—General Controls

Step 1    The Control Panels window should still be on your desktop. If not, select Control Panels from the  menu. Double-click on the General Controls icon.

### What's Happening

A new window will appear, as shown in Figure 11.3. The **General Controls** panel is divided into four regions: **Desktop Pattern, Rate of Insertion Point Blinking, Menu Blinking,** and **Date and Time**. We will examine each one separately.

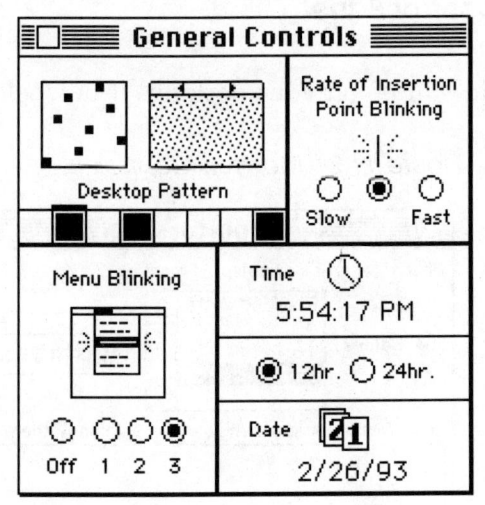

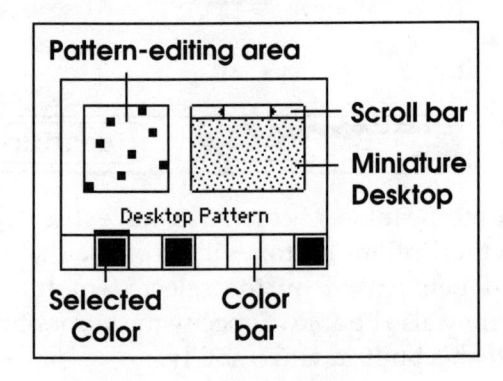

Figure 11.4—Background Pattern

### The Desktop Pattern

You may edit and set the background pattern on the desktop. The desktop may appear in the color(s) and pattern of your choice. Use the top left box of the General Controls window to set your desktop pattern. (Figure 11.4)

## Activity 11.4—Setting the Desktop Pattern

Step 1   Click several times on one of the small triangles on the scroll bar.

## What's Happening

Each time you click, a new desktop pattern appears on the miniature desktop. The triangle on the left displays the desktop patterns in reverse order. In other words, if you pass a pattern you like, click on the left triangle to backup.

Step 2   Click on the triangle until you see a sample desktop pattern you like.

Step 3   Click on the miniature desktop.

## What's Happening

The Macintosh's desktop pattern has been changed to match the sample. If you don't like it, repeat steps 2 and 3.

### Editing a Pattern

Step 4   Click on several of the dark squares and blank spots in the pattern-editing area.

## What's Happening

The pattern in the miniature desktop changes. By clicking on a square in the pattern-editing area you can customize the desktop pattern. If you find one you like, click on the miniature desktop to change your Macintosh's desktop pattern.

*Optional Activity*

### Editing the Pattern using Color

If you have a color or gray-scale monitor and it has been instructed to display multiple colors/grays through the Monitors control panel, proceed with steps 5 through 15. Otherwise proceed to step 16.

Step 5   Examine the **color bar**. The color with a horizontal line over it is the current selected color. Select a different color by clicking on it.

Step 6   Click on several squares in the pattern-editing area.

## What's Happening

The current selected color is assigned to each square you click on. The miniature desktop displays the new design.

Step 7    Click on a different color in the color bar.

Step 8    Click on several squares in the pattern-editing area.

Step 9    Repeat steps 7 and 8 until you create a desktop pattern you like.

Step 10   Click on the miniature desktop.

## What's Happening
The Macintosh desktop displays your customized pattern.

### Changing colors on the color bar
Step 11   Double-click on one of the colors you have been using in the color bar.

## What's Happening
If your monitor has been set to display sixteen or more colors/grays, the color wheel dialog box like the one in Figure 11.5 appears.

*Figure 11.5—Color Wheel Dialog Box: 16 or more Colors/Grays*

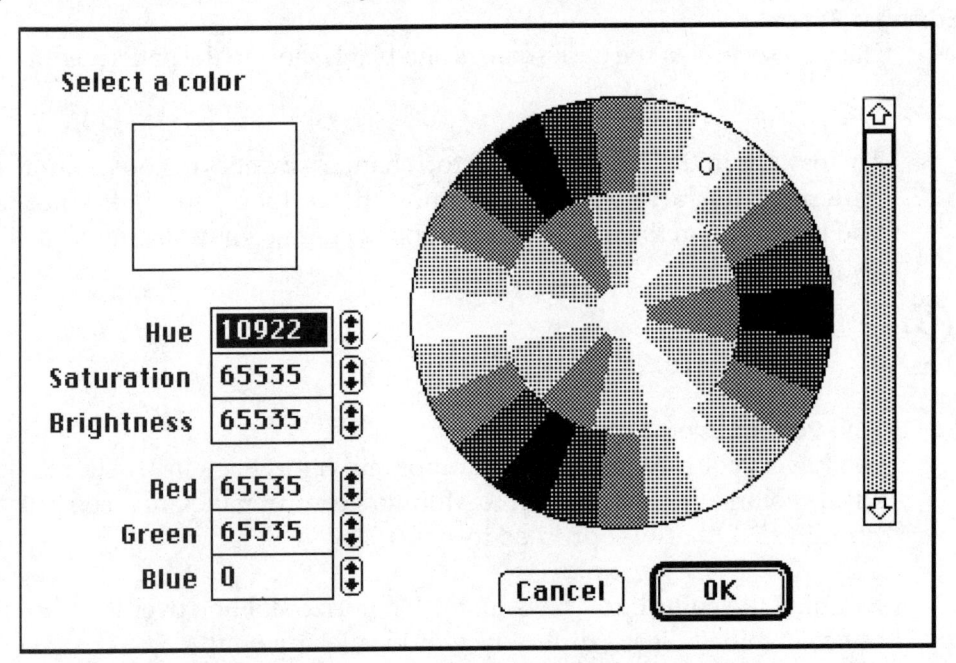

If your monitor has been set to display less than sixteen colors/grays, a color wheel dialog box like the one in Figure 11.6 appears.

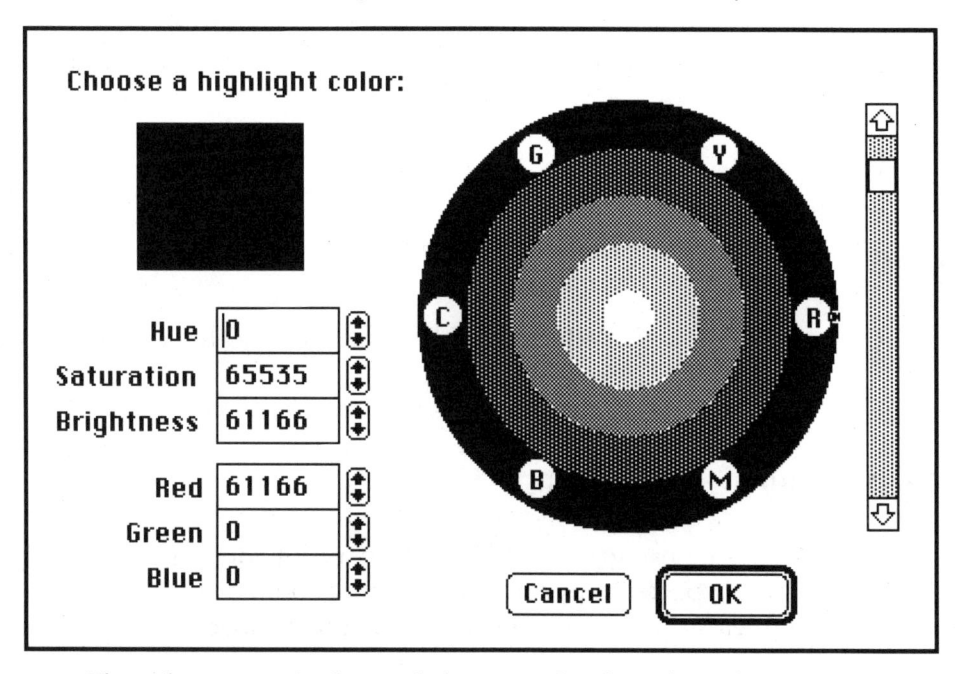

*Figure 11.6—Color Wheel Dialog Box: Less than 16 Colors/Grays*

The color square in the top left corner displays the current color. The boxes below the color square contain numbers corresponding to the current color. The color wheel can display over sixteen million colors, though not all at once. The small circle in the color wheel indicates the current selected color. The scroll bar controls the color brightness.

To change the brightness and to see other colors and grays, drag the scroll box or use the scroll arrow keys on the scroll bar. To select a color, click on the desired color in the color wheel or click on the arrows next to each box (Hue, Saturation, Brightness, Red, Green, Blue).

If your monitor has been set to display black and white, all the numbers will be set to 0. The letters on the color wheel stand for colors: Y is for yellow, R is for red, M is for magenta, B is for blue, C is for cyan, and G is for green.

Step 12   Click on a different color in the color wheel.

## What's Happening

The new color is displayed in the top half of the color square and the old color is in the bottom half. The numbers correspond to the new color.

Step 13   Repeat step 12 until you see a color you like.

Step 14   Click on the OK button.

### What's Happening

The Color Wheel dialog box disappears. The new color has replaced the old color on the color bar, in the pattern-editing area and in the miniature desktop.

Step 15   Click on the miniature desktop to change the color on the Macintosh's desktop.

☞ *Very Important: Restore the original settings*

Step 16   Click on the Desktop Pattern scroll bar until you locate the original pattern.

Step 17   Click on the miniature desktop to change the Macintosh desktop pattern.

### Rate of Insertion Point Blinking

When you are entering text, the **insertion point** identifies where the next character you type will appear. The insertion point, also called the cursor, generally appears as a flashing **vertical line.** You can specify how fast the cursor will blink.

### Activity 11.5—Setting the Rate of Insertion Point Blinking

Step 1   Click on any one of the three buttons to set how fast the cursor will blink. (Figure 11.7)

*Figure 11.7—Rate of Insertion Point Blinking*

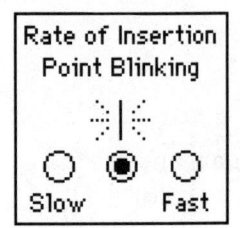

### What's Happening

As you click on the three buttons, the sample cursor will demonstrate the selected speed. Some Macintosh users feel the fast speed makes them nervous. Others dislike the slow speed because the cursor disappears for a longer time. Perhaps the middle one is just right.

☞ *Very Important: Restore the original settings*

Step 2   Click on the appropriate button to restore the original setting.

## Menu Blinking

When you select commands from menus, you have the option of the selected command blinking 0, 1, 2, or 3 times before the command is executed. Macintosh users who are interested in time saving features will usually turn menu blinking off.

### Activity 11.6 — Set Menu Blinking

*Figure 11.8— Menu Blinking*

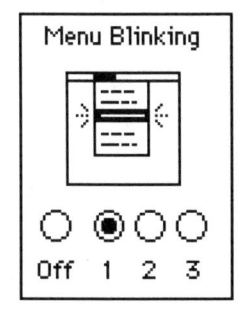

Step 1  Click on the buttons 1 to 3, depending on how many times you would like menu items to blink before executing. You can also select Off so they won't blink at all. (Figure 11.8)

*What's Happening*

The sample pull-down menu demonstrates the number of blinks that will occur before the command is executed.

*Very Important: Restore the original settings.*

Step 2  Click on the appropriate button (0, 1, 2, or 3) to restore the original setting.

## Time and Date

Remember, we discussed the importance of setting the correct date and time on your Macintosh. You can set the date and time here in the General Controls panel, in the Date & Time control panel, or by accessing the Alarm Clock DA. You can only set the time for the Alarm and turn the alarm on or off in the Alarm Clock DA. You can specify how dates are to be displayed in the Date & Time control panel.

### Activity 11.7—Setting Time and Date

*Figure 11.9—Time and Date*

Step 1  Click 12hr. or 24hr. to set time format. (Figure 11.9)

Step 2  Click on the hour, minute, or second (double arrows appear) and then click on the arrows or type the desired number to scroll the numbers. Click on the small clock in the top panel to set the new time (double arrows disappear).

Step 3  Click on the month, day, or year (double arrows appear) and then click on the arrows or type the desired number to scroll the numbers. Click on the numbers 21 to set the new date (double arrows disappear).

*Very Important: Restore the correct date and time.*

Step 4  Set the Time and Date to the current time and date.

Step 5  Click on the close box to close the General Controls window.

## Startup Disk

If you have more than one hard drive, you need to use the **Startup Disk control panel** to identify which one to use as the startup disk. You can attach up to seven hard disks to most Macintosh systems. The selected hard disk must contain a System Folder.

### Activity 11.8—Using the Startup Disk Control Panel

Step 1  The Control Panels window should still be on your desktop. If not, select Control Panels from the  menu.

*Figure 11.10—The Startup Disk*

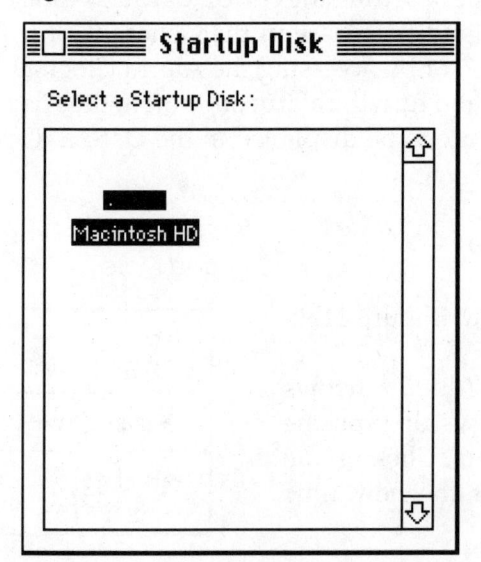

Step 2  Double-click on the Startup Disk icon.

*What's Happening*

The Startup Disk window appears. (Figure 11.10) If you have multiple hard disks, there will be more than one hard disk icon in the window. The highlighted icon is the selected booting disk. To select a different hard disk, click on its icon. (*Don't change Startup disks.*)

Step 3  Close the Startup Disk window by clicking on the close box.

## Keyboard

The **Keyboard control panel** is used to set the following keyboard controls.
- **Key Repeat Rate** is used to determine how fast a character repeats itself across the screen, when you press a key.
- **Delay Until Repeat** is used to set the amount of time the computer waits, once you hit a key, before it starts repeating the character.
- **Keyboard Layout**. Your Macintosh may include other choices (British, Deutsch, Italiano) depending on when and where it was purchased.

### Activity 11.9—Using the Keyboard Control Panel

Step 1   The Control Panels window should still be on your desktop. If not, select Control Panels from the menu.

*Figure 11.11—Keyboard Controls*

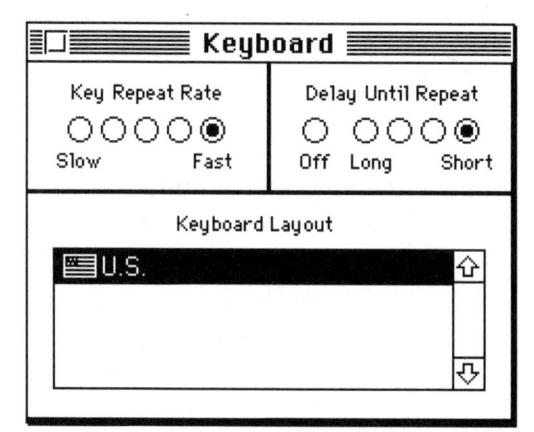

Step 2   Double-click on the Keyboard icon.

*What's Happening*

The Keyboard control panel window appears. (Figure 11.11) If you are working on your own Macintosh, you can adjust the settings by clicking on the appropriate button. Otherwise, do not change this control panel.

Step 3   Click on the close box to close the Keyboard window.

## Mouse

The **Mouse control panel** is used to set the following mouse controls.

**Mouse Tracking.** This control allows you to set how far you have to move the mouse on the tabletop to move the mouse pointer on the screen.
- **Slow.** If you move the mouse one inch, the pointer moves one inch. (Good for new Macintosh users.)
- **Fast.** If you move the mouse one inch, the pointer moves two inches. (Good for experienced Macintosh users.)

- **Very Slow/Tablet.** As you move the mouse on the table top, the pointer moves at a slow, constant speed. (Good for drawing with the mouse.)

**Double-Click Speed.** How fast do you double-click? Clicking the mouse twice quickly is used as a shortcut for many operations. If you are clicking twice and the Macintosh is interpreting it as two single clicks, use this control panel to adjust the double-clicking speed.

### Activity 11.10—Using the Mouse Control Panel

Step 1    The Control Panels window should still be on your desktop. If not, select Control Panels from the menu.

*Figure 11.12—Mouse Controls*

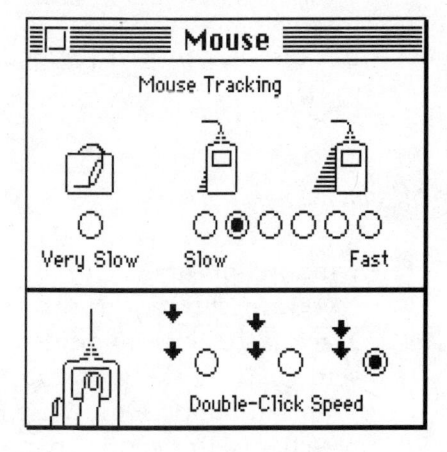

Step 2    Double-click on the Mouse icon.

### What's Happening
The Mouse window appears, as shown in Figure 11.12.

**Set the Mouse Tracking Speed**

Step 3    Click on the Fast button.

### What's Happening
The new mouse tracking speed takes effect immediately.

Step 4    Move the mouse on your desktop and watch how quickly the pointer moves on the screen.

Step 5    Click on the Slow button.

Step 6    Move the mouse on your desktop and watch how slowly the pointer moves on the screen.

**Set Double-Click Speed**

Step 7    Click on the Double-Click Speed buttons one by one.

### What's Happening
The sample mouse demonstrates each double-click speed you select.

☛ *Very Important: Restore the original settings*

Step 8   Click on the appropriate Mouse Tracking and Double-Click Speed buttons to restore the original setting.

Step 9   Click on the close box to close the Mouse window.

## Sound

Because the Macintosh will sound off to get your attention, the Macintosh system comes with several **alert sounds** for you to select from. The **Sound control panel** is used to set the volume and to choose which alert sound to use. A shaded scroll bar indicates additional sounds are available. Use the scroll bar to display them.

Some Macintosh systems are equipped with a sound input port and a microphone. On other Macintoshes, you will have to buy additional equipment to record sounds. Alert sounds may be added or removed by using this control panel.

### Activity 11.11—Using the Sound Control Panel

Step 1   The Control Panels window should still be on your desktop. If not, select Control Panels from the  menu.

Step 2   Double-click on the Sound icon.

*What's Happening*

The Sound control panel window appears. (Figure 11.13) It is divided into three parts: **Speaker Volume, Alert Sounds,** and **Microphones**. If your Macintosh does not have a sound input port, the bottom section (microphones) will not be included in the window.

**Setting the Speaker Volume**

Step 3   Drag the Speaker Volume knob to 4. Release the mouse button.

*What's Happening*

The selected alert sound plays at volume 4. The selected alert sound is highlighted.

*Figure 11.13—Sound Controls*

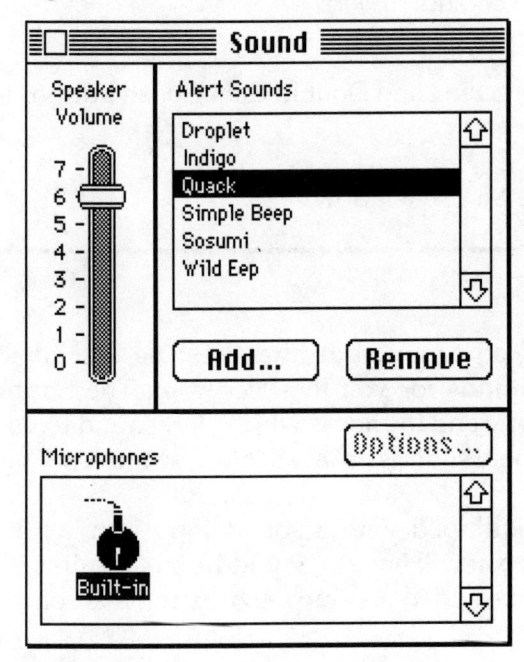

Step 4   Drag the Speaker Volume knob to 0.

*What's Happening*
You have turned the sound off. The menu bar will flash instead.

Step 5   Drag the Speaker Volume knob to 7. Release the mouse button.

*What's Happening*
The selected alert sound plays at volume 7.

### Selecting the Alert Sound
Step 6   Click on one of the other alert sounds.

*What's Happening*
The selected alert sound will play at the selected volume.

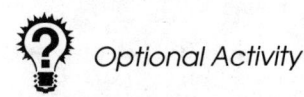

*Optional Activity*

**Adding Alert Sounds**
If your Macintosh does not have sound input capability or you do not have a microphone, skip steps 7 through 16 and proceed to step 17.

Step 7   Click on the Add button.

*What's Happening*
The Record dialog box appears. (Figure 11.14) Let's record your voice saying "Caution, Beware, Watch Out". Have your microphone in hand. Once you click on the Record button you have 10 seconds to completely enter your new alert sound.

Step 8   Click on the Record button. Say "Caution, Beware, Watch Out."

Step 9   Click on the Stop button.

*What's Happening*
> As you record your sound, the time **bar** along the bottom of the dialog box shows how long you have been recording.

Step 10   Click on the Play button.

*What's Happening*
> The new sound will be played back.

*Figure 11.14—Record Dialog Box*

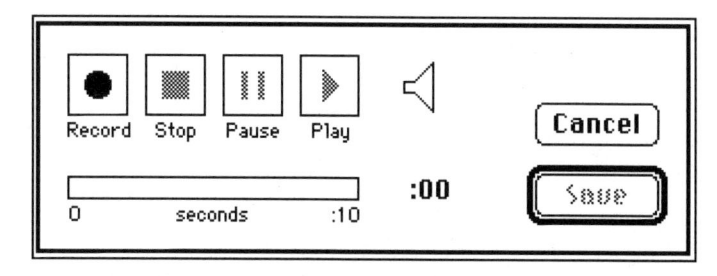

Step 11   If you are satisfied with the new sound, click on the Save button. If you wish to redo the sound, repeat steps 8 through 10 and then click on the Save button.

*What's Happening*
> A dialog box appears requesting a name for the new alert sound.

Step 12   Key in the name, Watch out. (Figure 11.15) Click on the OK button.

*What's Happening*
> The new alert sound has been added to the list of available sounds in the Sound window.

*Figure 11.15—Naming New Sound*

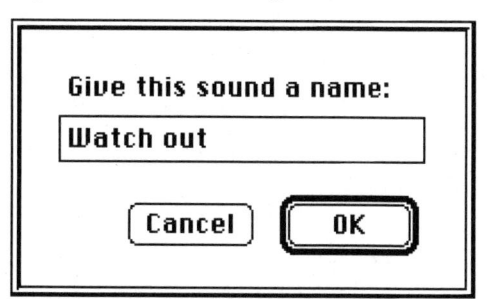

Step 13   Click on the new sound to hear it one last time.

*What's Happening*
> Your new sound will play at the selected volume setting.

*Optional Activity*

**Removing Alert Sounds**

If you are not working on your own Macintosh and you added the Watch out sound, you need to remove it. If you are using your own Macintosh and wish to keep the alert sound, proceed to step 17.

Step 14   The sound, Watch out, should be highlighted. If not, click on it.

Step 15   Click on the Remove button.

*What's Happening*

An alert dialog box appears verifying your request to delete the sound. (Figure 11.16)

Figure 11.16—Removing an Alert Sound

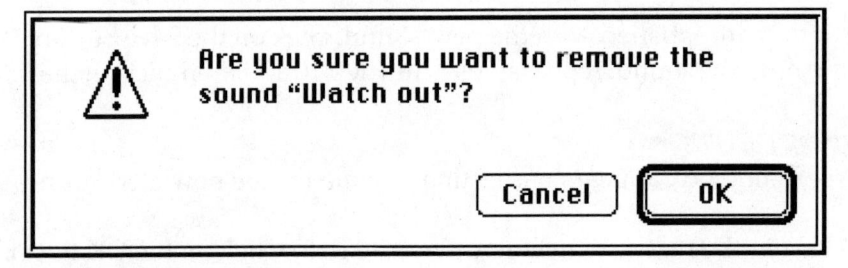

Step 16   Click on the OK button.

*Very Important: Restore the original settings*

Step 17   Drag the Speaker Volume knob to the original setting. Click on the original alert sound.

Step 18   Click on the close box to close the Sound window.

# Color

The **Color control panel** is used to specify the color/gray to use for highlighting text and window borders. Obviously if you do not have a color or gray-scale monitor or if it isn't set to display multiple colors/grays, read but do not do this Activity.

*Optional Activity*

### Activity 11.12—Using the Color Control Panel

Step 1   The Control Panels window should still be on your desktop. If not, select Control Panels from the menu.

Step 2   Double-click on the Color icon.

*Figure 11.17—Color Controls*

```
╔════════════════ Color ════════════════╗
                                         
  Highlight color:  [■  Red         ▼]  
  [Sample text]                          
                                         
  Window color:     [□  Gold        ▼]  
                                         
╚═══════════════════════════════════════╝
```

*What's Happening*
The Color control panel window appears. In Figure 11.17, the current Highlight color is Red (notice the sample text square). If the **Window color** is Gold, the box surrounding the word Gold and the Color control panel window will be bordered in gold. When a disk, folder, or document window is open, numerous items will appear in the selected window color: the window outline, scroll box, scroll arrows, close box, zoom box, and size box.

Step 3   Point to the triangle in the **Highlight color bar.** Press and hold the mouse button.

*What's Happening*
A pop-up menu appears displaying other colors to select from. (Figure 11.18) **Pop-up menu** names do not appear on the menu bar; instead, they are attached to dialog boxes, windows, and so on. The triangle indicates the existence of a menu. If you select Other, the color wheel dialog box appears. (Figure 11.5 or 11.6)

*Figure 11.18—Highlight Color*

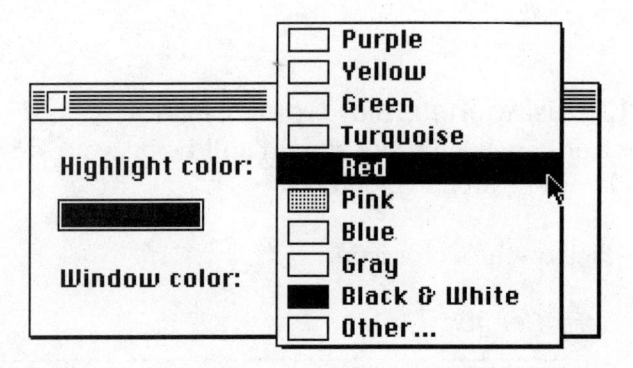

Step 4   Drag the mouse up or down the list and select a different color. Release the mouse button.

## What's Happening

The Sample text square displays the new color.

Step 5   Point to the triangle in the Window color bar. Press and hold the mouse button.

## What's Happening

The window in Figure 11.19 appears.

*Figure 11.19—Window Border Color*

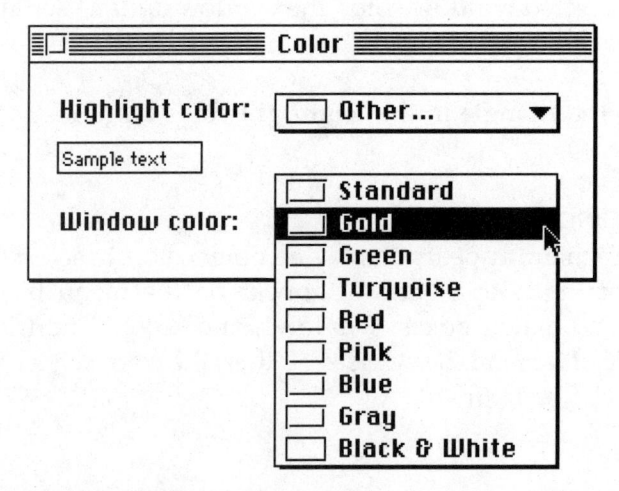

The window border color may be set to one of nine colors. There is no Other entry. You can not access the color wheel and change color selections.

Step 6   Drag the mouse up or down the list to select a different color and release the mouse button.

## What's Happening

The Color control panel window's border matches your selected color.

☞ *Very Important: Restore the original settings*

Step 7   Set the Highlight color and the Window color back to their original settings.

Step 8   Click on the close box to close the Color window.

## Memory

The **Memory control panel** allows you to:
- Increase or decrease disk cache
- Turn virtual memory on and off
- Turn 32-bit addressing on and off.

Any changes in this window do not take effect until you restart the system.

☞ *Very Important: Do not make any changes in this window*

### Activity 11.13—Using the Memory Control Panel

Step 1   The Control Panels window should still be on your desktop. If not select Control Panels from the  menu.

Step 2   Double-click on the Memory icon.

## What's Happening

The Memory control panel window appears. (Figure 11.20) Do not change any entries in this window. If your Macintosh is not capable of using virtual memory or 32-bit addressing, those two sections will not appear.

*Figure 11.20—Memory Control*

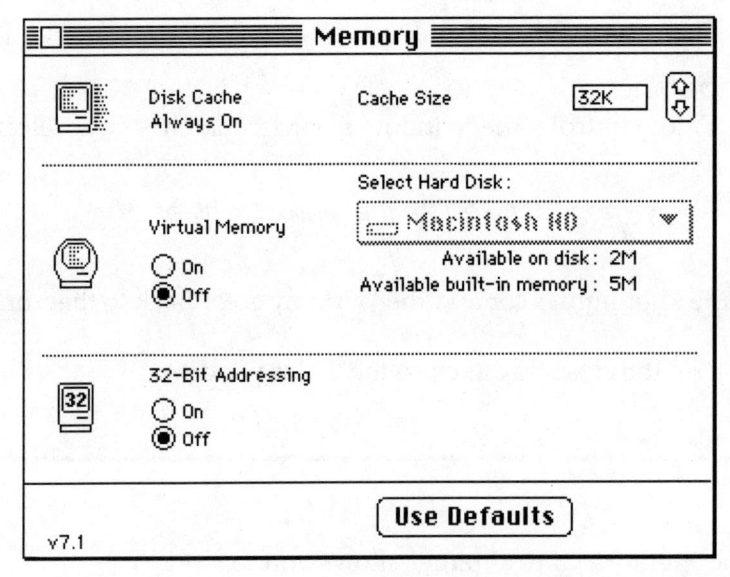

```
┌─────────────────── Memory ───────────────────┐
│                                              │
│   ▯  Disk Cache         Cache Size   [ 32K ] │
│      Always On                               │
│  ────────────────────────────────────────    │
│                      Select Hard Disk:       │
│   ▯  Virtual Memory  [≡ Macintosh HD   ▼]    │
│      ○ On            Available on disk: 2M   │
│      ● Off           Available built-in memory: 5M │
│  ────────────────────────────────────────    │
│   [32] 32-Bit Addressing                     │
│       ○ On                                   │
│       ● Off                                  │
│  ────────────────────────────────────────    │
│                        [  Use Defaults  ]    │
│   v7.1                                       │
└──────────────────────────────────────────────┘
```

**Disk Cache** is always on, but you must specify how much memory to use. Disk Cache is memory that is set aside to store frequently-used data. It reduces the number of times the system needs to retrieve information from the disk because it is already in memory. Be careful not to set Disk Cache too high. The memory you set aside is not available for opening additional application programs or documents. If you are low on memory, set Disk Cache very low (16K minimum allowed). Your system software may run slower but you will be maximizing the amount of memory available for application programs.

The Virtual Memory controls will be included in the Memory control panel if your Macintosh can use virtual memory. Not all Macintoshes are capable of using this feature. **Virtual Memory** is disk space that is being used to store open application programs and documents in a way that is similar to RAM. Of course, this disk space is not available for permanently storing files. If you have more than one hard disk, you can access a pop-up menu under Select Hard Disk. Virtual Memory is most effective for Macintosh users who wish to work with several small application programs concurrently.

**32-Bit Addressing** is available if you have a newer Macintosh with the 68030 or 68040 processor chip. Newer Macintoshes can use 32-bit numbers to specify memory addresses instead of 16-bit numbers. This feature is useful if you need to use large amounts of RAM (over 8MB). Besides turning 32-bit addressing on, you must purchase and install extra RAM.

Step 3     Click in the close box to close the Memory window.

## Views

Disk, folder, and Trash windows may be viewed in an icon (by Small icon or Icon) or list view (by Name, Size, Kind, Label, or Date). Use the Views control panel to adjust how the contents of these windows appear.

The three regions of the **Views control panel** allow you to specify:
1. Fonts for views
    - The font and point size to use for icon and list view windows (icon names and information).
    - You can not change the font or point size for window titles and menu names.

2. Icon Views
    - The default layout of icons in a window (straight or staggered).
    - Whether icons are to line up on the invisible grid when moved.

3. List Views
    - Whether to calculate folder sizes and display this information in the list view.
    - Whether to show the information bar in list view windows.
    - What information to display in list view windows: size, kind, label, date, version, comments.
    - How large the icons are to appear in the window.

### Activity 11.14—Using the Views Control Panel

Step 1  The Control Panels window should still be on your desktop. If not, select Control Panels from the  menu. Use the size box to make the Control Panels window almost fill the screen. If the Control Panels window is not in list view, choose by Name from the View menu.

Step 2  Double-click on the Views icon.

### What's Happening

The Views control panel window appears.

Step 3  Examine the options containing an X in the List Views section in Figure 11.21. Compare these entries to the column headings displayed in the Control Panels window in Figure 11.21 (displayed under the Views window): Name, Size, Kind, Label, and Last Modified (date).

*Figure 11.21—List View Window*

```
                        Control Panels
   Name               Size   Kind           Label    Last Modified
 □ Color               12K   control panel    —      Thu, Aug 13, 1992, 12:00 PM
 □ Date & Time         36K   control panel    —      Fri, Feb 26, 1993, 5:00 PM
 □ File Sharing Monitor 4K   control panel    —      Thu, Aug 27, 1992, 12:00 PM
 □ General Controls
 □ Keyboard                       ▬▬▬▬ Views ▬▬▬▬
 □ Labels
 □ Memory              Font for views:  Geneva  ▼    9 ▼
 □ Monitors            ┌─ Icon Views ───────────────────────────┐
 □ Mouse               │ □ □ □ □  ● Straight grid               │
 □ Numbers             │                       □ Always snap to grid │
 □ Sharing Setup       │ □ □ □ □  ○ Staggered grid              │
 □ Sound               └────────────────────────────────────────┘
 □ Startup Disk        ┌─ List Views ───────────────────────────┐
 □ Users & Groups      │                         ☒ Show size    │
 ▣ Views               │    ◇     ◇     ◈        ☒ Show kind    │
                       │                         ☒ Show label   │
                       │    ●     ○     ○        ☒ Show date    │
                       │ □ Calculate folder sizes □ Show version │
                       │ □ Show disk info in header □ Show comments │
                       └────────────────────────────────────────┘
```

Step 4   If necessary, move the Views window on your desktop in order to see the contents of your Control Panels window. Now compare the options containing an X in your Views control panel to the Control Panels window on your desktop.

## What's Happening

You are about to modify these settings. Please record the current settings here or on a separate sheet of paper.

*Font for views* _____

*Point Size* _____

*Icon Views* _____

*List Views* _____

*Icon Size* _____

Did the following checkboxes contain an X? (Yes or No) _____

*Calculate folder sizes* _____

*Show disk info in header* _____

*Show size* _____

*Show kind* _____
*Show label* _____
*Show date* _____
*Show version* _____
*Show comments* _____

**Modify the List Views region**

Step 5   Click on the button under the largest icon in the List Views region. (Figure 11.22)

*What's Happening*
The icons on the Control Panels window will be larger.

Step 6   Verify there is an **X** in the *Show size*, *Show kind*, and *Show date* checkboxes. Remove the X from *Show label, Show version*, and *Show comments* (if necessary). Click once on a checkbox to place or remove the X. (Figure 11.22)

☒ Show size
☒ Show kind
☐ Show label
☒ Show date
☐ Show version
☐ Show comments

*What's Happening*
Your Control Panels window should display only the name, size, kind, and date of each icon.

Step 7   If an **X** does not appear in the *Show Disk Info in Header* entry, click on this checkbox.

*What's Happening*
The information bar appears under the title bar on the Control Panels window. Figure 11.22 displays all your selections in the List View section of the Views window: large icon, show disk info in header and show size, kind, and date. Figure 11.23 shows the results of your new settings on the Control Panels window.

*Figure 11.22—Modifying the List View*

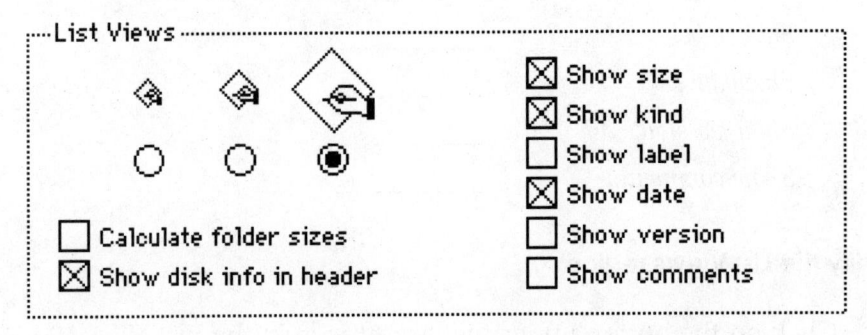

*Figure 11.23—Modified List View in the Control Panels Window*

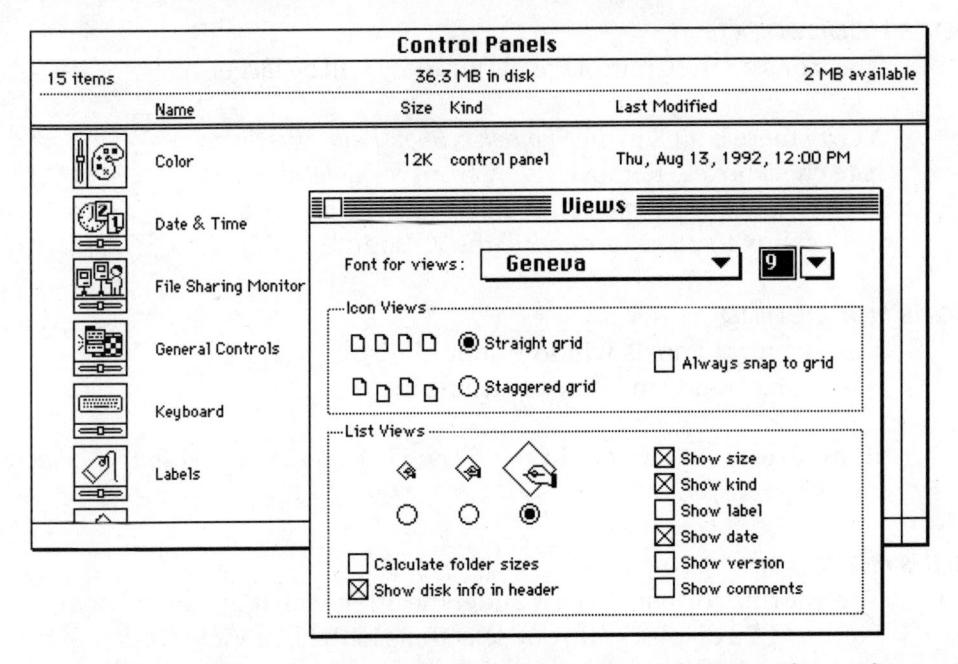

The *Calculate folder size* option is a useful System 7 feature. If you choose this option, the Macintosh will calculate and display the number of bytes (characters) each folder contains. This does tend to slow down the performance of the Macintosh. Another way to see the size of selected folders is to use the Get Info command on the File menu.

### Changing font and point size

Step 8    Position the pointer on the triangle in the first panel, Font for views. Press and hold the mouse button.

*What's Happening*

A pop-up menu containing available fonts appears. (Figure 11.24) The current font has a check mark next to it.

*Figure 11.24—Available Fonts*

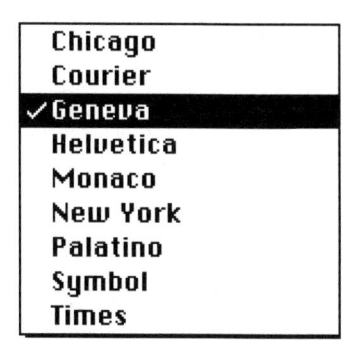

```
Chicago
Courier
✓ Geneva
Helvetica
Monaco
New York
Palatino
Symbol
Times
```

Step 9   Drag the pointer up or down the list to highlight the Helvetica font. Release the mouse button.

*What's Happening*

Look at the Control Panels window. The icon names are now displayed using the Helvetica font.

*Figure 11.25— Point Sizes*

Step 10   Position the pointer on the triangle next to the point size number. Press and hold the mouse button.

*What's Happening*

A pop-up menu containing available point sizes appears. (Figure 11.25) The current point size has a check mark next to it. Numbers displayed as solid numbers, not outlined, will not display the font very well.

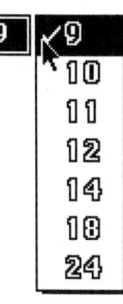

```
9
10
11
12
14
18
24
```

Step 11   Drag the pointer up or down the list to highlight 14. Release the mouse button.

*What's Happening*

Look at the Control Panels window. The icon names are now displayed in 14-point Helvetica. Figure 11.26 shows all your changes.

*Figure 11.26—Views Panel and List View Window*

☞ *Very Important: Restore the original settings*

If you are not working on your own Macintosh, locate where you wrote down the original settings and reset everything you have changed in the Views window.

Step 12  Set the font and point size back to the way you found them.

Step 13  Set the icon size back to the way you found it.

Step 14  Set all checkboxes in the List Views region to the way you found them.

Step 15  Close the Views window.

## Labels

Labels may be assigned to icons for quick identification. You assigned labels to a couple files in Chapter 9. A Label consists of a name and a color, if you have a color or gray-scale monitor. The **Labels control panel** is used to change the name of available labels and to change the color assigned to each.

## Activity 11.15—Using the Labels Control Panel

Step 1   The Control Panels window should still be on your desktop. If not, select Control Panels from the  menu.

Step 2   Double-click on the Labels icon.

*Figure 11.27—Labels Control*

### What's Happening

The Labels control panel window appears. (Figure 11.27) Remember the Label column in the list view window. (Figure 11.21) There were no labels assigned. Let's quickly examine how you would make changes to this window.

*Optional Activity*

If you are not working on your own Macintosh, *Do Not* change any entries in this window.
- To change a Label name, highlight the label name and type the new name.
- To change a Label color, click on the color you wish to change, the color wheel dialog box will appear, click on the desired color.

Step 3   Click on the close box to close the window.

## Numbers

The **Numbers control panel** allows you to specify the format to be used when displaying numbers and currency. This control panel is new in System 7.1. If you have an older version of System 7, you may not have this control panel.

### Activity 11.16—Using the Numbers Control Panel

Step 1   The Control Panels window should still be on your desktop. If not, select Control Panels from the  menu.

Step 2   Double-click on the Numbers icon.

## What's Happening

The Numbers control panel window appears. (Figure 11.28) Use this control panel to specify:
- The language version installed in your system.
  (The standard format for numbers in that language will appear in the window).
  If you change any entry in this window, the Number Format will change to Custom.
- The character to use as the Decimal and Thousands separator.
- The character to use as the Currency Symbol.
- Where to place the currency symbol.

*Figure 11.28—Numbers Control Panel*

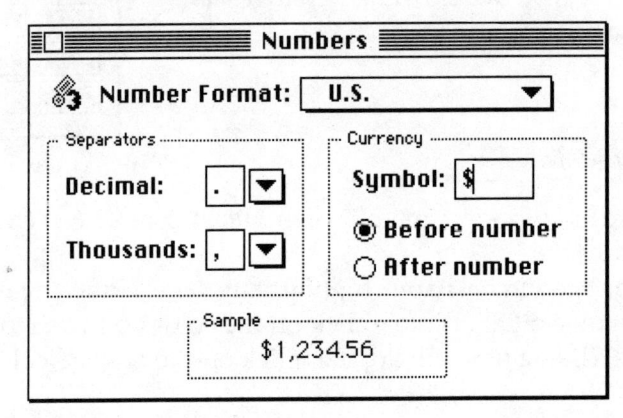

[Numbers control panel dialog showing:
Number Format: U.S.
Separators — Decimal: . Thousands: ,
Currency — Symbol: $ ● Before number ○ After number
Sample: $1,234.56]

Three pop-up menus are included: Number Format, Decimal, and Thousands. You may select an entry from one of these menus or type the character you want. The sample number on the bottom of the window displays your selections.

Step 3  Position the pointer on the triangle next to Decimal. Press and hold the mouse button.

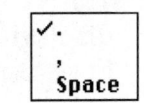

[Pop-up menu: ✓ . , Space]

## What's Happening

A pop-up menu appears containing a variety of separators.

Step 4  Drag the pointer down the list to highlight **Space**.

[Sample: $1,234 56]

## What's Happening

The sample number is now displayed with a space instead of a decimal point. The Number Format entry has changed to Custom.

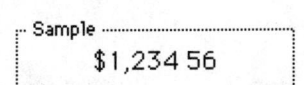

Step 5  Press the Tab key twice to highlight the dollar sign ($) Symbol character. Press the Space Bar.

*Sample*
1,234 56

### What's Happening
The dollar sign has been removed from the sample number.

Step 6  Position the pointer on the triangle next to Thousands. Press and hold the mouse button.

### What's Happening
A pop-up menu appears containing a variety of separators.

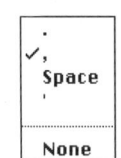

```
.
✓ ,
  Space
  '
  None
```

Step 7  Release the mouse button.

☞ *Very Important: Restore the original settings*

Step 8  Position the pointer on the triangle next to Number Format. Press and hold the mouse button. Drag the pointer up or down to highlight the original language version (U.S.).

### What's Happening
All settings on this control panel have been restored to the standard format for this language.

Step 9  Click on the close box to close the Numbers window.

## Date & Time

The **Date & Time control panel** can be used to set the System date and time and to change the way they are displayed on your Macintosh. This control panel is new in System 7.1.

### Activity 11.17—Using the Date & Time Control Panel

Step 1  The Control Panels window should still be on your desktop. If not, select Control Panels from the  menu.

Step 2  Double-click on the Date & Time icon.

*Figure 11.29—Date & Time Control Panel*

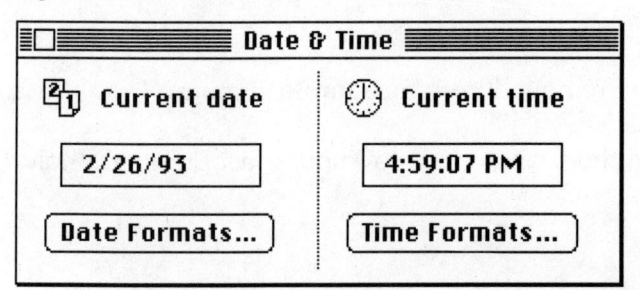

```
┌─────────── Date & Time ───────────┐
│  🕐 Current date    🕐 Current time │
│   ┌─────────┐       ┌──────────┐   │
│   │ 2/26/93 │       │4:59:07 PM│   │
│   └─────────┘       └──────────┘   │
│  [ Date Formats... ] [ Time Formats... ] │
└────────────────────────────────────┘
```

### What's Happening

The Date & Time control panel window appears. (Figure 11.29) Your system's current date and time will be displayed in the window.

If you need to enter the correct date and time, click on the incorrect number (month, day, year, hour, minutes, or second). The number will be highlighted and a double-arrow will appear. Type the correct number and press the Return key.

Step 3  Click on the Date Formats... button.

### What's Happening

The Date Formats dialog box appears. In Figure 11.30, the selected Date Formats are displayed in standard U.S. format. If any entry in this dialog box is changed, the Date Formats entry will change to Custom. The dialog box is divided into two major sections: Long date and Short date. Examples of the selected formats are displayed in the Samples section (long date, abbreviated long date, and short date).

*Figure 11.30—Date Formats Dialog Box*

```
┌──────────────────────────────────────────────────┐
│  🕐 Date Formats: [ U.S.          ▼]             │
│  ┌─ Long date ──────────┐  ┌─ Short date ──────┐ │
│           Prefix: [    ]    [Month/Day/Year ▼]   │
│    [Weekday ▼] , [    ]    Separator: [ / ]      │
│    [Month   ▼]   [    ]    ☐ Leading zero for day│
│    [Day     ▼] , [    ]    ☐ Leading zero for month│
│    [Year    ▼]   [    ]    ☐ Show century        │
│    ☐ Leading zero for day                        │
│  └──────────────────────┘  └───────────────────┘ │
│  ┌─ Samples ──────────────────────┐  [ Cancel ]  │
│       Thursday, January 2, 1992                  │
│           Thu, Jan 2, 1992           [   OK   ]  │
│               1/2/92                             │
│  └────────────────────────────────┘              │
└──────────────────────────────────────────────────┘
```

In the Long date section, you can specify the order of elements in the long date format from pop-up menus. You can also specify which separators will appear between elements in the long date and whether or not to enter the leading zero in front of the day. For example, look at the Long Date specification in Figure 11.30. Read it starting at the top and working your way to the right and down: Weekday, Month, Day, Year.

**Change the Long Date Format**

Step 4   Position the pointer on the triangle next to Weekday. Press and hold the mouse button.

*Figure 11.31—Long Date Menu*

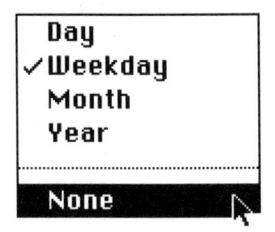

*What's Happening*

A list of possible entries appears in a pop-up menu.

Step 5   Drag the pointer down the list to highlight **None**. (Figure 11.31) Release the mouse button.

*What's Happening*

The sample long date and abbreviated long date is now displayed in the new format (the day of the week is gone). The Date Formats entry has changed to Custom.

Step 6   Display the Short Date pop-up menu. Select the entry **Year/Month/Day**. (Figure 11.32)

*Figure 11.32—Short Date Menu*

*What's Happening*

The sample short date is now displayed in the new format. (Figure 11.33)

The other entries in the dialog box allow you to specify the separator to use in the short format, to enter leading month and day zeroes, and to show the century. (Figure 11.34)

*Figure 11.33—New Date Formats*

*Figure 11.34—Short Date Options*

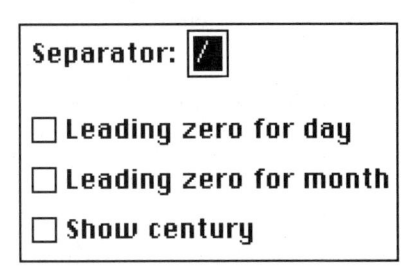

☛ *Very Important: Restore the original settings*

Step 7   Display the Date Formats pop-up menu. Select the entry U.S.

## What's Happening

Standard U.S. formats are now displayed in the dialog box.

Step 8   Click on the OK button.

## What's Happening

The Date Formats dialog box closes and the Date & Time control panel becomes the active window.

Step 9   Click on the Time Formats button.

## What's Happening

The Time Format dialog box appears. (Figure 11.35) This dialog box can be used to specify how time is to be displayed.

*Figure 11.35—Time Format Dialog Box*

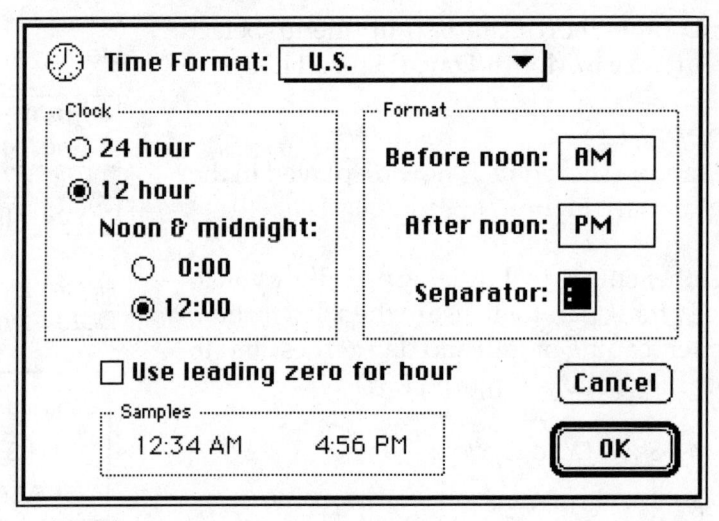

```
┌──────────────────────────────────────────────┐
│  🕐  Time Format: │ U.S.        ▼ │          │
│  ┌─ Clock ──────────┐ ┌─ Format ────────────┐│
│  │  ○ 24 hour       │ │ Before noon: │ AM │ ││
│  │  ● 12 hour       │ │                     ││
│  │  Noon & midnight:│ │ After noon:  │ PM │ ││
│  │     ○ 0:00       │ │                     ││
│  │     ● 12:00      │ │ Separator:   │ : │  ││
│  └──────────────────┘ └─────────────────────┘│
│   ☐ Use leading zero for hour    ┌─────────┐ │
│  ┌─ Samples ──────────────────┐  │ Cancel  │ │
│  │   12:34 AM    4:56 PM      │  ┌─────────┐│
│  └────────────────────────────┘  │   OK    ││
└──────────────────────────────────────────────┘
```

Step 10  Do not change any entries in this dialog box. Click on the Cancel button to close the dialog box.

Step 11  Click on the close box to close the Date & Time window.

# Computer Network Control Panels

The other three control panels (Sharing Setup, File Sharing Monitor, and User & Group) may be used if your Macintosh is connected to a computer network. A computer network consists of a group of computers and peripherals (printers, disks, CD-ROM drives, and so on) that are connected. This connection may be accomplished through cables, telephone, or satellite links and so on. Communication software is also required. System 7 provides several networking capabilities including file sharing between computers and printer sharing. The network control panels are beyond the scope of this book so only a brief explanation is presented. If you want more details refer to the Macintosh Networking Reference book that came with your System 7 software.

## Sharing Setup

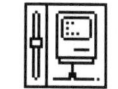

Use the **Sharing Setup control panel** to name your Macintosh, name yourself as owner and to enter a password. The password will prevent other users from accessing your files without permission. Other entries in this control panel allow you to turn File Sharing and Program Linking on and off. (Figure 11.36)

*Figure 11.36—Sharing Setup Controls*

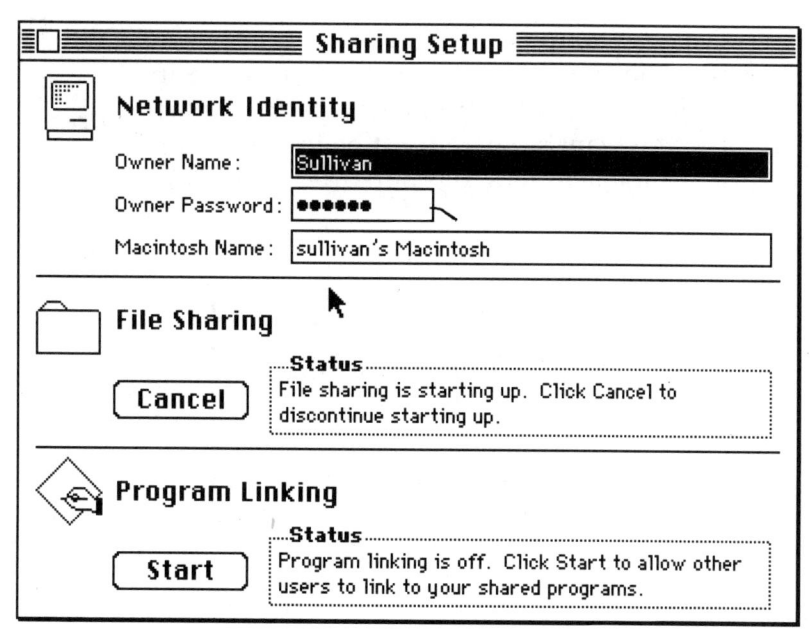

## File Sharing Monitor

The **File Sharing Monitor control panel** can be used to see who is connected to your Macintosh and what folders and/or disks you are sharing. (Figure 11.37)

*Figure 11.37—File Sharing Monitor Controls*

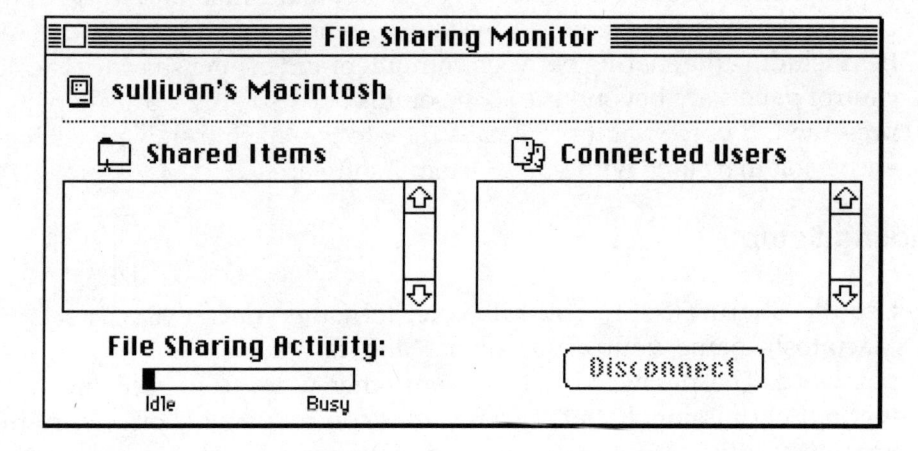

## Users & Group

Use the **Users & Groups control panel** to restrict who may access certain folders and hard disks. You can specify from one to 100 individual users and groups. Each folder or hard disk you want to share must be identified and given a list of eligible users and groups. (Figure 11.38)

*Figure 11.38—Users & Groups Controls*

## Key Terms

| | |
|---|---|
| 32-bit addressing | Labels control panel |
| Alert Sounds | List views |
| Color bar | Memory control panel |
| Color control panel | Menu Blinking |
| Color wheel | Monitor control panel |
| Control panels | Mouse control panel |
| Date & Time control panel | Mouse Tracking |
| Delay Until Repeat | Numbers control panel |
| Desktop Pattern | Pop-up menus |
| Disk Cache | Rate of Insertion Point Blinking |
| Double-Click Speed | Speaker Volume |
| File Sharing Monitor control panel | Sharing Setup control panel |
| General control panels | Sound control panel |
| Highlight color | Startup Disk control panel |
| I-beam | System Folder |
| Icon views | Time bar |
| Insertion point | Users & Groups Control Panel |
| Key repeat rate | Views control panel |
| Keyboard control panel | Virtual Memory |
| Keyboard layout | Window color |

## Discussion Questions

1. Discuss the advantages of using Disk Cache.
2. Discuss the possible hazards of setting Disk Cache too high.
3. Which control panels should you reset before shutting down the system?
4. Discuss the importance of setting control panels back to the way you found them when working on a shared Macintosh.
5. Discuss the possible advantages and disadvantages of virtual memory.
6. Discuss adding RAM to a Macintosh system. Is it expensive? Is it a difficult task? Is there a limit to how much memory can be added? Are there different kinds of memory chips (speed)?

## True/False Questions

For each question, circle the letter T if the statement is true and the letter F if the statement is false.

T F 1. You can design your own desktop pattern.
T F 2. The color wheel you see on your system will vary depending on whether you have a color, gray-scale, or monochrome monitor and how it is set.
T F 3. Every time you execute a command, it will blink three times before executing.
T F 4. You can use the Alarm Clock DA to set the time format to 24 hour.
T F 5. Additional alert sounds can be added to your Macintosh system.
T F 6. The color wheel can be accessed from the Monitors control panel.
T F 7. You can access the Control Panels programs from the _____ menu.
T F 8. You can specify the font and point size to be used when displaying window titles, menu names, and icon names.
T F 9. You can specify what icon information is to be included in a list view window.
T F 10. The information bar can only be displayed in an icon view window.
T F 11. Unlike most control panels, changes you make in the Memory control panel do not take effect until you restart the system.
T F 12. One quarter of RAM should be set aside to be used as Disk Cache.

## Completion Questions

Write the correct answer in each blank space.

1. Fifteen control panel programs are located in the _____ _____ folder, which is stored in the _____ folder on the _____ disk.
2. The General Controls panel can be used to set four items:
   A.
   B.
   C.
   D.
3. The color wheel can be accessed from the _____ _____, _____, and _____ control panels.
4. _____ _____ is disk space that is being used to store open application programs and documents (similar to RAM).
5. Use the _____ _____ control panel to specify which hard disk to use during the boot process.
6. Slow mouse tracking moves the pointer _____ inch(es) for every inch you move the mouse on the table top.

7. Fast mouse tracking moves the pointer _____ inch(es) for every inch you move the mouse on the table top.
8. _____ menus do not appear from the menu bar, unlike _____ menus. They are attached to _____ and _____.
9. Use the Color control panel to select the color to be used when _____ _____ and for _____ _____.
10. _____ _____ _____ is used to set the amount of time the computer waits, once you hit a key, before it starts repeating the character.
11. Use the _____ control panel to direct the Macintosh to calculate and display folder sizes in the list window.
12. Use the _____ control panel to set the volume and to select the _____ _____.

## Assignments

There is no hands-on assignment for this chapter. Instead, write a brief statement, in your own words, summarizing the purpose of each control panel.

1. Color
2. File Sharing Monitor
3. General Controls
4. Keyboard
5. Labels
6. Memory
7. Monitors
8. Mouse
9. Sharing Setup
10. Sound
11. Startup Disk
12. Users & Groups
13. Views

**Introduced in System 7.1**

14. Date & Time
15. Numbers

# 12  The System Folder

## Learning Objectives

**After completing this Chapter you will be able to:**

1. Explain the importance of having only one System Folder per disk.
2. Describe the contents of the System Folder.
3. Add and remove fonts and sounds.
4. Explain the difference between TrueType and fixed size fonts.
5. Add and remove items in the Apple Menu Items folder.
6. Add and remove items in the Startup Items folder.
7. Explain how alias files can be useful when stored in the Apple Menu Items or Startup Items folders.

## Introduction

Previously, we have discussed the process of booting up the Macintosh. When you turn the power on, the Macintosh hardware looks for the operating system programs. The hardware is useless without the operating system. The system software is found in two locations. ROM-BIOS stores the initial instructions on how to start the computer, how to control the disk drives, how to interpret keyboard and mouse input, and how to display information on the screen. However, the majority of the operating system programs are stored in the System Folder on your Startup disk.

The System Folder is not a place to experiment, especially if you are not using your own Macintosh. However, it should not be a complete mystery, even to Macintosh beginners. This chapter will briefly describe the System Folder and discuss its importance. You will learn how to add and remove fonts, sounds, and print drivers to the System Folder and you will also learn how to add and remove items to the Apple Menu Items and Startup Items folders. The usefulness of aliases in relationship to the System Folder will be examined.

## The Startup Disk

Any floppy or hard disk that contains a System Folder configured for your hardware may be used to start or boot your Macintosh. Every time you turn on your Macintosh, it will search for this folder and for the programs contained inside it. The first System Folder found will be used. The Macintosh searches for the System Folder on available disks in the following order:

- Internal 3.5-inch floppy drive
- External 3.5-inch floppy drive
- Startup device named in the Startup Disk control panel
- Internal hard disk on SCSI (small computer system interface) port
- Other devices connected to SCSI ports (from 6 to 0).

There is a reason for this order of precedence. If anything happens to the System Folder on your hard drive, or if you have a head crash (read/write heads come in contact with the hard disk recording surface), you can still use your Macintosh. A floppy disk containing a System Folder inserted in the floppy drive before powering on your system will boot your Macintosh.

Macintosh owners can quickly and easily expand the power of their Macintosh system by connecting SCSI devices. **SCSI** (commonly pronounced skuh-zee) is an acronym for **Small Computer System Interface**. All Macintoshes have the capability of connecting peripherals through a port (plug-in socket) on the back of the system unit using the SCSI system. This system provides high-speed communication between the computer and the peripherals. Up to eight devices (including the Macintosh) can be **daisy-chained** (connected one after the other by cables) off of one SCSI port. Peripherals that are commonly found on a SCSI system include: internal and external hard disk drives, CD-ROM drives, printers, and tape drives. An **internal floppy** or **hard drive**, is installed inside your system unit. An **external drive** usually comes with its own case, cables, power supply and is installed outside the system unit. External drives usually costs more than internal drives.

Each peripheral you add to your system is assigned a unique address (0 through 6), usually specified by a switch on the peripheral. The Macintosh system unit is always assigned address 7 and the internal hard drive's address is 6. This is necessary because although the SCSI system allows for the seven devices to be connected to the Macintosh simultaneously, only one can be sending data at a time. A **device ID number** is used to determine the device's communication priority. The device with the highest ID number has priority when sending data.

# The System Folder

You should not have more than one System Folder on any Startup disk. Two folders will confuse the Macintosh—the computer will randomly select the one to use. If you accidentally damage or erase your System Folder you can recreate it at that time. You should have a backup copy of your System Folder on floppy disks or magnetic tape. If not, simply reinstall the software from the original floppy disks. The System Folder files determine which devices you can access in the Control Panels, which fonts and sounds are available, which desk accessories (DA) appear in the Apple Menu, which printers you can use, which application programs will be opened during the booting process, the contents of the Scrapbook, and which version of the System and Finder will be used.

How do you know if you have more than one System Folder on your disk? If, one day, you have ten fonts available, and the next day you only have six, or if you had the Alarm Clock and Calculator DAs available yesterday and now they've disappeared, there is a good chance that your Startup disk has multiple System Folders. How does this happen? Occasionally, Macintosh users accidentally place an additional System Folder on the hard disk by dragging a floppy disk icon to the hard disk icon. This process copies everything from the floppy to a folder on the hard disk, including any System Folders hidden inside. Always open a floppy disk icon before dragging it to your hard disk and verify that a System Folder is not stored on the floppy disk. If there is a System Folder on the floppy disk, don't drag the floppy disk icon to the hard disk. Instead, open the floppy disk icon and select only the files you want to copy from the floppy and drag them to the hard disk.

If you think you have more than one System Folder on the Startup disk, use the Find command to locate and display all System Folders. Then open the System Folders and examine their contents to determine which one(s) to throw away. The location of the folders on the disk can also indicate which one(s) should be removed. The System Folder located on the disk level is probably the one you want to keep.

## System Folder Contents

What's inside the System Folder? The System Folder contains a variety of files. The System Folder is custom designed to meet your hardware and software needs, so the System Folder on one Macintosh will not necessarily be the same as the System Folder on another Macintosh. Figure 12.1 shows the contents of a System Folder after it has been installed on a new Startup disk along with a brief explanation of the twelve items.

**Apple Menu Items**—Stores items found in the  menu.

**Clipboard**—Stores text or graphics you have copied or cut to the Clipboard.

**Control Panels**—Stores all Control Panels.

**Extensions**—Stores items found in the Chooser and Init files.

**Finder**—The Finder program creates, maintains, and allows access to the desktop.

**Fonts**—Stores screen and printer fonts. This folder is new in System 7.1.

**Note Pad File**—Stores information in the Note Pad DA.

**Preferences**—Stores special setting files for application programs.

**Print Monitor Documents**—Stores documents for printing in the background.

**Scrapbook**—Stores text or graphics you have placed in the Scrapbook.

**Startup Items**—Stores items that are to be executed at boot time.

**System**—Stores sounds, keyboard layouts, and other essential system files.

Figure 12.2 shows the contents of the System Folder after several application programs were installed on the hard disk drive. Examine the items in the bottom half of the window. As you can tell, application programs place files in the System Folder. Do not remove items from your System Folder unless you know what you are doing. For example, if you remove the Claris folder, the Claris Works program will not work.

*Figure 12.1—New System Folder*

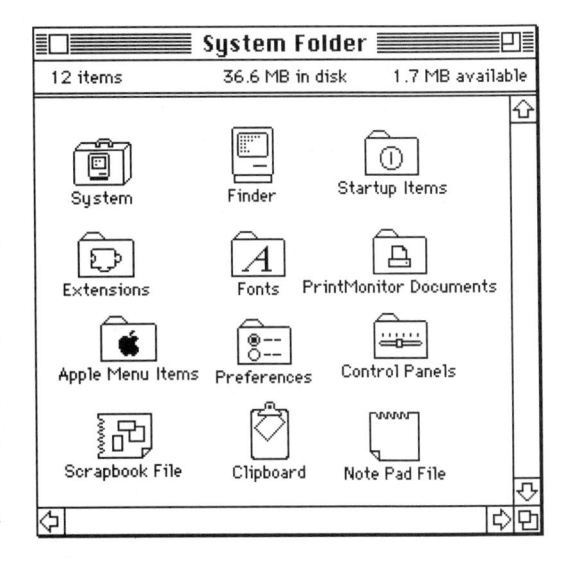

*Figure 12.2—Used System Folder*

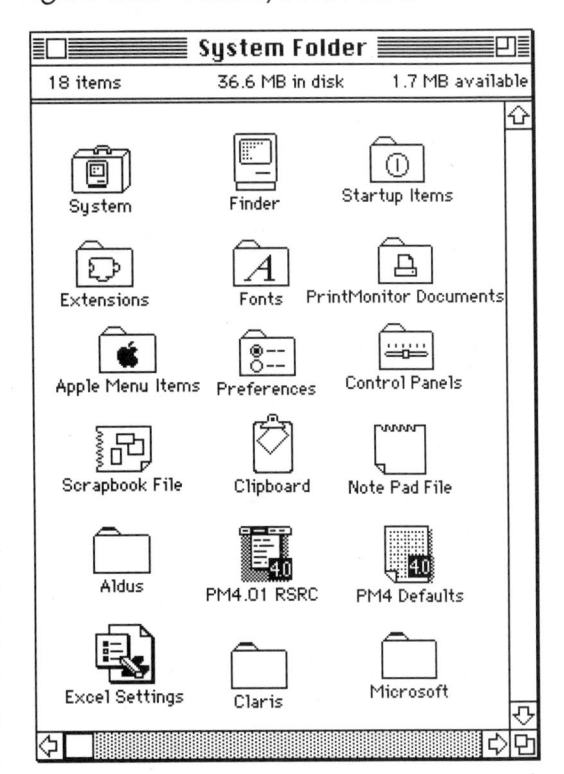

Some items in the System Folder need to be discussed in greater detail, while some items are self-explanatory and some, such as the Clipboard, Scrapbook, Note Pad File, and Control Panels folder, have been discussed previously.

## The Finder File

The Finder creates, maintains and allows access to the desktop. It provides the visually oriented interface that allows Macintosh users to feel less intimidated—and more comfortable—with the computer.

Finder tasks include:
- Creating and maintaining the desktop.
- Controlling disk resources: initializing, copying, renaming, ejecting and erasing disks, opening, closing, copying, locking, moving, renaming, deleting files and folders, obtaining information about and locating files and folders.

## The System File

The System suitcase file is an essential file that must be in the System Folder of the Startup disk. Generally, the **suitcase** icon is assigned to files that store one or more fonts, sounds, and/or DAs. The System suitcase file stores sounds, keyboard layout files and startup information. Prior to System 7.1, the System file also stored screen fonts and the Extension folder stored printer fonts. System 7.1 stores screen and printer fonts in a new Fonts folder.

Your direct interaction with the System file will be to add and remove sounds. To add a new sound, simply drag its icon to the System Folder. A dialog box will appear informing you the sound should be placed in the System Folder. Click on the OK button. To remove a sound, open the System Folder, then open the System file and drag the appropriate sound icon to the Trash. Figure 12.3 shows a portion of a System suitcase file containing multiple sound files and a keyboard layout file (U.S. - System 6). If you double-click on any of the sound icons, you will hear a sample of the sound stored inside.

*Figure 12.3—System Suitcase*

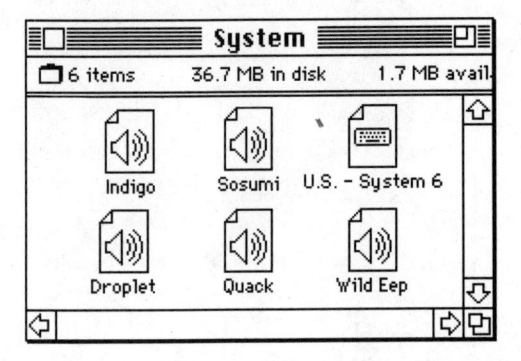

## Preferences

Many application programs automatically place files in the Preferences folder during the program's install process. These files contain special settings needed by the application program. Settings you have chosen for sharing files with users or groups, and Finder Preferences are also stored here. (Figure 12.4)

*Figure 12.4—Preferences*

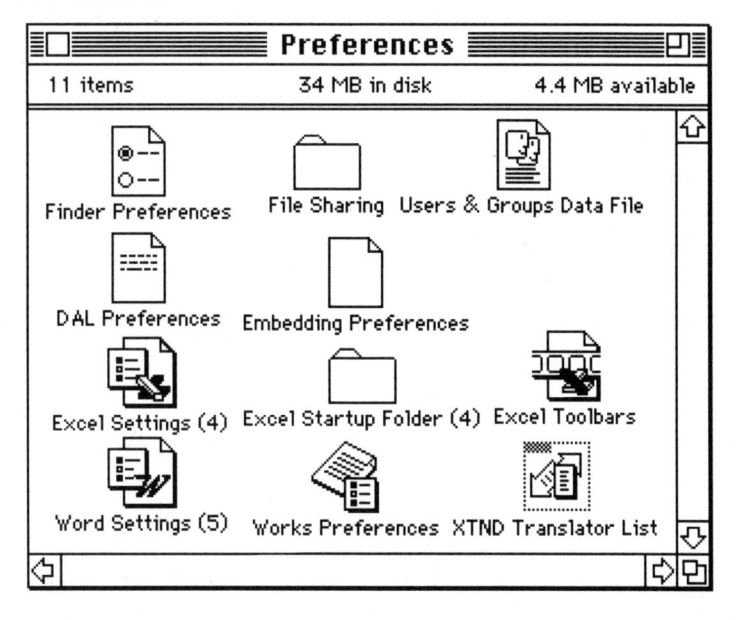

## Extensions

The Extension folder stores all Chooser resources (print driver, scanner, and networking files) and Init files. **Inits,** short for **initialization**, programs automatically load during the boot process and instruct the System to perform operations that it normally wouldn't do. System 7 refers to these files as **system extensions**. For example, the Apple CD-ROM Init program needs to be placed in this folder so that the Macintosh recognizes the CD-ROM storage device.

The print driver icons in Figure 12.5 may look familiar. You probably see one or more of them every time you access the Chooser DA.

*Figure 12.5—Extensions*

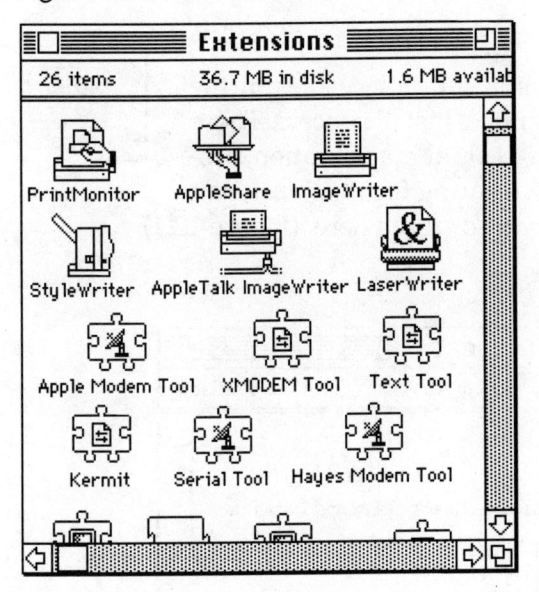

To add additional system extension files, drag their icon to the System Folder icon. A dialog box will appear informing you the system extension file should be placed in the Extension folder. Click on the OK button. To remove an extension file, open the System Folder, the Extension folder, and drag the appropriate extension file to the Trash.

## PrintMonitor Documents

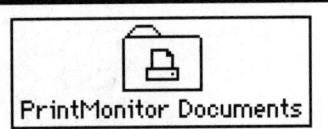

If Background Printing is turned on in the Chooser DA window, the PrintMonitor program automatically creates this file. **PrintMonitor** is the **print spooler program** that comes with the Macintosh operating system. It intercepts print files and writes them quickly to the PrintMonitor Documents folder on disk. You can continue to work on another task in the **foreground** while the Macintosh prints in the **background** (behind the scene). You don't have to wait for the document to print. The PrintMonitor Documents folder will be empty unless there is a document waiting to be printed.

*Figure 12.6—Application Menu*

### PrintMonitor Program

We did not discuss the PrintMonitor program in the Printing chapter because it is an advanced feature. Let's examine it here.

In order to use background printing:
- the PrintMonitor program must be in the Extensions folder.

- the selected printer must be able to work with the PrintMonitor program.
- Background Printing must be turned on in the Chooser window.

The PrintMonitor program starts automatically when background printing begins and closes automatically when printing is completed. The PrintMonitor name and icon will appear on the Application menu. (Figure 12.6)

Selecting PrintMonitor in the Applications menu will open the PrintMonitor window. This window (Figure 12.7) gives you the following controls over background printing:
- Check on the status of printing and waiting documents.
- Cancel the printing of document(s).
- Set the date and time for a specific document to print.
- Postpone indefinitely the printing of a document(s).
- Printer problems that may occur (printer not ready, out of paper, paper jam, feed paper manually).

*Figure 12.7—PrintMonitor Window*

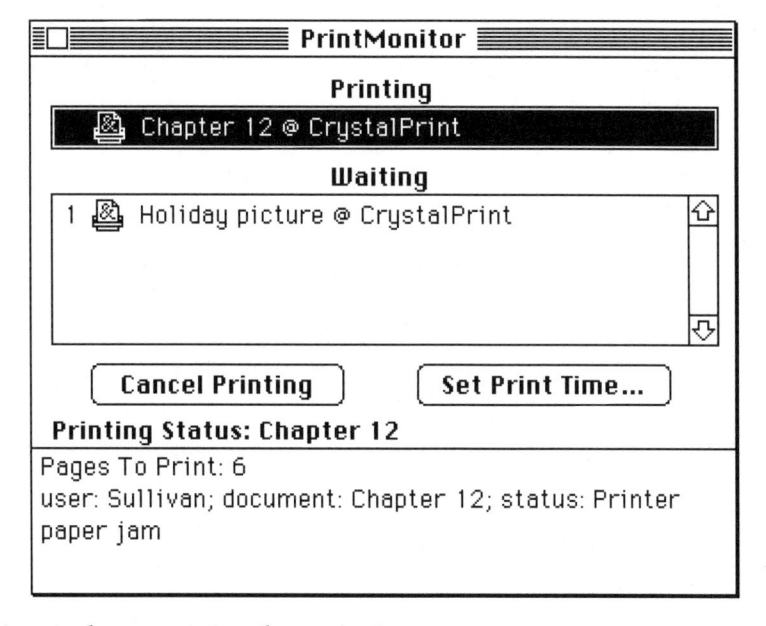

```
┌─────────────── PrintMonitor ───────────────┐
│                   Printing                 │
│  ▓ Chapter 12 @ CrystalPrint               │
│                   Waiting                  │
│  1 ▓ Holiday picture @ CrystalPrint        │
│                                            │
│  [ Cancel Printing ]   [ Set Print Time... ]│
│  Printing Status: Chapter 12               │
│  Pages To Print: 6                         │
│  user: Sullivan; document: Chapter 12; status: Printer
│  paper jam                                 │
└────────────────────────────────────────────┘
```

This window contains three sections:
- Printing—The name of the currently printing document.
- Waiting—A list of waiting documents and the name of the printer they are to print on.
- Printing Status—This sections keeps you informed on how many pages of the current document remain to be printed, user name (if names assigned in Users control panel), and printer status.

*Figure 12.8—Set Print Time Dialog Box*

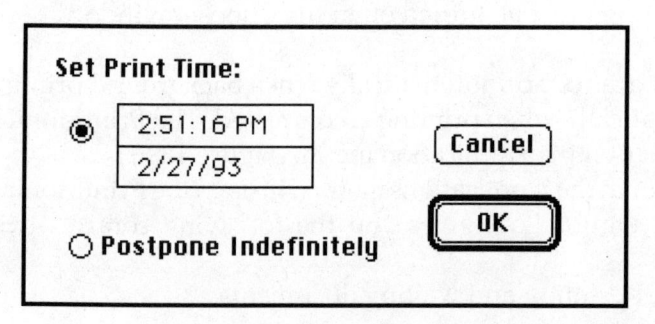

```
Set Print Time:
  ⦿  2:51:16 PM
     2/27/93           [ Cancel ]
                       [   OK   ]
  ○ Postpone Indefinitely
```

Examine the Printing Status section in Figure 12.7. The document has stopped printing because the printer has a paper jam.

Two buttons are available on the PrintMonitor window.

- Cancel Printing—Highlight the document you don't want to print, and click on the Cancel button.
- Set Print Time—Click on this button to specify when to print the highlighted document. (Figure 12.8)

If you send a document to the printer and it doesn't print, try to find out why before attempting to print again. There are several ways the PrintMonitor program can report a printing error message: a ◆ symbol will display next to the PrintMonitor listing in the Application menu, the PrintMonitor's icon may blink over the top of the Application menu icon (right end of the menu bar), and/or an alert box may appear on your desktop. Use the Preferences command in PrintMonitor's File menu to specify which method to use. (Figure 12.9)

*Figure 12.9—Preferences Dialog Box*

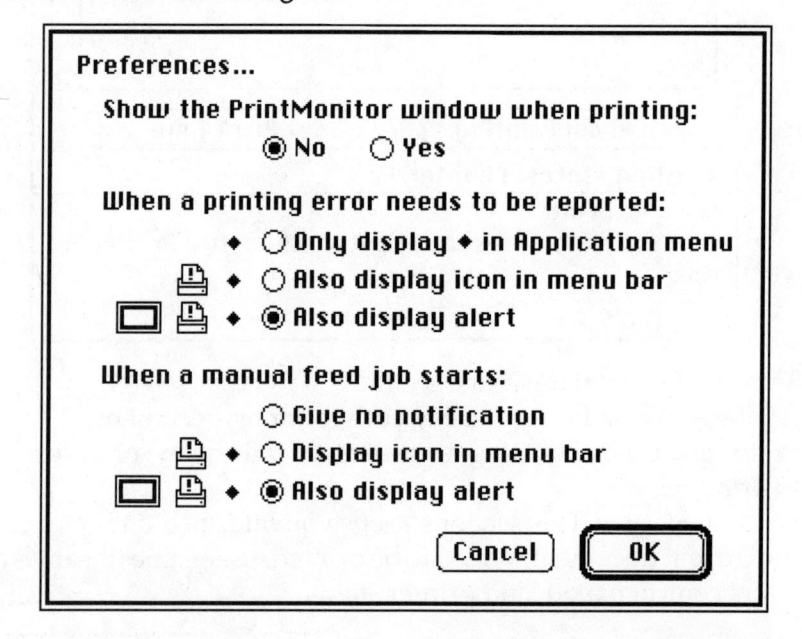

```
Preferences...
   Show the PrintMonitor window when printing:
           ⦿ No    ○ Yes
   When a printing error needs to be reported:
        ◆ ○ Only display ◆ in Application menu
     🖨 ◆ ○ Also display icon in menu bar
   ▭ 🖨 ◆ ⦿ Also display alert
   When a manual feed job starts:
           ○ Give no notification
     🖨 ◆ ○ Display icon in menu bar
   ▭ 🖨 ◆ ⦿ Also display alert
                      [ Cancel ]  [   OK   ]
```

## Fonts Folder

System 7.1 stores screen and printer fonts in the new Fonts folder. Earlier versions of System 7 stored screen fonts in the System file and printer fonts in the Extensions folder. A font is a set of characters (letters, numbers, and symbols) in the same typeface, style (italic), weight (bold), and point size. Typeface refers to the design of the characters (such as Geneva, Helvetica, or Times). Fonts are measured in points. Point size refers to the size of the font. Each point is one 72nd of a inch. Figure 12.10 shows several suitcase icons.

There are two basic types of fonts included with System 7: **TrueType fonts** (also known as variable-size, outline, or scalable fonts) and **Fixed Size fonts** (also know as bitmapped fonts). TrueType fonts are known for their smoothness and quality. A mathematical formula is used to display the requested font in any point size. A separate file is not necessary for each point size. Fixed Size font files store the font in one point size, indicated by its name. You can use both types on the screen and the printer. Figure 12.11 shows the contents of the open Palatino Suitcase (by icon).

You can easily distinguish TrueType font files from fixed size font files by their icon and name. TrueType font files do not have a point size specified in their name and are assigned the icon displaying multiple *A*s. (Figure 12.12.)

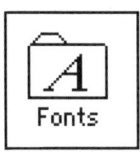

*Figure 12.10—Fonts Folder*

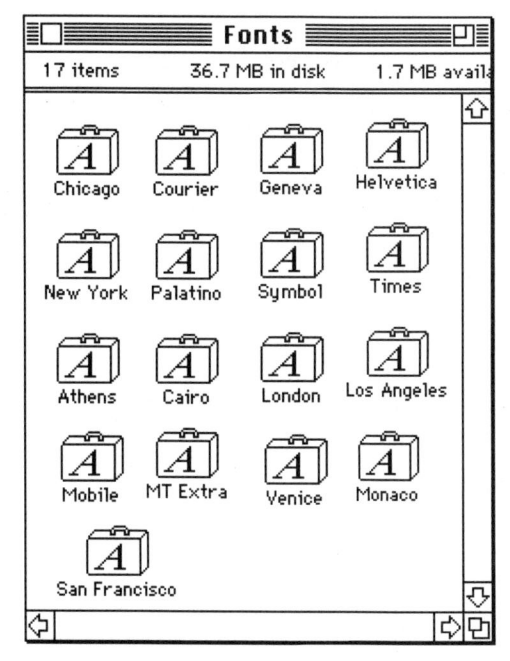

*Figure 12.11—Palatino Suitcase*

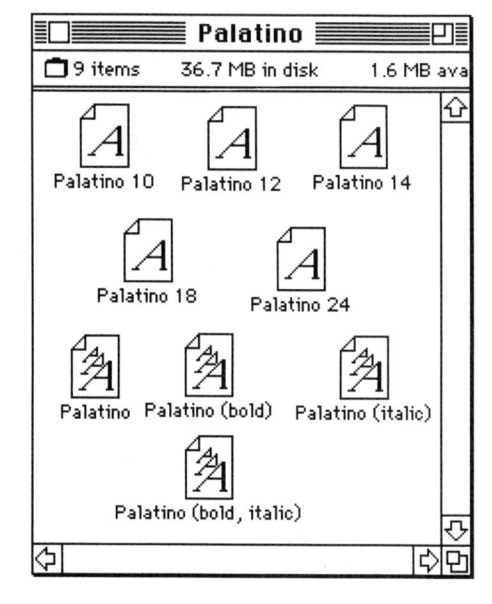

*Figure 12.12—Sample Font Icons*

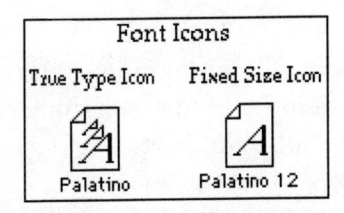

Double-clicking on a font file will open a window displaying a sample of the font. A window displaying a TrueType font will show the font in three sizes. A window displaying a Fixed Size font will show the font in that one size. (Figure 12.13)

*Figure 12.13—Sample Fixed Size and TrueType Font Files*

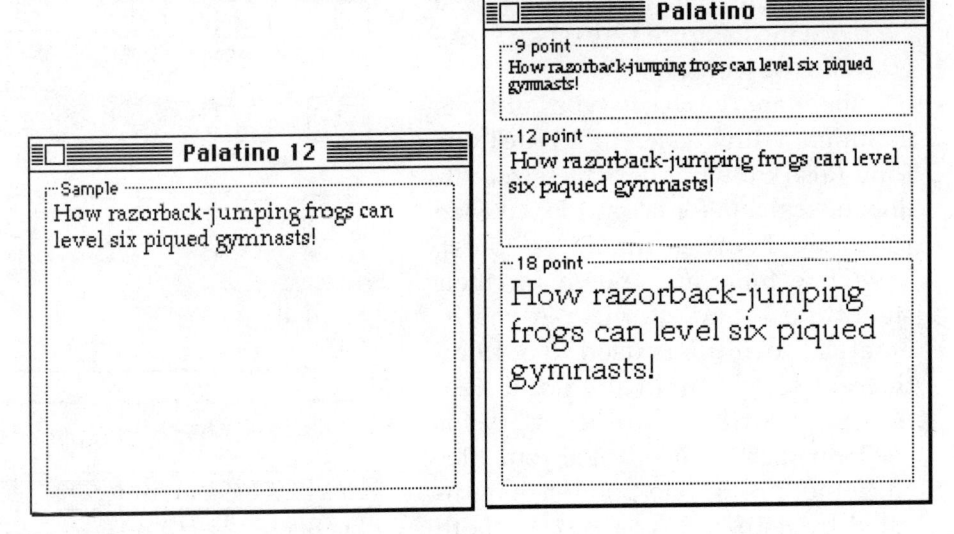

To Add a Font:
- Quit all application programs.
- Drag the font file or font suitcase to the System Folder.
- A dialog box will appear confirming your desire to install the font in the Fonts folder. Click on the OK button.

or
- Open the System Folder.
- Drag the font file or font suitcase to the Fonts folder.

To Remove a Font:
- Quit all application programs.
- Open the System Folder and the Fonts folder.
- Drag the desired suitcase or font file to the Trash.

There are hundreds of fonts available. Adobe Systems' PostScript outline fonts are a major font competitor. As more TrueType fonts become available, Macintosh users may switch exclusively to them.

## The Apple Menu Items Folder

Anything you place in the Apple Menu Items folder will appear on the  menu. You may place an unlimited number of DAs, programs, documents, or aliases on the menu. An **alias** is a small file (approximately 2K in size) that represents the original document, folder, program, disk, or Trash item. When you double-click on an alias, the original item is located and opened.

Anything you need access to quickly and easily can be placed in the Apple Menu Items folder. Simply drag the icon representing the item into the folder. Common sense should tell you not to place all your application programs in this folder. Most Macintosh users place application programs and their related files in separate folders. If you wish to have access to an application program from the  menu, place an alias of the program file in the Apple Menu Items folder.

Figure 12.14—Apple Menu Items

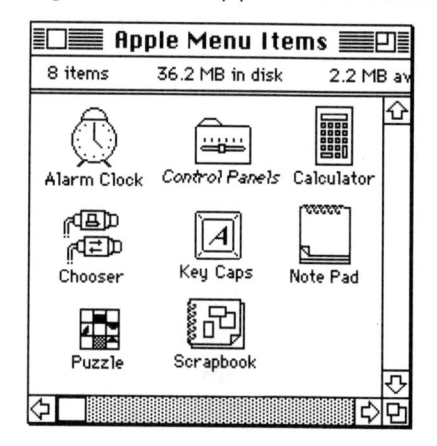

An example of the Apple Menu Items folder is shown in Figure 12.14. It contains the seven desk accessory programs you studied in Chapter 5: Alarm Clock, Calculator, Chooser, Key Caps, Note Pad, Puzzle, Scrapbook. An alias for the Control Panel folder is also in the menu. Choosing this entry in the  menu opens the real Control Panels folder stored in the System Folder of the Startup disk.

## The Startup Items Folder

Any document, DA or program that you want to automatically open on your desktop when you boot your Macintosh should be placed in this folder.

For example, placing an alias file for the MacPaint and Microsoft Word application programs in this folder will cause the programs to be located, and opened the next time you boot. (Figure 12.15) Placing a document in the Startup Items folder will cause the application program that created the document to be located, and loaded into memory. The document will then appear in an open window on your desktop.

*Figure 12.15—Startup Items*

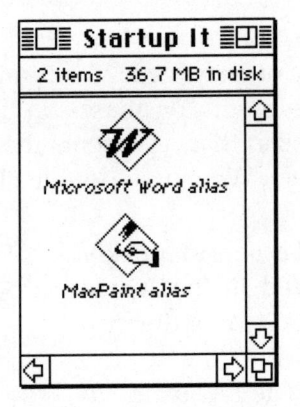

There are a few limitations to consider before you place an item in this folder. First, how much memory does your Macintosh have? Every program you open takes up memory space. Do you really want the program to open every time your boot? Do not place a folder in the Startup Items folder. If you do, the next time you boot, the Macintosh will try to open everything stored inside the folder. Holding down the Shift key during booting will prevent these programs from opening.

To place an item in this folder, simply drag the item's icon to the Startup Items folder.

## Alias Files

Alias files are one of the many useful features included in System 7. You have seen two examples of where alias files can be used: Apple Menu Items and Startup Items folders. Figure 12.16 provides possible additional uses for alias files.

To create an alias, click on the original icon and choose **Make Alias** from the File menu. To remove an alias, drag it to the Trash. Dragging an alias to the Trash does not remove the original item. Removing the original item from the disk does not remove the alias.

*Figure 12.16—Alias Files*

<table>
<tr><td colspan="3" align="center">Possible Alias Uses</td></tr>
<tr><td>**Alias for**</td><td>**Place alias**</td><td>**Why?**</td></tr>
<tr><td>Application program</td><td>Apple Menu Items</td><td>Easy access from  menu.</td></tr>
<tr><td></td><td>Startup Items</td><td>Opens and loads during boot process.</td></tr>
<tr><td></td><td>Desktop</td><td>Easy access at desktop.</td></tr>
<tr><td>DA</td><td>Desktop</td><td>Easy access at desktop.</td></tr>
<tr><td>Control Panel</td><td>Apple Menu Items</td><td>Easy access from  menu.</td></tr>
<tr><td>Folder</td><td>Apple Menu Items</td><td>Easy access from  menu.</td></tr>
<tr><td></td><td>Desktop</td><td>Easy access at desktop. Place items in and remove items from folder without opening other folders.</td></tr>
<tr><td>Hard disk</td><td>Apple Menu Items</td><td>Easy access from  menu. No need to close or move windows to locate and open disk icon.</td></tr>
<tr><td>Document</td><td>Apple Menu Items</td><td>Easy access from  menu.</td></tr>
<tr><td></td><td>Startup Items</td><td>Open and loads during boot process.</td></tr>
<tr><td>Document or program stored on a separate disk</td><td>Anywhere on your primary disk</td><td>When opened, the system will request the name of the disk where the item is stored. Once the disk is inserted, the item will be opened.</td></tr>
<tr><td>Trash</td><td>Apple Menu Items</td><td>Easy access from  menu. No need to close or move windows to locate and open the Trash.</td></tr>
</table>

## Key Terms

| | |
|---|---|
| Alias | Make Alias |
| Apple Menu Items | Note Pad File |
| Background | PostScript fonts |
| Clipboard | Preferences |
| Control panels | PrintMonitor program |
| Daisy-chained | Print Spooler program |
| Device ID number | Scrapbook |
| Extensions folder | SCSI |
| External drive | Small Computer System Interface |
| Finder | Startup Items |
| Fixed Size fonts | Suitcase icon |
| Fonts folder | System extensions |
| Foreground | System Folder |
| Init | System suitcase |
| Internal drive | TrueType fonts |

## Discussion Questions

1. Discuss why it is inadvisable to randomly add or remove items from the System Folder.
2. Explain why the contents of System Folders vary.
3. Explain how easy it is to accidentally place an extra System Folder on the hard drive.

## True/False Questions

For each question, circle the letter T if the statement is true and the letter F if the statement is false.

T F  1. The hard drive is the first place the Macintosh searches for the System Folder during booting.
T F  2. Fonts and sounds are stored in the System file.
T F  3. Up to 8 items can be daisy-chained off of one SCSI port.
T F  4. Only 20 items may appear in the Apple menu.
T F  5. Holding down the Control and Option keys while booting prevents programs from opening automatically.
T F  6. Use the Make Alias command from the Special menu to create an alias of the selected item(s).

T F  7. Internal drives are installed inside the system unit.
T F  8. When you trash the original item, its alias is automatically removed from the disk.
T F  9. Background printing permits you to continue working in the foreground while documents print in the background.
T F 10. Dragging a floppy disk icon on to a hard disk icon places a copy of the entire contents of the floppy on the hard drive.
T F 11. You should always have a backup copy of the System folder on the hard drive.
T F 12. All system files are locked to prevent you from erasing them.
T F 13. Fonts do not take up much disk space, so you can add as many as you like to your disks.

## Completion Questions

Write the correct answer in each blank space.

1. System software is stored in two locations: in _____ and the _____ folder of the _____ disk.

2. _____ _____ font files store the font in one point size.

3. Anything you place in the _____ _____ _____ folder will appear in the Apple menu.

4. If you want an application program to automatically open on the desktop when you boot, place an alias of the program in the _____ _____ folder.

5. The _____ folder stores all Chooser resources.

# Security Issues

## Learning Objectives

**After completing this Chapter you will be able to:**

1. Compare and contrast Trojan Horses, Worms, and Viruses.
2. Explain the honor system used with Shareware software.
3. List some simple rules to follow to help prevent your system from catching a virus.
4. Explain why it is illegal to write virus programs and the possible penalties involved if you are caught.
5. Describe the procedures to follow with original application or system disks.
6. Compare and contrast the reasons for saving data files on your hard drive.
7. Define the term backing up and list the three methods used to backup floppy disk files.
8. Compare and contrast Global backup and Incremental backup.
9. Describe a variety of ways to protect your data.

## Introduction

In this chapter we will discuss three major computer software security issues: computer viruses, original copies of programs, and data files. The topic of computer security could take up an entire book and course by itself. You will only be introduced to the topic and provided with some suggestions on how to protect your computer and files.

# Computer Viruses

A computer virus is a computer program designed to plant itself into the computer's operating system or in an application program. It directs the computer to alter or destroy data and copies itself onto other programs. A typical virus tells the computer to keep running, but instructs it to continue making copies of the virus until millions of bits of information are created, jamming the computer. Some viruses are fairly harmless—showing an innocent message on the monitor. More aggressive ones eat information and make the computer system useless.

The first computer virus was planted in 1940, but in the last decade, with the explosion in personal computer use, virus outbreaks have become more common. For example, in 1988 over 76,000 cases of computer viruses were reported to the Computer Virus Industry Association, an association that tracks virus outbreaks. The number of cases continue to go up every year. The name **virus** comes from the program's ability to replicate and infect other computers. Computer users who write virus programs are often doing it as a prank or a challenge, but a few write virus programs in a deliberate attempt to destroy data.

The increase in virus outbreaks has lead many states to create legislation aimed at prosecuting the creators of viruses. For instance, on January 1, 1988, California enacted section 502 of the Penal Code which declares that anyone who "knowingly accesses and without permission, adds, alters, damages, deletes, or destroys any data, computer software, or computer programs which reside or exist internal or external to a computer, computer systems, or computer network..." is guilty of a public offense. Individuals found guilty of authoring or knowingly distributing a virus in California can receive a $10,000 fine, loss of computer equipment, and three years in jail. Other states have enacted similar penalties.

## Three main families of viruses

**Trojan Horses** are not true viruses. They appear to be legitimate programs but they have hidden agendas. They may display messages, destroy programs, or erase information. Trojan Horses do not reproduce themselves and cannot contaminate other programs. The damage is localized—removing the program usually solves the problem.

A **Worm** is a destructive program routine that corrupts programs and databases. Worms can tunnel their way through memory like moles eating through a carrot patch. The Macintosh is not susceptible to worms, but Apple II systems are prone to worms that paralyze programs and tie up systems.

A true **virus** has two primary objectives: one is to replicate, and the other is determined by the creator of the virus. To replicate, the virus copies itself to a valid program. When the infected application is copied to a sterile system (virus free), the virus invades the system files. As other application programs are opened, the virus attacks and infects them.

## Anti-Viral Programs

An **anti-viral** program should be used regularly to check for and erase (eradicate) viruses. These programs seek out where the original code is hidden and erases it. Some anti-virus programs can be set to automatically scan every floppy disk you insert in the drive. Computer "bug-busters" have identified over 30 viruses that attack personal computers and have developed programs to fix most of them. Sometimes an infected program can not be restored. Anti-virus programs are available on bulletin boards, as shareware, mail order or in computer stores.

**Shareware** are application programs you can purchase for a fraction of the cost of most software. There are several companies that specialize in shareware. This is how it works. You obtain a catalogue from a shareware company. After reviewing the catalogue, you order several programs and pay a nominal fee to cover the price of the disks and postage. When the programs arrive, you try them out. If you like a program and intend to use it, you mail the requested fee to the programmer. If the program does not meet your needs, you are not required to pay for it but you should erase the disk. Shareware is based on the "honor system."

There are a variety of anti-virus programs available and new ones are written every year. It is impossible to mention all these programs, but we will examine a couple.

**SAM (Symantec AntiVirus for Macintosh)** is a powerful and effective protection program with several nice features. Symantec Corporation's 24-hour Virus Newsline allows registered SAM users to update the SAM program to fight new viruses. The system extension (Init) portion of the program, known as SAM Intercept, loads when you boot the Macintosh and keeps watch over what goes on. If anything questionable occurs the program will intercept the process and inform you of the event. For example, if an attempt is made to change the System Folder, you will be notified. Newly inserted floppy disks are automatically scanned for possible viruses. The program can usually erase a located virus.

**Virex**, from Microcom Utilities Product Group, is another virus preventer, detector and eradicator program. It is easily installed and can be installed on a AppleShare file server.

**Rival,** from Inline Design, is a system extension (Init) program that constantly checks open files for viruses. Additional features include its ability to scan disks and perform some file repair operations.

## Spreading Viruses

A computer virus is spread in several ways. Borrowing software from a friend can lead to the infection of your own system. It is illegal to copy application programs to give to friends. This is called **Pirated Software.** You know how easy it is to copy floppy disks—it may be difficult to refuse a friend's request for a copy of a program you own. But it is illegal to give copies of programs away. The original programmer and company that created the application software deserve to be paid for their work. Think of it this way. If everyone bought application software instead of sharing it, perhaps the prices would go down.

Computer networks can quickly spread a virus through shared programs, electronic mail, and so on. A computer network is a set of multiple computers that are connected to each other. **Electronic mail (e-mail)** is application software that allows you to send messages or entire documents to other users on the network. They can read the mail at their convenience and send you a message back via electronic mail.

**Computer Bulletin Boards** are another common source of infection. By using a modem and data communication software, you can connect your Macintosh to other computer systems to access commercial subscriber services and/or bulletin boards. **Modem** (pronounced "mow-dum") is short for **Modulator-Demodulator.** This input/output device allows you to send information stored on your computer through the phone lines to other computers. Data is stored on the computer as **digital signals,** (electronic pulses in which 1 = on and 0 = off). Telephones were created to send human voices—they use analog signals, or electronic waves. The modem converts the digital sounds (pulses) to **analog signals** (waves) to transmit data over the phone lines. On the other end the analog sounds must be converted back to digital sounds for the computer to accept them.

Several commercial subscriber services are available, such as **CompuServe** and **Prodigy.** For a fee, you can use your Macintosh to call these services. The features provided by each service can vary but often include games, shopping services, e-mail, stock exchange data, reference material, databases (on restaurants, hotels, sights to see), and airline reservation services. A computer bulletin board is similar to a normal bulletin board hanging on your office wall. It is used to post advertisements, announcements, inquiries, documents, programs, and so on, which you wish to share with others. Most commercial bulletin boards have system administrators who are responsible for maintaining the bulletin board. One of their primary responsibilities is to make sure the bulletin board is virus free. When you use a non-commercial bulletin boards you should take extra care and be virus aware.

## Simple rules to follow to help prevent your computer from catching a virus

1. Don't copy pirated software. It is illegal, and you may be getting more than you expected—a virus, for example.
2. Don't download free software or shareware from a computer bulletin board unless you know that the system administrator of the bulletin board checks the software. You might want to copy it to a floppy and then check it for bugs by using an anti-viral program. Do not download it to your hard disk. **Downloading** is the process of copying information from another computer system to yours. **Uploading** is copying software from your computer system to another system.
3. Use only commercially operated bulletin boards like CompuServe or Prodigy.
4. Don't leave your system up and running all the time with a modem attached, unless you have taken special precautions. Anyone with a computer, a modem, and your phone number can call your Macintosh. Once they are connected, it is easy to wreak havoc with your files.
5. Use an anti-viral program frequently to check your disks and to fix viruses.
6. If you bring work home, check out all disks for viruses before using them on your home system.
7. Run virus checks before backing up. Back up frequently.
8. Never work with original master disks. Write protect them and make copies.
9. Make a backup copy of your uninfected System Folder and put it away for future use as necessary.

## Original Program Issues

Any time you buy a new operating system, application, or developmental software program, you should:

1. Fill out the registration card and mail it.
2. Make a copy of all included floppy disks.

Floppy disks can be corrupted or destroyed. When the floppy is being read, the drive's read-write heads are touching the disk surface—eventually the disk will wear out. Occasionally a drive may malfunction and destroy your disk. You could lose or misplace the disk. Anything could happen, so why take the chance?

Any time you purchase new software, you should make a copy of the disk(s), put the original disk(s) away, and use the copies. If anything happens to the copies, you still have the originals. You can simply make yourself a new copy. You may come across a few application programs that will not allow copies to be made. Be sure to complete the registration card for all purchased software and mail it in. If the disks can not be copied and get ruined, the manufacturer may offer you a new set at a reduced price. Manufacturers also keep known customers informed on program improvements and may offer reduced prices for upgrades.

## Data File Issues

Any time you create a data file (document) that has any worth you should also create a copy of that file on a separate disk. Should you store original document files on your hard disk or on floppies?

**There are several advantages to storing documents on hard disks:**
- The system reads and writes faster to a hard disk.
- The document's size may make it a necessity, as it may be too large to store on a single floppy.
- You don't have to look for the floppy on which the document is stored.

**There are also disadvantages to storing documents on the hard disk:**
- It may not be the best usage of your hard disk space. Hard disk space needs to be saved for large application programs that must be stored on the hard disk.
- The documents can be accessed and/or modified by anyone having access to the system. If your Macintosh is in the office and you store employee files on the disk, anyone who knows how to use your Macintosh can access the document files and find out sensitive information.

There are a variety of programs available that may minimize the disadvantages of storing document files on the hard disk, file compression, security, and data recovery software. File compression programs compact information so that it takes up less storage space on the disk. A common compression technique replaces each frequently occurring word (the, here, you and so on) with a 2 character substitute. This saves one or more storage position(s) for each occurrence of the word. The compressed file must be decompressed in order for you to use it the next time. Security software allows you to protect a file, folder, or an entire disk from intrusion.

There are many good compression and security programs available. Only a couple are mentioned here for discussion purposes.

**AutoDoubler** from Salient Software, Inc., installs as a control panel. This program automatically and transparently compresses and decompresses files. You can direct the program to not compress certain files and folders.

Two good shareware programs to quickly compress files on your disk are **Compact Pro** from Cyclos Software and **StuffIt Lite** from Aladdin Systems, Inc.

**FolderBolt** from Kent Marsh Ltd., protects the contents of folders. You assign one of three levels of security to a folder. **Password protected folders** can only be accessed by the user(s) that knows the key (password) to open it. **Read-only folders** may be read but not modified. **Drop-only folders** allows users to add to the folder.

**DiskLock** from Fifth Generation Systems allows you to password protect your entire hard drive.

**FileGuard** from ASD Software Inc., can be used to protect folders, applications, and data files.

**NightWatch** from Kent Marsh Ltd., locks the hard drive by using a floppy startup disk and password. You must have the floppy startup disk and know the password to gain access to the disk.

**Complete Undelete** from Microcom Utilities Product Group can be used to recover deleted files and fragments of partially overwritten files.

**Norton Utilities for the Macintosh** from Symantec Corp., provides a variety of features to protect and restore data on a hard drive.

Another kind of security problem seems so obvious that it is often overlooked. Leaving sensitive information on your screen while you walk away from the computer leaves the information open to all wandering, prowling eyes. One simple solution to this problem is a screen saver program. These programs address two concerns: security and monitor screen maintenance. Generally, it is not advisable to allow the same information to remain on the screen for an extended length of time. Screen saver programs automatically change the display on your screen after you have not touched the mouse or keyboard for a specified length of time (**delay time**). Upon returning to your computer, you touch a key and the information reappears on the screen. AfterDark and Pyro! are two popular screen saver programs.

**After Dark** from Berkeley Systems, Inc., has 31 different color display modules including the fish aquarium, flying toasters, and rainstorm. You select the module and control the speed, sound level, and the delay time.

**Pyro!** from Fifth Generation Systems has twelve adjustable display modules. It continues to handle background tasks (such as printing) while displaying the color screen saving image on the screen.

# Backing Up

The process known as **backing up** involves making a copy of an original file to another disk. It's a type of disaster preparedness. Just in case disaster strikes you have a copy of the file(s) on another disk. If you leave your floppy disk in the car and it melts, you have a copy of those files on another disk. If your hard drive crashes, you have a copy of those files on another disk.

## Backing Up Floppy Disk Files

Floppy disk backup is relatively simple and was discussed earlier in the book. Three methods are available.

1. Floppy to Floppy Copy (copying the entire contents of one floppy disk to another).
2. Copying a group or a single file or folder to another disk.
3. Using the Save As Command. Most application programs have two save commands. Save writes the active data file to the current folder and disk. The Save As... command allows you to change drives, create new file folders, eject the current disk and insert another, and change the file's name. This means that while you are in the application program you can save the file to the primary location and immediately follow-up by creating a back up copy by saving it to another disk.

## Hard Disk Backup

Because of size considerations, hard disk and large file backups are a little more difficult to do. If you have a hard disk or a data file that won't fit on a single floppy you need to purchase an application program that will allow you to backup. The Macintosh operating system does not provide this utility. Make sure that the program you purchase can perform three types of backups.

There are three types of hard disk backups.

1. A **Global Backup** is the process of copying the entire hard disk to numerous 3.5 inch floppies, magnetic tape, or to another hard disk.

2. An **Incremental Backup** is the process of copying only the files that have been created, modified, or copied to your hard disk since the last global backup to numerous 3.5 inch floppies, magnetic tape, or to another hard disk.

3. A **Data File** backup programs will only copy documents, not application programs or system software.

**Magnetic tape** is a practical and inexpensive way to store large amounts of information. It is commonly used for backing up hard disks, or for transporting large amounts of data. Its usage is usually limited to these tasks because information on magnetic tape must be accessed in sequential order. **Sequential access** means that when you are searching for a specific piece of information on the tape, you must start reading the tape from the beginning, unlike the **random access** method disk drives use.

Different backup programs provide different features. For example, examine the following short list of available backup programs.

Whenever you save or activate a data file, **Autoback** from TerraNetics, automatically copies the file onto another hard disk or magnetic tape.

**Backmatic** from Magic Software, Inc, is a system extension (Init) program. Whenever you shut down the Macintosh, it scans the hard disk and backs up all changed files to floppies, a folder on your hard disk, or to a file server.

**Fastback Plus** from Fifth Generation Systems, will perform incremental and full backups. It also provides a range of file compression levels.

**Redux** from Inline Design, lets you backup files, folders, or entire disks.

**Retrospect** from Dantz Development Corp., is another excellent backup program that supports a variety of storage devices.

## Key Terms

Analog signals
Anti-Viral programs
Bulletin boards
Computer virus

Computer security
Data file backup
Digital signals
Download

E-Mail
Electronic mail
Global backup
Incremental backup
Magnetic tape
Modem
Original programs
Password-protected

Pirated software
Sequential access
Shareware
Trojan horses
Upload
Virus
Worms

## Discussion Questions

1. Why should you not give copies of programs to friends?
2. How frequently should you backup data files and/or application programs?
3. What precautions should you take to protect your hardware and software from infection?

## True/False Questions

For each question, circle the letter T if the statement is true and the letter F if the statement is false.

T F 1. Individuals guilty of authoring a virus in many states can receive a fine and a jail term.
T F 2. Anti-viral programs should be used regularly to check for and fix viruses found on your disks.
T F 3. It is OK to copy and share programs among friends.
T F 4. Shareware are sets of programs you can test before paying the programmer's fee.
T F 5. The term shareware means it is OK to share these programs with friends.
T F 6. Trojan Horse programs replicate themselves and spread quickly.
T F 7. You should always make a copy of original program disks and then put the original disks away for safe keeping.
T F 8. A global backup is the process of copying the entire source disk to one or more destination disks.
T F 9. An incremental backup will copy only files that have been created, modified, or copied to your hard drive since the last backup.
T F 10. Non-commercial Bulletin Boards and Computer Networks are great places to catch viruses.

## Completion Questions

Write the correct answer in each blank space.

1. A _____ file can only be accessed by the user(s) that knows the key to open it.
2. The process of making a copy of an original file on another disk is known as _____ .
3. A virus program has two major objectives: _____ and _____.
4. List two advantages of storing data files on your hard disk.
   a.
   b.
5. List two possible disadvantages of storing data files on your hard disk.
   a.
   b.

## Assignment

Gather the necessary information for the following questions by checking with local computer stores, reading Macintosh magazines or sales catalogs, and by talking to friends with Macintoshes. You may use TeachText or any other word processing program on the Macintosh to create and print this report.

1. Write a short paragraph listing available anti-viral programs for the Macintosh. Wherever appropriate, include the price and a brief description of the program.

2. Write a short paragraph listing available security programs for the Macintosh. Wherever appropriate, include the price and a brief description of the program.

3. Write a short paragraph listing available backup programs for the Macintosh. Wherever appropriate, include the price and a brief description of the program.

4. Write a short paragraph describing the security concerns you would have if you owned a Macintosh. What types of programs discussed in this chapter would you need to purchase?

# 14 Word Processing Applications

## Learning Objectives

**After completing this Chapter you will be able to:**

1. Create a document using one or more word processing application programs.
2. Save your document to disk.
3. Print your document.
4. Edit the document by inserting, copying, moving, and deleting text.
5. Use bold and italic styles to emphasize text.
6. Perform simple formatting operations by changing line spacing and text alignment.

## Introduction

Word processing application programs are one of the most popular software packages available. Many people write letters or create reports. Word processing software allows you to create, save, print, and modify text. The capabilities of the programs vary. Some word processing packages allow you to create footnotes, a table of contents, an outline, a row and column table, and so on, while others do not.

The spell checking features of word processing programs also differ greatly. Some programs not only check your spelling and offer synonym choices, but also count the number of characters, words, lines and paragraphs in your document. (Do you remember having to type several 500 word essays for school and counting each word by hand?) A few word processing programs include simple paint and draw features.

## Word Processing

In the following exercises, three different word processing packages—ClarisWorks, Microsoft Works, and Microsoft Word—will be used to create the same letter. You will not be exposed to all the wonderful features of each program, but hopefully you will see the advantages of using a word processing program to create your text documents. Conceptually, the steps in creating a letter are the same in all packages, but the menus and/or keystrokes necessary to accomplish each task will vary from program to program.

Check with your instructor to see which program(s) you will be using and how to access the program(s).

### Activity 14.1—Creating, Saving and Printing a Document.

In this activity you will open a new word processing document, type in the text, correct mistakes as necessary, save, and print the document. You need access to either ClarisWorks, Microsoft Word, or Microsoft Works and a new unformatted disk.

**Opening a new word processing document**

Step 1    Boot your Macintosh.

Step 2    Place your new disk in the available floppy disk drive. Follow the instructions provided by the Macintosh to format your disk. Name the disk Lastname's Applications. (For example, Sullivan's Applications.)

*What's Happening*

The Macintosh guides you through the formatting process. If you don't remember how to format a disk, refer to Chapter 3.

Step 3    Follow your instructor's directions to locate the word processing program icon. Double-click on the appropriate program icon.

ClarisWorks          Microsoft Works 3.0          Microsoft Word

*What's Happening*

An untitled document window appears on your desktop if you are using Microsoft Word. ClarisWorks and Microsoft Works will display a greeting dialog box. Both Works programs are integrated application packages that allow you to create a database, word processing, graphics/draw, or spreadsheet document. They also have communication capabilities. You must specify the type of document you wish to create.

Step 4   Follow the instructions for your specific program to open a new word processing document.

*Figure 14.1—ClarisWorks New Document Dialog Box*

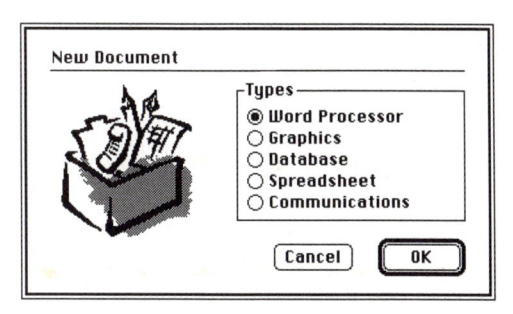

**ClarisWorks**—Verify that the button next to Word Processor is selected. (Figure 14.1) If it isn't, click on it. Click on the OK button to open a new word processing document.

*Figure 14.2—Microsoft Works Greeting Screen*

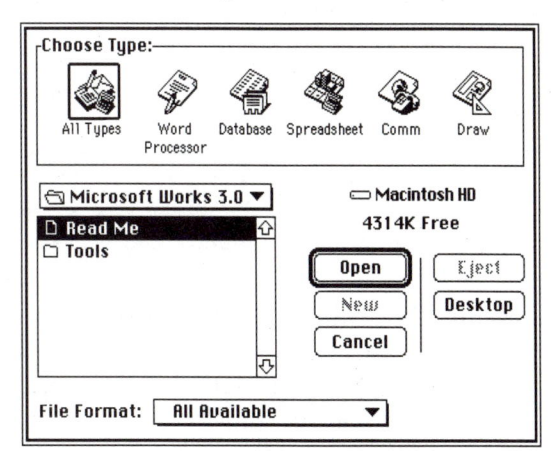

**Microsoft Works**—Double-click on the word processor icon. (Figure 14.2) A new Untitled document window will appear. If Microsoft Works' ruler bar is not displayed under the title bar, choose Show Ruler from the Window menu.

**Microsoft Word**—An untitled document is on your desktop.

Step 5   Spend a little time looking through the pull-down menus and examining the ruler.

## What's Happening

The Application menu icon displays the icon of the active program. The menu bar across the top of the screen varies slightly from one program to the next but essentially each program can perform the same basic word processing functions.

For example, the File menu on each program allows you to open, close, save, and print your document. The Quit command is also on this menu. The editing tools (undo, cut, copy, paste, and clear) are available on the Edit menus.

The **Format, Style, Font,** or **Size menus** are used to change the appearance of the document and to emphasize text. You can emphasize text by underlining, outlining, shadowing, bolding, or italicizing selected text.

The capabilities of the **ruler bars** vary greatly.

*Figure 14.3—ClarisWorks' Menu Bar and Ruler*

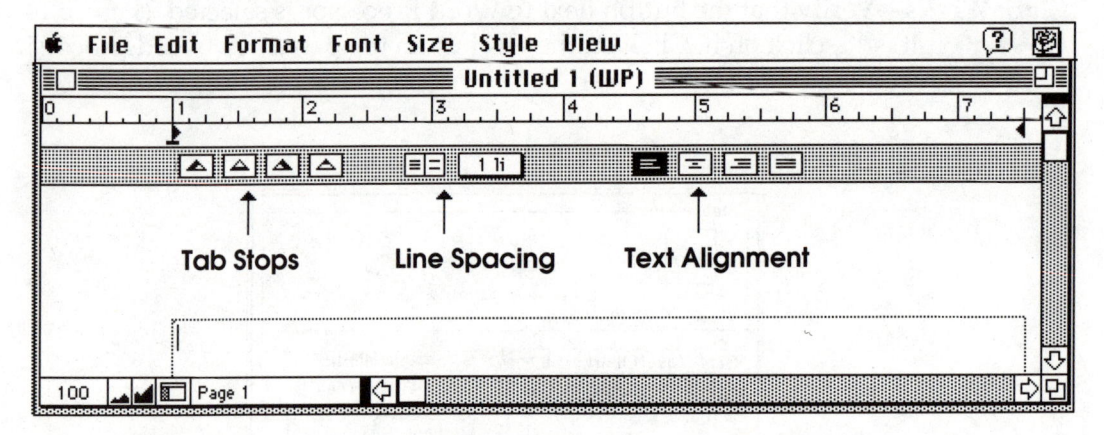

**ClarisWorks' ruler bar** (Figure 14.3) can be used to set **Tab Stops, Line Spacing,** and **Text Alignment**. Tab Stops can be created to line up columns and lines on a page. Line Spacing can be set by .5 increments from single line spacing to 10 lines. Text can be aligned to either **left flush, centered, right flush,** or **justified** on the page.

WORD PROCESSING 321

*Figure 14.4—Microsoft Works Menu Bar and Ruler*

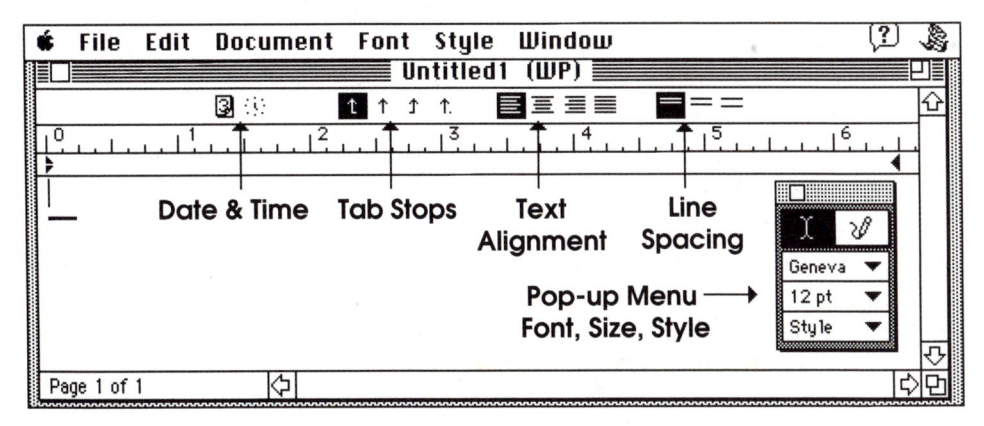

[Screenshot: Microsoft Works window showing menu bar with File, Edit, Document, Font, Style, Window. Ruler labeled with Date & Time, Tab Stops, Text Alignment, Line Spacing, and Pop-up Menu Font, Size, Style (Geneva, 12 pt, Style).]

**Microsoft Works' ruler bar** (Figure 14.4) can be used to enter the date and time in the document, set tab stops, align text, and set line spacing.

A **pop-up Tools menu** may appear when you open a new document. In **text mode,** the menu contains several pop-up lists to set the document's font, size, and style. In **draw mode,** an extended menu will appear containing several drawing tools. If the pop-up Tools menu is on your desktop, click on the close box in the pop-up Tools menu.

*Figure 14.5—Microsoft Word Menu Bar and Ruler*

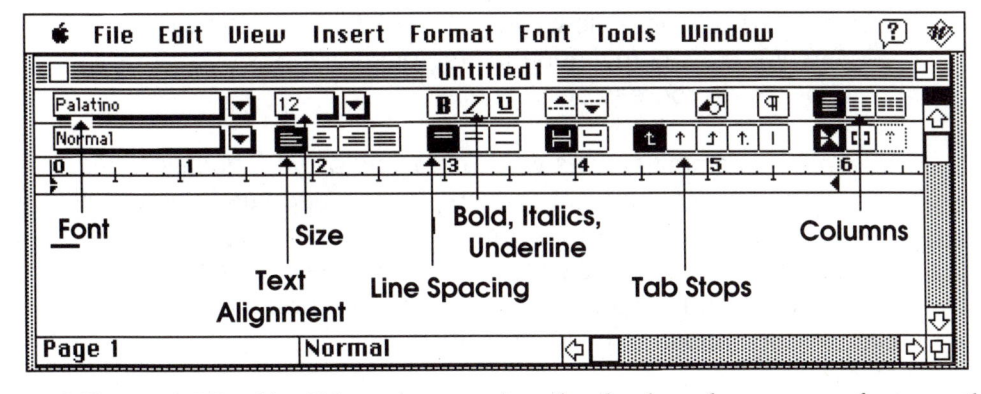

[Screenshot: Microsoft Word window showing menu bar with File, Edit, View, Insert, Format, Font, Tools, Window. Ribbon and ruler labeled with Font (Palatino), Size (12), Text Alignment, Line Spacing, Bold, Italics, Underline, Tab Stops, Columns; style set to Normal.]

**Microsoft Word's ribbon** (top row) and **ruler bars** have many features that are not included in the other two rulers. If Word's ribbon or ruler bars are not displayed, choose the appropriate command, Ribbon or Ruler, from the View menu.

Some of these features have been identified in Figure 14.5.

**Keying in your new document**

Before you key in this document, let's clarify a few issues.

- The flashing, vertical line under the left side of the ruler identifies your insertion point. Remember, the insertion point indicates where the next character typed will appear.
- Use wordwrap. Do not press the Return key within the body of a multiple line paragraph.
- Insert your name and address where appropriate (wherever the document says Your Name).
- Do not be concerned if your lines do not break on the right margin at the same place as the sample document. A different font or margin may be used by your application program. This will cause line advancement to be different.
- To insert a blank line, press the Return key. This is known as a **hard return** versus a **soft return** (wordwrap).
- Use the original default settings for line spacing, tab stops, margin settings, page length, font, and point size for each program.

*Figure 14.6—Congrats Letter*

Your Name
Your Street Address
Your City, State Zip

Dear Your Name,

It was a pleasure to interview you last week for a position with our company. We have completed the first round of interviews. A reference check is in progress on all finalists.

The interview committee was very impressed by your qualifications and enthusiasm. Your educational preparation appears to be exactly what we are looking for. Some committee members are a little concerned about your practical experience. If you have any additional information concerning the jobs you have held during the last ten years, please send it to me immediately.

The President of the company is conducting the final round of interviews next week. Please call our office at your earliest convenience to schedule the second interview.

Sincerely,

Christopher Michaels

Step 6    Key in the letter in Figure 14.6.

Step 7    Look over the document to see if you made any mistakes. Correct them as necessary, using the text selection, cut, copy, paste, and clear techniques you learned in Chapters 6, 7, and 8.

**Saving a Word Processing Document**

Step 8    Choose the Save command from the File menu.

*What's Happening*

The program's directory dialog box will appear. You must direct the Macintosh where to save your file, and what to name the document.

Figure 14.7, 14.8, and 14.9 show the directory dialog boxes for all three programs. All of them contain the same basic information. The disk, folder, and file names that appear in your dialog box are probably different from the examples. Make sure that you save your files on your Lastname's Applications floppy disk.

*Figure 14.7—ClarisWorks' Directory Dialog Box*

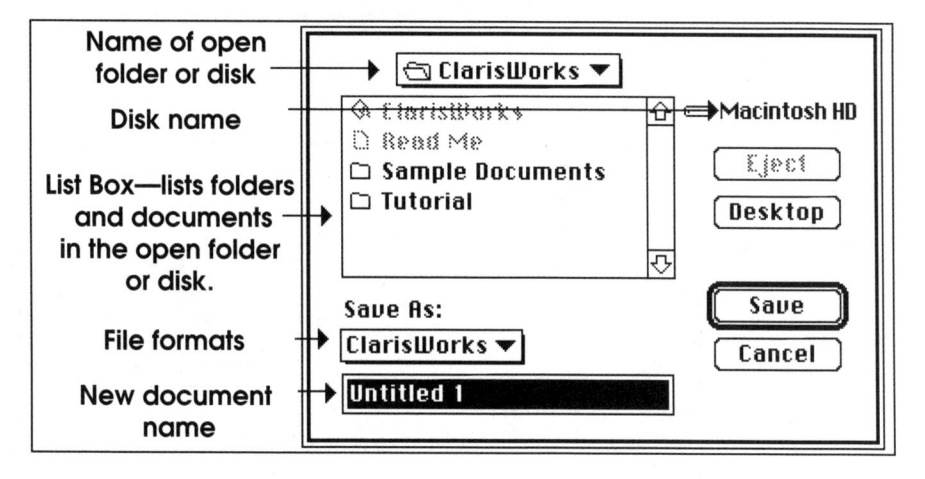

Figure 14.7 describes the different parts of a directory dialog box.
- The name of the open window (disk or folder) or desktop appears in the top left corner.
- The name of the active disk appears in the top right corner. The active disk name is probably the hard disk the application program is stored on.
- The list box contains an alphabetic list of files and folders in the open window.

- The File Format entry provides a pop-up list of different file formats. If you create the document in ClarisWorks but later want to access it in Microsoft Word, you need to save the document in a format Microsoft Word can read.
- An entry is available for you to name the new document.
- Several buttons are available to direct the Macintosh to perform specific tasks.

*Figure 14.8—Microsoft Works' Directory Dialog Box*

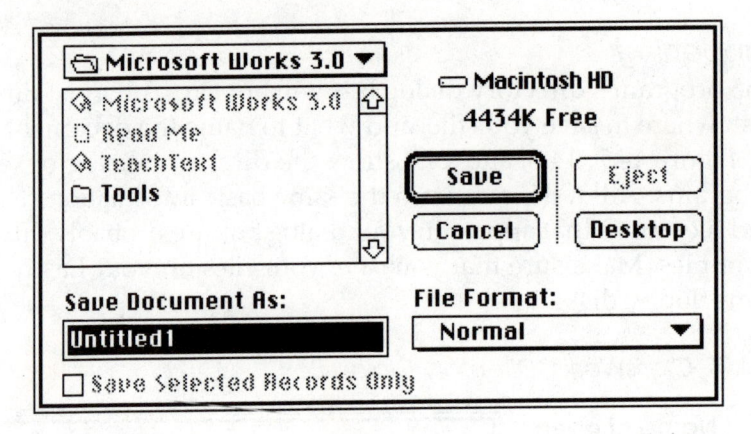

*Figure 14.9—Microsoft Word's Directory Dialog Box*

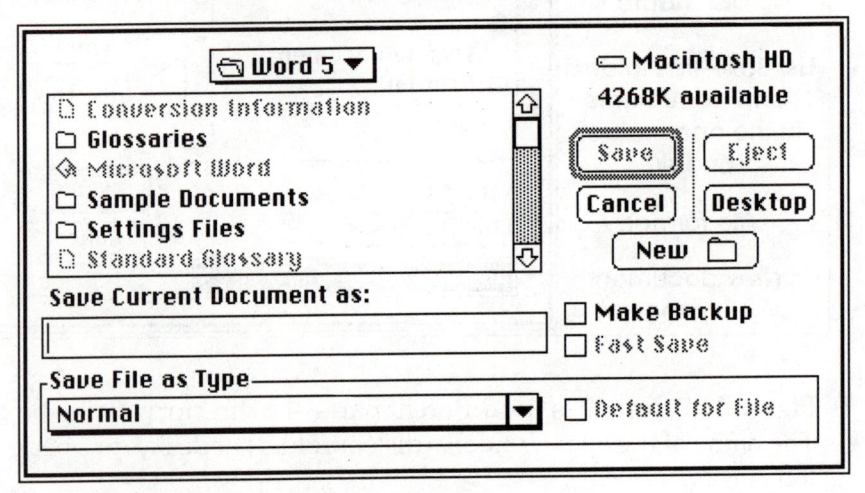

Step 9   Click on the **Desktop** button.

## What's Happening

An alphabetic list of all items on the desktop appear in the list box. An example of ClarisWorks' directory dialog box is shown in Figure 14.10.

Step 10   Click on Lastname Applications in the list box. Click on the Open button.

*What's Happening*

The disk name displayed in the directory dialog box changes to your Lastname's Applications disk. The list box will be empty.

Step 11   Press the Tab key to highlight or to display the flashing insertion point in the new name box. Key in the name of your new document—Congrats. Click on the Save button. (Figure 14.11) Microsoft Word may display a Summary Info dialog box. Just leave the box empty and click on the OK button.

*Figure 14.10—Desktop Level*

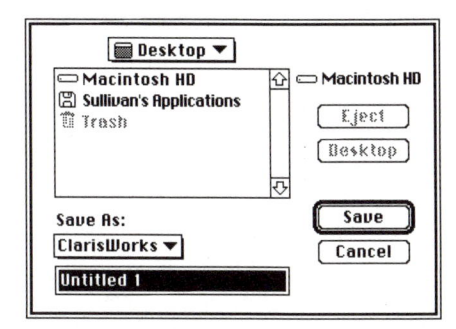

*Figure 14.11—Last Name's Application Disk*

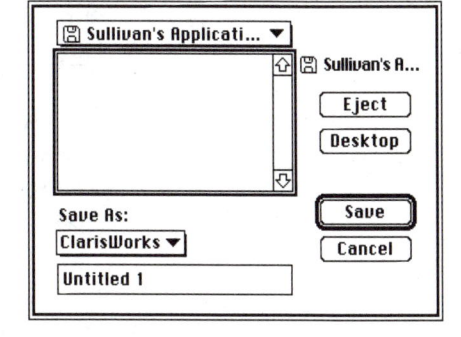

*What's Happening*

The document is written to your disk and the directory dialog box disappears.

**Printing your document**

Step 12   Verify there is paper in the printer and that it is properly aligned if necessary. Verify that the printer is turned on and ready.

Step 13   If you have multiple printers available, select Chooser from the  menu and identify the printer you wish to use. Close the Chooser window.

*What's Happening*

Refer to the Chapter 7 and 8 if you need to refresh your memory on how to print a document.

Step 14   Choose Print from the File menu. Click on the OK or Print button to print your document.

Step 15   Retrieve your document from the printer.

## Activity 14.2—Editing, Saving, and Printing a Document

The next activity guides you through the following editing techniques: inserting, copying and pasting, and cutting and pasting text. You will also change the style of the document by selecting a different font and point size. As you complete this activity, refer to the document in Figure 14.12 to make sure you are on the right track. The underlined text indicates changes from the original document.

*Figure 14.12—The Edited Letter*

> Your Name
> Your Street Address
> Your City, State Zip
>
> Dear Your Name,
>
> It was a pleasure to interview you last week for a position with our company. We have completed the first round of interviews. <u>Congratulations on **surviving** the interview.</u>
>
> The interview committee was very impressed by your qualifications and enthusiasm. Your educational preparation appears to be exactly what we are looking for. Some committee members are a little concerned about your practical experience. If you have any additional information concerning the jobs you have held during the last ten years, please send it to me immediately.
> The President of the company is conducting the final round of interviews next week <u>after a reference check is completed on all finalists.</u> Please call our office at your earliest convenience to schedule the second interview.
>
> Sincerely,
>
>
> Christopher Michaels
> <u>1010 Palm Drive</u>
> <u>Los Angeles, CA 92233</u>
> <u>(213) 999-1111</u>
>
> <u>Congratulations on surviving the interview.</u>

**Inserting text**

Step 1   Position the I-beam immediately following the period (.) at the end of the second sentence in the first paragraph. Click once to identify the new insertion point. Move the I-beam off to the side of the desktop for better viewing.

Step 2       Press the Space Bar twice.

Step 3       Key in the following sentence.

　　　　　　　　　Congratulations on surviving the interview.

Step 4       Position the I-beam at the bottom of the page immediately following the closing (Christopher Michaels). Click once to identify the new insertion point. Press the Return key to advance to the next line.

Step 5       Key in the following address and phone number immediately below Christopher Michaels.

　　　　　　　　　1010 Palm Drive
　　　　　　　　　Los Angeles, CA 92233
　　　　　　　　　(213) 999-1111

**Copying and Pasting Text**

Step 6       Position the I-beam at the beginning of the Congratulations sentence you just keyed into the first paragraph. Press and hold the mouse button while dragging the I-beam over the entire sentence.

*What's Happening*

You have selected the sentence for further action. It should be highlighted. If you make a mistake, click anywhere in the window to deselect all text and try again.

Step 7       Choose Copy from the Edit menu.

*What's Happening*

A copy of the sentence has been placed on the Clipboard.

Step 8       Position the I-beam at the bottom of the page immediately after the phone number and click once.

Step 9       Press the Return key twice to move you to the next line and to leave one blank line.

Step 10      Choose Paste from the Edit menu.

*What's Happening*

The Congratulations sentence appears at the bottom of the document.

**Cutting and Pasting Text**

Step 11   Select (highlight) the fourth sentence in the first paragraph (A reference check...).

Step 12   Choose Cut from the Edit menu. If you accidentally remove the hard return and the blank line between the paragraphs, put them back in.

*What's Happening*

The sentence is eliminated from your document and placed on the Clipboard.

Step 13   Position the I-beam immediately after the period (.) in the first sentence of the last paragraph (The President...) and click once. Press the Delete key once to remove the period (.).

Step 14   Press the Space Bar once and type

after

Step 15   Press the Space Bar once to insert a blank space.

Step 16   Choose Paste from the Edit menu.

*What's Happening*

The sentence now reads:
The President of the company is conducting the final round of interviews next week after A reference check is in progress on all finalists.

Step 17   Delete the capital A and replace it with a lowercase a.

Step 18   Select the text

in progress

Replace the selected text with the following word:

completed

*What's Happening*

The sentence now reads:
The President of the company is conducting the final round of interviews next week after a reference check is completed on all finalists.

WORD PROCESSING    329

### Save As a Different Name
Step 19   Choose the Save As... command of the File menu. Type in the new name—Congrats 1. Verify that the document is being saved to your Lastname's Applications disk, and click on the Save button.

## What's Happening
When you save the document under a new name, the original document, Congrats, is not changed on the disk. Microsoft Word will display a Summary Info dialog box, click on the OK button.

### Add Style To Emphasize the Word Surviving
Step 20   Select the word *surviving* in the first paragraph by double-clicking on the word. The word is highlighted.

Step 21   Depending on the word processor you are using, select one of the following methods to italicize and bold the word.

**ClarisWorks** and **Microsoft Works**
  Choose *Italic* from the Style menu.
  Choose **Bold** from the Style menu.

**Microsoft Word**
  Click on the **B** in the ribbon bar.
  Click on the *I* in the ribbon bar.

Step 22   Click anywhere on the text to deselect the word.

### Change the Document's Font and Point Size
Step 23   Select the entire document. Choose Select All from the Edit menu.

Step 24   Depending on the word processor you are using, select one of the following methods to change the font and point size. The check mark next to a font name indicates it is the current selected font.

**ClarisWorks**
  Select a different font from the Font menu.
  Choose 10 from the Size menu.

**Microsoft Works**
  Select a different font from the Font menu.
  Choose 10 from the Style menu.

**Microsoft Word**
Use the ribbon bar to change the font and point size.

`Helvetica ▼`

Select a different font from the font pop-up menu.

`14 ▼`

Select 10 from the size pop-up menu.

Step 25   Click anywhere on the window to deselect the document.

**Saving and Printing your Document**
Step 26   Press ⌘ S

*What's Happening*
You used keyboard equivalent keys to save your revised document to disk, replacing the old Congrats 1.

Step 27   Print your document.

## Activity 14.3—Text Alignment and Line Spacing

In this activity, you will justify the text alignment of the entire document and change the line spacing of the three paragraphs.

Step 1   Select the entire document (Select All command). (The entire document is highlighted).

Step 2   Follow the instructions specific to your program to justify the text.

**ClarisWorks**—Click on the fourth icon in the third group of icons on the ruler.

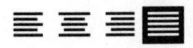

**Microsoft Works**—Click on the fourth icon in the third group of icons on the ruler.

**Microsoft Word**—Click on the fourth icon in the first group of icons on the ruler.

WORD PROCESSING 331

Step 3  Click anywhere in the first paragraph of the document to deselect the block of text.

Step 4  Place the I-beam in front of the first word in the first paragraph (It) and hold down the mouse button while you drag the I-beam down the document to highlight the three paragraphs through the closing (Sincerely). Release the mouse button.

## What's Happening

All three paragraphs plus the closing should be highlighted. If you made a mistake, click anywhere on the document to deselect the paragraphs and try again.

Step 5  Follow the instructions specific to your program to double space the selected text.

**ClarisWorks**—Click on the second icon in the second group of icons to increase line spacing from 1 li to 1.5 li. Click on the same icon again to increase the line spacing to 2 li.

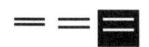

**Microsoft Works**—Click on the third icon in the fourth group of icons on the ruler.

**Microsoft Word**—Click on the third icon in the second group of icons on the menu bar.

Step 6  Choose the Save As command of the File menu. Type in the new name—CONGRATS 2. Verify that the document is being saved to your data disk. Click on the Save button.

Step 7  Compare your document to the one in Figure 14.12. Make corrections as necessary. Print your document. (Figure 14.12)

### Undo Command

Step 8  Select the entire document (Select All command). Press the A letter key.

*What's Happening*

>Your entire document has been replaced with the letter A. This is a very common mistake. Anytime you press a key when you have selected text, the text is replaced by the character typed.

Step 9   Choose Undo or Undo Typing from the Edit command.

*What's Happening*

>The last operation you performed (deleting text) is canceled. Your document reappears on your window.

Step 10   Close your document. Choose Quit from the File menu.

*What's Happening*

>A dialog box will appear asking if you want to save the changed document. You really have not changed this document since you saved the document in step 6.

Step 11   Click on No.

Step 11   Close folder and disk windows as necessary.

## Key Terms

| | |
|---|---|
| Center alignment | Ribbon bar |
| Double space | Right flush |
| Draw mode | Ruler bar |
| Font menu | Size menu |
| Format menu | Soft Return |
| Hard return | Style menu |
| Insertion point | Tab stops |
| Justification | Text alignment |
| Left flush | Text mode |
| Line spacing | Tools menu |
| Margins | Undo Ccommand |
| New Document dialog box | Undo Typing command |
| Point size | Wordwrap |

## Discussion Questions

1. Describe the advantages of using the Macintosh and a word processing program to create documents.
2. Explain the difference between the Save and Save As commands.
3. Discuss the word processing features that you would look for in a word processing program.
4. How do you direct the Macintosh to save the document on a specific disk?
5. Explain the steps to copy and paste text.
6. Explain how to emphasize text.
7. Discuss the available features on the various word processing rulers.
8. Explain text alignment: flush left, flush right, centered, justified.

## Assignments

Boot your Macintosh. The Macintosh desktop should be clean—no open windows. For this assignment you will use your Lastname's Applications disk. Open a new document in the word processing program you used in this chapter.

1. Hand in the three printed documents from this Chapter.

2. Write a double-spaced, one page document, containing at least four paragraphs on any subject. Use the original default settings for tab stops, margin settings, page length, font, and point size. Save and Print the document. Include your name and the date (top of page).

3. Use the document you just created and change the line spacing to one. Cut paragraph 1 and paste it to the end of the document. Save and Print the document.

Close all open windows.

# 15 Database Management Applications

## Learning Objectives

**After completing this Chapter you will be able to:**

1. Define common database terms.
2. Describe the advantages of using a database program.
3. Create a new database using one or more database application programs.
4. Create a record (form) design.
5. Add multiple records to the database.
6. Print a single record.
7. Sort and print a columnar report.

## Introduction

A database management program allows you to store, organize, and manage information. A database file is a collection of related information. For example, your personal phone book could easily be converted to a computer database file. An instructor's record of student names, student identification numbers, phone numbers, and grades makes a good database file. If you have a favorite collection of books, works of art, figurines, dolls, musical compact disks, or recorded VCR tapes, it can be recorded in an electronic database file. Any collection of related items can become a useful database file.

In the following exercise, two different database packages are used to create an identical database file. You can use ClarisWorks or Microsoft Works. These exercises will introduce you to database management but will not show you all the wonderful and powerful features of the programs. As you look through the following pages you will notice that conceptually the process to create and use a database file is the same, but the menus and keystrokes vary greatly.

Check with your instructor to see which program(s) you will use and how to access the program(s). Use the data disk, Lastname's Applications, you created in Chapter 14 to store the documents you create. Follow the instructions carefully.

## Database Uses

If you want to gather information on people or objects, you should probably create a list of questions and then collect the answers. A database program works much the same way. First you create the form design (the list of questions), then you gather the data and enter it into the computer, and then you use the database program to manage and organize the information.

In the following activity, you will create a simple database form consisting of seven pieces of information: Last Name, First Name, Street Address, City, State, Zip, and Home Phone. Each piece of information will be stored in a **field**. Once the form has been created you will enter ten records. (Figure 15.1) Each completed form containing information about one individual is a **record**. You will then be instructed to print a single record and a columnar report consisting of all ten records.

Separate instructions have been provided for Microsoft Works and ClarisWorks. The menus and keystrokes necessary to complete the assignment are very different.

*Figure 15.1—Ten Names and Addresses to Enter in the Database*

| Record 1= Smith Pat | 10 Palm Avenue | Long Beach | CA 90311 | (213)433-9000 |
| --- | --- | --- | --- | --- |
| Record 2= Vu Ty | 1077 9th Street | Sacramento | CA 95814 | (916)345-1212 |
| Record 3= O'Malley Fay | 1 Penn Avenue | Detroit | MI 21022 | (222)888-1111 |
| Record 4= Nguyen Thi | 15 Hill Street | San Francisco | CA 94132 | (415)333-4444 |
| Record 5= Lane Bettye | 35 Blue Avenue | El Toro | CA 92630 | (714)999-4545 |
| Record 6= Lee Chien | 12 Flower Lane | Wilsonville | OR 97060 | (503)888-3334 |
| Record 7= Sanchez Lupe | 23 W. N. Loop | Austin | TX 78756 | (512)111-2345 |
| Record 8= Rodriquez Jose | 1022 10th Street | Redding | CA 96001 | (916)232-9991 |
| Record 9= Webb Kate | 45 Ocean Drive | San Juan | CA 92692 | (714)555-0000 |
| Record 10= Spigut Irene | 456 Forest Drive | District Heights | MD 20831 | (301)991-2255 |

Activities 15.1 through 15.3 provide instructions on how to create a database using the ClarisWorks program. Activities 15.4 through 15.5 describe how to create a database using Microsoft Works. Follow the instructions for the database program you have available.

# ClarisWorks

## Activity 15.1—Using ClarisWorks to Create and Save the Form Design (layout)

Step 1  Boot your Macintosh. All windows should be closed on the desktop. Place your Lastname's Applications disk in the floppy drive.

Step 2  Follow the instructions provided by your instructor to locate the ClarisWorks program icon. Double-click on the icon.

*Figure 15.2—ClarisWorks New Document Dialog Box*

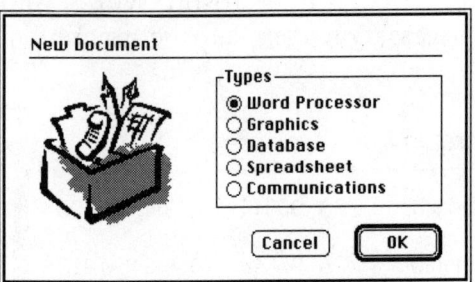

### What's Happening

ClarisWorks will display a greeting dialog box. ClarisWorks is an integrated application package that allows you to create a database, word processing, graphics/draw, spreadsheet, or communication document. You must specify the type of document you wish to create. (Figure 15.2)

Step 3  Verify the button next to Database is selected. If it isn't, click on it. Click on the OK button to open a new database document.

*Figure 15.3—Define Fields Dialog Box*

### What's Happening

The **Define Fields** dialog box appears. Use this box to specify your fields. (Figure 15.3)

Step 4  Type in the first field name, Last Name, and press the Return key to create the field.

CLARISWORKS 337

*What's Happening*
>The name will appear in the field name box.

Step 5   Type in each of the other field names and press the Return key after each.

>First Name
>Street Address
>City
>State
>Zip
>Home Phone

Step 6   Click on the Done button. (Figure 15.4)

*Figure 15.4—Field Names Entered*

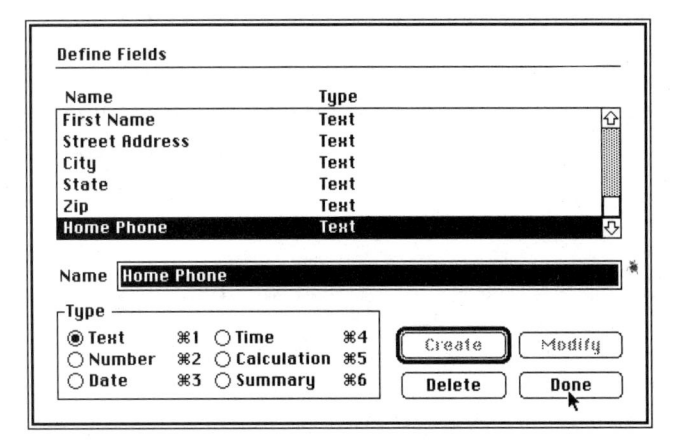

*What's Happening*
>A new window appears displaying all field names and an empty, outlined, field data box next to each. The cursor will be flashing in the Last Name field. (Figure 15.5)

*Figure 15.5—Entering First Record*

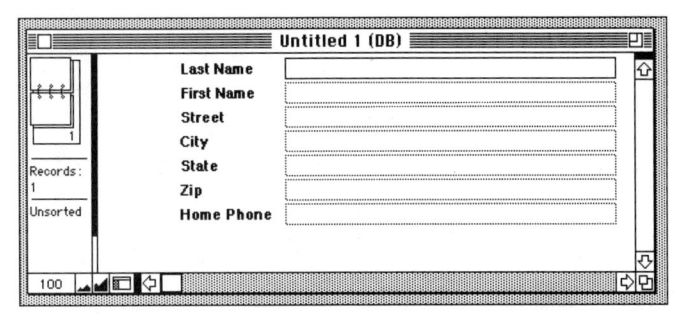

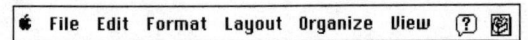

338　CHAPTER 15 • DATABASE MANAGEMENT APPLICATIONS

```
 File  Edit  Format  Layout  Organize  View  ?
```

Step 7　Most of the menus on the menu bar are now accessible. Browse through the menus to see the available commands.

Step 8　Choose Save from the File menu to save your database form design to your Lastname's Applications disk.

## What's Happening

The Directory dialog box that we discussed in Chapter 14 will appear. Make sure your Lastname's Applications disk name appears in the window. Refer to Chapter 14 if you need to refresh your memory on how to work with this dialog box.

Step 9　Key in the database document's name—Friends. Verify you are saving it to your Lastname's Applications disk. Click on the Save button.

### Adding ten records to your document

Step 10　If the **field data boxes** (appearing next to the field name) have disappeared, press the Tab key. Type in the last name Smith. Press the Tab key to move to the next field. If you accidentally press the Return key, don't worry—just press the Delete key.

Step 11　Type in the rest of the information for this record.

|  |  |  |
|---|---|---|
| First name | = | Pat |
| Street Address | = | 10 Palm Avenue |
| City | = | Long Beach |
| State | = | CA |
| Zip | = | 90311 |
| Home Phone | = | (213)433-9000 |

Step 12　Double-check the information in this record to verify its accuracy. (Figure 15.6) If any changes are necessary, use standard editing techniques to fix them.

*Figure 15.6—Completed First Record*

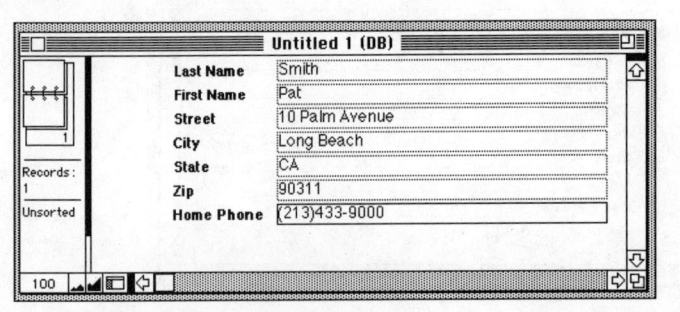

Pressing the Tab key will move you from one field to the next.

```
┌─────────────────────────────────────┐
│           Untitled 1 (DB)           │
├─────────────────────────────────────┤
│         Last Name  │Smith         │ │
│         First Name │Pat           │ │
│         Street     │10 Palm Avenue│ │
│         City       │Long Beach    │ │
│ Records:│State     │CA            │ │
│ 1       │Zip       │90311         │ │
│ Unsorted│Home Phone│(213)433-9000 │ │
│                                     │
│ 100                                 │
└─────────────────────────────────────┘
```

CLARISWORKS    339

Step 13    Choose New Record from the Edit menu.

### What's Happening
Record 2 appears with empty field data boxes. (Figure 15.7) In the future, you may use the keyboard equivalent command (⌘ R) for New Record.

*Figure 15.7—Second Record*

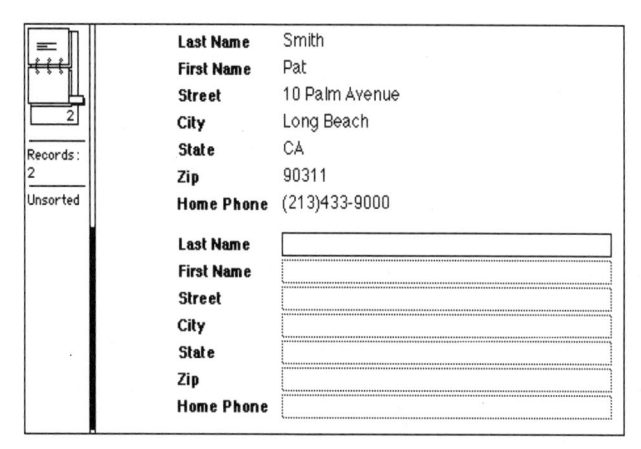

| | |
|---|---|
| Last Name | Smith |
| First Name | Pat |
| Street | 10 Palm Avenue |
| City | Long Beach |
| State | CA |
| Zip | 90311 |
| Home Phone | (213)433-9000 |
| Last Name | |
| First Name | |
| Street | |
| City | |
| State | |
| Zip | |
| Home Phone | |

Records: 2
Unsorted

Step 14    Repeat steps 10 through 13 to key in the other 9 records (refer to Figure 15.1 provided earlier in this chapter for the data).

Step 15    Review all records and verify that the information has been entered correctly. Use the scroll bar to display different records. If you find an error, simply click on the data you wish to change. The data field box will appear. Enter the new text.

Step 16    Choose Save from the File menu.

### What's Happening
Your revised Friends database is written to disk.

## Activity 15.2—Using ClarisWorks to Print Record Number 5 (Lane)

Step 1    Use the book icon in the top left corner to locate record 5. Either click on the top page to select the previous record, the down page to view the next record or drag the Slide Control.

### What's Happening
Lane's record has a bold vertical line to the left of the record. Boxes may appear around the field data.

Records: 10
Unsorted

Step 2    If boxes do not appear around the data, click on the name Lane.

Step 3    Turn the printer on. If necessary, use the Chooser to specify which printer to print to. Choose Print from the File menu.

*What's Happening*
The Print window appears.

Step 4    Click on the Current Record button. Click on the OK or Print button for your one record to print.

### Activity 15.3—Using ClarisWorks to Sort and Print a Columnar Report of All Records.

Step 1    Choose **New Layout** from the **Layout** menu.

Step 2    Click on the Columnar report button and click on the OK button. (Figure 15.8)

*Figure 15.8—New Layout*

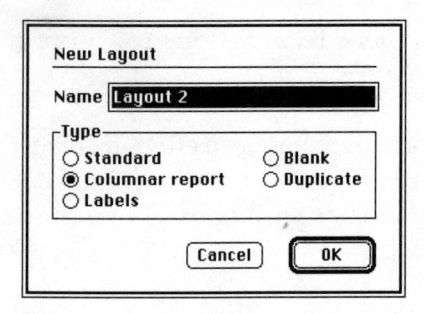

*What's Happening*
The **Set Field Order** dialog box will appear.

Step 3    Click on Last Name in the Field List box, then click on the Move button.

*What's Happening*
The Last Name field appears in the Field Order box. (Figure 15.9)

*Figure 15.9—Set Field Order Box*

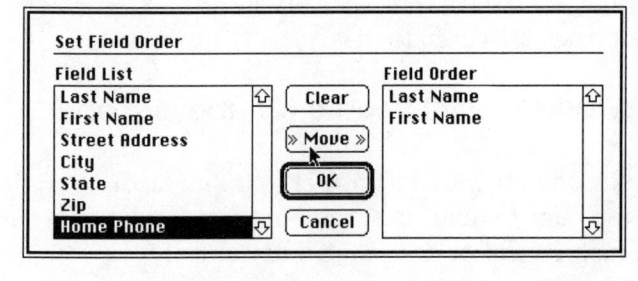

Step 4    Repeat step 3 to place the field names, First Name and Home Phone, in the Field Order box. (Figure 15.9)

Step 5    After all three names appear in the Field Order box, click on the OK button.

*What's Happening*
The Set Field Order dialog box disappears. The records are now displayed in a columnar report. (Figure 15.10)

Step 6    Choose **Sort Records**... from the **Organize** menu.

## What's Happening

A new dialog box will appear requesting Sort Order.

Step 7    Click on Last Name in the Field List. Verify the Ascending Order button is selected, and click on the Move button. Click on the OK button. (Figure 15.11)

## What's Happening

A list of your records in ascending order by Last Name should appear on your desktop. (Figure 15.12)

Step 8    Choose Print from the File menu.

## What's Happening

The Print dialog box appears.

Step 9    Click on the Visible Records button. Click on the OK or Print button to print a columnar report with all 10 names and phone numbers.

Step 10   Choose Save from the File menu.

Step 11   Choose Close and then Quit from the File menu.

Step 12   Close folder and disk windows as necessary.

*Figure 15.10—Columnar Layout*

| Last Name | First Name | Home Phone |
|---|---|---|
| Smith | Pat | (213)433-9000 |
| Vu | Ty | (916)345-1212 |
| O'Malley | Fay | (222)888-1111 |
| Nguyen | Thi | (415)333-4444 |
| Lane | Bettye | (714)999-4545 |
| Lee | Chein | (503)888-3334 |
| Sanchez | Lupe | (512)111-2345 |
| Rodriquez | Jose | (916)232-9991 |
| Webb | Kate | (714)555-0000 |
| Spigut | Irene | (301)991-2255 |

Records: 10 Unsorted

*Figure 15.11—Sort Records Box*

Sort Records

Field List: Last Name, First Name, Street Address, City, State, Zip, Home Phone

Sort Order: Last Name

Clear  « Move «  OK  Cancel

● Ascending order
○ Descending order

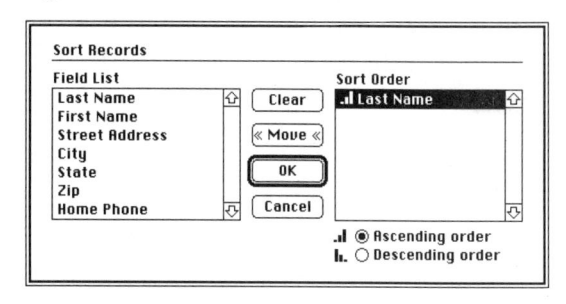

*Figure 15.12—Sorted Columnar List*

| Last Name | First Name | Home Phone |
|---|---|---|
| Lane | Bettye | (714)999-4545 |
| Lee | Chein | (503)888-3334 |
| Nguyen | Thi | (415)333-4444 |
| O'Malley | Fay | (222)888-1111 |
| Rodriquez | Jose | (916)232-9991 |
| Sanchez | Lupe | (512)111-2345 |
| Smith | Pat | (213)433-9000 |
| Spigut | Irene | (301)991-2255 |
| Vu | Ty | (916)345-1212 |
| Webb | Kate | (714)555-0000 |

Records: 10 Sorted

If you do not wish to create a database using Microsoft Works, proceed to Key Terms at the end of this chapter.

## Microsoft Works

### Activity 15.4—Using Microsoft Works to Create and Save the Form Design (Layout)

In this activity you will be opening a new database document and adding field names.

Step 1   Boot your Macintosh. All windows should be closed on the desktop. Place your Lastname's Applications disk in the floppy drive.

Step 2   Follow the instructions provided by your instructor to locate the Microsoft Works program icon. Double click on the icon.

*Microsoft Works 3.0*

*What's Happening*

Microsoft Works will display a greeting dialog box. (Figure 15.13) Microsoft Works is an integrated application package that allows you to create a database, word processing, graphics/draw, communication or spreadsheet document. You must specify the type of document you wish to create.

*Figure 15.13—Microsoft Works Greeting Box*

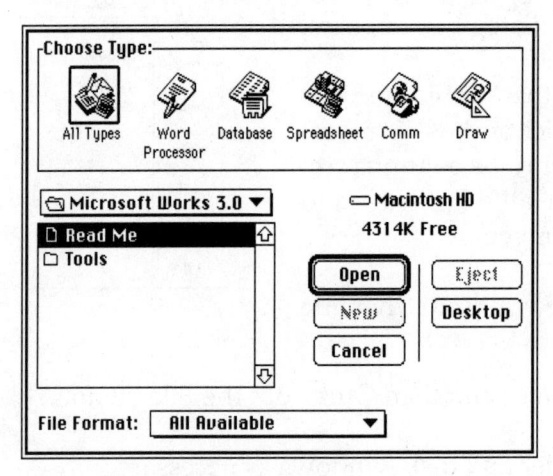

Step 3   Double-click on the Database icon.

*What's Happening*

A New Field box appears. (Figure 15.14)

MICROSOFT WORKS    343

Step 4    Key in the first field name—Last Name. Press the Return key or click on the Create button to create this field.

*Figure 15.14—New Field Dialog Box*

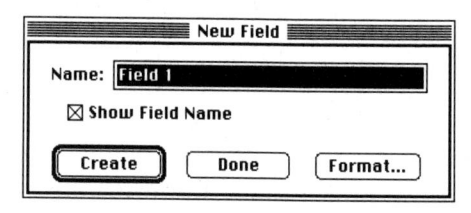

*What's Happening*

The field will appear on the Untitled (DB) window and another New Field box appears.

Step 5    Enter the next six fields the same way.
> First Name
> Street Address
> City
> State
> Zip
> Home Phone

Step 6    Once you have entered all field names they should appear on the Untitled (DB) window. Click on the Done button in the New Field box.

*What's Happening*

The New Field dialog box disappears. All field names appear in the Untitled1 window. The field name Home Phone may not be entirely visible.

```
 File  Edit  Form  Data  Report  Window
```

Step 7    Examine the menu bar and display each menu to get an overview of the available commands.

Step 8    Choose Save from the File menu to save your database form design to your Lastname's Applications disk.

*What's Happening*

The directory dialog box that we discussed in Chapter 14 will appear. Make sure your Lastname's Applications disk name appears in the window. Refer to Chapter 14 if you need to refresh your memory on how to work with this dialog box.

Step 9    Key in the database document's name—Friends. Verify you are saving it to your Lastname's Applications disk. Click on the Save button.

344   CHAPTER 15 • DATABASE MANAGEMENT APPLICATIONS

**Adding ten records to your document**

Step 10   Click on the Last Name data area and type in the last name Smith. The name will appear in the entry bar under the menu bar.

*What's Happening*

The entry bar contains an X and a check mark. Clicking on the X directs the Macintosh to ignore what you just typed in. Clicking on the check mark will place the data in the field but will not advance you to the next field. Pressing the Return key is the easiest and quickest way to place the data in the field and to move to the next field.

Step 11   Press the Return key to place the name in the Last Name field and to move to the next field.

Step 12   Type in the rest of the information for this record. (Figure 15.15) When you press the Return key after entering the Home Phone field information, a new empty record will appear on your window.

*Figure 15.15—First Record*

| Last Name | Smith |
| First Name | Pat |
| Street | 10 Palm Avenue |
| City | Long Beach |
| State | CA |
| Zip | 90311 |
| Home | (213)433-9000 |

```
First name      =   Pat
Street Address  =   10 Palm Avenue
City            =   Long Beach
State           =   CA
Zip             =   90311
Home Phone      =   (213)433-9000
```

Step 13   Key in the information for the other 9 records (refer to the data provided in Figure 15.1).

Step 14   Use the Previous Record (⌘ -) and Next Record (⌘ =) commands in the Data menu to review the records.
          If you need to fix information in one of the fields, click on the field's data area, type the new information and press the Return key.

Step 15   Choose Save from the File menu.

*What's Happening*

Your revised Friends database is written to disk.

## Activity 15.5—Using Microsoft Works to Sort and Print a Columnar Report of All Records

Step 1   Choose List View from the Form menu.

### What's Happening
A columnar list of your records appears on the screen. (Figure 15.16) An entire field or only partial information may be out of view.

*Figure 15.16—A Columnar List*

| Last Name | First Name | Street Address | City | State | Zip | Home Phone |
|---|---|---|---|---|---|---|
| Smith | Pat | 10 Palm Avenue | Long Beach | CA | 90311 | (213)433-9000 |
| Yu | Ty | 1077 9th Street | Sacramento | CA | 95814 | (916)345-1212 |
| O'Malley | Fay | 1 Penn Avenue | Detroit | MI | 21022 | (222)888-1111 |
| Nguyen | Thi | 15 Hill Street | San Francisco | CA | 94132 | (415)333-4444 |
| Lane | Bettye | 35 Blue Avenue | El Toro | CA | 92630 | (714)999-4545 |
| Lee | Chein | 12 Flower Lane | Wilsonville | OR | 97060 | (503)888-3334 |
| Sanchez | Lupe | 23 W.N. Loop | Austin | TX | 78756 | (512)111-2345 |
| Rodriquez | Jose | 1022 10th Street | Redding | CA | 96001 | (916)232-9991 |
| Webb | Kate | 45 Ocean Drive | San Juan | CA | 92692 | (714)555-0000 |
| Spigut | Irene | 456 Forest Drive | District Heights | MD | 20831 | (301)991-2255 |

Step 2   Choose New Report.. from the Report menu.

*Figure 15.17—Name Report Box*

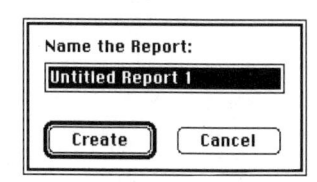

### What's Happening
A Name the Report dialog box will appear. (Figure 15.17)

Step 3   Key in the name—Name and Address—and click on the Create button.

Step 4   If you cannot see all seven fields, you must size the columns. Position the mouse at the top of the window on the vertical line separating the two field names (the pointer will become a two-way arrow). To increase or decrease the column width, hold the mouse button down and drag this separator line. Size the window as needed.

Step 5   Size the fields as small as possible while still displaying all the information.

Step 6   Position the vertical line following the zip field name on position 65 (6.5) of the ruler bar. (Figure 15.18) Size the columns to show the Last Name through Zip fields.

*Figure 15.18—Sizing Fields*

| Last Name | First Name | Street Address | City | State | Zip |
|---|---|---|---|---|---|
| Smith | Pat | 10 Palm Avenue | Long Beach | CA | 90311 |
| Yu | Ty | 1077 9th Street | Sacramento | CA | 95814 |
| O'Malley | Fay | 1 Penn Avenue | Detroit | MI | 21022 |
| Nguyen | Thi | 15 Hill Street | San Francisco | CA | 94132 |
| Lane | Bettye | 35 Blue Avenue | El Toro | CA | 92630 |
| Lee | Chein | 12 Flower Lane | Wilsonville | OR | 97060 |
| Sanchez | Lupe | 23 W.N. Loop | Austin | TX | 78756 |
| Rodriguez | Jose | 1022 10th Street | Redding | CA | 96001 |
| Webb | Kate | 45 Ocean Drive | San Juan | CA | 92692 |
| Spigut | Irene | 456 Forest Drive | District Heights | MD | 20831 |

### Sort the database by last name

**Step 7** Move the pointer over the top of the Last Name field name. The pointer will become a hand. Click once to select the entire column—the column is highlighted.

**Step 8** Choose Sort from the Data menu.

## What's Happening

The Sort Criteria dialog box appears. (Figure 15.19) The list box should display the Last Name field name. If the Descending checkbox has an **X** in it, your records will be sorted in reverse order (Z to A). If an X appears in the checkbox, click on the checkbox to remove it.

*Figure 15.19—Sort Dialog Box*

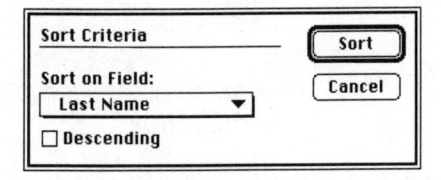

```
Sort Criteria                    [ Sort ]
Sort on Field:                   [ Cancel ]
 Last Name  ▼
☐ Descending
```

**Step 9** Click on the Sort button.

## What's Happening

Your records are now in alphabetical order by last name. (Figure 15.20)

*Figure 15.20—Sorted Records*

| Last Name | First Name | Street Address | City | State | Zip |
|---|---|---|---|---|---|
| Lane | Bettye | 35 Blue Avenue | El Toro | CA | 92630 |
| Lee | Chein | 12 Flower Lane | Wilsonville | OR | 97060 |
| Nguyen | Thi | 15 Hill Street | San Francisco | CA | 94132 |
| O'Malley | Fay | 1 Penn Avenue | Detroit | MI | 21022 |
| Rodriguez | Jose | 1022 10th Street | Redding | CA | 96001 |
| Sanchez | Lupe | 23 W.N. Loop | Austin | TX | 78756 |
| Smith | Pat | 10 Palm Avenue | Long Beach | CA | 90311 |
| Spigut | Irene | 456 Forest Drive | District Heights | MD | 20831 |
| Yu | Ty | 1077 9th Street | Sacramento | CA | 95814 |
| Webb | Kate | 45 Ocean Drive | San Juan | CA | 92692 |

**Step 10** Choose Print from the File menu to print this screen.

**Step 11** Save your database. Close the window. Choose Quit from the File menu. Close folder and disk windows as necessary.

## Key Terms

Database
Define Fields dialog box
Columnar report
Field
Form
Layout menu
New Layout
Record
Set Filed Order
Sort

## Discussion Questions

1. Explain the purpose of a database program.
2. Describe the steps necessary to create a database file.
3. Discuss the differences and similarities between ClarisWorks and Microsoft Works.
4. Explain the difference between the terms field and record.
5. List five database files that would be of value to you.

## Assignments

Boot your Macintosh. The desktop should be clean—no open windows. For this assignment you will use your Lastname's Applications disk. Open a new document in the database program you used in this chapter.

1. Hand in the report you created in this Chapter.
2. Create a new database.
   a. Use the following field names.
      Last Name
      First Name
      Home Phone
   b. Enter the names and phone numbers of ten friends.
   c. Sort the records by Last Name.
   d. Save your database.
   e. Print a report containing all ten records. Use all fields.

3. Create a new database containing your ten favorite movies.
   a. Use the following field names.
      Movie Name
      Leading Actor
      Leading Actress
      Category
   b. Enter the information for ten movies. Place one of following categories in the Category field of each record: Comedy, Musical, Romance, Thriller, Western.
   c. Sort the records by Movie Name.
   d. Save your database.
   e. Print a report containing all ten records. Use all fields.
   f. Sort the records by Category.
   g. Print a report containing all ten records. Use all fields.

   Close all open windows.

# 16 Spreadsheet Applications

## Learning Objectives

**After completing this Chapter you will be able to:**

1. Define common spreadsheet terms such as worksheet, cells, formulas, functions.
2. Create a new worksheet using one or more spreadsheet application programs.
3. Format a worksheet.
4. Enter formulas and functions to perform calculations.
5. Print and save the worksheet.
6. Change the contents of cells to see how fast the Macintosh recalculates.

## Introduction

A **spreadsheet** application program allows you to manipulate numbers. Accountants have traditionally used columnar pads of paper, pencils, erasers, and calculators to keep accounts. Today, many people use a Macintosh and a spreadsheet program to accomplish these tasks. The most significant difference between the two methods is the amount of time necessary to enter numbers, perform calculations, manipulate the numbers, and prepare reports.

This chapter will take you on a quick tour of three spreadsheet programs: ClarisWorks, Microsoft Works, and Excel. The full power of these programs take many hours to learn, but you can see the advantage of using a spreadsheet by creating a simple worksheet. Check with your instructor to see which program(s) you should use and how to access it. Carefully follow the instructions provided.

## Using ClarisWorks, Microsoft Works, or Microsoft Excel

### Activity 16.1—Creating and Saving a Simple Worksheet

Note:  Boot your Macintosh. All windows should be closed.

Step 1  Follow the instructions provided by your instructor to locate the ClarisWorks, Microsoft Works, or Microsoft Excel program icon. Double-click on the icon.

ClarisWorks        Microsoft Works 3.0        Microsoft Excel

*What's Happening*

**ClarisWorks** and **Microsoft Works** will open a New Document dialog box. (Figure 16.1 and 16.2) Both Works programs can be used for a variety of applications. You must specify the type you want to work on.

**Microsoft Excel** will automatically open a new worksheet document called Worksheet1. (Figure 16.5)

Step 2  Follow the instructions for your specific program to open a new spreadsheet document.

*Figure 16.1—ClarisWorks New Document*

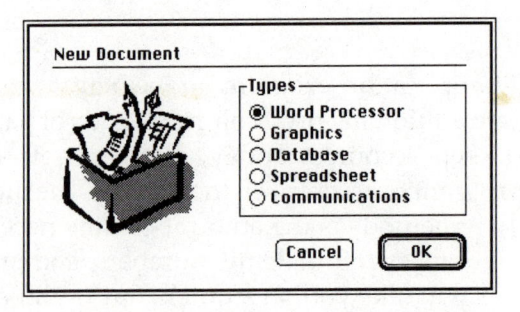

**ClarisWorks**
> Click once on the button next to Spreadsheet. (Figure 16.1) Then click on the OK button to open an Untitled 1 (SS) document. (Figure 16.3)

**Microsoft Works**
> Click once on the Spreadsheet icon. (Figure 16.2) Then click on the New button to open a new Untitled 1 (SS) document. (Figure 16.4)

*Figure 16.2—Microsoft Works New Document*

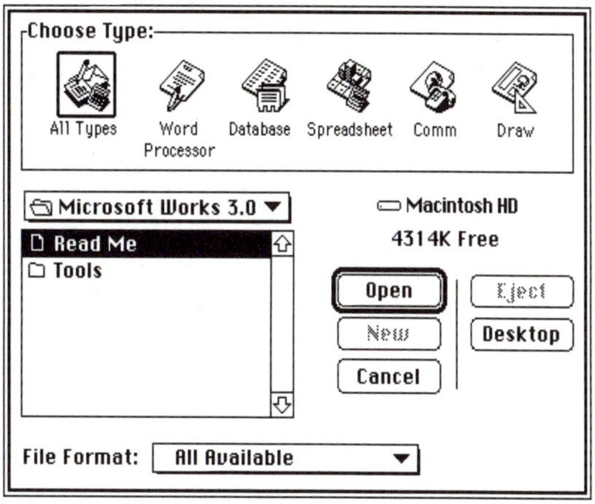

**Microsoft Excel**

A new spreadsheet document is automatically opened on your desktop. (Figure 16.5)

## What's Happening

Examine the worksheet window. The **worksheet** that appears on the desktop is similar to a columnar pad of paper. It is divided into rows and columns. The **intersection** of the **rows** and **columns** are called **cells**. Each cell on the worksheet has a unique address. Spreadsheet programs assign each cell a column letter followed by a row number such as A1, B2, F5.

Figure 16.3 shows ClarisWorks spreadsheet menu bar, the entry bar (under the title bar), and a portion of the worksheet. The entry bar shows the address of the active cell, A1 (Column A, Row 1). The active cell, A1, has a bold outline around it.

*Figure 16.3—ClarisWorks Worksheet*

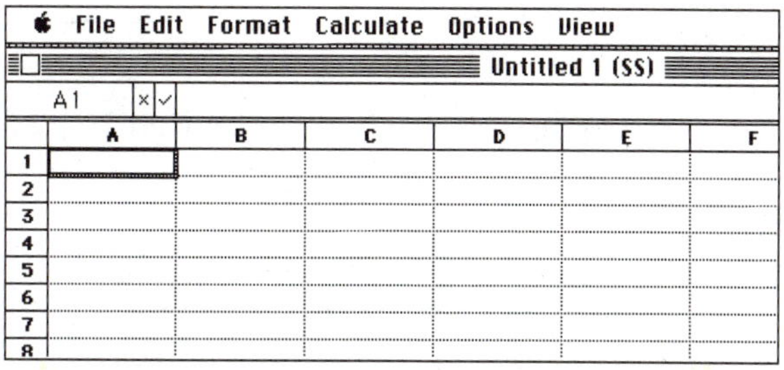

Figure 16.4 shows Microsoft Works spreadsheet menu bar, the entry bar, and a portion of the worksheet. The name of the active cell, A1, appears in the entry bar. The active cell, A1, appears in a bold outline.

*Figure 16.4—Microsoft Works Worksheet*

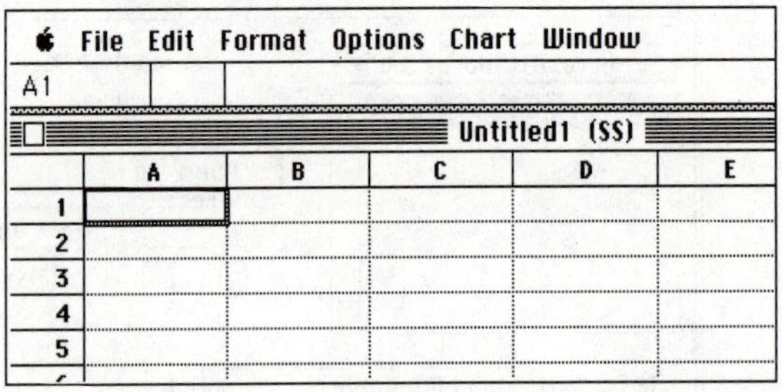

Figure 16.5 shows (from the top down) Microsoft Excel's spreadsheet menu bar, tool bar, formula bar, and a portion of the worksheet. The name of the active cell, A1, appears in the formula bar. The active cell, A1, appears in a bold outline.

*Figure 16.5—Microsoft Excel Worksheet*

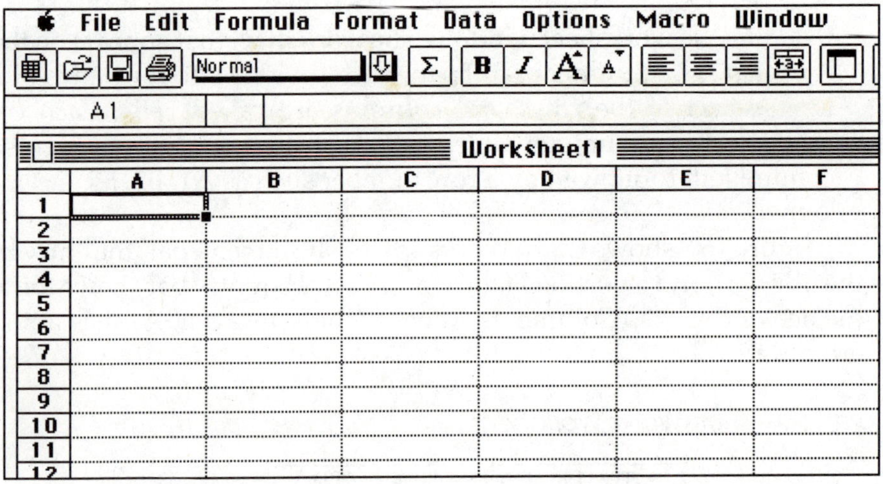

Step 3    Click on cell A1. Key in **Months**. Press the Return key to move to cell A2.

## What's Happening

As you key in text it appears in the entry/formula bar. Pressing the Return key places the text in the active cell and moves you down the column to cell A2. Pressing the Tab key will activate the cell to the right. Pressing an arrow key will activate the next cell in the direction of the arrow.

Step 4  Enter the information in cells A1 through F11 shown in Figure 16.6. Microsoft Works may convert the month name to numbers (1/01/93).

*Figure 16.6—Microsoft Works Spreadsheet Information*

|    | A | B | C | D | E | F |
|---|---|---|---|---|---|---|
| 1 | Months | January | February | March | Total | Average |
| 2 | Rent | 650 | 650 | 650 | | |
| 3 | Electric | 75 | 60 | 64 | | |
| 4 | Gas | 45 | 38 | 55 | | |
| 5 | Water | 38.24 | 25.5 | 34.73 | | |
| 6 | Phone | 39.5 | 38.75 | 23 | | |
| 7 | Charge Cards | 200 | 200 | 200 | | |
| 8 | Food | 350 | 350 | 350 | | |
| 9 | Car-gas | 56.89 | 89.96 | 45.6 | | |
| 10 | Insurance | 125 | 125 | 125 | | |
| 11 | Total | | | | | |
| 12 | | | | | | |

Step 5  Choose Save from the File menu. Insert your Lastname's Applications disk in the floppy drive. Verify your disk name appears in the Directory dialog box. Name the worksheet **Expenses**. Click on the Save button.

## Activity 16.2—Formatting the Worksheet and Entering Formulas and Functions.

To select a single cell, click on the cell. To select a group (block) of cells, position your mouse pointer on the first cell to be included in the group, hold the mouse button down, drag over the other cells to be included, release the mouse button. If you accidentally select the wrong cells, click on any cell and start over.

**Formatting your worksheet**

Step 1  Select the block of cells B2 through F11. Point to cell B2, press and hold the mouse button as you drag down the B column to row 11, then across column C, D, E, and F. Release the mouse button.

*What's Happening*

Cells    B2, B3, B4, B5, B6, B7, B8, B9, B10, B11,
C2, C3, C4, C5, C6, C7, C8, C9, C10, C11,
D2, D3, D4, D5, D6, D7, D8, D9, D10, D11,
E2, E3, E4, E5, E6, E7, E8, E9, E10, E11,
F2, F3, F4, F5, F6, F7, F8, F9, F10, F11
should be highlighted or have a box outline surrounding them.

**354**   CHAPTER 16 • SPREADSHEET APPLICATIONS

Step 2   Follow the instructions for your specific program to format this block of cells on the worksheet as numeric with 2 decimal positions. When you apply a format to a cell(s), the cell assumes the format. Characters currently stored in the cell plus future characters placed in the cell will automatically be displayed in the assigned format.

**ClarisWorks**

Choose Number from the Format menu. In the Numeric dialog box, click on Fixed, verify Precision is 2 and click on the OK button. (Figure 16.7)

*Figure 16.7—ClarisWorks Numeric Dialog Box*

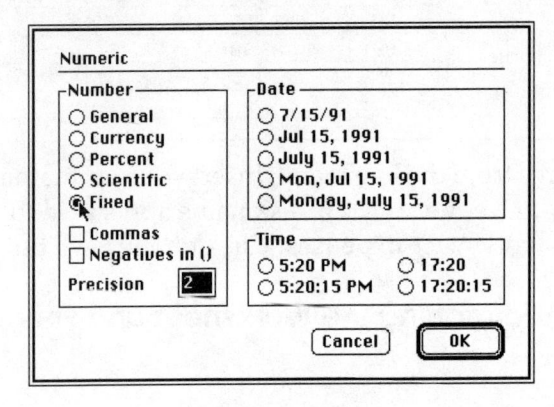

**Microsoft Works**

Choose Format Cells from the Format menu. Click on the Number button in the Format Cells dialog box. Click on 1234.56 in the Appearance list box. Verify Decimal Places is 2 and click on the OK button. (Figure 16.8)

*Figure 16.8—Microsoft Works Format Cells Dialog Box*

## Microsoft Excel

Choose Number from the Format menu. A Number Format dialog box will appear. Click on the format **0.00** in the Format Codes list box. (Figure 16.9) Click on the OK button.

*Figure 16.9—Microsoft Excel Number Format Dialog Box*

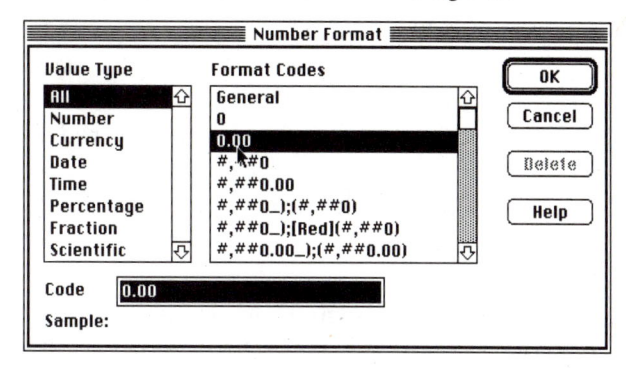

**Step 3**  Click anywhere on the worksheet to deselect the cells.

## What's Happening

All numbers on your worksheet should now have 2 decimal positions. (Figure 16.10)

*Figure 16.10—Worksheet with Two Decimal Places*

|   | A | B | C | D | E | F |
|---|---|---|---|---|---|---|
| 1 | Months | January | February | March | Total | Average |
| 2 | Rent | 650.00 | 650.00 | 650.00 | | |
| 3 | Electric | 75.00 | 60.00 | 64.00 | | |
| 4 | Gas | 45.00 | 38.00 | 55.00 | | |
| 5 | Water | 38.24 | 25.50 | 34.73 | | |
| 6 | Phone | 39.50 | 38.75 | 23.00 | | |
| 7 | Charge Cards | 200.00 | 200.00 | 200.00 | | |
| 8 | Food | 350.00 | 350.00 | 350.00 | | |
| 9 | Car-gas | 56.89 | 89.96 | 45.60 | | |
| 10 | Insurance | 125.00 | 125.00 | 125.00 | | |
| 11 | Total | | | | | |
| 12 | | | | | | |

### Entering the formula =B2+C2+D2 in cell E2

There is no need to use a calculator when you have a spreadsheet program. Formulas allow the program to calculate for you.

**Step 4**  Don't type in the formula. You are going to use the point and click method to place the formula in the cell. Click on cell E2 and type the equal sign.   =

356   CHAPTER 16 • SPREADSHEET APPLICATIONS

*What's Happening*

The equal sign (=) should appear in the entry/formula bar across the top of the window.

Step 5   Click on cell B2 (B2 should now appear in the entry/formula bar). Release the mouse button. Click on cell C2. Release the mouse button. Click on cell D2. Release the mouse button.

*What's Happening*

The entry/formula bar should now display the desired formula, =B2+C2+D2.

Step 6   Press the Return key to place the formula in cell E2.

*What's Happening*

The result of the calculation, 1950.00, appears in cell E2.

**Pasting the formula down the column**

A short cut to placing this formula in cells E3 through E11 is to copy the formula.

Step 7   Select cells E2 through E11. Follow the instruction for your program to place the formula in the selected cells.

**ClarisWorks**

Choose Fill Down from the Calculate menu.

**Microsoft Works**

Choose Fill Down from the Edit menu.

**Microsoft Excel**

Choose Fill Down from the Edit menu

*What's Happening*

The formula is copied down the column and will change according to the row it is in. The result of the calculations should appear in cells E2 through E11. Cell E11 will have 0.00 stored in it.

**Entering the column total function and copying it right across the row**

Step 8   Click on cell B11.

Step 9   Use the SUM function to total the columns. Follow the instructions for the program you are working in. Functions are listed in alphabetic order.

## ClarisWorks

Choose **Paste Function** from the Edit menu. The Paste Function dialog box will appear. Use the scroll bar to locate the **Sum(number1, number2...)** function. Click on the Sum function when you find it. Click on the OK button. (Figure 16.11)

*Figure 16.11—ClarisWorks Paste Function*

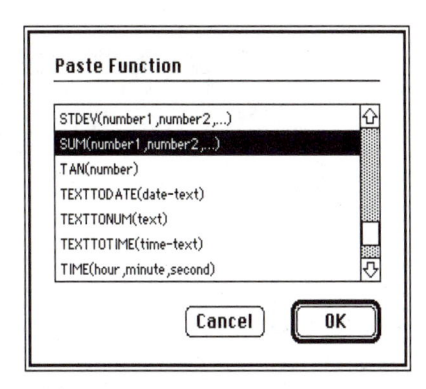

## Microsoft Works

Choose Paste Function from the Edit menu. The Mathematical button should be highlighted in the Paste Function dialog box. Use the scroll bar to locate the **Sum(v1,v2...)** function. Click on the Sum function when you find it. Click on the OK button. (Figure 16.12)

*Figure 16.12—Microsoft Works Paste Function*

## Microsoft Excel

Choose Paste Function from the Formula menu. (Figure 16.13) Use the scroll bar to locate the SUM function in the Paste Function list box. Click on the Sum function. Click on the OK button.

358  CHAPTER 16 • SPREADSHEET APPLICATIONS

*Figure 16.13—Microsoft Works Paste Function*

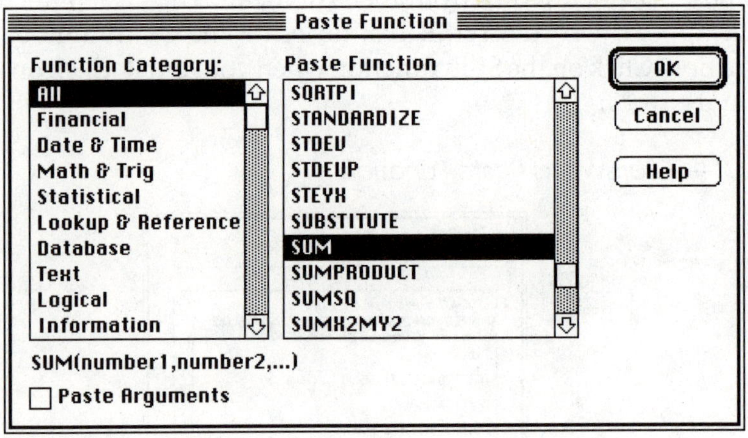

```
┌─────────────────── Paste Function ───────────────────┐
│ Function Category:      Paste Function               │
│  All                 ▲   SQRTPI              ▲   ┌──────┐ │
│  Financial               STANDARDIZE              │  OK  │ │
│  Date & Time             STDEV                    └──────┘ │
│  Math & Trig             STDEVP                   ┌──────┐ │
│  Statistical             STEYX                    │Cancel│ │
│  Lookup & Reference      SUBSTITUTE               └──────┘ │
│  Database                SUM                      ┌──────┐ │
│  Text                    SUMPRODUCT               │ Help │ │
│  Logical                 SUMSQ                    └──────┘ │
│  Information         ▼   SUMX2MY2            ▼           │
│  SUM(number1,number2,...)                                │
│  ☐ Paste Arguments                                       │
└──────────────────────────────────────────────────────┘
```

### What's Happening

The function now appears in the entry/formula bar.

**Step 10**  In the entry/formula bar, highlight everything between the parentheses (if it isn't already highlighted). Press the Delete key.

### What's Happening

The function should read =Sum(). The flashing insertion point is positioned between the parentheses. If it does not, click on the **X** in the entry/formula bar and try again.

**Step 11**  Select cells B2 through B10. Point to cell B2, press and hold the mouse button as you drag down the B column to row 10, then release the mouse button.

### What's Happening

The entry/formula bar should read =Sum(B2:B10) or =Sum(B2..B10).

**Step 12**  Press the Return key to place the result of the function (1579.63) in cell B11.

**Step 13**  Select cells B11 through D11 (B11, C11, D11).

**Step 14**  Follow the instruction for the program you are working with to copy the function across the row.

  **ClarisWorks**—Choose Fill Right from the Calculate menu.

  **Microsoft Works**—Choose Fill Right from the Edit menu.

  **Microsoft Excel**—Choose Fill Right from the Edit menu.

*What's Happening*
> The function is copied to the other two cells (C11, D11).

Step 15  Click on cell F2. Follow the instruction for the program you are working with to complete the Average calculation.

**ClarisWorks**
> Choose Paste Function from the Edit menu. The Paste Function dialog box will appear. Use the scroll bar to locate the **Average(number1, number2...)** function. Click on the function when you find it. Click on the OK button.

**Microsoft Works**
> Choose Paste Function from the Edit menu. The Paste Function dialog box will appear. Click on the Statistical button to display a list of statistical functions. Click on the **Average(v1,v2..)** function. Click on the OK button.

**Microsoft Excel**
> Choose Paste Function from the Formula menu. The Paste Function dialog box will appear. Click on **Statistical** in the Function Category list box. Click on **Average** in the Paste Function list box. Click on the OK button.

*What's Happening*
> The function now appears in the entry/formula bar.

Step 16  In the entry/formula bar, highlight everything between the parentheses (if it isn't highlighted already). Press the Delete key.

*What's Happening*
> The function should read =Average(). The flashing insertion point is positioned between the parentheses. If it does not, click on the X in the entry/formula bar and try again.

Step 17  Select cells B2 through D2. Point to cell B2, press and hold the mouse button as you drag across row 2 to column D, then release the mouse button.

*What's Happening*
> The entry/formula bar should read =Average(B2:D2) or =Average(B2..D2).

Step 18  Press the Return key to place the result of the function (650.00) in cell F2.

Step 19  Copy the function down the column (F2 through F11) by using the Fill Down command. Click anywhere on the worksheet to deselect the cells. (Figure 16.14)

Figure 16.14—Completed Worksheet

|   | A | B | C | D | E | F |
|---|---|---|---|---|---|---|
| 1 | Months | January | February | March | Total | Average |
| 2 | Rent | 650.00 | 650.00 | 650.00 | 1950.00 | 650.00 |
| 3 | Electric | 75.00 | 60.00 | 64.00 | 199.00 | 66.33 |
| 4 | Gas | 45.00 | 38.00 | 55.00 | 138.00 | 46.00 |
| 5 | Water | 38.24 | 25.50 | 34.73 | 98.47 | 32.82 |
| 6 | Phone | 39.50 | 38.75 | 23.00 | 101.25 | 33.75 |
| 7 | Charge Cards | 200.00 | 200.00 | 200.00 | 600.00 | 200.00 |
| 8 | Food | 350.00 | 350.00 | 350.00 | 1050.00 | 350.00 |
| 9 | Car-gas | 56.89 | 89.96 | 45.60 | 192.45 | 64.15 |
| 10 | Insurance | 125.00 | 125.00 | 125.00 | 375.00 | 125.00 |
| 11 | Total | 1579.63 | 1577.21 | 1547.33 | 4704.17 | 1568.06 |

## Activity 16.3—Saving, Modifying and Printing the Worksheet

Step 1  Press ⌘ S to Save the worksheet.

Step 2  Turn the printer on. Select Chooser from the  menu. Select the printer you wish to use and close the Chooser window. Choose Print from the File menu. Click on the OK or Print button.

### Changing the charge card payments to 50.00

One of the reasons spreadsheet software is so popular is its ability to play the "what if" game. You can enter different numbers in cells and the spreadsheet program will automatically recalculate all effected calculated fields. For example, what if charge card payments were reduced to $50.00? How would this change the budget?

Step 3  Click on cell B7 and type 50.00. Press the Tab key to move to cell C7 and key in 50.00. Enter 50.00 in cell D7. The Macintosh recalculates the totals and averages. Save the worksheet.

Step 4  Print the worksheet.

### Closing and quitting the program

Step 5  Choose Close and then Quit from the File menu.

Step 6  Close all open folder and disk windows.

## Key Terms

>Average function
>Cells
>Columns
>Fill Down
>Fill Right
>Formulas
>Functions
>Rows
>Spreadsheet
>Sum function
>Worksheet

## Discussion Questions

1. Discuss the value of a spreadsheet program.
2. Define the following spreadsheet terms: worksheet, cells, formulas, functions.
3. Explain how to select a block of cells.
4. Give examples of how you can format a cell (for example 0.00).
5. Explain the commands: Fill Down and Fill Right.
6. What's the difference between functions and formulas?

## Assignments

Note: Boot the Macintosh. The Macintosh desktop should be clear—no open windows. For this assignment you will use your Lastname's Applications disk. Open a new worksheet in the spreadsheet program you used in this chapter.

1. Hand in the two printed worksheet documents from this Chapter.
2. Create the following worksheet. Enter the text and numbers as shown except for rows 5, 17, and 19. Enter formulas or functions in rows 5, 17, and 19.
   - Row 5, Branch Revenue, is a calculated row.
     =B3+B4.
   - Row 17, Branch Expenses, is a calculated row.
     =Sum(B8:B16)
     or =Sum(B8:..B16)
   - Row 19, Branch Profit, is a calculated row.
     =B5-B17

3. Format the numeric cells to display two decimal positions.
4. Save your worksheet frequently to your Lastname's Applications disk.
5. Print the document.
6. Close all open folder and disk windows.

## Worksheet

|    | A | B | C | D | E |
|----|---|---|---|---|---|
| 1  |   | Medford | District Heights | Mission Viejo | Placerville |
| 2  | Revenue |  |  |  |  |
| 3  | Sales | 26000.00 | 28000.00 | 40000.00 | 33000.00 |
| 4  | Repair | 1200.00 | 1900.00 | 2900.00 | 700.00 |
| 5  | Branch Revenue | 27200.00 | 29900.00 | 42900.00 | 33700.00 |
| 6  |   |   |   |   |   |
| 7  | Expenses |   |   |   |   |
| 8  | Rent | 760.00 | 1200.00 | 2500.00 | 650.00 |
| 9  | Utilities | 200.00 | 185.00 | 135.00 | 155.00 |
| 10 | Phone | 120.00 | 100.00 | 180.00 | 160.00 |
| 11 | Insurance | 200.00 | 200.00 | 200.00 | 200.00 |
| 12 | Payroll | 7150.00 | 7600.00 | 9250.00 | 8925.00 |
| 13 | Office Supplies | 175.00 | 200.00 | 65.00 | 180.00 |
| 14 | Advertising | 500.00 | 500.00 | 500.00 | 500.00 |
| 15 | Inventory | 8000.00 | 8500.00 | 10000.00 | 13000.00 |
| 16 | Misc. | 360.00 | 420.00 | 566.00 | 230.00 |
| 17 | Branch Expenses | 17465.00 | 18905.00 | 23396.00 | 24000.00 |
| 18 |   |   |   |   |   |
| 19 | Branch Profit | 9735.00 | 10995.00 | 19504.00 | 9700.00 |
| 20 |   |   |   |   |   |

# 17 Desktop Publishing Applications

## Learning Objectives

### After completing this Chapter you will be able to:

1. Open a new publication window in PageMaker.
2. Explain the Toolbox.
3. Draw, size, and move graphic images.
4. Place text and graphics.
5. Save and print your publication.
6. Alter the document's existing format.
7. Change the style of selected text.

## Introduction

Desktop publishing is page layout software used to create, format, and print written communications. The printed document may include text and graphics. The publishing industry uses desktop publishing software to layout pages in books, magazines, newspapers, brochures, fliers, and so on. You will be using the desktop publishing program, PageMaker, for this exercise. Two files on your Lastname-Sys 7 disk will be used in this exercise: Newsletter and Store Logo Alias.

## Using PageMaker 4.01

### Activity 17.1—Opening a New Document and the Toolbox

Step 1    Boot your Macintosh.

Step 2        Insert your Lastname-Sys 7 disk in the floppy drive.

Step 3        Follow your instructor's directions to locate the PageMaker program icon. Double-click on the icon.

*What's Happening*

The PageMaker greeting screen flashes on the screen, and PageMaker's menu bar appears.

Step 4        Choose New from the File menu.

*What's Happening*

The Page Setup dialog box appears. (Figure 17.1)

*Figure 17.1—The Page Setup Dialog Box*

```
Page setup                                              [   OK   ]
Page:  [Letter]                                         [ Cancel ]
Page dimensions:  [8.5]  by  [11]  inches               
Orientation:  ● Tall   ○ Wide                           [Numbers...]
Start page #:  [1]     # of pages:  [1]
Options:  ☒ Double-sided   ☒ Facing pages
          ☐ Restart page numbering
Margin in inches:  Inside  [1]      Outside  [0.75]
                   Top     [0.75]   Bottom   [0.75]
```

Step 5        Click on the **Double-sided** button to remove the X from Double-sided and Facing Pages.

*What's Happening*

You will be creating a single-sided document. An X in the Double-sided checkbox directs PageMaker to create a document with information on the front and back side of each page. The X in the Facing Pages checkbox will automatically disappear when you remove the X from Double-sided. When you create a double-sided document and need the pages facing each other, you would specify **Facing pages**. Examine the other entries in this window but do not change them.

Step 6        Click on the OK button.

## What's Happening

The Page Setup dialog box closes. A PageMaker Publication window appears.

Step 7   Display the Page pull-down menu. Verify that a checkmark appears next to the **50% size** command in the Page menu. If not, select this command.

## What's Happening

Examine the Untitled PageMaker window on your desktop. The area in the middle of the window (**image area**) is displayed at 50% size and shows one page of your document. The broken line surrounding the image area shows you where your margins are located. The surrounding area is known as the **Pasteboard**. It is used for temporary storage of text and graphics. A Toolbox appears in the top right corner. (Figure 17.2)

*Figure 17.2—The PageMaker Menu Bar and Window*

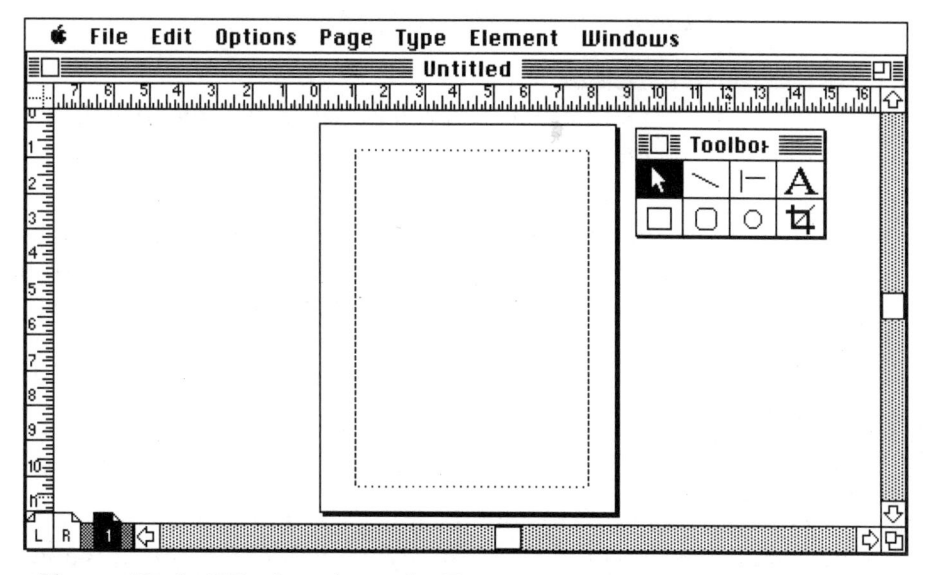

Step 8   Choose **Fit in Window** from the Page menu.

## What's Happening

The image area now fills your window. You control the size of the image area.

Step 9   If the Toolbox is not on the window, choose Toolbox from the Windows menu.

## What's Happening

The Toolbox contains tools to edit, type, and draw. Each tool has a purpose.

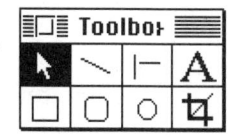

**Pointer icon**—used to select text and graphics.

**Diagonal-line tool**—used to draw lines at an angle.

**Perpendicular-line tool**—use to draw vertical, horizontal and 45-degree lines.

**Text tool**—used to enter, select and modify text.

**Square-corner tool**—used to draw squares and rectangles.

**Rounded-corner tool**—used to draw squares and rectangles with rounded corners

**Oval tool**—used to draw circles and ovals.

**Cropping tool**—used to trim (crop) graphics.

### Experimenting with the Toolbox

Step 10  Click on the Diagonal-line tool. As you move the pointer on to the image area it assumes the shape of crossbars.

Step 11  Position the center of the crossbars wherever you want the line to start on the image area. Hold the mouse button down and drag the crossbars to where you want the line to end. (Hint: if you hold the shift key down while dragging, you will get a straight line.) Continue to hold the mouse button, and move the crossbars around the image area (line changes size and direction). Release the mouse button.

## What's Happening

As long as you continue to hold the mouse button down, you can change the length and direction of the line (or any other item you are drawing).

Step 12  Click on the Rounded-corner tool. The pointer is in the shape of crossbars.

Step 13  Position the center of the crossbars where you want a corner of the square or rectangle to appear on the image area. Hold the mouse button down and drag the crossbars diagonally (up, down) or sideways until you have the shape you want. Release the mouse button.

Step 14  Click on the Text tool. As you move the pointer off the Toolbox on to the image area, the pointer assumes the shape of an I-beam.

USING PAGEMAKER 4.01   367

Step 15   Position the I-beam on the image area near the bottom left corner. Click once to position the insertion point. Key in your name and the date.

Step 16   Try the other drawing tools if you wish (Perpendicular-line tool, Square-corner tool, Oval tool).

*What's Happening*

Your document should contain at least a square/rectangle, a line, your name and the date.

**Printing your document**

Step 17   Turn on the printer. Choose Chooser from the  menu and select the printer you wish to use. Choose Print from the File menu.

*What's Happening*

The Print dialog box will appear.

Step 18   Do not change any options on the Print dialog box. Click OK or Print.

Step 19   Retrieve your printed document from the printer.

**Size and move the square/rectangle graphic**

Step 20   Click on the Pointer icon in the Toolbox.

*What's Happening*

The pointer assumes the shape of an arrow.

Step 21   Position the tip of the arrow pointer on one of the lines on the square or rectangle you previously drew. Click once.

*Figure 17.3— Graphic Handles*

*What's Happening*

Graphic handles appear on the four corners of the image and in the middle of each line. (Figure 17.3)

Step 22   Position the tip of the arrow pointer on one of the graphic handles. Hold the mouse button down. The pointer will assume the shape of a two-way arrow. (Figure 17.4) Drag the pointer up, down, left, or right to resize the image. Release the mouse button.

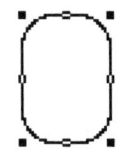

*Figure 17.4—Sizing a Graphic Image*

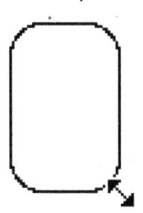

*What's Happening*
> You have resized the original image.

*Figure 17.5—Moving a Graphic Image*

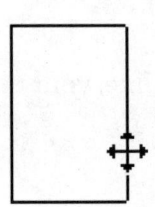

Step 23  Position the tip of the arrow pointer on one of the lines in the square, but not on a graphic handle. Hold the mouse button down. The pointer assumes the shape of a four-head arrow. (Figure 17.5) Drag the image to a new location on the window. Release the mouse button. Click anywhere on the image area to deselect the graphic image.

**Delete the line image and print the new document**

Step 24  Position the tip of the arrow pointer on the line you previously drew. Click once.

Step 25  Press the Delete key.

*What's Happening*
> The line disappears from the window.

Step 26  Print your document.

**Close your document window**

Step 27  Choose Close from the File menu.

*What's Happening*
> A dialog box will appear asking if you wish to save your document.

Step 28  Click on the No button in the dialog box. Do not save this document.

## Activity 17.2—Creating, Saving and Printing a Simple Document

Step 1  Choose New from the File menu.

*What's Happening*
> The Page Setup dialog box appears. (Figure 17.6)

*Figure 17.6—The Page Setup Dialog Box*

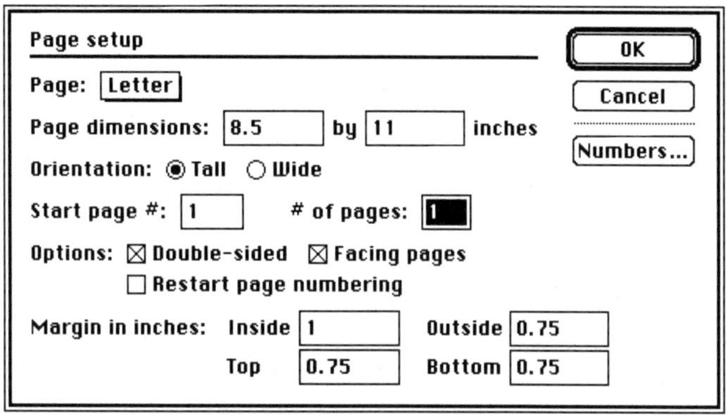

```
Page setup                                          OK
Page: [Letter]
                                                  Cancel
Page dimensions: 8.5  by  11   inches
Orientation: ● Tall  ○ Wide                      Numbers...
Start page #: 1       # of pages: 1
Options: ☒ Double-sided  ☒ Facing pages
         ☐ Restart page numbering
Margin in inches: Inside  1    Outside 0.75
                  Top    0.75  Bottom  0.75
```

Step 2   Click on the Double-sided button to remove the X from Double-sided and Facing Pages.

Step 3   Click on the OK button.

## What's Happening

A PageMaker publication window appears.

Step 4   Verify a checkmark appears next to the **50% size** command in the Page menu. If not, select this command.

Step 5   If the vertical and horizontal scroll bars are not on the Untitled window, choose Scroll Bars from the Windows menu.

Step 6   Access the menus on the menu bar to see the commands available in Page-Maker. Some of the commands will look familiar, but many of them will not.

Step 7   Choose Column Guides from the Options menu.

## What's Happening

The Column Guides dialog box appears. (Figure 17.7) Your document will use two columns on the page.

*Figure 17.7—Column Guides Dialog Box*

```
Column guides                              OK
                                         Cancel
Number of columns:       1
Space between columns: 0.167  inches
```

Step 8   Key 2 into the Number of Columns box. Click OK.

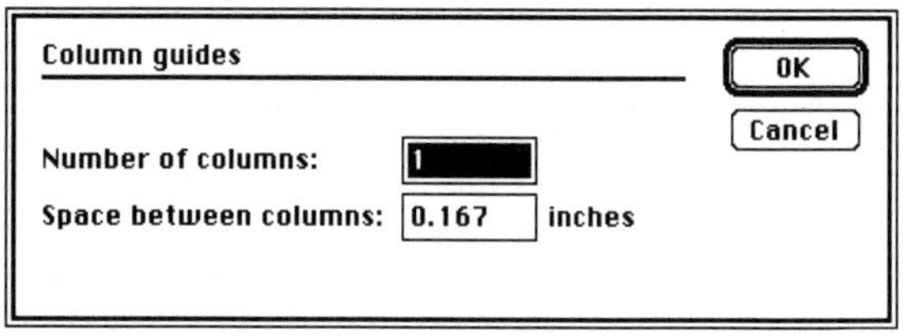

*Figure 17.8—
Two Columns*

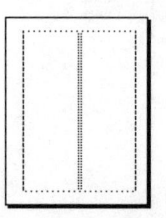

### What's Happening
The page on the publication window has been split into two columns with a small space in-between (0.167 inches). (Figure 17.8)

**Placing the Store Logo on the page**

Step 9    Choose Place from the File menu.

### What's Happening
The Place document dialog box appears. The Place command allows you to access text and graphic documents created in other application programs. The Open command is used to open a document that was created in PageMaker. The graphic, Store Logo, was created in the application program Mac Paint from Claris Corporation.

*Figure 17.9—Place Dialog Box*

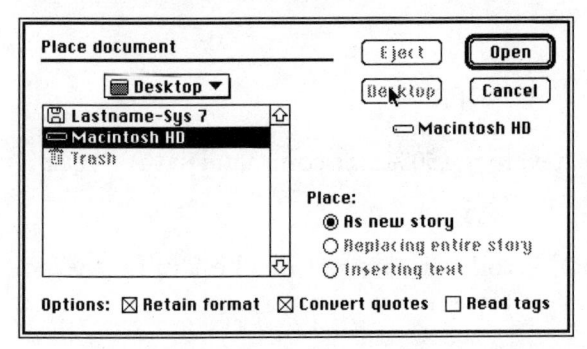

Step 10    Click on the Desktop button. Click on the disk name, Lastname-Sys 7, in the list box. (Figure 17.9) Click on the Open button.

### What's Happening
The dialog box should display your disk's name.

Step 11    Use the scroll bar to locate the Store Logo Alias document. Double-click on Store Logo Alias.

### What's Happening

*Figure 17.10—
Placing the Logo*

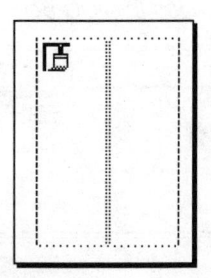

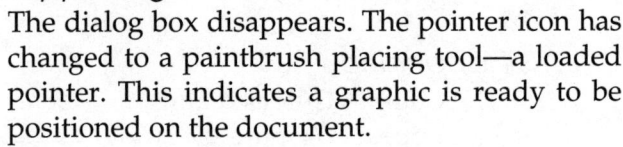

The dialog box disappears. The pointer icon has changed to a paintbrush placing tool—a loaded pointer. This indicates a graphic is ready to be positioned on the document.

Step 12    Move the paintbrush placing tool up to the top left side of the page. (Figure 17.10) Click once.

### What's Happening
The logo has been placed on the page.

Step 13    If you didn't place the logo just right, position the pointer in the middle of the graphic image, click once, and drag it to a new position.

**Placing text in the current document**

Step 14    Choose Autoflow from the Options menu.

*What's Happening*

By selecting the **Autoflow Mode**, imported text will fill the first page or column you identify and then automatically flow into the next until the entire story is placed.

Step 15    Choose Place from the File menu.

*What's Happening*

The Place Document dialog box will reappear. Your Lastname-Sys 7 disk should be open. The text document, Newsletter, was originally created in Microsoft Word. Therefore, you must use the Place command (not the Open command) to import the document. The button **As New story** is selected. You will import this document as a new story.

Step 16    Scroll until you locate the Newsletter document. Double-click on Newsletter.

*What's Happening*

The Place Document dialog box will disappear. The loaded **automatic text flow icon** replaces the arrow pointer.

Step 17    Place the automatic text flow icon immediately below the Store Logo on the image area. Click once.

*What's Happening*

Different status boxes will appear as this Microsoft Word document is converted to a PageMaker document. The text from the Newsletter document will fill column one and most of column two. (Figure 17.11)

*Figure 17.11—Autoflow Text*

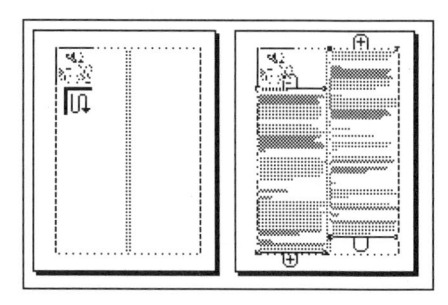

The story has been placed in several text blocks. A **text block** is a continuous string of words that can be manipulated as a unit (moved, formatted, copied, and so on). Each text block ends and begins with a **windowshade**.

Examine the image area on your screen. At the top and bottom of each column of text you see a horizontal line with a loop handle (**windowshade handle**) in the middle. You can drag the windowshade handles up or down to adjust the location and length of the text block. The location and content of the handles provide information.

- The empty windowshade handle at the top of column one (left column), indicates this is the beginning of the story. There are no previous text blocks related to this story. This handle may be difficult to see because the graphic image is underneath it.

- The windowshade handle on the bottom of column one contains a plus sign (+) indicating there is additional related text.

- The windowshade handle at the top of column two contains a plus sign (+) indicating this is a continuation of the story.

- The empty windowshade handle at the bottom of column two indicates you have reached the end of the story.

**Saving your document to disk**

Step 18   Choose Save from the File menu.

*Figure 17.12—Saving the document*

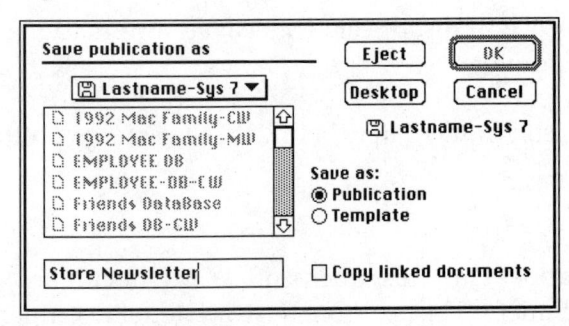

*What's Happening*

The **Save Publication as** dialog box appears. Verify your Lastname-Sys 7 disk is open. (Figure 17.12)

Step 19   Key in the document's name—Store Newsletter. Click on OK.

*What's Happening*

Your document has been saved to disk and the publication window now displays the name.

**Viewing and printing your document**

Step 20   Choose Actual Size from the Page menu.

*What's Happening*

You can now read your document. Use the scroll bars to scroll through the document.

Step 21    Turn on the printer. Choose Chooser from the  menu and select the printer you wish to use. Choose Print from the File menu.

*What's Happening*
The Print dialog box will appear.

Step 22    Do not change any options on the Print dialog box. Click OK or Print.

Step 23    Retrieve your printed document from the printer.

## Activity 17.3—Modifying, Saving, and Printing the document

Step 1    Click on the Text Tool in the Tool box.    **A**

*What's Happening*
The windowshade handles surrounding the text blocks disappear. As you move the arrow pointer back on to the document, it turns into an I-beam.

Step 2    Click anywhere on the document's text.

Step 3    Choose Select All from the Edit menu.

*What's Happening*
The entire story is highlighted.

Step 4    Choose Alignment from the Type menu. When the submenu appears, choose Justify.

*What's Happening*
The entire story is now justified between the left and right margins in each column.

Step 5    With the text still highlighted, choose Font from the Type menu and select Helvetica from the Font submenu.

Step 6    Click once in the image area to deselect the text.

Step 7    Drag the I-beam over the line **Growing, Growing,...** under the graphic image.

*What's Happening*
The line is highlighted.

Step 8    Choose Size from the Type menu. When the submenu appears, choose 12.

*Figure 17.13—Formatting Text*

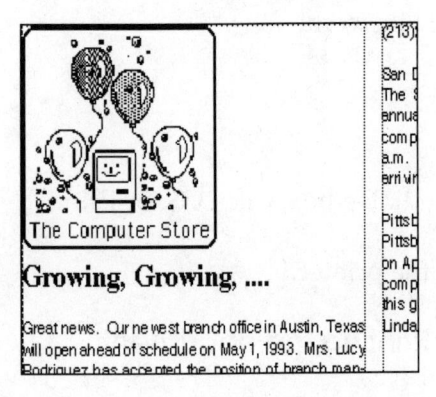

Step 9  Choose Type Style from the Type menu. When the submenu appears, choose Bold.

## What's Happening

The selected text line is now larger and bold. (Figure 17.13)

Step 10  Repeat steps 6 through 9 to increase the size and style to the following two lines: Branch Coming Events, Congratulations.

Step 11  Position the I-beam in front of the word Porterville (column one, under Branch Coming Events). Drag the I-beam over the word to highlight the word. Release the mouse button.

Step 12  Use the keyboard shortcut to apply the bold style to the selected text. Hold down the Shift key and the ⌘ key and type the letter B. Click once in the image area to deselect the text.

## What's Happening

The text now appears in **bold** style.

Step 13  Apply the **bold** style to the following lines:
    Los Angeles
    San Diego
    Pittsburgh
    Anniversaries and Wedding Bells
    Baby

**Saving and printing the document**

Step 14  Choose Save from the File menu.

Step 15  Print your document.

Step 16  Retrieve your printed document from the printer.

### Activity 17.4—Move the Windowshade Handles and Resize the Graphic Image

Step 1  Click on the Pointer tool in the Toolbox, the pointer assumes the shape of an arrow.

Step 2     Click anywhere on the document's text.

## *What's Happening*

The windowshade handles appear around the text blocks.

Step 3     Position the tip of the arrow pointer on the windowshade handle on the top of column one. Press and hold the mouse button down while dragging the windowshade down. Look at the ruler along the left side of the window. Release the windowshade handle when it is lined up at 3.5 on the ruler.

### Resizing the graphic

Step 4     Position the arrow pointer in the middle of the the computer store graphic and click once.

## *What's Happening*

Graphic handles appear around the graphic image.

Step 5     Position the tip of the arrow pointer on the bottom, middle graphic handle. Hold the Shift key down, while dragging this graphic handle down the window. Release the mouse button when the graphic image is located right above the text.

## *What's Happening*

Holding the Shift key down while dragging the graphic handle proportionally sizes the graphic image, otherwise some graphic images will appear distorted. The graphic image may be partially in the margin.

### Moving the graphic

Step 6     Position the arrow pointer on one of the lines surrounding the image, but not on one of the graphic handles. Hold the mouse button down and drag the graphic image to the middle of the column.

Step 7     Print your document.

Step 8     Retrieve your printed document from the printer.

### Closing the document and quitting PageMaker

Step 9     Close the Publication Window.

Step 10   Choose Quit from the File menu. Close file folder and disk windows as appropriate.

## Key Terms

| | |
|---|---|
| 50% size command | Oval tool |
| As New Story | Pasteboard |
| Autoflow mode | Perpendicular-line tool |
| Automatic text flow icon | Place command |
| Cropping tool | Pointer icon |
| Crossbars | Rounded-corner tool |
| Desktop publishing | Save publication as |
| Diagonal-line tool | Square-corner tool |
| Double-sided button | Text block |
| Facing pages button | Text tool |
| Fit in Window | Toolbox |
| Graphic handles | Windowshades |
| Image area | Windowshade handles |

## Discussion Questions

1. Discuss some of the reasons for using PageMaker instead of a normal word processing program.
2. Describe the different shapes the pointer assumes when placing graphics and text.
3. List five possible uses for the PageMaker program.

## Assignment

1. Hand in the printed documents from this Chapter.

2. Follow the instructions in this Chapter to place the Poem 1 file in a Page-Maker Publication window. Change Text Alignment, fonts, and styles as desired. Use the drawing tools as desired. Save and print the document.

3. Use the draw tools to create a new document consisting of squares, rectangles, circles, ovals, and lines. Use the text tool to enter your name and the date in the top left corner. Save and print your document.

   Close all open windows.

# Appendix: Quick Lookup

## The Finder Menu Bar

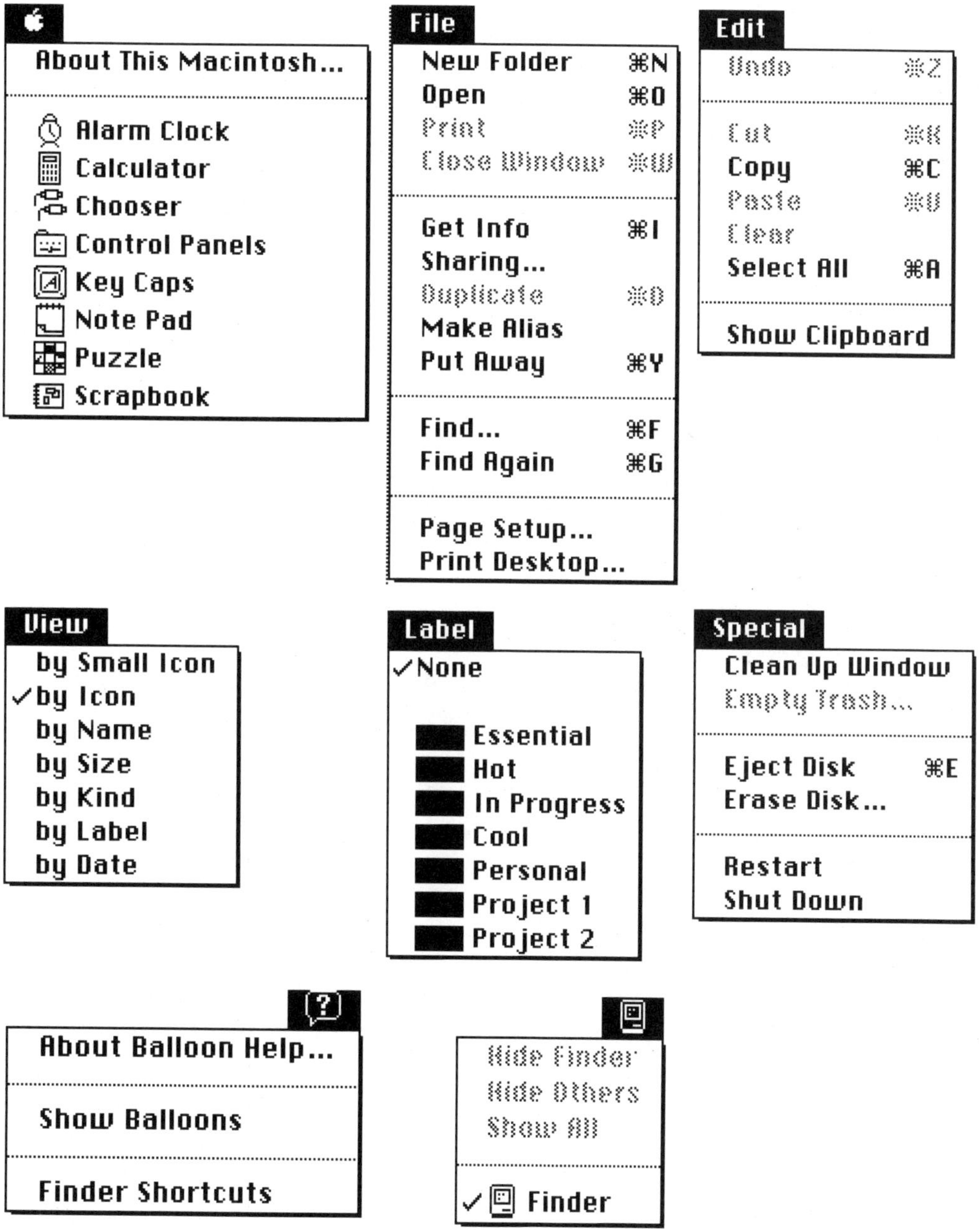

**Apple Menu**
- About This Macintosh...
- Alarm Clock
- Calculator
- Chooser
- Control Panels
- Key Caps
- Note Pad
- Puzzle
- Scrapbook

**File**
- New Folder ⌘N
- Open ⌘O
- Print ⌘P
- Close Window ⌘W
- Get Info ⌘I
- Sharing...
- Duplicate ⌘D
- Make Alias
- Put Away ⌘Y
- Find... ⌘F
- Find Again ⌘G
- Page Setup...
- Print Desktop...

**Edit**
- Undo ⌘Z
- Cut ⌘X
- Copy ⌘C
- Paste ⌘V
- Clear
- Select All ⌘A
- Show Clipboard

**View**
- by Small Icon
- ✓ by Icon
- by Name
- by Size
- by Kind
- by Label
- by Date

**Label**
- ✓ None
- Essential
- Hot
- In Progress
- Cool
- Personal
- Project 1
- Project 2

**Special**
- Clean Up Window
- Empty Trash...
- Eject Disk ⌘E
- Erase Disk...
- Restart
- Shut Down

**Help (?)**
- About Balloon Help...
- Show Balloons
- Finder Shortcuts

**Application**
- Hide Finder
- Hide Others
- Show All
- ✓ Finder

377

## Finder Menu Bar Commands

| Command | Keyboard Shortcuts | Menu |
|---|---|---|
| About Balloon Help | | Help |
| by Date | | View |
| by Icon | | View |
| by Kind | | View |
| by Label | | View |
| by Name | | View |
| by Size | | View |
| by Small Icon | | View |
| Clean Up ... | | Special |
| Close Window | ⌘ W | File |
| Clear | | Edit |
| Copy | ⌘ C | Edit |
| Cut | ⌘ X | Edit |
| Duplicate | ⌘ D | File |
| Eject Disk | ⌘ E | Special |
| Empty Trash | | Special |
| Erase Disk | | Special |
| Find | ⌘ F | File |
| Find Again | ⌘ G | File |
| Finder Shortcuts | | Help |
| Get Info | ⌘ I | File |
| Hide Balloons | | Help |
| Make Alias | | File |
| New Folder | ⌘ N | File |
| Open | ⌘ O | File |
| Page Setup | | File |
| Paste | ⌘ V | Edit |
| Print | ⌘ P | File |
| Print Desktop | | File |
| Put Away | ⌘ Y | File |
| Restart | Control + ⌘ + Power on Key | Special |
| Select All | ⌘ A | Edit |
| Sharing | | File |
| Show Balloons | | Special |
| Shut Down | | Special |
| Undo | ⌘ Z | Edit |

# Basic Menu Operations

| Operation | Steps |
|---|---|
| Access a menu | Point at menu name. Press and hold mouse button. |
| Execute a command | Access the necessary menu. Drag arrow down menu bar to highlight command. Release mouse button. |
| Dimmed commands | Not available for execution. |
| Ellipsis (...) after command | Additional information required. Dialog box will be provided. |
| ⌘ + a letter | Command keyboard shortcut. |
| ✓ in front of a command | Identifies current selection. |

Miscellaneous Keyboard Shortcuts

| Action | Results |
|---|---|
| Shift Key + ⌘ + 3 | Takes a snapshot of the screen and places it in a TeachText file on the startup disk. (This may not work on some color monitors.) |
| Control + ⌘ + power on key | Restarts the system without powering down. Use when System freezes up. |
| Hold Shift Key during Startup process | Prevents Startup Items and System Extensions (Inits) from opening. |
| Shift + Option + ⌘ during Startup process | Rebuilds desktop during booting. Perform on Startup Disks once a month. Helps the Macintosh keep track of files. |

# Working with Icons

Selecting an Icon

| Method | Action |
|---|---|
| Click on the icon | That icon becomes active. |
| Press an arrow key | The next desktop icon in that direction becomes active. |
| Press the Tab key | The next desktop icon in alphabetic order becomes active. |
| Press a letter key | The first desktop icon with a name that begins with the letter becomes active. |

Selecting Multiple Icons

| Method | Group includes |
|---|---|
| Shift-Click | Each icon clicked on. |
| Box | Any icon in or touched by the box. |
| Menu command—Select All | All icons on the desktop or active window. |

Deselecting Icons

| Method | Action |
|---|---|
| Click on another icon | That icon becomes active and the original icon is deselected. |
| Click on any empty desktop area | Everything becomes inactive. All icons become deselected. |

Opening a Window to an Icon

| Method | Steps |
|---|---|
| File menu command | Click on the icon you want to open. Choose the File menu command—Open. |
| Mouse shortcut | Double-click on the icon you want to open. |
| Keyboard shortcut | Click on the icon you want to open. Press ⌘ O or Click on the icon you want to open. Press ⌘ down arrow. |

Closing the Active Window

| Method | Steps |
|---|---|
| File menu command | Choose the Close Window command from the File menu. |
| Mouse shortcut | Click on the window's close box. |
| Keyboard shortcut | Press ⌘ W (This does not work in all application programs.) |

## Manipulating Files and Folders

**To Duplicate a file or folder**
    A. Select the icon(s).
    B. Choose Duplicate from the File menu.
    C. Rename the duplicate icon.

**To Copy a file or folder from one floppy disk to another floppy**
  Single floppy drive system configuration
    A. Insert the destination disk in the drive.
    B. Open the destination disk and folders as necessary.
    C. Select the destination disk icon and choose Eject Disk from the Special menu.
    D. Insert the source disk in the drive.
    E. Open the source disk and folders as necessary.
    F. Select the desired icon(s) and drag them to the destination disk, folder, or window.
    G. Swap disks as directed.

Dual floppy drive system configuration
  A. Insert the destination disk in one drive and the source disk in the other.
  B. Open the source disk and folders as necessary.
  C. Open the destination disk and folders as necessary.
  D. Select the desired icon(s) and drag them to the destination disk, folder, or window.

**To Lock or Unlock a file or folder**
  A. Select the icon(s).
  B. Choose Get Info from the File menu.
  C. Click in the Locked checkbox.
  D. Close the Info window.

**To Erase a file or folder**
  A. Drag the icon(s) to the Trash.
  B. Choose Empty Trash from the Special menu.

**To Rename a file or folder**
  A. Click on the icon's name.
  B. Key in the new name or use editing techniques to modify the current name.

## Trash Hints

**To throw away items**
  A. Select the icon(s) to remove and drag it to the Trash icon.

**Steps to recover items from the Trash**
  A. Open the Trash window.
  B. Drag the selected icons out of the Trash window to the desired window or disk.
     or
     Select the items to be removed from the Trash and use the Put Away command to place the items back where they came from.

**Emptying the Trash**
  A. Trashed items remain on the disk and in the Trash until you execute the Empty Trash command (Special menu). Therefore, the disk space the files are using is not available to store other files until you empty the Trash.
  B. The Empty Trash Warning dialog box usually appears whenever you empty the Trash.

C. The Empty Trash Warning may be temporarily avoided by holding down the Option key while executing the Empty Trash command. This will erase locked items in the Trash.
D. The Empty Trash Warning can be turned off by using the *Warn Before Emptying* checkbox in the Trash Info window (Get Info command).

## Customizing Icons

### To Change an icon
A. Create or locate the new icon, and copy it to Clipboard.
B. Select the icon to be changed.
C. Choose Get Info from the File menu.
D. Click on the existing icon in the Info window (top left corner).
E. Choose Paste from the Edit menu.
F. Close the Info window.

### To Assign a Label to an icon
A. Select the icon(s).
B. Choose the appropriate label from the Label menu.

### To Size an icon
Affects all icons in all windows
A. Choose Control Panels from the Apple menu.
B. Double-click on the Views icon.
C. Click on the desired icon size.
D. Close the Views and Control Panels windows.

### To Change Font and/or Point Size
Affects all icons in all windows
A. Choose Control Panels from the Apple menu.
B. Double-click on the Views icon.
C. Select the desired font or point size from the pop-up menus.
D. Close the Views and Control Panels windows.

## Locating Files and Folders Using the Find and Find Again Commands

A. Choose the Find command from the File Menu.
B. Click on More Choices button to display expanded Find Dialog Box.
C. Specify Search Criteria, Search Area.

D. Select "all at once" if desired.
E. Click on Find button.

Search Criteria and Possible Uses for Each

| Search Criteria | Use this Option when: |
|---|---|
| Name | You know the exact filename or only remember a portion of the name.<br>You want to locate a group of files that contain the same characters. |
| Size | You are running out of disk space and wish to locate the largest files to copy to another disk or to compress before removing them from the disk. |
| Kind | You wish to locate all aliases, applications, documents, folders, or stationary pad files. |
| Label | You use labels to group related files and/or folders. |
| Date Created and/or Date Modified | You need to locate older files to remove from the disk or newer files to backup. |
| Version | You wish to locate an item by version number. |
| Comments | You remember the comment you entered in the Get Info's comment box. |
| Lock | You wish to locate locked files in order to unlock them. |

# Handling Floppy Disks

**To erase a disk**
 A. Click on the disk icon that you want to erase (the icon turns dark).
 B. Choose the Erase Disk command of the Special menu.
 C. Read the dialog box carefully and confirm the name of the disk to be erased.
 D. Click on the appropriate button.
- Cancel—if you changed your mind.
- One-sided—if your system uses 400 KB floppy disks

- Two-sided—if your system uses 800 KB floppy disks
- Initialize—if your system uses 1.4 MB floppy disks
E. Rename the disk.
F. Prepare a new paper label. Remove the old label and place the new label on the disk.

## To completely rename a disk icon
A. Click on the name of the disk icon you want to rename.
B. Type the new name.

## To partially change the name
A. Click on the name of the disk icon you want to rename.
B. Position the pointer on the name where the change is to be made (pointer changes to an I-beam).
C. Click to identify insertion point.
D. Modify the name with one of the following methods.
 1. Use the Delete key to delete 1 character to the left of the I-beam.
 2. Type the additional characters in at the insertion point.
 3. Use the Cut, Copy, Paste, Clear commands, from the Edit menu.

## To lock and unlock a floppy disk
A. To lock a disk—Slide the tab (on the back of the disk) towards the outside edge of the disk. A hole appears in the disk cover.
B. To unlock a disk—Slide the tab (on the back of the disk) towards the center hub of the disk. The hole in the disk cover disappears.

Ejecting Floppy Disks

| Method | Results |
| --- | --- |
| Trash the disk icon | Ejects floppy disk. Icon disappears from desktop. |
| Eject Disk command | Ejects active floppy disk. Icon remains on desktop. * |
| ⌘ E | Ejects active floppy disk. Icon remains on desktop. * |
| Shift ⌘ 1 | Ejects floppy disk in internal drive. Icon remains on desktop. * |

| | |
|---|---|
| Shift ⌘ 2 | Ejects floppy disk in external drive. Icon remains on desktop. * |
| Shift ⌘ 0 | Ejects floppy disk in third drive. Icon remains on desktop. * |
| Restart command | Ejects all floppy disks. System reboots. |
| Shut Down command | Ejects all floppy disks. System ready to power down. |

\* Do not use this method to eject the disk if you are finished and you intend to leave the computer on and booted for the next person.

Copying Floppy Disks

**Copying Floppy Disks using Two Floppy Drives**
A. Insert the locked source disk in the top or left drive and the destination disk in the bottom or right drive.
B. Drag the icon of the source disk over the top of the destination disk icon.
C. Answer dialog boxes as they appear.
D. If you had to remove a floppy Startup disk from one of the drives to perform this copy, the Macintosh may request the Startup disk in order to complete the copy.

**Copying Floppy Disks using a Single Floppy Drive**
All Macintosh systems can use this method.
A. Place the locked source disk in the floppy drive.
B. Eject the disk with the Eject Disk command so that a dimmed disk icon is left on the desktop.
C. Insert the destination disk in the floppy drive. Both disk icons now appear on the desktop.
D. Drag the icon of the source disk over the top of the destination disk icon.
E. Answer dialog boxes as they appear.
F. Switch disks in the floppy drive as directed.

**Copying Floppy Disks using a Single Floppy Drive and a Hard Drive**
A. Place the locked source disk in the floppy drive.
B. Drag the source disk's icon on to the hard drive's icon. This will not erase the hard drive.

C. Respond to the dialog box that appears informing you that the two disks are different types and that the source disk's data will be placed in a file folder on the hard drive.
D. Once the copy is complete, drag the source disk to the Trash.
E. Double-click on the hard disk icon to display the hard disk window.
F. Insert the floppy destination disk and drag the file folder from the hard drive to the floppy destination disk icon.
G. Remove the file folder from the hard drive by dragging it to the Trash.
H. Use the Empty Trash command on the Special menu to remove the folder from the Trash.

# Windows

### Sizing Finder Windows

| **Method** | **Results** |
|---|---|
| Size Box | Point to the size box and drag the window to any size. |
| Click on zoom box | Window gets just large enough to show contents. |
| Option Key + zoom box | Window almost completely fills desktop |

### Scrolling Windows

| **Mouse Techniques** | **Results** |
|---|---|
| Clicking scroll arrow | Window scrolls one-half inch per click. |
| Pointing & holding mouse button on scroll arrow | Window scrolls slowly until button is released. |
| Dragging scroll box | Window information displayed relative to the scroll boxes position on the scroll bar. |
| Clicking on scroll bar next to the scroll box | Scrolls the window one full window in that direction. |

| Keyboard Techniques | Results |
| --- | --- |
| Pressing Home key | Top of window displayed. Scroll box at the top of the scroll bar. |
| Pressing End key | Bottom portion of window displayed. Scroll box at the bottom of scroll bar. |
| Pressing Page Down key | Contents of next window is displayed. |
| Pressing Page Up key | Contents of previous window is displayed. |

## Parts of the Window

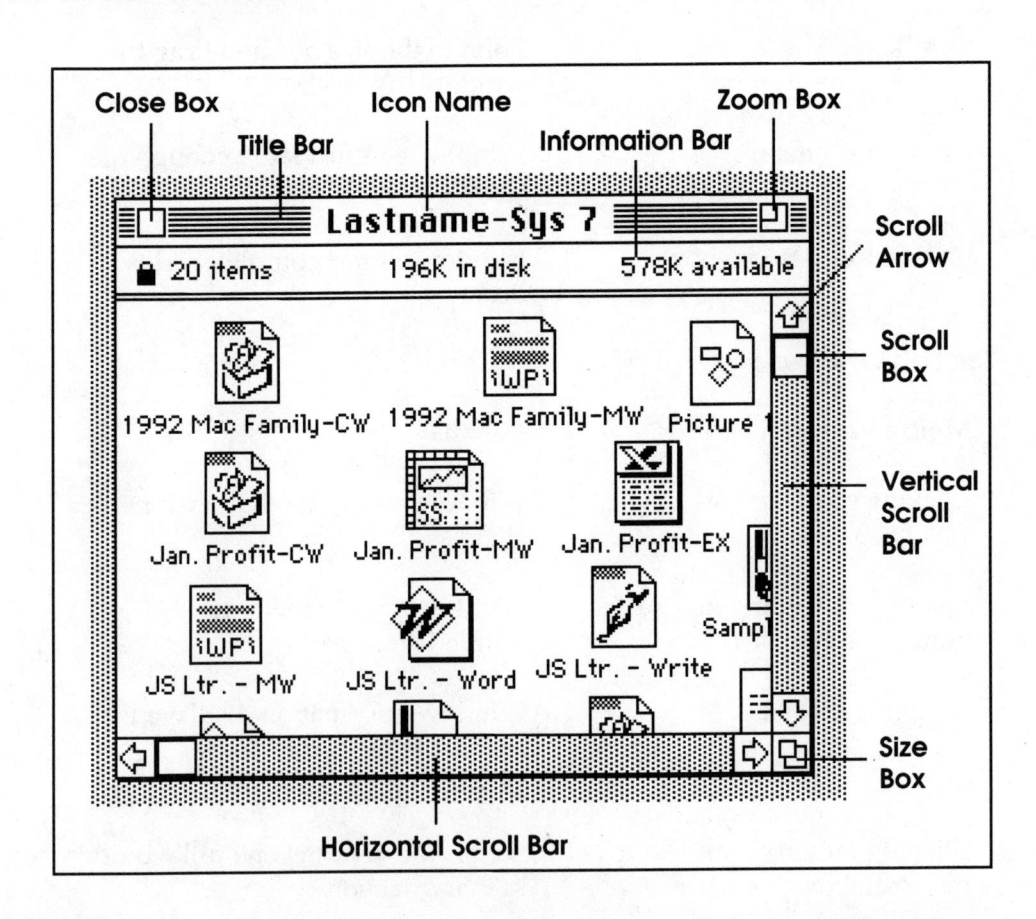

## Hierarchical Filing System Pop-up Menus

| Process | | Results |
|---|---|---|
| ⌘ + | Position pointer on window title and press the mouse button. | Displays the window's hierarchy. |
| ⌘ + | Position pointer on window title, press the mouse button, drag the pointer to highlight desired folder or disk, and release button. | Opens highlighted folder or disk. |
| ⌘ + | Option key + Position pointer on window title, press the mouse button, drag the pointer to highlight desired folder or disk, release button. | Opens highlighted folder or disk and closes the window that was active. |

## Hierarchical Filing System Keyboard Shortcuts

Displaying Outline Views

| Key(s) | Action |
|---|---|
| ⌘ → | Displays an outline view of the selected folder. * |
| ⌘ ← | Closes/hides the outline view of only the selected folder. * |
| ⌘ Option key → | Displays an outline view of the selected folder and all folders stored within the selected folder. * |
| ⌘ Option key ← | Closes/hides the outline view of the selected folder and all folders stored within the selected folder. * |

* Window must be displayed in a list view by Name, Size, Kind, Label, or Date

## Opening, Closing, and Activating Windows

| Key(s) | Action |
| --- | --- |
| ⌘ ↓ | Opens the selected icon. |
| ⌘ Option key ↓ | Opens the selected icon and closes the active folder/window. |
| ⌘ ↑ | Opens the folder that contains the active folder. |
| ⌘ Option key ↑ | Opens the folder that contains the active folder and closes the active folder. |

## Powering Down

**Steps to Power down the Computer**
    A. Close any open document files you have been working on.
    B. Quit all open application programs.
    C. Close all open windows.
    D. Select the Shut Down command in the Special Menu.

**Steps Performed by the Shut Down Command**
    A. Closes all open application program documents and programs.
    B. Closes all operating system files in an orderly fashion.
    C. Adjusts the hard drive's read/write heads so that the drive can safely be powered down.
    D. Ejects all floppy disks from the drives.
    E. Turns off the power on some Macintosh models.

# Glossary

**32-bit Addressing**   This feature is available on newer Macintoshes with the 68030 or 68040 processor chip. 32-bit Addressing is useful if you need to use large amounts of RAM (over 8 MB). Use the Memory control panel to turn this feature on or off.

**About Alarm Clock**   This is the first entry in the Apple menu when the Alarm Clock DA is active. When selected, a dialog box appears containing the programmer's names and copyright information.

**About Balloon Help**   This first entry in the Help menu provides a brief explanation on how to turn help on.

**About TeachText**   This is the first entry in the Apple menu when the TeachText program is active. When selected, a dialog box appears containing the programmer's names and copyright information.

**About This Macintosh**   When you are operating at the Finder level, this is the first entry in the Apple menu. Selecting this option will open a window containing information about your Macintosh System, including the version number of the operating system, the total amount of installed RAM and how RAM is currently being used.

**Access Time**   Disk storage access time is the amount of time required to retrieve a file(s) from the disk into RAM.

**Accessory Cards**   Printed circuit cards or boards that must be installed inside the Macintosh system unit, when you add certain peripherals to your computer system, such as a printer, monitor, or modem.

**Active Icon**   Clicking once on an icon selects or activates that icon for future action—the icon turns dark.

**Active Scroll Bar**   A shaded scroll bar indicates you are not seeing everything there is to see in that window, in that direction.

**Active Window**   You may have several windows open on the desktop but only one can be active. The scrolls bars, close box, zoom box, size box, and horizontal lines in the title bar appear in the active window.

**Adapter Cards**   See Accessory Cards.

**Alarm Clock DA**   This Apple menu Desk Accessory may be used to display the current date and time, to change the date or time, and to set an alarm.

**Alert Dialog Box**   A warning or error dialog box that appears on your desktop to provide you with information. The Macintosh may also beep. For example, an Alert Box will appear when you direct the Macintosh to erase a disk or to close a document you have not saved.

**Alert Sounds**   The Macintosh will produce a sound (sound off) to get your attention. Use the Sound control panel to select the sound to be used by the Macintosh to get your attention.

**Alias**   An alias is a small file (2K in size) that represents the original document, folder, program, disk, or Trash item. When you double-click on an alias, the original item is located and opened.

**Align**  Many application programs allow you to specify where to position text on a line. The most common types of alignment are left, center, right and justified.

**Alphanumeric**  Letters, numbers, special characters (? . , " : ; ...) and blank spaces are considered Alphanumeric characters.

**Anti-Viral Programs**  Programs written to check for and eradicate virus programs on disks.

**Apple Extended Keyboard**  This keyboard contains the standard 94 alphanumeric character keys, some special keys (Shift, Command, Esc, Alt, Control, Option), a separate numeric keypad, F1 through F15 function keys, and cursor control keys.

**Apple Standard Keyboard**  This keyboard contains the standard 94 alphanumeric character keys, a separate numeric keypad and some special keys (Shift, Command, Esc, Alt, Control, Option).

**Apple Menu**  The Apple symbol on the far left side of the menu bar provides access to this menu. Desk Accessories, and information concerning memory or the currently active program is available from this menu.

**Apple Menu Items**  This folder is used to store items found in the Apple menu and can be found inside the System Folder.

**AppleTalk**  A relatively inexpensive local area computer network that provides an environment in which different kinds of computers and peripherals can communicate.

**AppleTalk Zones**  The AppleTalk Zones list box will only be displayed in the Chooser window if the you are using a Macintosh connected to a network that has established zones.

**Application Menu**  This menu is split into two sections: the top section controls which open application windows are visible, and the bottom section displays a list of open programs.

**Application Software**  Programs that have been written to solve a specific problem, such as word processing, database, spreadsheet, and communications.

**ASCII**  An acronym for American Standard Code for Information Interchange. ASCII is an 8 bit coding scheme that allows for information exchange between computers.

**Autoflow Mode**  Selecting this command from the PageMaker Options menu will cause imported text to fill the first selected page or column and then automatically flow into the next until the entire story is placed.

**Automatic Paper Feed**  Use this option on the ImageWriter Print dialog box to specify continuous feed paper is loaded in the printer.

**Average Function**  This spreadsheet function adds the contents of several cells and calculates the average.

**Backing up**  The process of making a copy of a disk, folder, or file. Backing up is a type of disaster prevention. You should always have at least two copies of important information.

**Background**  An activity that is going on "behind the scenes". For example, some application programs allow you to have more than one document open at the same time but only one document can be "active", the inactive windows or documents are in the background. The system continues to work in the background when you are working with an application program in the foreground.

**Background Printing**  The Background Printing option appears in the LaserWriter and StyleWriter Chooser windows. If this option is turned on, print files are intercepted and written to the PrintMonitor Documents folder on disk. You can continue to work in the foreground while the Macintosh prints the documents in the background.

**Backup Disk**  A backup disk contains an exact copy of the information stored on the original disk.
**Balloon Help**  Balloon Help is used to learn about items on your screen. It can be turned on and off in the Help menu.
**Binary Digits**  The binary number system consists of two digits, 0 and 1.
**Bit-mapped**  Graphics and fonts, stored in memory as a set of dots are called bit-mapped.
**Bit**  The smallest unit a computer can recognize. Eight bits make a byte.
**Bold Button**  A bold, more defined, button in a dialog box represents the default answer. It represents the action that will be taken, should you choose to press the Return key instead of clicking on a button.
**Booting-up**  This process includes supplying power to the Macintosh, performing a quick hardware check, and reading the system from disk into memory.
**Box/Marquee**  One way to select multiple icons is to draw a box/marquee around them.
**Button**  A hot-spot in a window—clicking on this spot confirms or cancels an action.
**By Date**  Select this command from the View menu to display the contents of the active window in chronological order according to the Last Modified date and time.
**By Icon**  Select this command from the View menu to display the contents of the active window by icon. The size, kind or last modified date and time of each item in the window will not be displayed.
**By Kind**  Select this command from the View menu to display the contents of the active window by the kind of item it represents or by which application program was used to create it.
**By Label**  Select this command from the View menu to display the contents of the active window sorted by label. This view is useful if you have grouped files by assigning labels.
**By Name**  Select this command from the View menu to display the contents of the active window in alphabetic order by icon name.
**By Size**  Select this command from the View menu to display the contents of the active window by size from largest to smallest. Folders are listed last.
**By Small Icon**  Select this command from the View menu to display the contents of the active window by small icon. The size, kind or last modified date and time of each item in the window will not be displayed.
**Byte**  A byte is composed of eight bits and represents a letter, number or special character. Disk storage and memory is measured in bytes.
**Calculator DA**  This Apple menu Desk Accessory may be used to perform simple calculations.
**Cancel Button**  The Cancel button appears in many dialog boxes. If selected, the current operation will be aborted (canceled).
**Cap Lock Key**  Pressing the Cap Lock toggle key directs the Macintosh to use uppercase or lowercase letters. This key has no effect on number or special character keys.
**Case Sensitive**  Some commands and programs discriminate between upper and lower case characters.
**Cathode Ray Tube**  A technical name for a monitor.
**CD-ROM**  An Acronym for Compact Disk-Read Only Memory.
**Cell**  The intersection of a row and column creates a unique storage location on a spreadsheet document called a cell.

**Central Processing Unit**  The engine and brain of the computer. It interprets and executes instructions.

**Center Alignment**  See Align.

**Characters Per Second**  Print speed is measured in characters per second (CPS) or pages per minute (PPM).

**Checkbox**  A checkbox appears in many windows and dialog boxes. If an X appears in the checkbox, the option is active.

**Chooser**  Use this Apple menu Desk Accessory to select the printer or shared disk you wish to use.

**Circuit cards**  See Adapter Cards.

**Clean Up**  This Special menu command only works on the Finder desktop or when your disk or folder window is displayed in an icon view. The Clean Up command changes depending on what you have selected, whether you are using it in conjunction with the Option or Shift keys, and how the last list view was sorted.

**Clean Up All**  This Special menu command appears when you hold down the Option key while the desktop is active. When executed, the Startup disk icon will be placed in the top right corner of the desktop, and the Trash icon will be placed in the lower right corner of the desktop.

**Clean Up Desktop**  This Special menu command appears if the desktop is active. Upon executing the command, all desktop icons will be moved to the next available space on the invisible grid.

**Clean up by Name/Size/Kind/Label/Date**  This Special menu command appears when you hold down the Option key while a window or icon in a window is selected. The command will vary depending on which column your last list view was sorted on.

**Clean Up Selection**  This Special menu command is available when your window is displayed By Icon or By Small Icon. Selected icons will be arranged in rows and columns along an invisible grid.

**Clean Up Window**  This Special menu command arranges all icons in the active window in neat rows and columns along an invisible grid.

**Clear**  An Edit menu command used to cut selected text or graphics. A copy of it will not be placed on the Clipboard.

**Clicking**  The process of pressing and releasing the mouse button is one of the three basic Macintosh skills. Clicking once on an icon selects it for future action. Clicking twice on an icon will initiate an action.

**Clipboard**  A temporary storage location in memory. The last text or graphic selection you cut or copied from a document is stored here until replaced with a new selection or the Macintosh is powered down. The Clipboard folder can be found inside the System Folder.

**Close Window**  This File menu command will close the active window.

**Close Box**  Clicking on this small box, located on the left corner of the Title Bar, will cause the active window to close.

**Color Bar**  The General Controls panel color bar displays eight colors or shades of gray to be used in creating a desktop pattern.

**Color Control Panel**  Use the Color control panel to specify the color/gray to use for highlighting text and window borders.

**Color Wheel**  The color wheel can be accessed from the Color control panel when establishing a highlight color or from the General Controls panel when creating a desktop pattern.

**Command**  An instruction to a computer program that when executed causes an action to occur. Each menu on the menu bar contains numerous commands.

**Command Key**  This key, located on the keyboard next to the space bar, has a four-leaf clover and/or apple symbol on it. Some commands may be executed by using the keyboard instead of the menu system, keyboard equivalent commands. Holding down this key while pressing a specified letter key will execute the desired command.

**Computer Network**  A group of computers and peripherals that are connected in order to communicate and share information.

**Computer Security**  Computer security includes the protection of hardware and software from unauthorized use.

**Computer Virus**  A computer program designed to plant itself into the computer's operating system or application program, direct the computer to do its bidding, and to replicate and infect other computers.

**Computers**  A machine that accepts and processes data to produce useful information.

**Control Key**  This special key can be used in combination with other keys to perform special functions.

**Control Panels**  The Control Panels entry in the Apple menu allows you access to at least fifteen control panel programs: General Controls, Startup Disk, Keyboard, Mouse, Sound, Monitors, Color, Memory, Views, Labels, Numbers, Date & Time, File Sharing Monitor, Sharing Setup, User & Group. Each control panel program allows you to modify/customize one part of your Macintosh work environment. The Control Panels folder can be found inside the System Folder.

**Copy**  This Edit menu command places selected text or graphics on the Clipboard.

**Cover Page**  Some printer Page Setup Dialog Boxes permit you to print a cover page before your document prints.

**CPS**  An acronym for Characters Per Second. The printing speed of dot-matrix and ink-jet printers are measured in CPS.

**CPU**  See Central Processing Unit.

**Cropping Tool**  Use this PageMaker tool to trim (crop) graphics in the active PageMaker document.

**Cursor Control Keys**  The cursor control keys are located on the extended keyboard between the main keyboard and the number pad. This group of keys includes, help, home, end, page up, page down, del and the four directional arrow keys.

**Customized Application Programs**  Some computer users find it necessary to hire a programmer to write computer programs to meet their specific needs. Off-the-shelf application programs are far less expensive.

**Cut**  This Edit menu command removes the selected text or graphics from its current document location and places it on the Clipboard.

**DA**  See Desk Accessory.

**Daisy-chained**  Up to eight devices (including the Macintosh) can be daisy-chained (connected one after the other by cables) off one SCSI port.

**Database Management**  This popular type of application software is often referred to as record management software.

**Date & Time Control Panel** Use this control panel to set the System date and time and to change the way they are displayed on your Macintosh.

**Default Answer** The darker, more defined button in a dialog box is the default answer. Pressing the Return key will execute this action.

**Define Fields Dialog Box** This ClarisWorks (spreadsheet application program) menu is used to create fields in the database record.

**Delay Until Repeat** Use this feature of the Keyboard control panel to set the length of time the Macintosh waits before repeating a typed character.

**Deselected Icon** To deselect an icon, click on an empty spot on the window or desktop or select another icon.

**Desk Accessories** A small program written to operate at any time, even from within an application program. It is available on the Apple menu.

**Desktop** Your computer workspace on the screen is called the desktop because it is similar to your table top workspace.

**Desktop Pattern** Select the pattern to be displayed on your computer desktop from the General Controls panel.

**Desktop Publishing** This page layout software is used to create, format, and print written communication. The printed document may include text and graphics.

**Destination Disk** The disk you are copying files to.

**Diagonal-line Tool** Use this PageMaker tool to draw lines at an angle.

**Dialog Box** A window provided by the operating system or the application program to provide information and to solicit your response.

**Dimmed Commands** Commands that appear dimmed on a menu are currently not available for execution.

**Directory** The Directory File is created during the disk initialization process. It contains a list of items on the disk, including characteristics associated with each item (name, kind of item, date and time of last modification).

**Directory Dialog Box** A Directory Dialog Box will appear when you open or save a document. Use this box to identify the name and location of the document.

**Directory Path** The directory path specifies the icons exact location on the disk.

**Disk** The primary storage media for computers are floppy and hard disks.

**Disk Cache** Disk Cache is always on but you can use the Memory control panel to specify how much memory to use. Disk Cache is memory that is set aside to store frequently-used data.

**Disk Drive** The hardware device necessary to read and write information to a disk.

**Documentation** Written instructions explaining how to use the associated program(s).

**Dot-Matrix Printer** This common type of impact printer creates characters by using many tiny individual dots.

**Double-click** Double-clicking on an icon will cause an action to occur. For instance, double-clicking on a file folder will cause a new folder window to open on your desktop.

**Double-click Speed** Use the Mouse control panel to adjust the double-clicking speed.

**Double-sided Button** This PageMaker Page Setup dialog box button is used to create a double-sided document.

**Download** The process in which your computer receives information through the phone lines from another computer.

**DPI** An acronym for Dots Per Inch. Printer and monitor quality is measured in DPI. DPI represents how many dots appear within one linear inch on the screen or printed page.

**Draft** Printing a document in draft mode produces a rough draft document of low print quality.

**Dragging** One of the three basic mouse operations. The process of moving the mouse while holding the mouse button down. Dragging allows you to move icons on the screen, use pull-down menus and highlight text.

**Draw Mode** Many application programs have a draw mode where you can use drawing tools to create lines, squares, rectangles, circles, ovals, and so on.

**Drop-down Menu** A menu that drops from the menu bar when accessed.

**DS-DD** Acronym for Double Sided-Double Density. A 3 1/2 inch, DS-DD floppy disk stores 800K characters.

**DS-HD** Acronym for Double Sided-High Density. A 3 1/2 inch, DS-HD floppy disk stores 1.4 million characters.

**Duplicate** Use this File menu command to make a duplicate copy of the selected icon(s). The new icon(s) will be assigned the original icon name followed by the word copy, and will be located on the same window as the original.

**Edit Menu** The editing commands Undo, Cut, Copy, Paste, Clear, Select All, and Show Clipboard are located on this menu.

**Eject Button** This button appears on some directory and dialog boxes. If selected, the active floppy disk will be ejected from the drive.

**Eject Disk** Use this Special menu command to eject the selected floppy disk from the drive. The subdued image of the disk remains on the desktop.

**Electronic Mail** Also known as E-Mail, Electronic Mail provides an alternative way to communicate, via a computer, through a network or phone lines.

**Empty Trash** Use this Special menu command to discard items placed in the Trash.

**Erase Disk** Use this Special menu command to remove everything on the disk and to create a new disk directory.

**Esc Key** This special key can be used in combination with other keys to perform special functions.

**Expansion Cards** See Accessory Cards.

**Expansion Slots** Accessory Cards plug into expansion slots inside the system unit. (See Accessory Cards.)

**Extensions Folder** This folder is used to store items found in the Chooser (print drivers, scanner and networking files) and Init files. It can be found inside the System Folder.

**External Drive** An external floppy or hard disk drive is installed outside the system unit. (See Floppy Disk and Hard Disk.)

**Facing Pages Button** When selected, this PageMaker Page Setup button indicates document pages will appear side-by-side in the publication.

**Faster Bitmap Printing** A button on the LaserWriter Page Setup window. Text and graphics that use bitmaps will print faster if this option is turned on.

**FDHD** Acronym for Floppy Drive-High Density.

**Fewer Choices Button** Click this button in the Find command dialog box to close the expanded Find dialog box.

**Field** A single piece of information on a record in a database is considered a field.

**File** Documents you create, programs, and sets of records used by programs are stored on disk as files.

**File Folders** Disk file folders, like paper file folders, provide a way to file related objects together.

**File Menu** This Finder menu contains commands to create new folders, open and close windows, print documents and the desktop, get information on selected icons, create an alias or duplicate selected icons.

**File Menu** Commands available in this application program menu affect whole documents and files, including Open, Close, Save, Save As, and Print.

**File Server** A hardware device on a local area network that is used to store shared programs and documents, and to manage network users.

**File Sharing Monitor Control Panel** Use this control panel to see who is connected to your Macintosh and what folders and/or disk you are sharing.

**Fill Down** This spreadsheet application program command copies the information in the first selected cell down the column to all other selected cells.

**Fill Right** This spreadsheet application program command copies the information in the first selected cell right across the row to all other selected cells.

**Find** This Finder File menu command is helpful in locating disk documents and folders. You can specify what you are looking for (search criteria) and where to look (desktop, disk, folder).

**Find Again** This Finder File menu command locates and displays the next item that matches the search criteria specified in the Find command. (See Find.)

**Find Original Button** This button appears in Alias Get Info boxes. If selected, the original item will be located and selected.

**Finder** This program is loaded during the boot process and is working from boot to shut down. The Finder program creates, maintains and allows access to the Macintosh desktop. The Finder program is stored in the System Folder.

**Finder Menu Bar** The Finder program has its own menu bar consisting of the Apple, File, Edit, View, Label, Special, Help and Application menus.

**Finder Shortcuts** This Help menu command displays a dialog box describing keyboard shortcuts on working with icons, selecting icons, working with windows, working with outline views, and miscellaneous options.

**Firmware** The ROM-BIOS chip is an example of firmware, a combination of hardware and software. The chip is hardware and the set of instructions encoded on it is software.

**Fixed Drives** See Hard Disk.

**Fixed Size Fonts** These screen or printer font files store the font in one point size, indicated by its name (Palatino 10).

**Flawed Sectors** Storage locations on the disk that are considered damaged by the system and therefore unreliable for storing information.

**Flip Horizontal** A checkbox available on the LaserWriter Page Setup window. If selected, the document will be flipped horizontally when printed.

**Flip Vertical** A checkbox available on the LaserWriter Page Setup window. If selected, the document will be flipped vertically when printed.

**Floppy Disk** A flat, round, flexible piece of mylar used to store and transport information.

**Font Menu** This application menu contains a list of available fonts.

**Font Substitution**  A checkbox available on the LaserWriter Page Setup window. If selected, certain fonts will be substituted for fonts that produce higher print quality text.

**Fonts**  The collection of numbers, letters and punctuation characters presented in the same typeface.

**Fonts Folder**  This folder stores screen and printer fonts. This new System 7.1 folder can be found inside the System folder.

**Foreground**  The active program in control and currently responding to commands. For example, when you are working in the foreground on an application program document, the system is working in the background.

**Form Feed**  A push button on an ImageWriter printer used to advance the paper.

**Format Menu**  Commands on this application program menu can be used to change the appearance of the document and to emphasize text.

**Formatting**  The process of setting document margins, tab stops, fonts and character styles.

**Function Keys**  The F1 through F15 keys, located across the top of the extended keyboard, are assigned commands by application programs.

**General Controls Panel**  Use the General Controls panel to set the desktop pattern, rate of insertion point blinking, menu blinking, and data and time.

**Get Info**  Use this Finder File menu command to display information on the selected icon, including Kind, Size, Where, Created, and Modified. Other entries in this window varies depending on the type of icon selected. A Locked checkbox is provided for files. A Warn before emptying checkbox is provided for the Trash. A memory requirement section is provided for application programs.

**Gigabyte**  A unit of measurement used to describe memory and disk storage. A Gigabyte, 1 GB, is equal to 1024 MB or 1,073,741,824 storage positions.

**Global Backup**  A backup process used to copy the entire hard disk contents to another hard disk, floppy disks or magnetic tape.

**Graphical User Interface**  A visually oriented computing technique used by the Macintosh in which interaction between human and machine takes place in visual ways.

**Graphics Smoothing**  A checkbox on the LaserWriter Page Setup window. If selected, the jagged edges of graphic images will be smoothed.

**Gray-scale**  A series of shades ranging from black through white.

**GUI**  See Graphical User Interface.

**Hand Feed Paper**  This ImageWriter Print dialog box option may be used if you are feeding individual sheets of paper to the printer.

**Hard Copy**  A paper copy of a computer document.

**Hard Disk**  Inflexible recording surfaces known as platters that allow for the magnetic recording of data. Hard disks are used for permanent information storage.

**Hard Return**  A line break inserted by the user by pressing the Return key. (See Wordwrap and Soft Return.)

**Hardware**  The physical components of the computer system.

**Head Crash**  A head crash can occur when the read/write heads come in contact with a hard disk recording surface.

**Help Menu**  Use this Finder menu to toggle Show Balloons on and off and to view Finder shortcuts.

**HFS**  See Hierarchical File System.

**HFS Pop-up Menu** Press and hold the Command key while the pointer is on the active window's title to display the window's hierarchy.

**Hide Balloons** Use this Help menu command to turn balloon help off.

**Hide Finder** This Application menu command changes to display the name of the active program. If selected, the active program window is hidden from view.

**Hide Others** Selecting this Application menu command will cause all open program windows (other than the active program), to be hidden from view.

**Hierarchical File System** A filing system consisting of file folders that allows the Macintosh user to file related documents in an organized manner for easy retrieval.

**Highlight Color** Use the Color control panel to select the color to be used when highlighting text.

**I-Beam** The pointer assumes the shape of an uppercase I when working with text.

**Icon View** Disk and folder windows may be viewed in an icon or list view.

**Icons** Symbolic pictures that represent objects on your computer desktop.

**Image Area** The area within a PageMaker document window where text and graphics appear.

**ImageWriter II** A relatively inexpensive, dot-matrix, impact printer.

**Impact Printer** A printer that creates marks on the paper by pressing a fabric or cotton ribbon against the paper.

**Inactive Scroll Bar** A clear scroll bar indicates you are seeing everything there is to see in that window, in that direction.

**Inactive Window** You may have several windows open on the desktop but only one can be active. The scrolls bars, close box, zoom box, size box, and horizontal lines in the title bar do not appear in inactive windows.

**Incremental Backup** The process of copying disk files that have been modified since the last backup to a hard disk, floppy disks or magnetic tape.

**Information Bar** In disk or folder windows, this bar appears immediately below the title bar. It may contain a padlock, if your disk is locked, and also the number of items in the window and the amount of disk storage available.

**Init** Init, short for initialization, programs automatically load during the boot process and instruct the System to perform operations that it normally wouldn't do.

**Initialize** The process used to prepare a disk for use.

**Ink-jet Printer** An ink-jet printer forms characters by shooting tiny dots on to the paper.

**Input Devices** Peripherals used by you to provide data to the CPU. They convert data to electronic pulses and transmit the pulses to the CPU. The keyboard and mouse are examples of input devices.

**Insertion Point** A blinking vertical line on your screen that identifies where the next keyed in character will appear.

**Internal Drive** An internal floppy or hard disk drive is installed inside the system unit.

**Invert Image** An option on the LaserWriter Page Setup window. If selected, a negative image of the document will print.

**Justification** See Align.

**Key Caps DA** A desk accessory used to display the standard and optional characters for each available font on your system.

**Key Repeat Rate** An option available in the Keyboard control panel that permits the user to set how fast a character repeats itself across the screen, when the key is pressed.

**Keyboard**   A computer input device that resembles a typewriter keyboard.

**Keyboard Control Panel**   This control panel provides options to set Key Repeat Rate, Delay until Repeat and Keyboard Layout.

**Keyboard Equivalents**   Many Macintosh menu commands can be executed by holding down the Command key and the specified letter. For instance, pressing the letter O key while holding down the Command key will cause the selected icon to open.

**Kilobyte**   A unit of measurement used to describe memory and disk storage. A kilobyte, 1 K, is equal to 1024 characters or storage positions.

**Label Menu**   This Finder menu contains seven labels. You may assign any label from this menu to the active icon(s).

**Labels**   Labels are used to group related files. Labels may be assigned to documents, folders, or programs for quick recognition.

**Labels Control Panel**   Use this control panel to change the name of available labels and to change the color/gray assigned to each.

**Landscape Monitor**   A monitor that is wider than it is tall.

**Landscape Orientation**   Choose this orientation if you wish to view or print your document sideways.

**Laptop Computers**   A computer that is lightweight, battery powered, compact and portable.

**Larger Print Area**   A checkbox on the LaserWriter Page Setup window. If selected, the document will print on more of the total page area.

**Laser Printers**   A non-impact printer that uses xerographic copier technology to beam complete pages onto a drum, the paper picks up the image as it passes over the drum.

**Layout Menu**   Use commands on this ClarisWorks menu to create a database report.

**Left Flush**   See Align.

**Line Feed**   A printer push button that when pushed advances the paper one line.

**List Box**   A box that appears within a dialog box. Scroll bars may be used to display different items in the List Box. Open, Save As, and Delete dialog boxes contain List Boxes.

**Locked Checkbox**   Use the File menu command, Get Info, to display an information window on the selected file. If the Locked checkbox within the window contains an X, the file cannot be erased or modified.

**Locked Files**   Use the Get Info window to lock or unlock files. Locked files cannot be modified or deleted but they can be viewed or printed. (See Locked Checkbox.)

**Magnetic Tape**   A strip of Mylar used to store information.

**Make Alias**   This Finder File menu command is used to create an alias for the selected item.

**Megabyte**   A unit of measurement used to describe memory and disk storage. A Megabyte, 1 MB, is equal to 1024 K or 1,048,576 storage positions.

**Memory Control Panel**   Use this control panel to increase or decrease disk cache, to turn virtual memory on or off, and to turn 32-bit addressing on or off.

**Memory Minimum Size**   Use the File menu command, Get Info, to display an information window on the selected program icon. The Memory Current Size entry represents the smallest amount of memory that your Macintosh will allocate to the program.

**Memory Preferred Size**   Use the File menu command, Get Info, to display an information window on the selected program icon. The Memory Preferred Size entry represents the amount of memory you would like the Macintosh to allocate to the program, if available (if not allocated to other programs).

**Memory Suggested Size**   Use the File menu command, Get Info, to display an information window on the selected program icon. The Memory Suggested Size entry represents the amount of memory the program creators recommend in order to use the program.

**Menu**   Menu names appear in the menu bar and when accessed the menu displays a list of available commands.

**Menu Bar**   The menu bar appears across the top of the desktop and contains the names of the available menus.

**Menu Blinking**   Use the General Controls Panel to specify how many times (0,1, 2, or 3) the selected command blinks before the command is executed.

**Message Box**   A box provided within the Get Info window. You may enter a message in this box.

**Micro Floppy Disks**   See Floppy Disk.

**Modem**   Short for Modulator-Demodulator. This hardware device allows a computer to send and receive information through the phone lines.

**Monitor Control Panel**   A control panel used to specify the number of grays or colors to be displayed on your monitor.

**Monitors**   A computer output device used to visually display images.

**Monochrome**   Monochrome monitors display text and graphics in black and white.

**More Choices Button**   Click this button in the Find command dialog box to expanded the Find dialog box.

**Mouse**   A hand held input device with a ball-type roller on the bottom and one or more buttons on the top. The mouse is used to point at objects on the screen, to select menu options, to mark text for editing and to select items for further action.

**Mouse Control Panel**   A control panel used to set mouse tracking and double-clicking speed.

**Mouse Tracking**   Use this option of the Mouse control panel to change the speed of mouse tracking. If mouse tracking is set to slow, the pointer will move one inch on the screen for every inch you move the mouse. Fast mouse tracking will move the pointer two inches for every inch you move the mouse.

**MS-DOS**   An acronym for Microsoft Disk Operating System. The operating system used by IBM microcomputers and IBM clones.

**Multitasking**   A mode of operation where several operations appear to be executing at the same time.

**Nesting Folders**   The process of placing file folders within file folders. Nesting of folders may go more than twelve levels deep. Four levels is considered a practical limit.

**Near Letter Quality (NLQ)**   The best quality print available on a dot matrix printer. Characters are printed and then printed again in a slightly offset pattern to fill in the spots between the dots.

**Network Versions**   Multiple users can use network versions of application programs at the same time.

**New Folder**   Use this Finder File menu command to create a new empty folder.

**No Gaps Between Pages**   This checkbox appears in the ImageWriter Page Setup dialog box. If selected, the printer is directed to print up to the paper's perforation without a break.

**Nonvolatile**   ROM is nonvolatile. Information stored in ROM is not lost when power is interrupted.

**Note Pad**   This Apple menu desk accessory is similar to a scratch pad. Use this DA to write yourself notes for later reference. The Note Pad File is stored inside the System Folder.

**Numbers Control Panel** Use this control panel to specify the format to be used when displaying numbers and currency.

**Numeric Keypad** A separate numeric keypad can be found on the extended apple keyboard. This keypad can be used for rapid number input.

**Operating System** Operating System software coordinates and supervises the operation of the physical components of the computer and allows the hardware to run application programs.

**Open** Use this File menu command to open a window to the selected icon.

**Orientation** See Landscape Orientation or Portrait Orientation.

**Original Programs** See Customized Application Programs.

**Output Devices** Peripherals used to produce or display useful information. Printers and monitors are examples of output devices.

**Outline View** Folders in the list view window can be opened (in the same window) to display a list of items stored inside.

**Oval Tool** Use this PageMaker tool to draw circles and ovals in the active PageMaker document.

**Packaged Application Programs** Application programs that have been created to solve a specific problem. They are marketed and available for a wide range of computer uses.

**Padlock** This symbol will appear on an icon window's information bar if the icon is locked. It also appears to the right of locked files in a list view window.

**Page Per Minute** Print speed is measured in characters per second (cps) and pages per minute (ppm).

**Page Range** The option on the Print or Page Setup dialog boxes used to indicate specific document pages to print.

**Page Setup** Use this File menu command to enter specific printer features, including paper size and document orientation.

**Paper Feed** This ImageWriter Print dialog box option signifies you are feeding individual sheets of paper to the printer.

**Password-protected** Some software packages permit the user to assign a password to documents. To access the document, you must know the password.

**Paste** Use this Edit menu command to place the Clipboard's contents in the active document at the current insertion point.

**Pasteboard** The area surrounding the image area on a PageMaker document window. This area is used for temporary storage of text and graphics.

**Peripherals** Input, output and storage devices used to access the CPU.

**Permanent Storage** Disk and tape is used for permanent storage. Of course, you can direct the Macintosh to erase the information.

**Perpendicular-line Tool** Use this PageMaker tool to draw vertical, horizontal, and 45-degree lines.

**Pirated Software** Software that is illegally copied.

**Pixels** The image on a computer screen consists of tiny dots called picture elements or pixels.

**Platters** The rigid metal or glass recording surfaces of a hard disk.

**Pointer Icon** Use this PageMaker tool to select text and graphics in the active PageMaker document.

**Pointing** One of three basic mouse techniques. Pointing is the process of moving the mouse across a surface in order to position the pointer on the screen at the desired location.

**Points** A unit of measure used to identify the character size of the selected font. One point is approximately 1/72 of an inch high.

**Pop-up Menu** A menu that appears on the screen, but its name does not appear in the menu bar.

**Port** A port is a socket where you can plug in a cable to connect to a printer, another computer, a modem and so on.

**Portrait Monitor** A monitor that is taller than it is wide.

**Portrait Orientation** The default print orientation used by most printers. The document is printed vertically on the paper.

**Power-down** Powering down the computer system consists of several steps, including closing all open documents, quitting application programs, closing open windows, executing the Shut Down command, and turning off the electricity to the computer.

**Power-on** See Booting up.

**PPM** Short for Page Per Minute. Printer speed can be measured in PPM.

**Precision Bitmap Alignment** A checkbox on the LaserWriter Page Setup window. If selected, bitmap images will print at four times the resolution of the Macintosh screen.

**Preferences Folder** This folder stores special setting files for application programs and can be found inside the System Folder.

**Pre-formatted Disks** You can purchase floppy disks that have already been formatted by the manufacturer.

**Print** Use this File menu command to print your current document.

**Print Desktop** Use this Finder File menu command to print the directory of the current disk or folder window.

**Print Drivers** A print driver program contains the codes and commands to properly operate a specific printer.

**Print Quality** This entry on the ImageWriter Print dialog box allows you to specify the print quality (Best, Faster, Draft) to be used when printing the document.

**Print Servers** A computer with a hard drive can serve as a print server on a computer network. All print files would be sent to the print server, and stored there until a printer was available.

**Print Spooler Program** PrintMonitor is the print spooler program that comes with System 7.1. If background printing is turned on, print files will be intercepted and written to the PrintMonitor Documents folder on disk and then sent to the printer (when available).

**Printer Effects** This entry in the LaserWriter Page Setup dialog box allows you to request font substitution, text smoothing, graphics smoothing, and faster bitmap printing.

**PrintMonitor Documents** This folder stores documents for printing in the background. It is stored inside the System Folder.

**Program Language Processor** Programs that allow you to use programming languages to write application programs.

**Programs** A set of instructions that when executed in sequence directs the hardware to perform a specific task.

**Pull-down Menu** A menu that drops down from the menu bar and remains open until the mouse button is released.

**Put Away**  Use this File menu command to return selected icons to the folders and disks they came from.

**Puzzle DA**  This Apple menu desk accessory resembles a plastic puzzle cut into squares that you can rearrange to create a picture.

**Quit**  This application File menu command will close the application program and all open documents within the window.

**QWERTY**  Standard keyboard layout named for the first half row of letters, consisting of 94 alphanumeric characters.

**RAM**  An acronym for Random Access Memory. This volatile portion of memory can be read and written to by the computer and peripherals.

**Random Access**  Disk Drives use this access method to retrieve information.

**Random Access Memory**  See RAM.

**Rate of Insertion Point Blinking**  Use the General Controls Panel to specify how fast the cursor will blink on your computer desktop.

**Read Only Memory**  See ROM.

**Record**  A database record consists of a group of related fields containing information on a single item.

**Reduce/Enlarge**  An option in the LaserWriter Page Setup window. You can increase or reduce the print size of the document.

**Rename**  The process of changing the name of icons.

**Restart**  Use this Special menu command to clear RAM and to reload the system into memory without turning the Macintosh off and on.

**RGB**  Short for Red, Green, Blue. Used to describe color monitors.

**Ribbon Bar**  Application program ribbon bars provide fast access to a variety of frequently used features (tab stops, line spacing, fonts, point sizes, text alignment).

**Right Flush**  See Align.

**ROM**  An acronym for Read Only Memory. Instructions have been prerecorded on this portion of memory. This nonvolatile portion of memory can only be read.

**ROM-BIOS**  An acronym for Read Only Memory-Basic Input Output System. A prerecorded chip inside the system unit accessed during the boot-up process.

**Rounded-corner Tool**  This PageMaker tool is used to draw squares and rectangles with rounded corners.

**Ruler Bar**  The capabilities of application program ruler bars vary greatly. You may be able use the ruler bar to enter the date and time in the document, set tab stops, line spacing, text alignment.

**Save**  Use this application program File menu command to write the active document to disk.

**Save As**  Use this application program File menu command to specify where to save the active document, what to name it, and to write the document to disk.

**Save Publication As**  Use this PageMaker dialog box to name, and identify where to save the current document.

**Scanner**  An input device that takes a computer image, a picture, of paper placed in front of it. The image appears on your screen and can be modified, printed and saved to disk.

**Scrapbook**  A desk accessory used to permanently store text and graphics. Entries in the

Scrapbook may be copied and pasted into documents. The Scrapbook File is stored inside the System Folder.

**Scroll** The process of moving the contents horizontally or vertically within the window. (See Scroll Arrows, Scroll Bars, Scroll Box.)

**Scroll Arrows** Two scroll arrows are located on each scroll bar. Clicking on the arrow will scroll the window in the direction of the arrow.

**Scroll Bars** The vertical and horizontal scroll bars can be used to display different parts of a window. An active scroll bar will be shaded, an inactive scroll bar will not be shaded.

**Scroll Box** The small box located in the vertical and horizontal scroll bars. It shows the relative position of the window's contents compared to the whole picture. Dragging the scroll box along the scroll bar is a quick way to move through the window.

**SCSI** An acronym for Small Computer System Interface (pronounced scuzzy) that provides a way to attach peripherals to the System Unit.

**Search Criteria** If you wish to locate only certain records in a database, you must tell the Macintosh what you are looking for.

**Search Pop-up Menu** This menu in the Find command dialog box allows you to specify where to look for the selected item.

**Secondary Storage Devices** Hard disks and floppy disks are secondary storage devices.

**Sectors** Disk tracks are further divided into sectors.

**Select All** Use this Edit menu command to select everything in the active window. If there are no windows open, it will select everything on the desktop.

**Selected Icon** Active icons that have been selected for further action.

**Sequential Access** Magnetic tape drives use this type of access mode. Sequential Access means that you begin searching for a specific piece of information at the beginning of the tape and continue to read until you locate the desired information.

**Serial Port** A serial port transmits information from the computer to a printer in a single file, one bit at a time.

**Sharing Setup Control Panel** Use this control panel to name your Macintosh, name yourself as owner, to enter a password for protection, and to turn File Sharing and Program Linking on and off.

**Shift-click** A process of holding the shift key down while pointing and clicking on different icons. One of several ways to select multiple icons for future action.

**Show All** This Application menu command reverses the Hide command. All open windows will be displayed on the desktop.

**Show Balloons** Use this Help menu command to turn balloon help on.

**Show Clipboard** Use this Edit menu command to display the current contents of the Clipboard.

**Shut Down** Use this Special menu command to power down your Macintosh in an orderly fashion. You should never just cut the power to the Macintosh.

**Size Box** The small box in the lower right corner of the window. Use the mouse to point at this box and then drag the window to the desired size.

**Size Menu** Use this application program menu to select the font point size to be used in the document.

**Small Computer System Interface** See SCSI.

**Soft Return** A line break inserted by the application program at the right margin when inserting text. (See Wordwrap and Hard Return.)

**Software**   A set of instructions that tells the computer hardware what to do.

**Sort**   The process of organizing data in a particular order, such as alphabetic or numeric.

**Sound Control Panel**   Use this control panel to adjust speaker volume, to add and remove sounds, and to select which sound the Macintosh will use to get your attention.

**Source Disk**   During a disk to disk copy routine, the source disk is the disk being copied.

**Speaker Volume**   Use the Sound control panel to adjust speaker volume.

**Special Effects**   An entry in the ImageWriter Page Setup window. Use this entry to turn on Tall Adjusted, 50% reduction or No Gaps between Pages.

**Special Menu**   This Finder menu contains commands to Clean Up the window and desktop, Empty Trash, Eject Disk, Erase Disk, Restart and Shut Down.

**Spreadsheet**   A type of application program used for manipulating numbers. The programs ability to create formulas and to use the many built-in functions make calculations simple.

**Square-corner Tool**   Use this PageMaker tool to draw squares and rectangles in the active PageMaker document.

**Stand-alone Mac**   A Macintosh that is not attached to a computer network is a stand-alone.

**Startup Disk Control Panel**   Use this control panel to specify the disk drive to be used at boot time.

**Startup Items Folder**   This folder stores items that are to be executed at boot time. It is stored inside the System Folder.

**Stationary Pad Checkbox**   This checkbox appears in the Save and Save as Directory dialog box. If selected, the current document will be saved as a stationary pad (template to be used for future documents).

**Status Box**   During the execution of certain tasks, an information only status box will flash on the desktop to inform you of its progress.

**Status Light**   Green Num Lock, Caps Lock and Scroll Lock keyboard lights indicate the respective option is on.

**Storage Devices**   Input-output peripheral devices used to store data and programs for later access.

**Style Menu**   This application program menu can be used to change the appearance of the document and to emphasize text.

**StyleWriter   Printer**   An Apple ink-jet printer. (See Ink-jet Printer.)

**Subdirectories**   MS-DOS refers to file folders as subdirectories.

**Subdued Command**   See Dimmed Commands.

**Suitcase Icon**   This icon is assigned to files that store one or more fonts, sounds, and/or DAs.

**Sum Function**   This spreadsheet function will add the contents of the selected cells.

**System Boot disk**   A disk containing the System Folder and files necessary to boot the Macintosh.

**System**   The System suitcase stores sounds, keyboard layouts and other essential system files. It is stored inside the System Folder.

**System Folder**   A folder containing files used by the Macintosh during the boot process and other files necessary for the Macintosh to operate.

**System Software**   A set of programs that allow us to interact with the hardware. System software coordinates and supervises the operation of all physical components of the computer and permits the hardware to run application software.

**Tab Stops**  Create tab stops in documents to line up columns of text or numbers on the page.

**Tall Adjusted**  Select this ImageWriter Page Setup dialog box checkbox if you are printing graphics.

**TeachText**  A simple word processing program sold along with the Operating System. Used by software manufacturers to share the latest software documentation.

**Terabyte**  A unit of measurement used to describe memory and disk storage. A Terabyte, 1 TB, is equal to approximately 1 trillion storage positions.

**Text Alignment**  See Align.

**Text Smoothing**  A checkbox in the LaserWriter Page Setup window. Selecting this checkbox will improve the appearance of certain bitmapped fonts.

**Text Tool**  Use this PageMaker tool to enter, select, and modify text in the active PageMaker document.

**Thermal Printer**  This nonimpact printer uses heat generated by the printer to create whole letters on the paper.

**Time and Date**  The computer system time and date can be set in the General Controls panel, in the Date & Time control panel (System 7.1) or by accessing the Alarm Clock DA.

**Title Bar**  The bar located at the top of the window that contains the close box, the name of the icon and the zoom box.

**Toolbox**  A palette that contains a variety of tools for drawing, selecting, and editing text and graphics.

**Tools Menu**  This application menu frequently contains commands to automate editing tasks, such as Spelling and Grammar checking.

**Trackball**  A popular pointing device with a ball-type roller on top and one or more buttons.

**Tracks**  Concentric circles on a disk. Tracks are broken further down into sectors.

**Transfer Rate**  The amount of time necessary to transfer information from disk to RAM.

**Trash**  An icon on the desktop used to delete documents, and folders from the disk. Dragging a disk icon to the Trash will eject the disk.

**Trojan Horses**  Trojan Horse programs appear to be legitimate programs, but they actually have hidden agendas. They are not true computer viruses because they do not replicate themselves.

**TrueType Fonts**  TrueType fonts are know for their smoothness and quality. A mathematical formula is used to create the requested font in any point size.

**Undo**  Use this Edit menu command, when available, to cancel the last editing operation you performed.

**UNIX**  A popular operating system.

**Unlimited Downloadable Fonts**  A checkbox in the LaserWriter Page Setup window. If selected, the printed can use more fonts in your printed document.

**Upload**  The process of sending information from your computer through the phone lines to another computer.

**Users & Groups Control Panel**  Use this control panel to restrict who may access certain folders and hard disks.

**Utility Programs**  A program that provides routine maintenance work on the system.

**Version Numbers**  Instead of changing the name of a program every time an improved version of the program is released, a number is assigned. The highest version number assigned to a specific program indicates the latest version of that program.

**View Menu**  This Finder menu allows the Macintosh user to display the contents of the disk or folder By Icon, By Small Icon, By Name, By Size, By Kind, By Label, and By Date.

**Views Control Panel**  Use the Views control panel to specify how and what to display in icon and list view Finder windows.

**Virtual Memory**  Virtual Memory is disk space that is being used to store open application programs and documents. Not all Macintoshes are capable of using this feature. Use the Memory control panel to turn this feature on and off and to select the hard disk to be used.

**Visually Oriented Computing**  A computing environment where human and computer communicate through visual means.

**Volatile Memory**  The portion of memory, RAM, that is wiped out when power is interrupted.

**Warn Before Emptying**  This checkbox can be found in the Trash Info window. If the X is removed from the checkbox, the System will empty the Trash without warning you.

**Window**  A region on the desktop that is associated with a specific icon.

**Window Color**  Use the Color control panel to select the window border color.

**Windowing Environment**  The Macintosh system works in this graphical environment.

**Windowshade Handles**  Horizontal lines with a loop handle that appear at the top or bottom of each column of text in a PageMaker document.

**Word Processing**  A very popular type of application program used to enter, modify, save and print text.

**Wordwrap**  A word-processing technique that allows the user to continually key in information while the program automatically controls line advancement when the text reaches the right margin.

**Worksheet**  A document created by and used by a spreadsheet program.

**Worms**  A program that duplicates itself in computer memory to disrupt the system's operations. Can cause the computer to "bomb" or "crash". (See Computer Virus.)

**Write-protect Tab**  A small tab on the underneath, top left corner of a floppy disk. Pushing this tab up so that a hole appears in the disk causes the disk to be write-protected—the disk can not be written to or erased.

**Zoom Box**  The small box on the right corner of the Title Bar. Clicking in this box will cause the window to switch between its original size to one that almost completely fills the screen.

# Index

32-bit Addressing, 271-272
50% Reduction, 160, 163

## A

About this Macintosh, 95-97, 102-103
About Alarm Clock, 100-101. See also Alarm Clock DA
About Balloon Help, 37-38, 139
About TeachText, 95, 171. See also TeachText
Access time, 10
Accessory cards,5
Active
  application, 140-143
  icon, 24-27, 87-88
  scroll bar, 77
  window, 83-84
Adapter Cards. See Accessory cards
Alarm Clock DA, 97-101. See also Date; Time
Alert dialog box, 70
Alert Sounds, 265-268
Alias, 302-303
American Standard Code for Information Interchange, 157
Anti-Viral program, 308-309
Apple extended keyboard, 6
Apple menu, 33, 94-109. See also Apple Menu Items folder; Desk Accessories; Scrapbook
Apple Menu Items folder, 301
AppleTalk, 155-159
  active/inactive, 159
  selecting devices, 158-159
  zones, 158
Application menu, 36, 140-143
  Hide Finders, 140
  Hide Others, 141
  Show All, 141

Application software, 12-14, 317-375
  Database Management, 13, 334-346
  Desktop Publishing, 14, 363-375
  Spreadsheet, 14, 349-360
  Word Processing, 12-13, 317-332
Arrow Pointer, 23
ASCII, 157

## B

Background printing, 158-159, 296-298
Background processing, 179
Backing-up, 59-62, 313-314
Balloon Help, 37-40
Bit, 157
Booting-up, 20-21. See also Startup Item folder
Box/Marquee, 29-31
Button, 54
by Date, 131, 133
by Icon, 74, 131-132
by Kind, 131
by Label, 131
by Name, 73-74, 131
by Size, 131
by Small Icon, 131-132
Byte, 157

## C

Calculator DA, 101-102
Cancel button, 164, 183
Calendar. See Date; Time
Cap Lock key, 6
Cell, 351
CD-ROM, 7
Central Processing Unit, 3-5
Chooser DA, 103, 154-159

  Using with AppleTalk printers, 158-159
  Using with directly connected printers, 155-157
Choosing a printer. See Chooser
Choosing commands from menus, 254
Clean Up command, 135-138
Clear command, 125-130
Clicking, 22-23
Clipboard, 125-130. See also System Folder-Clipboard
Close box, 76
Close Window command, 34, 72-73, 117
Color bar, 256-260
Color control panel, 268-271
Color Wheel, 256-260, 269-271
Command key, 6
Commands, 22
  About Balloon Help, 37-38, 139
  by Date, 133
  by Icon, 74, 131-132
  by Kind, 131
  by Label, 131
  by Name, 73-74, 131
  by Size, 131
  by Small Icon, 131-132
  Clean Up, 135-138
  Clear, 125-130
  Close Window, 34, 72-73, 117
  Copy, 125-130, 203-206, 327
  Cut, 125-130, 328
  Duplicate, 117, 201-203, 239-240
  Eject Disk, 50-51, 136, 230-231
  Empty Trash, 62-64, 136, 233, 240
  Erase Disk, 62, 136, 230-231
  Find, 118, 242-247, 383-384
  Find Again, 118, 242-247, 383-384

Finder Shortcuts, 139-140
Get Info, 117-123
Hide Balloons, 37-38, 139
Hide Finder, 140
Hide Others, 141
Make Alias, 117, 301-303
New folder, 116, 234-238
Open, 33-34, 70-73, 116, 225, 281
Page Setup, 118, 160-161
Paste, 125-130, 328
Print, 116-117
Print Desktop/Window, 118, 159-169
Put Away, 117, 123-125
Restart, 136
Save, 171-172, 191-192
Save As, 188
Select All, 36-37, 123-125, 130
Sharing, 117
Show All, 141
Show Balloons, 37-38, 139
Show Clipboard, 125-130
Shut Down, 40-42, 136
Undo, 125-130
Comment box, 118, 125-130
Computer Network, 155, 285-286
Control Panels, 253-286. See also System folder-Control Panels folder
 Color control panel, 268-271
 Date & Time, 281-284
 File Sharing Monitor control panel, 286
 General Controls panel, 256-262
 Keyboard control panel, 263
 Labels control panel, 278-279
 Memory control panel, 271-272
 Monitors control panel, 255-256
 Mouse control panel, 263-265
 Numbers control panel, 279-281
 Sharing Setup control panel, 285
 Sound control panel, 265-268
 Startup Disk control panel, 262
 Users & Groups control panel, 286

Views control panel, 273-278
Copy command, 125-130, 203-206, 327
Copying and pasting text. See Copy command; Paste command
CPU. See Central Processing Unit
Cursor control keys, 6
Cut command, 125-130, 328
Cutting and pasting text, 125-130, 328

## D

DA. See Desk Accessories
Daisy-chained, 291
Date
 Alarm Clock, 97-101
 General Controls panel, 256-262
 Date & Time control panel, 281-284
Date & Time control panel, 281-284
Database Management software, 13, 334-346
Default answer, 54
Delay Until Repeat, 263
Desk Accessories
 Activating and Closing, 95-96
 Alarm Clock, 97-101
 Calculator, 101-102
 Chooser, 103
 Control Panels, 95, 253-286
 Key Caps, 103-106
 Note Pad, 107
 Puzzle, 107
 Scrapbook, 108-109
Desktop, 21-22
Desktop button, 183-184
Desktop Pattern, 256-260
Desktop Publishing software, 14, 363-375
Destination disk, 57
Dialog boxes, 50
Dimmed
 commands, 31
 icons, 59
Directories, 54
 printing, 159-169
Directory dialog box, 182-186, 318-319, 323-325

Directory views. See Icon view; List view
Disk(s), 384-387
 backing-up, 313-314
 capacity, 8-9
 copying, 57-62, 230-231
 directory, 54
 drives, 8-10
 ejecting, 50-54
 erasing, 62, 230-231
 floppy, 8-10
 formatting, 53-75
 hard, 10
 head crash, 10
 inserting, 27-28, 50
 locking, 9, 52
 opening, 70-73
 pre-formatted, 53
 reinitializing, 62-64
 renaming, 65
 start-up, 20-21, 262, 291
Disk Cache, 271-272
Document icon. See Icon
Documents. See File
Dot-Matrix printer. See Printer
Double-click, 73, 129
Double-Click Speed, 264-265
Download, 310
DPI, 152-153
Draft, 161-162
Dragging, 24, 28-29, 31
Duplicate command, 117, 201-203, 239-240

## E

Edit menu, 125
 Clear command, 125-130
 Copy command, 125-130, 203-206, 327
 Cut command, 125-130, 328
 Paste command, 125-130, 328
 Select All command, 36-37, 123-125, 130
 Show Clipboard command, 125-130
 Undo command, 125-130
Eject button, 56, 183
Eject Disk command, 50-51, 136, 230-231
Electronic mail, 309
Empty Trash command, 62-64, 136, 233, 240, 382-383

## INDEX

Erase Disk command, 62, 136, 230-231
Expansion slots, 5
Extensions folder, 154, 295-296

### F

Faster Bitmap Printing, 164
Field, 335
File, 381-382
  copying, 203-206, 215
  data, 311-313
  duplicating, 201-203, 215
  erasing, 213-216
  Get Info, 119, 120, 200-201, 210-213
  locking, 119, 200-201, 216, 239
  renaming, 206-208, 216
  unlocking, 119, 200-201, 214-215
File Folders, 69-70
  copying, 230, 231
  creating, 185, 234-238
  duplicating, 239-240
  naming, 234-238
  nesting, 234-238
  removing, 232-233, 240-242
File menu, 33-34
  Close Window command, 34, 72-73, 117
  Duplicate command, 117, 201-203, 239-240
  Find command, 118, 242-247, 383-384
  Find Again, 118, 242-247, 383-384
  Get Info command, 117-123
  Make Alias, 117, 301-303
  New folder command, 116, 234-238
  Open command, 33-34, 70-73, 116
  Page Setup command, 118, 160-161
  Print command, 116-117
  Print Desktop/Window command, 118, 159-169
  Put Away command, 117, 123-125
  Sharing command, 117
File Server, 155
File Sharing Monitor control panel, 286

Find command, 118, 242-247, 383-384
Find Again command, 118, 242-247, 383-384
Finder, 20-21, 294
Finder menu bar, 31, 114-143
Finder Shortcuts, 139-140
Firmware, 20-21
Fixed Size Fonts, 299-301
Flawed Sectors, 54
Flip Horizontal, 165
Flip Vertical, 165
Floppy Disk. See Disk
Font Substitution, 164
Fonts, 104, 291-301
Fonts folder, 299-301
Foreground, 179
Formatting disks. See Disk
Function keys, 6

### G

General Controls panel
  Date & Time, 261-262
  Desktop Pattern, 256-260
  menu Blinking, 261
  Rate of Insertion Point Blinking, 260
Get Info command
  alias, 120-121
  application programs, 123
  disk, 118
  documents, 119-120, 200-201, 210-213
  folders, 121-122
  trash, 119
Global backup, 313-314
Graphical user interface (GUI), 20
Graphics Smoothing, 164

### H

Hard disk. See Disk
Hardware, 2-11
Head Crash. See Disk
Help menu, 35, 139-140
  About Balloon Help, 37-38, 139
  Show Balloons, 139
  Hide Balloons, 37-38, 139
  Finder Shortcuts, 139-140
Hierarchical file system, 221-247
  creating, 234-238

  dismantling, 232-233
  keyboard shortcuts, 225, 389
  navigating, 223-229
  pop-up menu, 223-227, 389
HFS Pop-up menu, 163, 191-192, 223-247
Hide Balloons, 37-38, 139
Hide Finder, 140
Hide Others, 141
Highlight Color, 269-270
Hot Spot, 24-25
Horizontal scroll bar. See Scroll bars

### I, J

I-beam, 126
Icon(s), 22, 380-383
  changing icons, 210-213
  changing font and point size, 217, 273-278
  closing, 72
  dragging, 24-25, 28-31
  labeling, 208-210, 216
  opening, 70-73
  renaming, 206-208
  selecting a single, 24-26, 87-88
  selecting a group of, 29-30
  sizing, 217, 273-278
Icon view, 73-75, 273-278
ImageWriter, 152-154
  Page Setup dialog box, 160
  Print dialog box, 161-162
Inactive scroll bar. See Scroll bars
Inactive window. See Window
Incremental backup, 313-314
Information bar, 76, 273-278
Initializing disks. See Disk-formatting
Ink-jet printer. See Printer
Input devices, 6-7
Insertion point, 127
Invert Image, 164-165

### K

Key Caps DA, 103-106
Key Repeat Rate, 263
Keyboard, 6
Keyboard control panel, 263
Keyboard equivalents, 32-33

## L

Labels, 208-210, 216
Labels control panel, 278-279
Label menu, 35, 135
Landscape monitor. See Monitor
Landscape orientation, 161, 164, 167
Larger Print Area, 165
Laser printers. See Printer
LaserWriter, 152
    Options dialog box, 164-165
    Page Setup dialog box, 162-164
    Print dialog box, 166
List box, 156, 158
List view, 73-74, 273-278
Locked checkbox, 119. See also Files-locking
Locking. See Files-locking; Disk-locking

## M

Magnetic tape, 314
Make Alias, 117
Memory
    RAM, 4-5, 170
    ROM, 5
Memory control panel, 271-272
Memory Current Size, 123
Memory Preferred Size, 123
Memory Suggested Size, 123
Menu, 31-32, 379
Menu bar
    See Apple menu; Applications menu; Edit menu; File menu; Finder menu; Help menu; Label menu; Special menu; View menu
Menu blinking, 261
Menu operations, 32
Modem, 157, 309-310
Monitors control panel, 255-256
Monitors, 7-8. See also Monitors control panel
Mouse, 7
Mouse control panel, 263-265
Mouse tracking, 263
MS-DOS, 221
Multitasking, 12

## N

Naming icons. See Icon
Near Letter Quality, 154
Nesting folders, 234-238
Network, 155
New button, 183, 185
New folder command, 116, 234-238
Note Pad DA, 107
Note Pad File, 293
Numbers control panel, 279-281
Numeric Keypad, 6

## O

Open button, 185
Open command, 33-34, 70-73, 116, 186-187, 225, 281
Orientation, 161, 164, 167
Outline View, 133-134, 227-229
Output devices, 3, 7-8

## P

Padlock, 76, 201
Page Range, 162
Page Setup command, 118, 160-168
Paste command, 125-130, 328
Pattern. See Desktop pattern
Peripherals, 3, 6-11
Points, 104. See also Control Panels-Views
Pop-up menu, 163, 191-192, 223-227
Port, 157
Portrait monitor. See Monitor
Portrait Orientation, 161, 164, 167
Post Script Fonts, 301
Power-down, 40-42, 390
Power-on, 20-21
Precision Bitmap Alignment, 165
Preferences folder, 295
Print command, 116-117
Print Desktop/Window command, 118, 159-169
Print dialog box. See ImageWriter; LaserWriter; StyleWriter
Print drivers, 154
PrintMonitor Program, 296-298
PrintMonitor Documents folder, 296-298
Printers, 8, 152. See also Chooser; ImageWriter; LaserWriter; StyleWriter
Put Away command, 117, 123-125
Puzzle DA, 107

## Q

Quit command, 186

## R

RAM. See Memory
Rate of Insertion Point Blinking, 260
Recovering items from Trash. See Trash
Record, 335
Reduce/Enlarge, 163-164
Reinitializing disks. See Disk
Renaming. See Icon; File
Restart command, 136
Ribbon bar, 320-321
ROM. See Memory
ROM-BIOS, 20
Ruler bar, 320-321

## S

Save As command, 188
Save command, 183
Scrapbook, 108-109, 189-194. See also System folder
    adding to, 189
    copying from, 190-191
    removing from, 194
Scroll arrows, 77, 79-80
Scroll bars, 77
Scroll box, 77, 80-81
SCSI. See Small Computer System Interface
Sectors, 53
Select All command, 36-37, 123-125, 130
Sharing command, 117
Sharing Setup control panel, 285
Shift-click, 29-31
Show All, 141
Show Balloons, 37-38, 139,
Show Clipboard command, 125-130

Shut Down command, 40-42, 136, 390
Size box, 77
Sizing windows, 77-78
Small Computer System Interface (SCSI), 291
Software, 2, 11-14
Sound control panel, 265-268
Source disk, 57
Speaker Volume. See Control panels- Sound
Special effects, 161
Special menu, 35, 135
   Clean Up command, 135-138
   Empty Trash command, 62-64, 136, 233, 240
   Eject Disk command, 50-51, 136, 230-231
   Erase Disk command, 62, 136, 230-231
   Restart command, 136
   Shut Down command, 40-42, 136
Spreadsheet software, 14, 349-360
Startup disk, 20-21, 262, 291
Startup Disk control panel, 262
Startup Items folder, 301-302
Stationary Pad checkbox, 119, 183
Status box, 55
Status light
   ImageWriter printer, 152-154
   keyboard, 6
Storage devices, 3, 8-10
StyleWriter, 152, 167
   Page Setup dialog box, 167
   Print dialog box, 168
Subdirectories, 222. See also Hierarchical File System
Subdued commands, 31
Suitcase icon, 293
System folder, 290-303
   Apple menu Items folder, 293, 301
   Clipboard, 293
   Control Panels folder, 293
   Extensions folder, 154, 293, 295-296
   Finder, 294
   Fonts folder, 299-301
   Note Pad File, 293

Preferences folder, 293, 295
PrintMonitor Documents folder, 293, 296-298
Scrapbook File, 293
Startup Items folder, 293, 203-302
System suitcase, 293-294
System suitcase, 293-294

**T**

TeachText, 170-174, 177-194
Text
   editing, 181
   entering, 181
Text Smoothing, 164
Text alignment, 330
Time
   Alarm Clock, 97-101
   General Controls panel, 256-262
   Date & Time control panel, 281-284
Title bar, 76
Trackball, 7
Tracks, 53
Trash, 217, 382-383. See also File; File Folders; Commands
Trojan Horses, 307
TrueType fonts, 299-301

**U**

Undo command, 125-130, 331-332
Unix, 221
Unlimited Downloadable Fonts, 165
Unlocking
   disks, 9, 52
   documents, 119, 200-201, 214-215
Upload, 310
Users & Groups control panel, 286
Utility program, 31

**V**

Version numbers, 11, 96-97
Vertical scroll bar. See Scroll bars
View menu, 35, 130-134
   by Date command, 133

   by Icon command, 74, 131-132
   by Kind command, 131
   by Label command, 131
   by Name command, 131
   by Size command, 131
   by Small Icon, 131-132
Views control panel, 273-278
Virtual Memory, 271-272
Viruses, 307-310
Visually Oriented Computing, 20
Volatile memory. See Memory-RAM

**W, X, Y**

Warn Before Emptying checkbox, 118-119, 242
Window, 70, 387-388, 390
   activating, 83-84, 225, 229
   close box, 76
   closing, 34, 72-73, 86-87, 225, 229, 381
   color, 269-271
   directories, 54
   environment, 70
   inactive, 76, 83-84
   information bar, 76
   moving, 84
   naming, 76
   opening, 33-34, 70-73, 116, 225, 381
   scroll arrows, 77, 79-80
   scroll bars, 77
   scroll box, 77, 80-81
   scrolling, 79, 81-82
   size box, 77
   sizing, 77-78
   title bar, 76
   zoom box, 77, 85-86
   zooming, 78-79, 84-85
Word Processing software, 12-13, 317-332
Wordwrap, 181
Worms, 307
Write-protect tab, 9

**Z**

Zones, 158
Zoom box, 77, 85-86
Zooming windows, 78-79, 84-85